Studies in the History of Law and Justice

Volume 17

The purpose of this book series is to publish high quality volumes on the history of law and justice. Legal history can be a deeply provocative and influential field, as illustrated by the growth of the European universities and the *Ius Commune*, the French Revolution, the American Revolution, and indeed all the great movements for national liberation through law. The study of history gives scholars and reformers the models and courage to question entrenched injustices, by demonstrating the contingency of law and other social arrangements. Yet legal history today finds itself diminished in the universities and legal academy. Too often scholarship betrays no knowledge of what went before, or why legal institutions took the shape that they did. This series seeks to remedy that deficiency.

Studies in the History of Law and Justice will be theoretical and reflective. Volumes will address the history of law and justice from a critical and comparative viewpoint. The studies in this series will be strong bold narratives of the development of law and justice. Some will be suitable for a very broad readership.

Contributions to this series will come from scholars on every continent and in every legal system. Volumes will promote international comparisons and dialogue. The purpose will be to provide the next generation of lawyers with the models and narratives needed to understand and improve the law and justice of their own era. The series includes monographs focusing on a specific topic, as well as collections of articles covering a theme or collections of article by one author.

More information about this series at http://www.springer.com/series/11794

Filip Batselé

Liberty, Slavery and the Law in Early Modern Western Europe

Omnes Homines aut Liberi Sunt aut Servi

Springer

Filip Batselé
PhD Fellow—FWO (Research
Foundation—Flanders)—Institute
for Legal History
Ghent University
Ghent, Belgium

ISSN 2198-9842 ISSN 2198-9850 (electronic)
Studies in the History of Law and Justice
ISBN 978-3-030-36854-8 ISBN 978-3-030-36855-5 (eBook)
https://doi.org/10.1007/978-3-030-36855-5

This Springer imprint is published by the registered company Springer Nature Switzerland AG
The registered company address is: Gewerbestrasse 11, 6330 Cham, Switzerland

In memory of my grandparents
Maria Degraeve (1937–2014)
and Johan Bockstaele (1934–2019)

Preface

In 1777, a family of three enslaved persons petitioned the States General, the most important institution of the Dutch Republic. In their petition, Blondin and his family, who had lived most of their lives on a Suriname plantation, asked the States General to reconsider a previous decision and grant him and his family their freedom. What were the grounds for their claim? The enslaved family believed that, because they had previously been in the Dutch Republic for a short while, they had become personally free. The case of Blondin and his family was not unique. In fact, especially during the eighteenth century, several enslaved persons in the Low Countries, England, France and several other European countries were making the same claim. They and some of their lawyers believed that a "freedom principle," which legally entailed that one became free upon touching the soil of a certain country, had saved them from continued slavery. This book traces both the origins and the development of that freedom principle in several jurisdictions, namely England, the Low Countries and France.

This book aims to contribute to a fuller understanding of the legal manifestations of slavery. While the field has been dominated, understandably so given the numbers, by the legal manifestations of the Atlantic slave trade in the New World, it has always been clear that metropolis and colony were closely connected with one another. A growing number of scholars have become interested in the presence of enslaved persons on European soil. This book aims to both synthesize and supplement that growing body of literature.

Over the years, European countries have wrestled with their colonial past and involvement in the slave trade. To name but a few examples, in the wake of US universities, several British universities have started enquiring into their involvement in the slave trade and considered if something can and should be done to compensate for past gains they had derived therefrom. Likewise, closer to my own home, the Netherlands has continued to debate the role the slave trade had for the Dutch Republic. For example, a very recent report concluded that 5.2% of the Republic's GDP in 1770 was fueled by the Atlantic slave trade. This and other reports have prompted the difficult questions of apologies and possible compensation by municipal, regional and national authorities. In all these discussions, an argument that is sometimes brought to the fore is the idea that “slavery was in the Americas,” and that European states themselves had banned the practice of slavery much earlier. This book undoubtedly problematizes that latest contention.

The uses of history can be many. While achieving a better understanding of the past is a goal of history in itself, historical writing also has bearing upon the present-day reality. Although it is my hope that this book can also help to inform the debate on how European states should deal with their slavery past, the normative implications one wishes to draw from this book for present purposes are for the reader to decide.

Ghent, Belgium

Filip Batselé

Acknowledgements

This monograph is borne from the master's thesis for the degree of Master of Laws that I submitted at Ghent University in 2017. Over the last two years, the original manuscript was extensively edited and expanded upon. As a young scholar, I particularly owe a ton of gratitude to various persons who have been seminal in the conception of this monograph.

In the first place, I wish to thank the staff of the Ghent Legal History Institute. During the course of my own law studies, the Legal History Institute invariably served as the perfect redoubt for a student interested in the contextual history of law, and the courses taught by its staff gave me a lasting interest for European legal history. Professor Dhondt, as the promoter of the original master's thesis, and Professor Heirbaut, as the secretary, deserve particular gratitude. Professor Dhondt possesses an encyclopedic knowledge of European legal history, and both his substantive comments, as well as his willingness to always help a young student, have greatly improved the quality of this monograph. Likewise, Professor Heirbaut's intellectual curiosity and experience have been of great importance in forming my academic background. I would also like to thank John Finlay, Professor of Scots Law at the University of Glasgow. An Erasmus+ exchange does not only give one a sense of appreciation for the EU's motto of "united in diversity," but also the opportunity to see things through "another lens," which helps to frame research questions. It was through the work of the late Alan Watson, as well as the seminal *Montgomery v. Sheddan* case, both to which Professor Finlay introduced me, that the topic for my dissertation was further refined. I am also indebted to the various academics who were willing to answer e-mails from a curious law student, as well as to the peer reviewer who gave various useful comments for the completion of this book. Over the past years, I have had the enormous opportunity to study and conduct research in three different countries and have greatly enjoyed from conversations with scholars, and assistance from library staff, at Ghent University, the University of Glasgow and the Fletcher School of Law and Diplomacy at Tufts University. I also had the chance to make use of some of the resources of the Free University of Brussels, where my promoter Prof. Dhondt currently teaches and where I have also been able to do an academic assistant internship. My year in the USA, which has greatly influenced my views on law and society, would have been impossible without the financial support of the Belgian American Educational Foundation (BAEF) and the Fletcher School's LL.M. fund. Finally, gratitude also goes to Springer, the series editors Prof. Georges Martyn and Prof. Mortimer Sellers, Ms. Viradasarani Natarajan and Ms. Anja Trautmann, all who have been very helpful in the publishing process of my first monograph.

Some thanks to friends are also due. As a person, one benefits not only from the academic assistance received, but also from friends with whom one shares the joys of life. My friends in Ghent from both secondary school, law school and student organizations, as well as those made in Glasgow and Boston, have been an incredible support during my life. Mats Cuvelier, Carlos Santana Rubino, Samir Salimzade, Philippe Baert, Glenn Deduytsche, Jonas Veys, Arno Buyse and my own sister An-Sofie Batselé have been willing to make various orthographical corrections to the original manuscript. Many thanks also to Rami Blair, who provided superb proofreading for the final manuscript of this book. Finally, a word of thanks to my parents. A stable and positive home environment is of incredible importance to a young student, and in my parents I have always found the most kind and loving people. I cannot thank them enough for the past 25 years.

Ghent, Belgium
October 2019

Filip Batselé

Contents

Chapter 1
Introduction

1.1 Research Question and Research Goals

My research focuses on the following question: how did the "freedom principle" develop in the Dutch, French and English legal order in the Early Modern Period? The main topic is thus a descriptive one, although I will also offer a legal comparison in the final chapter, on the basis of the conclusions derived from the countries that were researched.[1] To better indicate the scope of the undertaking, let us first divide the central question in several constituent parts.

First, what do I mean by the "legal order"? The aforementioned "freedom principle" has often been linked to local and popular traditions, but this popular notion will not be the main scope of my research. Rather, I am interested how the law dealt with this issue. Did courts, legislators and scholars believe that slaves became free upon arrival in Nantes, Amsterdam or London? Of course, laws are primarily made when there is a perceived problem that needs to be addressed, and courts mainly come into play in cases of conflict. To take this into account, historiography and legal-historical research that focuses on some of the other archival records associated with enslaved records (e.g. different forms of administrative records such as birth and marriage records, or notarial deeds), next to the by now rather extensive historical literature on this topic, can help us to fill the gaps that a law, case and doctrine focused approach leaves.

---

[1]Normally, one uses either a dogmatic or a functional approach when engaged in comparative law. In the dogmatic approach, the researcher solely looks at the rules as they can be found in the formal sources of law. If one uses a functional approach, one does not take the legal norms as one's starting point, but rather starts with a problem. To discover how this problem is solved in different legal orders, one then takes both the formal sources of law and the broader legal, economic and cultural context into account. The comparison I am conducting cannot be easily put within either one of these categories. Although I am primarily interested in comparing the operation of the freedom principle per se, I will also take the broader socio-political context into account. In general, see Zweigert and Kötz (1998), pp. 32–47.

F. Batselé, *Liberty, Slavery and the Law in Early Modern Western Europe*, Studies in the History of Law and Justice 17, https://doi.org/10.1007/978-3-030-36855-5_1

Second, why the Early Modern Period? There are two reasons. One is that the origins of nationwide enunciations of the freedom principle have been traced back to at least the sixteenth century.[2] A second reason is that this was the era during which France, England and the United Provinces became actively engaged in the Atlantic slave trade. For each of these countries, we know that colonial proprietors often wanted to take slaves with them to their respective metropolises. This offers us the possibility of seeing whether and how the law dealt with this crossing of legal boundaries. Moreover, for our purposes, the focus will be the period between the first enunciations of national freedom principle traditions in the sixteenth century, and the Age of Revolutions around 1800. Where useful, I will mention, albeit in brief, some material that stretches to the official abolition of slavery in the respective countries.[3]

Third, why France, England and the United Provinces? Several reasons compelled me to choose these countries.[4] First, all three were actively involved in the Atlantic slave trade. Some literature has already shown the tensions between this freedom principle tradition on the one hand, and the presence of slaves on the other hand for these countries. Second, the constraints of time and writing space also necessitated a choice, and as a result, some countries with an "Atlantic connection" such as Scotland will not be discussed.[5] Third, partially due to linguistic reasons (e.g. the Nordic countries), and partially due to some regions' very limited involvement in the Atlantic slave trade (e.g. the German speaking realm), the German and Nordic region are omitted as well.[6] Fourth, Portugal and Spain will also not be discussed, as the idea of the "freedom principle" simply did not exist there in most of the Early Modern Era, and only came up in the eighteenth and nineteenth century.[7]Finally, the United States is also omitted, with the exception of those aspects that are relevant to

---

[2]Peabody and Grinberg (2011), p. 332.

[3]1834 in England, 1794 for France (with a small *excursus* up to the second abolition in 1844) and 1863 for the Dutch Republic (and later Kingdom of the Netherlands).

[4]As the various provinces of the Dutch Republic and the Southern Netherlands were in a personal union starting from the Habsburg period until the 1581 Act of Abjuration, North and South will be treated together here. After the secession, the crux of the exposition will focus on the United Provinces (alternatively called the Dutch Republic). I will give some remarks on the (little) available material we know of regarding slavery and the law in the Spanish and Austrian Netherlands. When I refer to "Low Countries", I am talking about both the Northern and the Southern part.

[5]Persons interested in this matter will find satisfaction in i.a. the works of Professor Iain Whyte and Professor John Cairns. Professor Cairns also gave an introduction to the topic of slavery in Scotland as the speaker of the inaugural Alan Watson Memorial Lectures in 2019, and which are freely available online. I wish to thank Professor Cairns for having sent me all his articles related to slavery and the law. Private correspondence with Professor John Cairns, 30/05/2016.

[6]For Central Europe, see Brahm and Rosenhaft (2016). I should also mention here that the European Research Council is currently funding a project on "The Holy Roman Empire of the German Nation and its Slaves", the results of which will greatly enhance our knowledge on slavery and the freedom principle in the German-speaking sphere. On the Nordic countries, see Hall (1992); Palsson (2016).

[7]A generic overview can be found in Phillips (2014), pp. 10–27. On the freedom principle in Spain and Portugal more specifically, see Martín Casares and García Barranco (2011); Nogueira Da Silva and Grinberg (2011).

the British domestic response to slavery. The literature on the American experience with slavery from independence to the end of the Civil War is incredibly extensive.[8]

To answer the central question, I have divided the monograph into four main parts, one for each major issue (next to this introductory chapter, as well as a short concluding chapter).

In the first part, I provide the necessary background information for this study. First, I look at the legal definition of slavery as it has been fleshed out by twentieth century international law, and assess its relevance for the early modern era. Second, I examine the situation in Europe until the end of the Middle Ages (ca. 1500) both from a theoretical and a practical point of view. I ask if and how slavery as an institution was legitimised in law by European scholars. At the same time, I will also briefly assess whether slavery still existed "on the ground" in the countries discussed by the end of the fifteenth century. Third, we take a brief look at the situation at the other side of the Atlantic for the period between the end of the fifteenth century and the Age of Revolutions. How was slavery legally justified during the Atlantic slave trade from the point of view of legal doctrine? Likewise, if we wish to understand what the status of slaves coming to Europe was in the metropolis, we need to know which laws governed them in the colonies.

In the second part, I discuss whether the freedom principle had become part of the legal systems of England, France and the Low Countries by the mid-seventeenth century. Basically, this means that we have to ask ourselves whether the domestic laws of England, France, and the United Provinces still recognised slavery, as well as how the legal order of these countries reacted when faced with slaves coming from other countries.

In the third part, I investigate whether, and if so how, the domestic legal order's approach changed during the heyday of the Atlantic slave trade, which I broadly define as the period between 1650 and 1800. During this period, especially the latter part of the eighteenth century, slaves tended to show up more numerously in the metropolis through a variety of means (chiefly masters taking them with them during visits to the motherland, or stowaway slaves appearing when the ship in which they had hidden themselves appeared in a European port). We have to ask whether the law accommodated or opposed this. Given the amount of material, this part is divided in three chapters, one for each country (the United Provinces and the Southern Netherlands are dealt with together).

Finally, in the fourth part, I hope to set out some of the similarities and differences in the legal application of the freedom principle. I aim to compare the legal application of the "freedom principle" between England, France and the Low Countries in the following ways. First, was the freedom principle part of the domestic legal order of these countries by the middle of the seventeenth century? If so, in which source of law could it be found, and how did this come to be? Second, did anything change

[8] A generic overview is Rael (2015). Two works focusing on the legal aspects of slavery in the United States, the former on the formative period and the latter on the final decade of slavery, are Van Cleve (2011); Blumrosen and Blumrosen (2005). An extensive bibliography on American slavery can be found at the Oxfordbibliographies entry "The Growth and Decline of Slavery in North America".

during the time of the Atlantic slave trade? How did legislators react to this issue in the metropolis, and how did courts deal with it? Also, do these sources of law tell us the "whole story", or did the situation on the ground diverge? Are there any other notable similarities and difference between the discussed countries?

1.2 Status Quaestionis

The innovations of this book can obviously only build upon the solid foundations of past scholarship. Let me thus say a word or two about the state of the research. Using Watson's language, which "details or expressions of the law of slavery" have indeed already caught the attention of scholars in this field?

To keep the exercise manageable in scope, some exclusions must apply. In this overview, I mostly limit myself to writings on the freedom principle in England, the Low Countries and France during the period 1500–1800. The literature on slavery, even only in Europe, is simply far too vast to cover. To not completely brush this matter aside however, I would refer the reader to two sources in particular. First, there is the magisterial "Cambridge World History of Slavery", a 4-volume work (Volume 2 on the Medieval Period, 500–1420 is still in the making as of 2019), which gives coverage of all aspects of slavery. Second, as I will refer to later, Joseph Miller's *Slavery and Slaving in World History: A Bibliography, 1900–1991*, as well as the annual supplements to this bibliography that are published yearly in the journal *Slavery & Abolition*, are incredible tools for all research into slavery.

Even within this paired down exercise, a proliferation in studies is visible over the past decades. If the clear focus of the relationship between slavery and the law has tended to focus on the American side of the Transatlantic slave trade—with good reason, given the sheer numbers, Europe has come more to the fore in recent decades. Whilst the number of slaves on European soil in the Early Modern era was infinitely smaller, Europe did not stand separate from the evolutions in the New World. If anything, Atlantic history, as a separate sphere, has become a more popular strand of historical research, and historians of the transatlantic slave trade have certainly been seminal in this evolution.[9] As a result, some excellent recent works, such as Michael Guasco's *Slaves and Englishmen: Human Bondage in the Early Atlantic World*, Brett Rushfordt's *Bonds of Alliance: Indigenous and Atlantic Slaveries in New France* and Kwame Nimako, Glenn Willemsen and Stephen Small's *The Dutch Atlantic: Slavery, Abolition and Emancipation* incorporate both European and American aspects of slavery to a larger account than before.

French literature on the presence of enslaved persons on French soil dates back at least a century. Whilst the legal implications remained mostly in the background in these studies, Lucien Peytraud's 1897 *L'esclavage aux Antilles françaises avant 1789: d'après des documents inédits des archives coloniales*, Jules Mathorez' 1919

[9] On Atlantic history in general, see Games (2006).

Les étrangers en France sous l'Ancien Régime and Shelby McCloy's 1961 *The Negro in France* are but the three most extensive publications in this regard.

In more recent history, both the topics of Mediterranean slavery, as well as the presence of slaves on metropolitan French soil have been the subject of various monographs.

On the former topic, one could point to Robert C. Davis' *Christian Slaves, Muslim Masters* in general, and to Gillian Weiss' 2011 *Captives and Corsairs: France and Slavery in the Early Modern Mediterranean* in particular.

On the slave presence in France, the work of Sue Peabody and Pierre Boulle stands out in particular. Most importantly, Sue Peabody's *There Are No Slaves in France: The Political Culture of Race and Slavery in the Ancien Régime* is a seminal work. Peabody's work rests (primarily) upon a close reading of the slave cases that came before the Parisian Admiralty Court, as well as the legislative initiatives regarding the black presence in France. This can be supplemented by much of the work of Pierre Boulle, who has also written on legal aspects of the black presence in France but has equally well written more broadly on the black presence in France, such as in his 2007 *Race et Esclavage dans la France de l'Ancien Régime*. Most recently, the two have collaborated in the writing of a 2014 book, *Le droit des noirs en France au temps de l'esclavage*, containing many of the primary sources on the subject for France, as well as providing up-to-date summaries of the main episodes on the black presence in France.

Next to Peabody and Boulle (Peabody most recently also wrote a marvellous piece of micro-history on this topic, entitled *Madeleine's Children - Family, Freedom, Secrets, and Lies in France's Indian Ocean Colonies*), other authors have been prolific as well. The late Marcel Koufinkana, Dwain C. Pruitt and Erick Noël are but some of the more prominent names. Interestingly, some of the more recent literature has tended to veer away from a focus on Paris, and towards closer assessments of the French provinces bordering the Atlantic. Armel de Wismel and Dwain C. Pruitt have done so for Nantes for example, and Éric Saugera and Dominique Rogér have done the same for the Bordeaux area. Finally, I should mention the three-volume *Dictionnaire des gens de couleur dans la France moderne*, which was recently published under the editorial direction of Erick Noël. These three volumes provide a painstakingly researched list of all persons of colour who had set foot on French soil before the Revolution. It will undoubtedly be of interest for future micro-histories of the French slave trade and beyond.

The country with the most abundant volume of material on the unfree presence on metropolitan soil is certainly England.

First, there is a rather abundant literature dealing specifically with the black presence in England, and which to a more or lesser degree also engages with the legal debates. James Walvin's 1973 *Black and White: The Negro and English Society*, 1555–1945, Folarin Shyllon's 1974 *Black Slaves in Britain*, and Peter Fryer's 1984 *Staying Power: The History of Black People in Britain* are three of the best known examples here. A more recent example in this genre, drawing on an extensive database, is Kathleen Chater's 2011 *Untold Histories: Black People in England and Wales during the Period of the British Slave Trade, C. 1660–1807.*

Likewise, the legal literature is vast. The great majority of attention has been paid to the case of *Somerset v. Stewart*, by far the most well-known case of an enslaved person on metropolitan soil. Whilst the case was the subject of popular discussion in the eighteenth and nineteenth century, the "re-evaluation" of the case's importance can be said to have started with Edward Fiddes' 1934 article *Lord Mansfield and the Sommersett Case* in *Law Quarterly Review*. Ph.D. theses have been devoted to this single case, as well as monographs. For an extensive evaluation of the literature on Somerset up until 1973, I would refer to Carol P. Bauer's 1973 NYU PhD dissertation called *Law, Slavery, and Sommersett's Case in Eighteenth-Century England*. For the more recent literature, Steven M. Wise's 2005 monograph *Though the Heavens May Fall—The Landmark Trial That Led to the End of Human Slavery* (although certainly covering more than just Somerset) is a bit more of a popularized account, but very instructive. Much of the secondary literature is well described in this work, although I would also point to the importance of much of the work of James Oldham in this regard. Oldham has written meticulously on eighteenth century English law, Lord Mansfield, and Somerset's case.

Whilst *Somerset* certainly continues to dominate the debate, the past two decades have also seen much work that went beyond *Somerset*. This work has ranged from assessments of slavery in England before (i.a. Travis Glasson's article *"Baptism doth not bestow Freedom": Missionary Anglicanism, Slavery, and the Yorke-Talbot Opinion, 1701–30*) and after (i.a. Ruth Paley's article *After Somerset: Mansfield, Slavery and the Law in England 1772–1830*) Somerset's case, attempts to put the English law on slavery in its imperial context (George van Cleve's excellent article *Somerset's Case and Its Antecedents in Imperial Perspective*, as well as his book *A Slaveholders' Union: Slavery, Politics, and the Constitution in the Early American Republic* on the consequences of Somerset in the US particularly stand out), and evaluations of other actors' involvement in the English law of slavery (for example, on Parliament, Ruth Paley's article *Parliament and Slavery, 1660–c. 1710*). Whilst Scotland will not be treated extensively, I would point out that John W. Cairns and Iain Whyte, amongst others, are excellent authors treating these same issues for Scotland.

The same level of comprehensiveness does not yet exist on the black presence in the Low Countries, and the potential for research here has only recently been tapped. Reasons for this relative lack, in comparison with France and England, can probably be found both in the number of black people on Dutch soil (comparatively low, as we shall see), as well as linguistic reasons.

This is particularly the case for the Southern Netherlands, the territory of which more or less corresponds with current-day Belgium, where admittedly, the black presence in the eighteenth century must have been minimal. However, it must be noted that one of the greatest scholars of international law, Ernest Nys, in his little-known 1890 article *L'esclavage noir devant les jurisconsultes et les cours de justice* had already covered a lot of the field for the Southern Netherlands. The first half of the twentieth century also included some analysis of the sixteenth century slave presence in the then economically very important port of Antwerp (i.a. Jan Goris' 1923 article *Uit de Geschiedenis der vorming van het Antwerpsch stadsrecht: Slavernij te Antwerpen in de XVIde eeuw* in the Bijdragen tot de geschiedenis). Somewhat surprisingly, the primary material to re-evaluate this topic has been left untouched by historians for at least the past 50 years.

There is more to be found on the Dutch Republic, current day Netherlands. Some books do an excellent job of covering the presence of foreigners on Dutch soil, and tangentially touch upon the legal aspects. In particular, I refer to Gert Oostindie's and Emy Maduro's two volume work *In het land van de overheerser* for Dutch speakers, as well as Mark Ponte's recent work on the existence of a (very small) Afro-Atlantic community in seventeenth century Amsterdam. In the English language, Jonathan Schorsch' chapter on Amsterdam in his *Jews and Blacks in the Early Modern World* and Dienke Hondius' *Blackness in Western Europe: Racial Patterns of Paternalism and Exclusion* are instructive, recent examples. Professor Hondius has recently written much on the black presence in the Netherlands, and many of her articles complement the references to the Dutch Republic in this monograph.

Extensive treatment of the legal issues is scarcer to find. Of the older literature, especially Priester's 1987 *De Nederlandse houding ten aanzien van de slavenhandel en slavernij, 1596-1863: het gedrag van de slavenhandelaren van de Commercie Compagnie van Middelburg in de 18e eeuw,* is useful, mostly so for *Ideengeschichte* and the role of the province of Zeeland. In more recent times, Karwan Fatah-Black (who writes on many aspects of Dutch colonial history) and Dienke Hondius have included aspects of legal analysis in their articles and books on the subject. Next to this, monographs that deal with other areas of the Dutch colonial realm also sometimes include interesting chapters or paragraph of relevance to the metropolitan situation concerning slavery (for example, Han Jordaan's work on Curaçao, as well as the work by Karel Schoeman on the Dutch Cape Colony).

Many authors have attempted to make some comparative approaches between these case-studies. Often, these comparisons are shorter and more general[10], though some broader treatments do exists.[11] All in all, extensive legal comparison from a pan-European perspective is lacking. The most noteworthy approach (although again not with an exclusively legal angle) was the 2011 special issue of the journal Slavery & Abolition on the freedom principle. This issue has consequently been published as the book *Free Soil in the Atlantic World* in 2014, edited by Sue Peabody and Keila Grinberg. As a very useful point d'entrée for comparative approaches to the freedom principle, Peabody and Grinberg's article *Free Soil: The Generation and Circulation of an Atlantic Legal Principle* is indispensable. The other articles cover national experiences, but do not engage in extensive comparative work.

Given all this, I believe the relevance of this work to be threefold.

First, the book hopes to synthesise the wealth of available material on the application of the freedom principle by "judges, legislators and professors", to quote the

---

[10]For example Tugendhat (2017); Peabody (1996), pp. 3–10; Priester (1987), pp. 93–96.

[11]For example Drescher (2009), pp. 26–87; Hondius (2014), pp. 211–246. Treatment of the freedom principle in these works does not always focus on legal aspects. The same can also be said of David Brion Davis' impressive trilogy *The Problem of Slavery in Western Culture*, *The Problem of Slavery in the Age of Revolution* and *The Problem of Slavery in the Age of Emancipation*.

title of one of the late Professor Raoul Van Caenegem's works, in the Early Modern Period. Most of the current literature focuses on one country, or only engages in a very limited comparative exercise, and many scholars tend to remain within their own legal tradition. Likewise, legal-historical aspects of the freedom principle are often not the main focus. In that sense, this work will hopefully be able to serve as a more extensive entry point for the legal-historical study of this topic, and provide bibliographical material on not only the English, but also the French- and Dutch-language literature.

Second, as said, the literature on the application of the freedom principle in the Low Countries by courts and legislators is relatively scarce. Both the legal ramifications of the early black presence in the Southern Netherlands, as well as the background to the eighteenth century legislation on the black presence in the United Provinces, are understudied. I have re-assessed the existing scholarship and expanded upon it. Equally, I make use of hitherto undiscussed archival material to appreciate the role of the Dutch States General on the issue of black slaves arriving in the United Provinces.

Finally, my comparison between the legal application of the freedom principle by courts and legislators in the various countries goes further than existing literature. I theorise as to why legislators decided to intervene (or not) in this matter and try to explain some of the national peculiarities of the freedom principle. In this regard, my work can serve as a useful avenue for further research, which is especially needed for the hitherto unexplored material on the Low Countries.

I am cognisant of the limits of this work. My focus on the "judges, legislators, and professors" is somewhat biased in favour of addressing the law in the books. Furthermore, the monograph takes more of a national and regional rather than a local perspective, which means that decisions of local authorities and courts are certainly not always extensively treated. My focus likewise means that I do not fully treat the "law in society" and the many informal regulations that enslavers created on the ground to keep the enslaved under their power. Given the very limited written records that the enslaved themselves have left behind, our knowledge of this will always be imperfect and very dependent on the different glimpses of their lives which we can extract from the records (e.g. notarial deeds, birth and marriage registers, etc.). At several times, I will make reference to this difference between the law in books and the law in society approach, but much research on the latter remains to be done in coming years.

1.3 Methodology and Heuristics

The study is based upon a general historiographical literature study, supplemented by primary source material (legislation, case law, doctrine, and archival material).

General legal historical work, next to work on select aspects of the slavery and slave trade regime, added flesh to the legalist bones of this work. All these works are covered in the bibliography, though I would point the reader particularly at four works that were of immense use to this work. Jean Allain's *Slavery in International Law: Of Human Exploitation and Trafficking* contains an excellent survey of the international law aspects of slavery and the history of the slave trade. Likewise, Alan Watson's *Slave Law in the Americas* is pivotal to understand the colonial aspects of European slave law. Seymour Drescher's *Abolition: A History of Slavery and Antislavery* is a work of impressive breath and coverage which deals with abolition in general, but also provides a useful *point d'entrée* for freedom principle research specifically. Finally, Sue Peabody and Keila Grinberg's *Free Soil in the Atlantic World* contains must-read essays for initial research into the freedom principle. Besides for these books, secondary literature can most easily be found using Paul Finkelman's *Slavery and Slaving in World History*. This book serves as a massive bibliography for anything written related to slavery between 1900 and 1991. Since then, bibliographical supplements have been published annually in the periodical *Slavery & Abolition*.

In the first part (Chapter 2), I use a combination of primary and secondary materials. To assess the means by which slavery was legally justified, I have made use of the authoritative *Classics of International Law*-series. As the series is focused on the Early Modern Period, the choice of primary material for Classical Antiquity and the Middle Ages was more eclectic. Given the importance of Aristotle and Roman law in all of the Classics' remarks of slavery, I have discussed the legitimation of slavery that can be found in Aristotle's *Politics* and in the *Corpus Iuris Civilis*. Next to those, I have looked at the works of some of the most important Medieval thinkers on slavery, primarily on the basis of the references in the dated but still immensely useful R.W. Carlyle and A.J. Carlyle's *A History of Mediaeval Political Theory in the West* series. To collect the necessary secondary material, I extensively made use of the online database Oxfordbibliographies, which includes concise literature lists on many relevant topics (e.g. *Slavery in Dutch America and the West Indies*), written by academics.

For England, statutory law for this period can be found in two well-recognised collections, namely *The Statutes of the Realm* (pre-1713) and *The Statutes at Large*. The case law that I discuss can mostly be found in the first book of Catterall's *Judicial Cases Concerning American Slavery and the Negro* collection. Catterall only mentions cases that came before the superior courts of the common law (King's Bench and the Court of Common Pleas) and the Court of Chancery, Court of Star Chamber and Admiralty. For all cases in which Granville Sharp, the famous English abolitionist, was involved, Andrew Lyall's recent book *Granville Sharp's Cases on Slavery* is excellent. I have tried to refrain as much as possible from quoting unreported cases that I have not been able to consult myself (both from local and superior courts), only referencing them where I have felt it necessary. Though not primary sources of law, I use some of the pivotal treatises on English law: Glanvill, Bracton, Littleton's *New Tenures*, Coke's *Commentary on Littleton*, Hale's *History of the Common Law* and Blackstone's *Commentaries on the Laws of England*.

For France, the essential primary sources on this subject (especially royal law and customary law) are found in Sue Peabody and Pierre Boulle's *Le droit des noirs en France au temps de l' esclavage*. This book also contains parts of the *mémoires* of lawyers for the few court cases related to slavery where these were published.

As all of these published cases are related to proceedings before Parisian courts, I have counterbalanced this with secondary literature on the situation in other areas of France. This has been supplemented by works of seventeenth and eighteenth century French scholars.

For the Low Countries, legislation can be found in the *Recueil des ordonnances des Pays-Bas* for the Southern Netherlands, and the various *Groot placaet-boecken* for the United Provinces, which contain both the laws of the States General (*Staten Generaal*) and of the States of Holland related to slavery. There are no published collections of cases related to slavery. Additionally, I have analysed the *Generaale index op de registers der resolutien van de Heeren Staaten van Holland en West-vriesland* for the period 1524–1790, to see if the issue of slaves coming to the United Provinces was ever discussed by the central authorities of Holland. (As Holland was the province most involved in the Atlantic slave trade, it made more sense to look at these resolutions rather than those of another province.)[12] The results from that enquiry were then used to trace archival material for the States General, which can be found in the Dutch National Archives in The Hague.

Finally, before starting, a word on terminology. I have chosen to stay as close to the original sources in writing this work, and this also means that I sometimes employ the language of the (mainly eighteenth century) writers. When it comes to race relations, these writers used other words for the enslaved than we obviously would in the twenty-first century. English writers routinely called black slaves "blackamoor" or "negroe". Likewise, French writers sometimes went for "nègre" and Dutch writers for "neger". A variety of other terms were also used, which sometimes but not always also tell us more about the origins of the enslaved (which could come from Africa, but equally from the Americas or the East Indies). In my own analysis, I refer to black, coloured people, slaves or enslaved (the latter two obviously only if we know this personal status). However, when I quote primary material, I will refer to the words used by the contemporary writers, which will be made clear by italicising the word.

References

Blumrosen AW, Blumrosen RG (2005) Slave nation: how slavery united the colonies and sparked the American revolution. Sourcebooks Inc., Naperville

Brahm F, Rosenhaft E (2016) Slavery hinterland: transatlantic slavery and continental Europe, 1680–1850. Boydell & Brewer, Suffolk

Drescher S (2009) Abolition: a history of slavery and antislavery. Cambridge University Press, Cambridge

[12]It is certainly true that the province of Zeeland, in particular the cities of Vlissingen and Middelburg, were also heavily involved in the Atlantic slave trade, certainly so with the Middelburgse Commercie Compagnie after the Dutch West India Company lost its monopoly on the Dutch slave trade in 1730. However, whilst involved in the slave trade, none of the cities in Zeeland had a significant black presence, which explains the focus on Holland. Priester (1987), pp. 17–20.

Games A (2006) Atlantic history: definitions, challenges, and opportunities. Am Hist Rev 111:741–757

Hall NAT (1992) Slave society in the Danish West Indies: St. Thomas, St. John and St Croix. Aarhus University Press, Baltimore

Hargrave F (1772) An argument in the case of James Sommersett, A Negro. W.Otridge, London

Hondius D (2014) Blackness in Western Europe: racial patterns of paternalism and exclusion. Transaction Publishers, New Brunswick

Martín Casares A, García Barranco M (2011) Legislation on free soil in nineteenth-century Spain: the case of the slave Rufino and its consequences (1858–1879). Slavery Abol 32:461–476

Nogueira Da Silva C, Grinberg K (2011) Soil Free from Slaves: Slave Law in Late Eighteenth-and Early Nineteenth-Century Portugal. Slavery Abol 32:431–446

Palsson G (2016) The man who stole himself: the slave Odyssey of Hans Jonathan. The University of Chicago Press, Chicago

Peabody S (1996) There are no slaves in France: the political culture of race and slavery in the ancien régime. Oxford University Press, New York

Peabody S, Grinberg K (2011) Free soil: the generation and circulation of an Atlantic legal principle. Slavery Abol 32:331–339

Phillips WD (2014) Slavery in medieval and early modern Iberia [middle ages series]. University of Pennsylvania Press, Philadelphia

Priester LR (1987) De Nederlandse houding ten aanzien van de slavenhandel en slavernij, 1596–1863 : het gedrag van de slavenhandelaren van de Commercie Compagnie van Middelburg in de 18e eeuw. Commissie Regionale Geschiedbeoefening Zeeland, Middelburg

Rael P (2015) Eighty-eight years: the long death of slavery in the United States, 1777–1865. University of Georgia Press, Athens

Tugendhat M (2017) Slavery and Comparative Law in Eighteenth Century England, University of Leicester Research Paper No. 17-08

Van Cleve G (2011) A slaveholders' union: slavery, politics, and the constitution in the early American Republic. University of Chicago Press, Chicago

Watson A (1989) Slave Law in the Americas. University of Georgia press, Athens, GA

Zweigert K, Kötz H (1998) An introduction to comparative law, 3rd edn. Oxford University Press, Oxford

Chapter 2
The Legal and Institutional Framework of Slavery

2.1 Defining Slavery in International Law

The first question posed here has proven to be one of the more difficult questions in debates on this topic: what, in law, constitutes slavery?

Some of the doyens of slavery studies have grappled with this question extensively, and a multitude of possible definitions have emerged. For example, for Orlando Patterson, slavery could most adequately be defined as the "permanent, violent domination of natally alienated and generally dishonoured persons".[1] Another of those doyens, the late David Brion Davis, saw things more in terms of a spectrum ("one can imagine a spectrum of states of freedom and dependency or powerlessness, with various types of serfdom and peonage shading off into actual slavery"), whilst simultaneously recognising that within slavery systems, large differences existed in the amount of protections and rights a slave did (or did not) enjoy.[2]

Likewise for many eighteenth century abolitionist, the question of defining slavery has proven to be an elusive task. Even Granville Sharp, counsel in the famous case of Somerset v. Stewart which we will discuss, struggled with defining the institution.[3] Since the beginning of the nineteenth century, the international community had started with progressively restricting the Atlantic slave trade, before it turned to the institution of slavery itself.[4]

Although the European powers themselves abolished slavery in their empires in the nineteenth century, the international legal framework regarding slavery mostly took shape in the twentieth century. In particular, the Slavery, Servitude, Forced

---

[1] Patterson (1982), p. 13.

[2] Brion Davis (2006), p. 36. Also see the discussion at Finkelman and Drescher (2017), pp. 766–770.

[3] Hargrave (1772), 13–16.

[4] Decaux (2009), pp. 35–80; Allain (2012), pp. 57–104. On international law and the abolition of slavery and the slave trade, also see Erpelding (2017).

F. Batselé, *Liberty, Slavery and the Law in Early Modern Western Europe*, Studies in the History of Law and Justice 17, https://doi.org/10.1007/978-3-030-36855-5_2

Labour and Similar Institutions and Practices Convention of 1926 (Slavery Convention 1926)[5] and the Supplementary Convention on the Abolition of Slavery, the Slave Trade and Institutions and Practices Similar to Slavery of 1956 (Supplementary Convention 1956)[6] have been used in past decades to define what slavery is, and more importantly, as some of the main instruments in the battle against slavery. One must keep in mind, however, that besides these conventions, there is general agreement that the prohibition of slavery has reached the status of *jus cogens* within customary international law.[7] Slavery itself is defined in Art. 1 of the Slavery Convention 1926, which states:

(a) Slavery is the status or condition of a person over whom any or all of the powers attaching to the right of ownership are exercised.[8]

The problematic aspect with this definition is that the exact meaning of "any or all of the powers attaching to the right of ownership" has never been properly defined in the *travaux préparatoires* of the Slavery Convention 1926.[9] An interesting debate has ensued, which has led different scholars towards a 1953 Report by the Secretary-General of the United Nations to the Council on slavery, the slave trade and other forms of servitude.[10] In this report, the Secretary-General drew a clear historical line from Roman times to the current era by concluding that what is meant with the powers attaching to the right of ownership is nothing more than the authority which a master had over his slave in Roman law, the so called *dominica potestas*.

Proceeding on this conclusion, the Secretary-General then described these powers as follows:

1. the individual of servile status may be made the object of a purchase;
2. the master may use the individual of servile status, and in particular his capacity to work, in an absolute manner, without any restriction other than that which might be expressly provided by law;
3. the products of labour of the individual of servile status become the property of the master without any compensation commensurate to the value of the labour;

---

[5]Slavery, Servitude, Forced Labour and Similar Institutions and Practices Convention of 1926, *League of Nations Treaty Series*, vol. 60, p. 253; entered into force on 9 March 1927.

[6]Supplementary Convention on the Abolition of Slavery, the Slave Trade and Institutions and Practices Similar to Slavery of 1956 (the Supplementary Convention), *United Nations Treaty Series*, vol. 226, p. 3; entered into force on 30 April 1957.

[7]Brownlie (1998), p. 515. For the prohibition of slavery as a norm of the *ius cogens*, also see *Barcelona Traction, Light and Power Company Ltd (Belgium v. Spain)*, Judgment, I.C.J. Reports 1970, para. 34.

[8]Given that the definition mentions both 'status' and 'condition', the former is meant to apply to *de jure* cases of slavery, which does not formally exist anymore in any domestic legal system around the world. The word condition, on the other hand, is used to address cases of de facto slavery. For a recent Australian case about sex slavery, with de facto slavery being addressed by the court, see The Queen v Tang [2008], *HCA 39*, 28 August 2008.

[9]On the travaux préparatoires of the Slavery Convention 1926 and the Supplementary Convention 1956, see Allain (2008).

[10]Some examples of this approach are to be found in: Allain (2012); Lassen (1988).

4. the ownership of the individual of servile status can be transferred to another person;
5. the servile status is permanent, that is to say, it cannot be terminated by the will of the individual subject to it;
6. the servile status is transmitted ipso facto to descendants of the individual having such status.[11]

Although other scholars have sometimes arrived at slightly different definitions, most recently through the 2012 Bellagio-Harvard Guidelines (which take the Slavery Convention 1926 as a starting point), the above characteristics are arguably a good benchmark to understand what exactly is meant with slavery.[12]

A clear definition is all the more important when taking into account that, during the long lifespan of slavery, the institution often existed besides other, sometimes similar ones. For our purposes, it is especially important to note the difference between slavery and serfdom, which permeated Medieval Europe. Alas, the two slavery conventions have proven to be rather confusing when it comes to defining the difference between the institutions of slavery and serfdom. On the one hand, serfdom had been categorized as a form of slavery for the purposes of the Slavery Convention 1926.[13] On the other hand, the Supplementary Convention 1956 then made a separate definition of serfdom, being:

(b) Serfdom, that is to say, the condition or status of a tenant who is by law, custom or agreement bound to live and labour on land belonging to another person and to render some determinate service to such other person, whether for reward or not, and is not free to change his status.

Given the confusion created, the Supplementary Convention went on to clarify that each State Party should strive towards the complete abolition or abandonment of serfdom, whether or not it was already covered by the definition of slavery in the Slavery Convention 1926.[14]

The term slavery in this book, given the historical link, will correspond with the characteristics ascribed to it by the UN Secretary General in 1953, although these six characteristics are evidently present to differing degrees at different times. As concerns serfdom, the provided definition covers some forms of medieval serfdom but not others (in particular, medieval serfdom did not necessarily have to be linked

---

[11] United Nations Economic and Social Council, Slavery, the slave trade and other forms of servitude: report of the secretary-general, E/2357.

[12] The Bellagio-Harvard guidelines are a set of principles that were established by a group of scholars from various backgrounds working in the field of slavery, so as to come to an internally consistent interpretation of the legal definition of slavery (the principles can be found in Allain (2012), pp. 371–379).

[13] Office of the United Nations High Commissioner for Human Rights, Abolishing Slavery and its Contemporary Forms, HR/PUB/02/4 (New York and Geneva: United Nations, 2002), p. 17.

[14] Although this might seem like an illogical approach, it has to be borne in mind that the Supplementary Convention 1956 tried to enlarge the scope of the 1926 Convention. In particular, a definition of serfdom was added so as to bring the Latin American institution of *peonage*, a somehow similar institution to medieval serfdom, within the scope of the two slavery conventions.

to being bound to live and labour on land). Second, although there is clearly some overlap between slavery and serfdom within current international legal practise, given the timeframe of the discussion, we will treat both institutions as being separate. The main question of this book is about slavery on European soil in the Early Modern Era, not about serfdom. That being said, the two institutions do have similarities and could be found concurrently during some eras. Thus, a short account of the historiographical research on the evolution from slavery to serfdom in medieval Europe will be discussed later in this chapter, so as to clarify the difference between medieval slavery and serfdom.

2.2 Slavery in Europe—From Antiquity to the End of the Middle Ages (Ca. 1500)

Before starting with a discussion on the freedom principle in Europe during the Early Modern Era, we need to know what the situation was at the end of the Middle Ages. First, how was slavery legally justified by the great European philosophers and scholars? Second, we need to know what the institutional reality was. Were slaves still part of the social fabric of fifteenth century England, France and the Low Countries?

2.2.1 Legitimising Slavery Before the Atlantic Slave Trade: Between Aristotle and the Romans

2.2.1.1 Greek Thinking on Slavery: Balancing Physis and Nomos

The first stop within our intellectual tour of European slavery ought to lie in Classical Greece. The Greek tradition is important in two ways. First, because of the first conscious theorising on the institution of slavery and second due to Aristotle's writings on slavery in *Politics*. His ideas would come to have a profound influence on European medieval thinkers within the scholastic tradition.[15]

Theorising on slavery only began long after the institution itself was established. This can be aptly seen in the Homeric world, where slavery was accepted as fact, without any underlying theory. However, in the ensuing centuries, the Greek view of slavery would change by two parallel evolutions: Hellenic nationalism and a disdain for certain banausic occupations.[16] This sense of Hellenic unity increased by a combination of factors: leagues, pilgrimages and festivals which gave the Greeks some sense of cultural unity as opposed to 'barbarian' outsiders, the Greek wars

---

[15]Aristotle's ideas were particularly important when it came to attempts to legitimise the enslavement by the Spaniards of the Indians in their new world colonies.

[16]An account of this evolution can be found in Schlaifer (1960), pp. 93–104.

believe that it is a general principle of law that anyone conquered in a war is rightly enslaved. On the one hand, no one would agree that it is right to enslave Greek noblemen in a war. On the other hand, reasoning in the context of wars between the Greeks and outsiders, everyone would agree that it is right to enslave barbarian noblemen. Again, Aristotle concludes that the common denominator must be that there exist natural slaves and natural masters.[30] In the end, Aristotle's final conclusion is that physical force in and of itself cannot justly make someone a slave of another person, but that the true justification is the difference in nature between master and slave. If this difference is present, then the use of force by the natural master is allowed against his natural slave.

2.2.1.2 Slavery in Roman Law: Institution of the Ius Gentium

If there has ever been an example of what is called a "slave society", Ancient Rome immediately comes to mind. Spurred by rapid conquest at the end of the Republican period, the trickle of slaves already present in Rome for centuries quickly grew to a steady flow of slaves, amounting to a conservative estimate of 2.000.000 slaves at the end of the Republic in Italy (about 35% of the Italian population).[31] Generally, the number sharply declined towards the end of the Roman Era.[32]

The Roman slave himself was seen as some form of hybrid creature: both a thing (*res*) and a human being (*persona*). On the one hand, given that the slave was subject to ownership (*dominium*), he could be judged as a *res* (more specifically, he fell within the economically more important category of the *res mancipi)*. On the other hand, the slave's personhood was not denied. Although in modern terms, the term *persona* might imply as a necessity the capacity for rights, for the Romans this term only meant "human being".[33] From a legal point of view, this hybrid status did not entail some inherent consistency, as it was perfectly possible to think of a human being as property, more specifically, thinking property.[34]

There were various means through which one could become a slave in the Roman system. The most common one, certainly since the early Imperial period, was by birth to a slave mother.[35] The second largest source, which however became less

---

[30] Aristotle (1932), 1255a 24–40, 1255b 1–4.

[31] Finley (1980), p. 80. One should bear in mind that the Italian Roman heartland is not representative for slavery throughout the Empire. Although it existed everywhere, nowhere were slaves as abundant as within the Italian part of the Empire, see Thompson (1960).

[32] On the decline of slavery, and the rise of the colonate, in Roman history, see Finley (1980), pp. 123–149.

[33] This hybrid status of the slave is discussed in full in William Warwick Buckland's exhaustive work on Roman slave law, where six chapters discuss the laws of the slave as a human being (as opposed to two chapters on the slave as a thing). Buckland (2010), pp. 1–9.

[34] Watson (1989), p. 33.

[35] Justinian (1985), Digest 50.2.9. Late Imperial law also allowed the sale of young children into slavery in some circumstances. See Cairns (2001), pp. 197–202. On enslavement in Roman law more generally, a brief summary can be found in Watson (1987), pp. 7–22.

important as the Roman Empire reached its maximum extent by the Early Imperial period, was through capture in war.[36] Finally, there were some other, more eclectic means of becoming a slave as well that were not in sway during the whole history of the Roman Empire, such as self-sale, or as a punishment for some crimes.[37]

Given the longevity of slavery within the Roman world, the law was never static, and two evolutions are relevant to the rest of our story:

First, the character of Roman slave law fundamentally changed throughout the centuries. In the Republic, there were little to none legal limitations on the power of the *dominus* towards his slave. This did not mean that slaves were necessarily treated cruelly: the number of slaves was still quite small, slaves' relationships with masters were often close, and the censor could provide a check on cruel masters.[38] However, starting from the Imperial period, legislation was devised to prevent abuse of dominial power by the master, meaning that the slave progressively acquired more rights, a process that was even noticed by the great Roman jurist Gaius (130–180).[39]

Second, between the fourth-sixth centuries, a distinct group called the *coloni* appeared in the classical texts. Originally free contractual tenants, the word came to be applied to a category of people that had been tied to their land as a result of administrative pressure and fiscal reasons, creating a group that would be reminiscent of the serfs of the later medieval period.[40] Although nominally free, the increasing burdens imposed on them made Justinian doubt whether their actually still was a difference between the *colonus* and the *servus*.[41]

As concerns the meta-level, the question of the legality of slavery as an institution, we have to turn back to natural law and *ius gentium*. Romans also knew of this distinction, but the content of the terms had changed considerably since the time of the Greeks.[42] In the *Digest*, Ulpian discusses the difference between the two kinds of law. To him, the *ius naturale* were those laws that are not only specific to mankind, but are observed by all species in the animal kingdom. The *ius gentium*, on the other hand, is confined to human beings.[43] More specifically, it is the law which all humans observe. To which category did slavery belong?

Although slavery had been discussed before by Cicero, Seneca and others, the continuing legacy of Roman slavery lay within the transmission of Justinian's sixth century *Corpis Iuris Civilis*. In the *Digest*, Gaius pronounced that the great division in the law of persons was that all men were either free or slaves, and this was followed

[36] Watson (1987), pp. 7–22.

[37] Ibid., pp. 7–22. Finally, reference is sometimes made to persons called "addictus" or "nexus" in sources. These terms were used for persons who had incurred debts and were assigned to their creditors. However, the sources are consistent in that these persons are seen as personally free. See Testart (2002).

[38] Buckland (2010), p. 36.

[39] Dig 1.6.1. I have made use of the 1985 translation of the Digest by Mommsen, Krueger and Watson.

[40] A full survey on the history of the colonate can be found in Mirkovic (1997).

[41] Codex Justinianus, XI 48.21.

[42] Neff (2014), pp. 44–49.

[43] Justinian (1985), Digest 1.1.3., 1.1.4.

by Florentinus' definition of what slavery exactly was: slavery is an institution of the *ius gentium*, whereby someone is against nature made subject to the ownership of another *(servitus est constitutio iuris gentium, qua quis dominio alieno contra naturam subicitur)*.[44] No longer was slavery thus grounded on the *ius naturale*: its basis ought to be found in the *ius gentium*. According to Watson, this change in legitimacy might have created some uneasiness, which is why another text by Florentinus was added next to his definition of slavery. He clarified that slaves are so called, because generals have a custom of selling their prisoners and thereby preserving rather than killing them.[45] The result is that slavery is justified by clarifying that the slave has received a benefit: instead of being killed, his life is spared.

2.2.1.3 Medieval Europe: Continuity, Sin, and the Return of Aristotelian Thinking

Catholic Doctrine and Slavery: Reconciling Equality and Slavery Through Sin
The collapse of the Western Roman Empire ushered in a period of intellectual stagnation in Europe. Mainly, it was the Catholic Church that succeeded in ensuring a measure of intellectual continuity with the previous period.[46]

Christian thinking on slavery started with St. Paul (ca. 5–64/67), who made a twofold distinction that would essentially remain in sway well until the twentieth century in catholic doctrine.[47] On the one hand, it was held that, fundamentally, all people are equal in Christ. This principle, namely that all human beings are equal as children of God, was affirmed by later theologians and canon lawyers at every moment.[48] On the other hand, despite this acknowledgement, slavery was condoned by St. Paul. However, he stressed the importance of fairness in the relationship between master and slave, and encouraged manumissions of slaves.[49] In the Council of Gangra of 340, this permission of slavery was mentioned in a decree, which subsequently became part of the *Decretum Gratiani*.[50]

The Patristic Fathers (first-seventh century) agreed with this approach, but adjusted their terminology more to the Roman way of thinking. Augustine (354–430) knew about the Roman *ius naturale*, although in his vision, it was identified as the law of God, and he did not pursue an abstract theory on the issue.[51] In Augustine's views, mankind did not owe the institution of slavery due to its original nature,

---

44 Justinian (1985), Digest 1.5.3., 1.5.4.

45 Watson (1987), p. 8; Dig. 1.5.4. At the same time, Watson clarified that he did not intent to say that the Romans considered that slavery itself was morally wrong. Watson (1989), p. 118.

46 Kelly (1992), pp. 88–89.

47 Maxwell (1975), p. 28. One might be surprised to learn that the common Catholic teaching on slavery only clearly prohibited all kinds of slavery after the Second Vatican Council in 1965.

48 Kelly (1992), pp. 104–105, 146–148, 191–193.

49 Maxwell (1975), pp. 27–30.

50 Ibid., p. 30.

51 Kelly (1992), p. 103.

but because of its own sin. After the fall of man, sin had arisen in this world and, as a result, slavery served as a disciplinary system to adjust the sinful tendencies of mankind.[52] Other Patristic fathers agreed with the idea that slavery was not part of the natural state of mankind. Isidore of Seville (560–636), for example, placed it squarely in the *ius gentium*.[53] Conceptions of what this *ius gentium* was, could differ. For Isidore, the *ius gentium* and the *ius naturale* were less closely related. The *ius gentium* was manmade law. The *ius naturale* was not. Furthermore, the *ius gentium* was related to activities of states, whereas the *ius naturale* pertained more to the conduct of individual persons. Some others scholars were inspired by Augustinian thinking and believed in a conception of the *ius gentium* as a debased form of *ius naturale*, more suitable to mankind in its fallen state.[54] But whatever the relationship between the two was, until the twelfth century, canonists broadly agreed that slavery was not to be seen as part of the *ius naturale*.[55]

Romanists and Coutumiers: Same Beliefs, but Different Unfreedom
Clergymen were not the only ones to discuss the issue of slavery. After the study of Roman law had first gained hold in Bologna and soon after in the wider region, we also find slavery discussed amongst the works of the Romanists. As slavery remained common in Southern Europe, it made sense that these lawyers took note of how the Corpis Iuris Civilis dealt with slavery. And they squarely fell in line with its treatment of slavery. Great jurists such as Bulgarus (ca. 1100–1167), Placentinus (1130–1192) and Hugolinus (d. 1233) simply restated what the Roman jurists said, holding that slavery was lawful, not according to the *ius naturale*, but according to the *ius gentium*.[56]

At the same time, there was a distinction between much of the doctrinal work of the Romanists, and the reality of law as it existed on the ground in the Middle Ages. In the thirteenth century, we also find the first great works on the customary laws of several realms. Most notable are Eike von Repgow's (c. 1180–1233) *Sachsenspiegel* in Germany,[57] Philippe de Beaumanoir's (1252/1254–1296) *Coutumes de Beauvaisis*

---

[52]Book XIX, XV. I have made use of the 1960 translation of Augustine's City of God by William C. Greene, Saint Augustine (1960).

[53]Carlyle and Carlyle (1915), pp. 118–119. The six volume work of the Carlyles still contains the most elaborate treatment of the legal justification of slavery in the Middle Ages, and the thinking of individual jurists. Much of this work has been summarised in Kelly (1992), pp. 104–105, 146–148, 191–193.

[54]Neff calls the first category "dualists", and the second category "substitutionists". Neff (2014), pp. 63–67.

[55]Carlyle and Carlyle (1915), pp. 111–124. I do need to clarify that before the twelfth century and Gratian's Decretum, it is difficult to speak of an independent science of canon law, as the separation between theology and law had not really happened before then. Wieacker (1995), pp. 48–51.

[56]For primary references, see Carlyle and Carlyle (1909), pp. 34–40. On the notion of continuity between the ancient tradition and the revival of Roman law, Wieacker (1995), pp. 25–27.

[57]For a succinct summary of Eike von Repgow's views on slavery and serfdom (the two sometimes difficult to distinguish, see Zeuske (2018).

in France and *Bracton* (c. 1210–1268) in England.[58] All three of them agree in holding that in the beginning, mankind was free. Unfreedom could thus only exist by convention, not nature. That being said, there is a difference. In contrast to the Romanists, when they talk about unfreedom in their regions, they are talking about serfs, not slaves.[59] Again, this made much sense, given that, as we will still see, slavery had perished in these countries by the time these works were written.

Thomas Aquinas and His Followers: The Return of Aristotle

The biggest change in legal reasoning on slavery took place in the thirteenth century, when the "rediscovery" of Aristotle's works gave rise to the school of Scholasticism and its most famous scholar, Thomas Aquinas (1225–1274). With the scholastics, we find yet another conception of the relationship between the *ius naturale* and the *ius gentium*. If anything, the Scholastics "rationalised" natural law. As in Antiquity, it was seen as being independent from the will of God, although the Roman vision of a law "common to all animals" was rejected as well. Natural law became external from the human frame, and its content could only be accessed by study and reasoning.[60] In this tradition, the *ius gentium* was closely linked to the *ius naturale*. The *ius gentium* was still recognised as man-made law, but only in the limited sense that humans had to employ their reason in order to discover what natural law required them to do in certain cases.[61]

On slavery, Aquinas endeavoured "to bring together the tradition which he inherited from the Stoics and the Fathers with what he had learned from Aristotle".[62] At one point, he maintained that, in the state of innocence, there was no slavery. Two other fragments from his *Summa Theologica* however, seem to indicate something else. In the first fragment, Aquinas tries to square the circle of his belief in a close connection between *ius naturale* and *ius gentium*, St. Isidore's broader distinction between *ius naturale* and *ius gentium*, and Aristotle's belief in natural slavery. He does this by making the (rather abstract) point of a belief in two kinds of natural law: natural law in the absolute sense and natural law in relation to its consequences. Slavery belonged to the latter category, not being natural in itself, but being natural in the sense that "it is useful for the slave to be controlled by the wiser man, and for the wiser man to be helped by the slave". In a final fragment, Aquinas seems to build on this belief, noting that slavery does not represent a contradiction, but rather an addition to natural law.[63]

---

58 Van Caenegem (2011), pp. 11–15. The three of them were influenced by their personal knowledge on the "learned laws" as well.

59 Carlyle and Carlyle (1916), pp. 87–91. The Carlyles do sometimes make the mistake of equating slavery with serfdom.

60 Neff (2014), pp. 61–63.

61 Ibid., p. 66.

62 Carlyle and Carlyle (1928), p. 21.

63 The referred to passages are I, Q. 96, Art.4; II-II, Q. 57, Art. 3; I-II, Q. 94, Art.5. I have made use of the 1947 translation of the Summa Theologica by the Fathers of the English Dominican Province, Aquinas (1947).

Whilst Aquinas' balancing act makes it difficult to come to a confident judgment on his views regarding slavery, one could try to summarise by saying that Aquinas seems to have recognised "two levels of naturalness". On a first level, slavery was not natural. If one looked at the consequences of slavery in particular cases, it could, however, be seen as natural.[64]

Some of Aristotle's pupils do not seem to have engaged in such sophistry and went wholesale with the Aristotelian conception. For example, Ptolomy of Lucca (ca. 1236–1327) and Egidius of Colonna (ca. 1243–1316) flatly held that slavery was part of natural law.[65]

2.2.1.4 A Changed Custom: Slavery and European just Wars

One final evolution regarding the legal aspects of slavery in Europe remains to be discussed: the treatment of the defeated in a war on European soil. The Romans used war as a means to legitimise slavery, as they held that the enslaved had actually received a benefit, namely not being killed.[66]

One of the crowning achievements of the Christian Middle Ages was the development of just-war doctrine, which tried to answer the question when armed force could be justified (the state of war was part of the *ius gentium*).[67] The doctrine fundamentally needed to explain how it was possible to combine the pacifist views of the New Testament Gospels with situations in which the individual seemed to have to resort to violence. Out of this conundrum, a whole body of law developed during the Middle Ages with a set of intricate rules on when exactly one party could wage a just war on another entity (aptly summarised by the five elements that were discussed by Raymont of Penafort: *auctoritas*, *personae*, *res*, *iusta causa* and *animus*).[68]

What concerns us is what just war doctrine had to say about the treatment of those who were defeated in battle: could these people still be enslaved by the victors?

During large parts of history, we do not find much on this question. In a first period (fifth-eighth century), this was mostly due to the fact that enslaving the vanquished in wars was considered too obvious to merit attention.

Following on this, the Romanists of the twelfth century generally did not add much to the old Roman doctrine on enslaving prisoners of war, with at most some exceptions to enslavement that were discussed by Placentinus and Accursius.[69]

---

[64] Kelly (1992), pp. 148–149.

[65] Carlyle and Carlyle (1928), pp. 23–24.

[66] Dig. 1.5.4.

[67] Neff (2014), pp. 67–72.

[68] For a short summary on the content of these five principles, see Neff (2005), pp. 49–54.

[69] Placentinus believed that a war prisoner who freed himself or was captured by enemies of his captors did not become a captive again, but could enjoy the rights of *postliminium*. This was a doctrine of Roman law that held that a prisoner of war who returned to Roman territory, could be restored to his old legal position, see Buckland (2010), pp. 304–311. For Accursius, wars between Italian city-states were the exception to enslavement, as he held that this conflicts lacked *publica*

Likewise, canon lawyers mostly stayed within the confines of what already been written before. Many Decretists contented themselves with discussing the question whether Saracens could legally take Christians as slaves during the Crusades.[70] Some Decretalists, however, believed that what happened to property and subjects captured in war merited a longer discussion of what had hitherto been provided by their predecessors. By all accounts, they made interesting treatises on how property rights were affected by warfare, but alas, the same could not be said of their treatment of the personal status of the captured, which was usually rather succinct. Johannes Teutonicus (d. 1245), for example, did acknowledge that only those who fought a just war were entitled to the right of capture, whereas the victims of those who waged unjust wars were not legally enslaved and were encouraged to escape.[71]

Likewise, even Thomas Aquinas provided a very unsatisfactory answer to the issue, by noting that only barbarians could be enslaved after being captured in war, a status that was unbefitting for nobles.[72] Again, this is a mere restatement of the Aristotelian doctrine of natural slavery. Some of Aquinas' students, such as Ptolomy of Lucca, likewise reiterated the doctrine of Roman law on the enslavement of war captives. Thus, legal reasoning on the subject had virtually gone back to its Roman starting point without much change.[73]

It is quite interesting then, that there was a remarkable change at the end of the fourteenth century. Consider John of Legnano (1320–1383), whose *Treatise Concerning War, Reprisal and the Duel* can be regarded as the first important work in Western civilisation that attempted to discuss "international law".[74] In one of his questions, Legnano asks whether persons that were captured in a war between two states became slaves. According to him, one had to make a distinction whether the war was between two states which are under the same ruler, or whether this was not so. In the first case, it was held that enslavement could not occur. In the second case, it was held that enslavement was possible, albeit with the exception that did this not apply in wars between Christian states. Why? Because "the customs of modern times, and the practices observed among Christians from an early age" had rendered this practise obsolete.[75] Such ideas were also confirmed in "popularised versions" of Legnano's treatise, such as Honoré Bonet's (ca. 1340–1410) *Arbre des batailles* and Christine de Pisan's (ca. 1364–1430) *Le livre des faits d'arme et de chevalerie* (ca. 1410).[76]

---

licentia, meaning that the parties who tried to capture persons from their opponents could not be seen as enemies, but rather as bandits, see Russell (1975), pp. 51–53.

[70] Huguccio believed that the Saracens could do so when fighting a just war, but added that he doubted whether Saracens could ever fight a truly just war against Christians. Russell (1975), pp. 120–121.

[71] Ibid., p. 162.

[72] Ibid., pp. 279–280.

[73] In general on this subject, see Gillingham (2008); Russell (1975).

[74] Neff (2014), p. 84.

[75] The Tractatus de Bello, Ch. LIX. I have made use of James Brierly's 1917 translation of the Treatise Concerning War, Reprisal and the Duel, Da Legnano (1917).

[76] On these two authors, see Neff (2014), pp. 83–86.

Capturing defeated troops did not disappear all of a sudden, but instead, the Christian states devised complex systems of ransom and hostage-taking, which eventually came in the place of enslaving prisoners of war.[77] What caused this sudden change is less clear and has not been well studied, though some authors propose a link with the Catholic Church. This matches with Giovanni Da Legnano's assessment of the disappearance of enslavement in Christian wars. Although the church had an ambiguous position towards enslaving Christians until the end of the Middle Ages, it had prohibited the trading of Christian slaves from the early Middle Ages onwards. When that prohibition was in place, Gillingham argues that over time, it must have made less sense to enslave persons in war in the first place. Likewise, he argues that it is impossible to arrive at a precise chronology, but is convinced enslavement of war prisoners must have slowly ceased to exist within some of the Christian core-countries (e.g. the Frankish state), before this norm slowly extended towards the periphery of Christendom (e.g. the Anglo-Scottish border at the thirteenth century).[78] Second, adding to Gillingham's argument, one could also point to the fact that slaves had virtually disappeared in some regions of Europe by the twelfth century due to a mix of economic, political and religious reasons. At this point then, these two arguments help to understand the disappearance of slavery in Christian wars.

In any case, this meant that enslavement in war had completely disappeared amongst Christian nations at the end of the Middle Ages, something that has been identified by one commentator as "the most striking innovation" in the legal conduct of hostilities during the Middle Ages.[79]

2.2.2 *Institutional Realities: From Slavery to Serfdom in Medieval Europe*

2.2.2.1 The Great Transition

For present purposes, we take the presence of slaves during the Roman period as granted and will not immerse ourselves in a broad discussion on that period. Slaves were to be found everywhere in the Roman Empire, although in areas such as France and Germany, rural labourers or day-wage labourers clearly outnumbered the slaves.[80]

[77] Conceptually, the hostage can be distinguished from the prisoner of war in that he is the guarantor of an agreement, not subject to ransom, is a third party (meaning, not one of the individuals whose performance is being guaranteed) and is theoretically given rather than taken. On hostages, see Kosto (2012).

[78] Gillingham (2011).

[79] Keen (1965), pp. X–1.

[80] Whittaker (1987). We will also not treat the slave laws of the "barbarian kingdoms". On those laws, see Nehlsen (1972).

By all accounts, the period in between the end of the Roman Empire and the so-called "Renaissance of the twelfth century" is the most confusing as concerns the institutional importance of slavery. Without a doubt, it was possible to be a slave on European soil at any point, but by the twelfth century, slaves had become an oddity in several parts of Europe. Often, this evolution is called the transition from slavery to serfdom in Europe. The debate on how, why and when this evolution spread throughout Europe is still far from resolved, and its full story is outside the framework of this book. However (and although prone to a strong measure of generalisation), we will briefly discuss the main tenets of the evolutions that were visible throughout the whole of North-western Europe, based primarily on the work of Marc Bloch (1886–1944).[81]

Bloch held that, at the end of the Carolingian Era (800–888), the central social unit had become the manor (*seigneurie*).[82] This was a kind of estate that was inhabited by the manorial lord's subjects. The manor itself was divided in two parts: the *reserve*, which was the part directly held for the purpose of the lord, and the tenements (*tenures*). These were small peasant holdings where, although the lord retained the highest property right, the holder was entitled to enjoy the fruits of the ground in exchange for certain services to the lord.[83] Later on, the glossators would say that the lord had the *dominium directum*, and the holder the *dominium utile*. What was the relationship of those subjects to the lord?

In Charlemagne's empire, some peasants were considered to be free, although many of them were already in a tenant-like relationship with their lord. Next to that, there were still many *allodia*, grounds that were free of seigniorial rule and held directly by a peasant. According to Bloch, these *allodia* were the first to disappear *en masse* following the chaos that had begun to erupt at the end of the ninth century amidst the breakup of the Carolingian Empire. *Allodia* started to fall within the seigniorial system through a combination of contracts and sheer use of force by petty lords.[84] At the same time, the formerly free peasants started searching for protection. For example, they made use of a contract called *commendatio*, through which they received protection from a lord in exchange for which they became dependent of him (*cum obsequio*).[85] In this way, formerly free peasants were little by little subjected to lordly power.

On the other side of the spectrum, Bloch discussed three factors that led to the disappearance of genuine slaves: religious, military and economic, with most attention having been paid to the last. The economic rationale of Bloch was that the end of the use of Roman slave gangs, working in *latifundia* (great landed estates), in favour of smaller tenant systems, meant that master's incentives changed. Masters gradually found it more interesting to extract rents and services, rather than exploiting and

---

[81] Marc Bloch is, by all standards, the person who revolutionised the study of the Middle Ages. His views on the evolution from slavery to serfdom can be found in Bloch (1989); Bloch (1947).

[82] Bloch (1989), pp. 242–248.

[83] Ibid., 165.

[84] Ibid., 242–248.

[85] Bloch (1989), pp. 255–260; Foviaux (1993), p. 284.

having to pay for slaves directly. Eventually, and with some help of Church doctrine, Bloch believed that this led many masters to enfranchise their slaves through manumissions. However, the master still wanted to retain some measure of control over his slave, which meant that he preferred to have a *manumissio cum obsequio*, meaning that the slave still owed him several services. Soon, this process would receive a hereditary character.[86]

In this way, both slaves and free peasants were subjugated and eventually called serfs.[87] Bloch has defined this status with three characteristics: *mainmorte,* a form of succession tax that was usually collected by the lord in the form of a piece of moveable property; *formariage,* the prohibition to marry outside the manor without permission of the lord; and *chevage*, a small head-tax. In return for these and other obligations, the serf received land, protection and manorial justice from his lord.[88] This shows that medieval serfdom was fundamentally different from ancient slavery: although definitely in a subjugated position, master and serf were inextricably bound together in a network of mutual rights and obligations.

Admittedly, Bloch's version of the demise of slavery and the rise of serfdom has been seminal, but it has also been subject to many variations and alterations in the past decades. Historians still disagree widely as to the how, when and why slavery almost fully disappeared in North-Western Europe. More recent accounts also tend to give more scope for regional variations, and see freedom and unfreedom as the extremes of a continuum, with a lot of gray areas in between the two.[89] Or, to quote the author of a recent book on the transition from slavery to serfdom:

[T]he whole spectrum of possible meanings [to slave or serf] could apply at the same time within the same early medieval society—and indeed within a single lordship, depending on what lord and dependants had been trying to achieve with these labels.[90]

As a result, it would prove impossible to cover the scholarly debate on this transition in full, which is why I will finish by summarizing some of the most important discussions, referring the reader to the footnotes for further commentary.[91]

First, the timeframe of the demise of slavery stretches over a period of 600 years. Bloch saw the demise of slavery as starting at the end of the Roman period, and continuing until the ninth and tenth century, when serfdom rose to the fore. Many Marxist historians would disagree, and rather refer to what they call a process of synthesis that happened after the Germanic invasions blended both German and Roman society. This, according to them, resulted in the birth of feudalism at an

86 Bloch (1947).

87 The terminology could differ from country to country. In England, for example, the term *villein* was used most often to denote the legal category of unfree peasants.

88 Bloch (1989), pp. 260–266.

89 Epstein (2018).

90 Rio (2017), p. 247.

91 For an excellent English language survey, focused on France but also of relevance for Western Europe at large, see Barthélemy (2009), pp. 68–136.

earlier time.[92] Others, especially within France, have argued for the idea of a feudal revolution, which holds that there was a feudal transformation of society around the year 1000. These scholars believe that this was the time when the manorial regime was at its strongest and the population was enserfed.[93] Though much scholarship of more recent vintage increasingly tends to doubt whether the year 1000 marked really as much of a "mutation" of feudal society as some have made it to be before, this debate still simmers in (mainly French) historiography.[94]

Likewise, there is much debate about how the evolution towards serfdom happened. Bloch, as we have seen, proposed a two-tier model whereby slaves were manumitted before and partially at the time when peasants were losing their independence. There was, essentially, a rupture between slavery and serfdom. One scholar has criticized the characterisation of serfdom by Bloch (*chevage*, *formariage*, *mainmorte*) and believes that processes of imposing ever rising burdens on peasants were continuously present between the fourth and eleventh centuries.[95] Verriest and Verlinden have proposed a line of continuity, arguing that serfs actually descended directly from slaves.[96] Meanwhile, Bonnassie has taken a unique view by claiming that slavery completely perished around the year 1000, and that peasants subsequently enjoyed a period of relative freedom, after which serfdom would set in.[97] Rio, finally, likened early medieval laws about unfreedom to a Swiss knife that "could do many different things without being ideally suited to any of them". She notes that it was only at the end of the twelfth and thirteenth centuries that, through the work of professional lawyers, a process of increasing homogenization in the meaning of unfreedom was set in.[98]

The role of the Church in the decline of slavery is another difficult factor. The church itself did not outlaw the institution of slavery. It did, however, lend its moral blessings to provisions of Roman law that limited the power of the master, added some constraints of its own, and at times also encouraged Christians to manumit their slaves.[99] Second, the Church imposed several restrictions on the slave trade in Europe. This started with prohibiting the sale of Christian slaves to non-Christians in the early seventh century. By the tenth century, this was subsequently extended to a blanket ban on selling fellow Christian slaves (for example, this was referred to in the Synod of Koblenz of 922), which was often repeated afterwards.[100] How

---

[92] For an overview of Marxist thinking on this subject, see Bonnassie (1991), pp. 8–12.

[93] This idea owes much to Marc Bloch, who proposed two feudal ages in his Feudal Society. One between the ninth and tenth century, and a second one in the twelfth and thirteenth century. Within French historiography, see in particular Poly and Bournazel (1980).

[94] An excellent survey is Mazel (2010), pp. 637–648.

[95] Davies (1996).

[96] Verriest even went further by claiming that only a relatively small percentage of the population ever had the status of serfs, whereas the majority of peasants stayed free. Taxes such as the *chevage* were no sign of serfdom, but rather of tenancy, he proposed in Verriest (1946).

[97] Bonnassie (1991).

[98] Rio (2017), pp. 241–245.

[99] Logan (1932), pp. 473–475.

[100] Gillingham (2011), p. 14.

the Church affected the practise of enslaving Christians in war is less clear, with one scholar arguing that, although there are little available documented stories, certain churchmen must have opposed enslaving Christian captives.[101] That being said, it was not until the fifteenth century that we find papal letters excommunicating Christians who tried to enslave their co-religionists in war. This can hardly be called a Christian innovation, given that scholars such as John of Legnano already mentioned this as a custom in European wars before these papal letters.[102]

Finally, Bloch's framework is most useful for France. The broad strokes of his theory can also be used for England and the Low Countries, but chronology and specifics slightly differ. With respect to the Low Countries, slavery declined earlier and had already mostly disappeared after the seventh century. This is mainly due to the fact that large-scale wars remained absent from this area, and to several socio-economic factors (a quicker spread of labour-saving instruments, the early rise of the manorial system, etc.).[103] In England, the transition happened a bit later. Slavery had been declining before the Norman Conquest, but this event accelerated the evolution.[104] Although the Domesday Book of 1086 still mentioned that there were about 25,000 slaves in England (a category which was then, rather confusingly, called *servus* or serf), this category would almost completely disappear in the first decades following the Norman takeover.[105] In its place came a new institution: *villeinage*.

Much uncertainty thus remains about the exact end of slavery in Europe, but many major institutional or social historians would agree that slavery had become a fringe phenomenon in the territories of England, (most of) France and the Low Countries by the early twelfth century at the latest.

2.2.2.2 1200-1500: Serfdom and Slavery: North-South Divide

As slavery perished in England, France, and the Low Countries, unfreedom did not-yet-. Serfdom, or villeinage in England, came in its place. Let us see what this kind of unfreedom exactly was, in order to be able to clearly distinguish it from slavery. It should not be presumed that slavery disappeared everywhere. The Ghent historian Charles Verlinden (1907–1996), wrote ground-breaking scholarship on the continued presence of slaves in Southern Europe, and it is useful to give this a brief look as well.

England—The Rise and Decline of the Unfree Villeins

Originally, villein was a term used to talk about a simple (free) villager. However, at the time when slavery disappeared, formerly free citizens were increasingly tied to the lord's manor in England as a levelling process set in and former slaves and

[101] Ibid., pp. 12–14.
[102] Maxwell (1975), pp. 51–52.
[103] Van Bavel (2010), pp. 76–77.
[104] Pelteret (1996), pp. 251–254.
[105] Baker (2002), p. 468.

free peasants were combined in the composite class of villein.[106] Though several of the Roman law concepts applicable to slaves were used on villeins in early English treatises such as Glanvill and (especially) Bracton, and though these writers also held that villeinage was the only kind of unfreedom English common law knew of, it should be borne in mind that the institution of villeinage ought to be compared rather with the French *serf* (as in unfree peasant) than with the Roman chattel slave. According to Bloch, the biggest difference between the French *serf* and the English villein was that the English lords, in the more centralised England, were far more effective at tying their villeins to the land.[107]

This slow separation of villeinage from slavery is seen aptly in the differences between the two classic works on early English common law, Glanvill and Bracton.[108] According to Glanvill (written ca. 1187–1189), when a villein was manumitted by his lord, the villein only became free *vis-à-vis* the lord and his heirs, but remained unfree in his relation to all other persons.[109] This view had changed by the time of Bracton (mainly written between ca. 1220–1230, but brought up to date in the ensuing decades), who adopted the three principal characteristics of the common law of villeinage. First, there was only one kind of villeinage, and all villeins were equally unfree.[110] Second, villeinage was relative, meaning that the villein was unfree

---

[106]Pollock and Maitland (1968), pp. 430–432; Holdsworth (1922), p. 491. One final note on terminology: several writers tend to use both the terms "villeinage" and "serfdom" when talking about the unfree peasantry in England. For the purposes of this chapter, when reference is being made to serfdom, it is meant in a broad way, encompassing the legal, social and economic system of unfreedom and dependence. When reference is made to villeinage, I am discussing the narrower, legal English institution itself.

[107]Bloch (1989); Holdsworth (1922), p. 491. The reason for this more in-depth overview of English villeinage is that in the Early Modern Era, questions of slavery in England would also be tied to the question whether and to what extent chattel slavery could be seen in connection with or legitimised by the institution of villeinage. Much of the claims of Francis Hargrave, one of the lawyers in *Somerset v. Stewart*, would be based on the institution of villeinage and the fact that it could not serve as a means to allow chattel slavery to exist in England. But defenders of slavery equally well tried to use the villeinage argument, as Dana Rabin noted that: "The argument for the legality of slavery in England was made on the basis of analogy between slavery and the "complete subjection to a feudal lord or superior", known as villeinage", see Rabin (2011), p. 11.

[108]Both Glanvill and Bracton were treatises written at the beginning of the development of the common law system. In the nascent system of royal justice, one could only commence proceedings in the royal courts if an action was available, which explains why both Glanvill and Bracton did not expound on villeinage very systematically, but rather talked about it when discussing the compilation of available royal writs and procedures which they initiated. Baker (2002), pp. 175–177. I have used the following editions of Glanvill and Bracton, and will use standardised references of both works when referring to any of them: for Glanvill (written approximately between 1187–1189), the 1965 translation by G.D.G. Hall, Glanvill (1965); for Bracton (written approximately between 1220–1230), the 1968 translation by Samuel E. Thorne, Bracton (1968).

[109]Glanvill (1965), Book V [5].

[110]Baker (2002), pp. 468–469.; Bracton (1968), F. 4, the first classification of persons. Much has been made at times of the distinction between a villein regardant and a villein in gross, the former tied to a manor and the latter tied to the lord of the manor. As Holdsworth has clarified, differences in applicable rules between the two were small and insignificant, and this difference did not constitute two separate kinds of unfreedom. Holdsworth (1922), p. 508.

only in his relation to his lord, yet free in his relation against all other persons.[111] Finally, a clear distinction was drawn between villein tenure of land and personal villein status (villeinage *de sank*).[112]

How did one become a villein? Although Bracton made reference to how persons, by virtue of the *ius gentium*, became bonded by capture in war, this ought to be seen as proof of the Romanesque influence to which the writer was prone, rather than a reality at the time of writing.[113] Instead, there were two chief means of becoming a villein: in case of servile birth and that of a voluntary confession of servile status. English law thus acknowledged a transmission of status from parent to child (with the issue of mixed marriages being an especially contentious issue).[114] Several cases also point to the fact that confession of villein status was sometimes used as a means to escape prosecution, or to enjoy protection at the price of liberty.[115]

Villein status was not a pleasant one in common law. Whatever property a villein acquired, could be seized by the lord. Second, though protected by criminal law, the villein could be subjected to corporal discipline by the lord. And, the villein could not run away from his tenement, and could be forcefully retaken by his lord. That is not to say that the villein's lot was one of subjection to complete arbitrary use of power by the lord as the lack of protection under common law was partially compensated through protection under manorial justice.[116]

As the villein's status was less then enviable, it is not surprising to see that a great many cases related to the status of an alleged villein came before the royal courts. Usually, when the lord was faced with a runaway villein, he would try to obtain a writ of neifty (*de nativo habendo*), which ordered the local sheriff to deliver an alleged villein up to the lord. This would only be executed after a hearing in the county court, during which the villein could claim that he was free. If a villein did so, the proceedings were stopped and transferred to one of the royal courts, either by the claimant lord through the writ *pone de nativis* or by the alleged villein through the writ *de homine replegiando*.[117] Both parties then had to prove their claim before the royal courts by presenting suit of kin. Simply said, this meant that both parties tried

[111]Bracton (1968), F. 197B and F. 198B, quoted in Pollock and Maitland (1968), p. 415.

[112]Baker (2002), pp. 468–469. Bracton (1968), F. 25. Villein tenure meant that the services connected with the tenure were uncertain and that the tenant did not hold in his own name, but in the name of his lord, and stood in contrast to socage tenure, where the services due to the lord of the manor were fixed. Tenure stood conceptually apart from villeinage *de sank,* which referred to personal status. Ibid., pp. 307–308.

[113]Bracton (1968), F. 5. Pollock and Maitland (1968), p. 424.

[114]Bracton (1968), F. 190.

[115]Pollock and Maitland (1968), pp. 424–425. Some claimed that there was also a third means through which villeinage arose, namely that prolonged villeinage de facto could generate villeinage *de jure*. Ibid., 425–426.

[116]Baker (2002), pp. 468–470.

[117]Hyams (1980), pp. 162–183. During the reign of Edward III, the possibility for the villein to use the writ *de libertate probanda*, very similar to *de homine replegiando*, was taken away by statute. Holdsworth (1922), p. 497.

to present at least two male kinsmen who attested to their own villein or free status, after which the court would judge on the status of the alleged villein.[118]

The law of villeinage showed remarkable continuity throughout the twelfth and thirteenth century, after which the institution would start to decline in the second half of the fourteenth century. Then, many villeins would gain their freedom.[119] First, the decreased availability of labour meant that the labour market became more competitive. Mobility sharply increased as peasants took the momentum and left their villages in favour of high wages in agriculture and industry elsewhere. Lords thus had a disincentive to enforce their rights too vigorously, for doing so might drive their peasants away. Second, the manorial system of labour rents became increasingly replaced by a system of money rents. The status of villeinage was no longer as necessary to lords as it had been before, and lords increasingly saw the Ordinance (1349) and Statute of Labourers (1351) as a means to claim their rights.[120]

Villeins, once the majority of the peasant population, would cease to be an identifiable social class by the beginning of the fifteenth century, a time when class distinctions increasingly became dependent on economic conditions rather than the free-unfree dichotomy.[121] As the Middle Ages came to a close then, English common law recognised unfreedom, but only through the increasingly moribund institution of villeinage. Slavery had disappeared earlier on, and though some of its provisions had been inserted into the laws of villeinage, there was no substantive slave law in England.

Serfdom in France and the Low Countries

Slavery had ceased to exist as an institutional reality in North and Central France by the eleventh century. The institution having perished, the only kind of unfreedom left was that of the French *serf*. Broadly speaking, the French serf can be compared to the English villein, though French servitude has usually been characterised by using Bloch's three characteristics of *chevage*, *formariage* and *mainmorte*. That in itself is already a gross oversimplification of the real situation in France, there being various characteristics of serfdom. One general distinction was that there were two kinds of servitude, namely *servitude réelle* and *servitude personelle* (also called the distinction between *serfs de corps* and *serfs d'héritage*). The former was connected to persons possessing a plot of land to which servile dues are connected (a *bien servile*), and this form of servitude disappeared as soon as the serf left the land or changed residence. The latter was a form of servitude which attached itself to both the person and his progeny.[122] Both categories were subject to a variety of dues, but there

---

118 If each party brought suit and both were deemed to be sufficient, the court decided between them on the basis of a jury verdict. Hyams (1974).

119 The process by which villeinage disappeared was set in motion in the fourteenth century, but endured well onto the era of Elizabeth I (1558–1603), which is why the legal means by which villeins achieved their freedom will be discussed in the next chapter.

120 Hilton (1969), pp. 32–43. For the influence of the Black Death on the English law of villeinage, see Palmer (2000), pp. 16–17.

121 Hilton (1969), pp. 55–59; Baker (2002), pp. 470–472.

122 Bély (2010), pp. 1160–1163; Olivier-Martin (2010), pp. 282–284.

was great local variation in the names (*chevage*, for example, was called *avenage* or *schaft* in some regions) and the application of these marks of servile status.[123] The decline of serfdom had set in starting from the thirteenth century, which, given its relevance to the idea of the French freedom principle, we will discuss in more detail in the next chapter.

The situation was broadly the same in the Low Countries. Mass slavery had disappeared early, and the last vestiges of slavery were gone by the beginning of the eleventh century.[124] Just as elsewhere, this resulted in the rise of serfdom. Again, we should point out that the situation was subject to local variety all over the different counties, duchies, etc. of the Low Countries. In some, manorialism became an important factor, whilst in others, this was much less so. For example, previous studies have compared the importance or unimportance of serfdom between the County of Flanders, the County of Hainaut and the area of Picardy.[125]

When it comes to the County of Flanders, historically one of the most important parts of the Low Countries, we know that primarily in the eleventh century, serfdom was widespread as lords were able to subject peasants to their authority.[126]

Serfdom has generally been defined by scholars in a comparable way as for France-that is *formariage*, *mainmorte* and a variety of dues to which the serf was subject-. The difference between *servitude personelle* and *servitude réelle* was also recognized here (with, for example, *servitude personelle* being dominant in Flanders).[127] As elsewhere, other characteristics could be subject to local variations.[128]

In comparison with other places in North-western Europe, serfdom declined very early in the Low Countries, as it generally started to perish from the twelfth century onwards. As elsewhere, no provisions regulating slavery can be found.

For France, one qualifier is needed. Verlinden and other historians have been able to trace some proof of continuity in the history of slavery for several regions of Southern France, namely Roussillon, Languedoc and the Provence.[129] The slaves themselves were primarily Moorish in origin, but a variety of other ethnicities were

---

[123]Gallet (2010), pp. 1160–1163.

[124]Nicholas (1992), pp. 23–26.

[125]In general, see Van Bavel (2010), pp. 76–82. There were marked differences even between those counties located next to each other. For example, Verriest's critical study on serfdom in the County of Hainaut can be compared with Warlop's discussion for Flanders, where serfdom was an important force. Likewise, Jacob has noted how the area around Picardy was more subject to *servitude réelle*, whereas in Flanders *servitude personelle* was dominant. Warlop (1975); Verriest (1946); Jacob (1990).

[126]Warlop (1975), pp. 70–78.

[127]Nicholas (1992), p. 106; Godding (1991), p. 48. I am leaving aside (and refer to Godding's work for) other categories such as the *hommes d'avouerie* or *voegtmannen,* who found themselves in some sort of intermediate status between liberty and slavery.

[128]For some of the particularities of Flemish serfdom, see Van Caenegem (1990).

[129]Verlinden (1955), pp. 748–752. As concerns Roussillon, one does have to bear in mind that after the demise of the formally independent kingdom of Majorca in 1343, Roussillon was annexed to the Kingdom of Aragon. It was only after the 1659 Treaty of the Pyrenees that Roussillon would be re-attached to France.

to be found as well (i.e. Russians, Turks, Greek, Tatars and some black Africans starting from the fifteenth century).[130] In the Languedoc, slavery only perished in the sixteenth century. It had completely disappeared in Roussillon as well by the beginning of the seventeenth century.[131] The only slaves remaining in France before colonial slaves started to arrive in the second part of the seventeenth century were to be found in the royal galleys in the Provence, a subject to which we will return later. It seems that there were no French *ordonnances* regulating the status of these slaves at this time, though that might have been unnecessary anyhow. This is so because all these regions were to be situated in the so-called *pays de droit écrit*, where the Corpis Iuris Civilis abundant in slavery provisions, had received the status of supplementary law by the middle of the thirteenth century.[132]

Not a Universal Pattern: Slavery in Spain and Portugal
Nonetheless, this situation was not the pattern in all of Europe. In many ways, the areas we discussed could even be considered as outliers. A lot of other regions in Europe did make legal provisions on slavery, as slaves never disappeared from their territory. This, for example, can be demonstrated by the examples of both Spain and Portugal, but holds equally true for Italy or the Byzantine Empire.[133]

For both Iberian countries, slavery remained a vivid institution during the Middle Ages, both countries likely even having had more slaves in the fifteenth century than they had in the thirteenth.[134] Due to the *Reconquista*, both Iberian powers always had a supply of slaves close at hand (Muslims that could be taken captive in a just war.) In addition to that, both countries were heavily engaged in the slave trade and slaving raids against the Northern African coast starting from the fifteenth century.[135] As a consequence, when the first legal codes were made in these countries, provisions related to slavery were part of them. In Spain, slavery was dealt with by both the *Fuero Juzgo* (the translation of the Visigothic *Liber iudiciorum* which was given as a legal code to several towns conquered from the Moors) and *Las Siete Partidas*, Alfonso X's thirteenth century attempt to create a unified law for Castile.[136] Portugal primarily developed its medieval slave law through municipal regulations, although there was more royal interference in this process during the fifteenth century (*Ordenações Manuelinas*).[137]

---

[130] Ibid., 748–792.

[131] Ibid., 846–848.

[132] Rigaudière (2010), pp. 449–451.

[133] In particular, see Verlinden (1977).

[134] Verlinden (1955), p. 427. This also explains why many Romanists talked about slavery in such a casual fashion in their works.

[135] Ibid., 252–278.

[136] Watson (1989), pp. 40–42.

[137] Saunders (1982), pp. 113–115.

2.2.3 *Conclusion: Slavery in Europe at the End of the Middle Ages: Legally Justified but Institutionally Marginalised*

Through Classical Antiquity and up to the end of the Middle Ages, slavery as an institution was legally justified by nearly every European scholar. If scholars disagreed on slavery, it was about its origin. Here, we have seen a pendulum swinging back and forth between two sides: one which grounded slavery in *ius naturale*, and another side which believed that it was not part of the "original state of mankind", but part of the *ius gentium* (however those two concepts were defined). Only one thing changed as at the end of the Middle Ages writers started taking account of the fact that Christian nations no longer enslaved each other's troops in war.

However, as time progressed, much of these writings on slavery became more fiction than reality in day-to-day life in North-Western Europe. All of these countries had known slaves on their soil in the Roman Era and the beginning of the Middle Ages, but the institution had started its long decline by then. As a result, by the twelfth century, slaves disappeared from the soil of these countries, and the only kind of unfreedom left was serfdom or villeinage. Only in Southern France did a marginal slave presence subsist. That being said, none of these countries explicitly "abolished" slavery in the Middle Ages.

2.3 The Continued Legality of Slavery: Europe's Atlantic Endeavours in the Early Modern Era

By 1500, slavery was thus practically dead in England, France and the Low Countries but theoretically still alive in legal writing. In this part, we discuss how slavery continued to exist both in theory and practice between 1500 and 1800, as the great European powers expanded outwards and acquired colonies all over the world. Common to all European powers was their interest in a peculiar sort of commodity: slave labour. Portugal and Spain were the forerunners. The former was the first colonial power to get an interest in exporting Africans to the colonies. The latter primarily faced issues as concerns the status of the native population in their American colonies, before they made the switch to African slaves. In their wake would follow the English, French and Dutch, who also made abundant use of slave labour. All in all, modern estimates believe that about 12.5 million Africans were shipped as slaves from the African coast to the colonies between the sixteenth and nineteenth century.[138]

[138] In 1969, Philip Curtin was the first one to attempt to quantify the Atlantic slave trade in Curtin (1969). Since then, various historians have tried to come to the closest possible approximation of the number of slaves that were shipped from the African shores to the Americas. Their work has been collected in the Transatlantic Slave Trade Database, a collaboration between a global community of scholars.

In essence, this part tries to give an answer to both a theoretical and practical question. The theoretical question asks how the legality of the institution of slavery was upheld in this era. To answer this question, we will continue evaluating what the writers of the *Classics of International Law*-series had to say on this issue.[139] Second, I will try to shed some light on how, in practise, the main colonisers erected slave regimes in the Atlantic. Given that the focus of this book are England, France and the United Provinces, the Spanish and Portuguese slaving ventures in the American colonies will not be discussed in detail.[140] Finally, although the Atlantic region was certainly not the only one where the European powers were engaged in slavery, our discussion will be limited to this region.[141]

---

[139] Whilst all of the Classics did have something to say on slavery, this was not a topic in all of their works. Therefore, no reference will be made to Gentili's *Hispanicae Advocationis Libri Duo* or *De Legationibus Libri Tres*, Grotius' *De Jure Praedae Commentarius*, Bynkershoek's *De Domino Mares Dissertatio* and *De Ford Legatorum Liber Sigularis* and Pufendorf's *De Officio Hominis et Civis Juxta Legem Naturalem Libri Duo*. As I have used these materials myself, reference will be made to the relevant parts of the text of these primary materials. I have found Jean Allain's treatment of this issue very instructive to understand the views of the Classics and to easily trace the relevant parts of their works. Therefore, for a broader discussion of the views of the Classics than the scope of this work permits, I would gladly refer the reader to his excellent treatment of the issue in Allain (2012). As a side note, I do wish to clarify that slavery was legitimised during this period in a variety of ways. Racism, the so-called Curse of Ham (the ancient idea that the black race was the progeny of the biblical figure Ham, who had been cursed by his father) and a variety of other means were also used to legitimise slavery, but this would lead us too far. In general, for other legitimations of slavery, I would refer the reader to the following books. For France Rushforth (2012). For England: Guasco (2014). For the United Provinces: Emmer (2007); Van den Boogaart and Emmer (1979); Priester (1987); Vink (2007).

[140] No reference is made to the Southern Netherlands in this part. Up to 1714, they were part of the Spanish Empire. After the war of the Spanish Succession, the Southern Netherlands came in Austrian hands. The Austrians did not have any substantial colonies.

[141] In particular, two other regions are interesting as concerns the legal history of slavery in relation to the European powers. They are largely subservient to the goal of this part, which is to show the continuity in legal thought on slavery as an institution. This can best be done by explaining the legal and institutional underpinnings of the largest slaving venture, the Atlantic slave trade. First, slavery would continue to be a part of the exchanges between Muslim forces and Christian nations in the Mediterranean region, especially so because of the activities of the Barbary pirates. This should be seen in the same context as the previously discussed issue of the Iberian Christian powers fighting a just war against the Muslims of Al-Andalus. This field of study has received more attention in recent years, with two landmark studies by Davis and Weiss. Davis (2003). Weiss (2011). Although the Barbary pirates were the primary enslavers (Davis estimates that between the sixteenth and the nineteenth century, between 1 and 1.25 million Europeans were captured by the Barbary pirates), the European Mediterranean powers would enslave Muslims as well. As this Mediterranean slavery is primarily of some relevance for the French legal order's reaction to slavery, I will make reference to this issue in the next chapter. Second, the European powers also had colonies in the East Indies

2.3.1 Legitimising Slavery During the Atlantic Slave Trade: Continuity from Beginning to End

Starting from the fifteenth century, lawyers had a new challenge in the legitimation of slavery. Portugal and Spain were the first major powers to explore the Atlantic in that century. Most importantly, the Tordesillas Treaty of 1494 divided the newly discovered lands between Spain and Portugal.[142] The majority of the Americas were apportioned to Spain. As Spaniards conquered parts of this territory, they came into contact with the native population. The question whether and how these people could be subjected to slavery became part of the so-called "Spanish struggle for justice in the conquest of America".[143] The attempts to answer these questions were given by the Salamanca school of international law, a distinct school of theological, philosophical, political and economic thought. Using Aquinas' *Summa Theologica* as the main object of study, adherents started a revival of Thomist thought, whilst using philosophy and theology to applied social and policy issues in a systematic fashion.[144] Within the Classics of International Law, we find Franciscus de Victoria and Francisco Suarez as their main representatives.

The Spaniards were hardly the only ones to be faced with the legitimacy of slavery. If sixteenth century theorists such as Pierino Belli and Alberico Gentili primarily discussed slavery in the context of just wars between European powers, seventeenth and eighteenth century theorists of international law faced a different reality. If Spain's "question" had largely been related to Indian slavery, all of the main European powers were heavily involved in draining a new source of slaves. Black Africans were brought *en masse* to the Americas to serve European masters. How did the Classics legitimise the Atlantic slave trade?

The Classics were also concerned with a fundamental issue that had been touched on from Antiquity onwards, namely the distinction between *ius naturale* and *ius gentium*. Whereas the Romans' conception had to do more with biological instinct, and whereas the Scholastics had posited a very close link between the two bodies of law, this distinction was set to change again during the Early Modern Period. To understand this, one has to bear in mind that by origin, *ius naturale* had always been more concerned with providing a set of rules that were useful for interpersonal relations, rather than interstate relations. This view worked well during the Middle Ages, but less so as nation-states came to be seen as distinct impersonal corporate

---

and on the Indian subcontinent, where they would use slave labour as well. As Van Welie noted, this subject is far less approachable than the Atlantic slave trade: there was no clear beginning and no clear end to this slave trade, there was no clear racial identification and the geographic direction of this trade was multidirectional, Van Welie (2008). Considering all this, I believe a focus on the transatlantic slave trade is the best choice. Finally, although limited and eventually prohibited, England, France and the United Provinces also experimented with enslaving native Indians.

[142]Treaty of Tordesillas between Spain and Portugal of 7 June 1494. Ratified by Spain July 2nd, 1494 and ratified by Portugal 5 September 1494 in Davenport (1917), pp. 84–100.

[143]Hanke (1949).

[144]Alves and Moreira (2010), pp. 1–6. For an extensive bibliography on Spanish scholasticism, see Decock and Birr (2016).

bodies during the fifteenth and sixteenth century. Therefore, the rules governing the conduct of states had, to a certain extent, to be found somewhere else. The *ius gentium* succeeded in filling the void, as it became a more practical and important tool during this era. Whereas before, most theories held that the *ius gentium* was very closely connected to the *ius naturale*, the *ius gentium* would now start to assert more independence. Slowly, it would eventually be seen as the law which governed the conduct that states observe in their mutual relations.[145] This evolution was initiated by Francisco Suarez and Hugo Grotius, but vehemently opposed by the followers of Thomas Hobbes, who stated that natural law was the sole body of law that is binding between states. This whole period can thus best be characterised as some sort of pendulum between *ius naturale* and *ius gentium*. Within this pendulum, neither theorist would claim that there was no *ius naturale*, as positivism would only have its breakthrough in the nineteenth century. The penultimate difference then, lay rather in the relative importance of *ius naturale* vis-à-vis the *ius gentium* as a source of interstate conduct, and undeniable, the long-term evolution here was in favour of the *ius gentium*.[146]

2.3.1.1 From Indians to Blacks: Victoria and Suarez

Franciscus de Victoria (1483–1546) took up the Chair in Theology at the University of Salamanca in 1526, and is considered by James Brown Scott as the true "father of international law".[147] On slavery, his work is centred on the "Indian question".

Without going into detail, Victoria's works have to be seen within the context of this "Spanish struggle for justice in the conquest of America", as Spanish theologians and lawyers alike wrestled with the question of the legitimacy of enslaving the native American population.[148] It was a contemporary of Victoria, Friar Bartolomé de Las Cases (1484–1566), who became most famous for his defence of the Indians. At the height of the controversy, this led to the famous (but largely inconclusive) "Valladolid debate" between de Las Casas and the Spanish humanist Juan Ginés de Sepúlveda (1494–1573), a proponent of natural slavery.[149]

In his *De Indis*, Victoria started by mentioning the idea that the Indians were true owners in public and in private law before the Spaniards had arrived. He continued by using Aristotle's theory of natural slavery in a curious way. According to him, Aristotle did not mean that "*those who are not over-strong mentally are by nature subject to another's power and incapable of dominion alike over themselves and*

[145] Neff (2014), pp. 151–153.

[146] In general, see Chapter 4 and 5 of Neff (2014).

[147] Scott (1934). Although De Victoria did not publish any works himself, Brown Scott has collected much of the lecture notes that were written down by his students. I have made use of the 1917 translation of *The Reflections in Moral Theology of the Very Celebrated Spanish Theologian, Franciscus de Victoria* by J.P. Bate. In the references below, I have made use of the original texts that are annexed to Brown Scott's book (such as *De Indis*).

[148] In particular, see Hanke (1949); Pagden (1986).

[149] Hanke (1974).

other things", but rather "*that by defect of their nature, they need to be ruled and governed by others*". He equated the situation with that of a son who is subject to his parents until he reaches the age of majority, or of a wife to her husband.[150] In other terms, Victoria held that whereas it was not permissible to seize the patrimony of the Indians and enslave them without a reason, it would be "wise" if they were to be ruled and governed by the Spaniards.[151] This is followed by two sections in which Victoria deduced both the titles which he deemed illegitimate to reduce the Indians to slavery, and the titles which might have been legitimate. In each of those cases, he did not make a pronouncement whether a legitimate reason was actually present in the case at hand. Out of the eight possible legitimate reasons, it is most noteworthy that Victoria accepted the legitimacy of just war theory itself (his first possible legitimation).[152] For present purposes, it is also interesting to see that, even though Victoria believed that the Indians were no natural slaves, he did not deny the validity of Aristotle's natural slavery thesis itself.

If slavery was at the centre stage of Victoria's work, it was not anymore in Francisco Suarez' (1548–1617) thinking. At the time of writing, Spain had started to make the change towards a regime of African slave labour. In comparison with the discussions on Indian slavery, it is astonishing to see how the legality of the African slave trade was routinely ignored by the Spaniards. Seymour Drescher noted the curious case of King Philip II of Spain, who consulted theologians in 1553 to address the lawfulness of the regime that Spain used to procure slaves, the so called *Asiento de negros*. In its essence, this was a system of trade monopoly licenses that allowed private companies to bring slaves to the Spanish colonies.[153] The theologians discussed the justice of a state monopoly and the rate of profit that was given to the license holder. However, nothing was to be found about the justice of the slave cargo itself.[154]

This same idea of casual neglect can be found when reading Francisco Suarez' discussion on slavery. Acknowledged as being the "last of the Scholastics", Suarez, in his 1612 work *De Legibus, Ac Deo Legislatore,* refrained from the sweeping discussions on slavery that had typified his predecessor Victoria. Slavery simply served as an example in Suarez' discussion on natural law and *ius gentium*, the institution of slavery falling squarely within the latter. While acknowledging that slavery was not

[150]*De Indis*, XIII–XIV.

[151]de Victoria (1917), 114.

[152]*De Indis*, XXXVI–XLIII.

[153]Later on, the *Asiento de negros* would become treaty based and amalgamated into one *Asiento*, as the Dutch, Portuguese, French and English would contend with each other for the privilege of delivering slaves (and illegally, other goods) to the Spanish colonial market. Scelle defined the *Asiento* as "Un contrat de droit public, par lequel un particulier ou une compagnie s'engage, vis-à-vis du Gouvernement espagnol, à le remplacer dans l'administration du commerce de la main-d'oeuvre noire, aux Index ou dans une region des Indes occidentales", Scelle (1906a), p. 27.

[154]Drescher, Abolition: A History of Slavery and Antislavery, 65.

part of natural law, he did accept that the *ius gentium* itself, as established through the habitual conduct of nations, was quite in accord with nature.[155]

2.3.1.2 Belli, Ayala and Gentili: Writers in the Law of War Tradition

These three authors can be seen as part of the same tradition, as Pierino Belli, Balthazar Ayala and Alberico Gentili all wrote their works on the laws of war. When dealing with this topic, as medieval writers did before, they were obviously confronted with the issue of slavery.

Pierino Belli (1502–1575), an Italian, wrote his work *De Re Militari et Belli Tractatus* in the service of King Philip II of Spain in 1563.[156] Whilst his work focused on the European context, he did notice the issue of the Spanish enslavement of the Indians. As concerns slavery itself, he believed that "*things captured in war belong to the captors*". He noted that this provision not only applied in war, but also when a person went amongst people with whom his countrymen had no ties of hospitality or friendship, thus implicitly approving the enslavement of Indians.[157] He continued his enquiry by asking himself whether this also applied as between Christians. First, he took note of the discrepancy between various authors, citing Baldus and Bartolus as proponents of slavery between Christians, without taking a clear position himself.[158] Later, he returned to the issue, and noted that it had become the rule amongst Christians to ask a ransom for prisoners, but not to enslave them. To legitimise this exception to slavery, Belli turned to the *Digest*. He drew an analogy with a provision of the *Digest*, which stated that Romans were not true enemies in civil disagreements and thus should not enslave each other and transplanted this view to his era. As Christians were no real enemies either, even when they went to war, they did not enslave each other.[159]

Balthazar Ayala (1548–1584), a Spaniard who was born in Antwerp and who studied at the University of Leuven, also wrote his work *De Jure et Officiis Bellicis et Disciplina Militari Libri Tres* while in the service of the Spanish army. He should still be seen as belonging to those scholars upholding the substitutionist (those who conceived of the conception of the *ius gentium* as a debased form of *ius naturale*) relationship between the *ius naturale* and the *ius gentium*, which is visible in his treatment of slavery.[160] In a chapter "Of Capture in War and the Law of Postliminy", Ayala questioned whether slavery should be seen as part of the *ius naturale* or the *ius gentium*. He believed the latter to be the correct idea, as liberty is an institution of the

[155]Suarez (1944), 341–350. I have made use of the 1944 translation by Williams, Brown and Waldron of Suarez' work.

[156]Neff (2014), pp. 148–149.

[157]Belli (1963), Part II, Ch. XII. I have made use of H.C. Nutting's 1936 translation of Pierino Belli's *A Treatise on Military Matters and Warfare* (originally from 1563).

[158]Ibid., Part II, Ch. XVIII.

[159]Ibid., Part IV, Ch. I.

[160]Neff (2014), p. 148.

law of nature. Slavery arose because of two reasons, namely that "the wickedness of man [in his fallen state] ought to be restrained by war and captivity and slavery", and also because of "its utility to the State as a means of repressing those who wage unjust war".[161] This, however, only applied when dealing with a just war.[162] Just like Belli, he noted the existing custom between Christians not to enslave each other during wars, but held that, in case Christians were fighting on the side of the Saracens and infidels against fellow Christians, the exception did not apply.[163]

Alberico Gentili (1552–1608) was an Italian law professor who left Italy due to his Protestant faith and eventually became a professor of Civil Law at the University of Oxford.[164] His *De Iure Belli Libri Tres* was an inquiry into the circumstances in which war was justly undertaken, conducted and terminated. All this was framed in a comprehensive natural law framework reminiscent of Aquinas' theories. When it comes to slavery, Gentili asked when slavery arose, whether it was a just condition, and which laws regulated the relationship between master and slave. With respect to the first question, he held that slavery did not exist in wars of Christian nations as all Christians are brothers in Christ. However, slavery did arise in case a person was captured by the enemy in another, non-Christian, war.[165] Regarding the second question, Gentili reverted to Aquinas' view.[166] Whereas Gentilli believed that slavery was a provision of the *ius gentium*, he was also convinced that he had to deal with the assertion, made by some, that natural reason (the basis of the *ius gentium*) could not introduce slavery if we are all free by nature.[167] To answer the objection, Gentilli referenced Aquinas: "slavery is really in harmony with nature; not indeed according to her first intent, by which we were all created free, but according to a second desire of hers, that sinners should be punished".[168] As he explicitly agreed with Aristotle's view in *Politics* as well, Gentili seemed to attempt the same balancing act as Aquinas concerning the question whether slavery was part of the *ius naturale* or the *ius gentium*. Furthermore, he tried to discredit the famous French political philosopher

---

[161] Ayala (1912), Book I, Ch. V, [16]. I have made use of J.P. Bate's 1912 translation of Balthazar Ayala's 1582 *On the Law of War and on the Duties Connected with War and on Military Discipline, Three Books*.

[162] Ibid., Book I, Ch. V, [18].

[163] Ibid., Book I, Ch. V, [19].

[164] Neff (2014), p. 149.

[165] Oddly enough, Gentili seems to claim that slavery never ever existed in wars between Christians, which is in any case wrong. He does not follow up on this assertion. Gentili (1933), Book III, Ch. IX. I have made use of Humphrey Milford's 1933 translation of Gentili's Three Books on the Law of War (originally from 1598).

[166] Whilst Neff does mention that Gentili's thinking was framed within a comprehensive natural law framework, he does not explicitly place Gentili within his category of emanationist thinkers. When it comes to slavery, however, his line of reasoning falls squarely within Aquinas' line of thought.

[167] As becomes clear later in the treatise, Gentili is referring to Jean Bodin's objection to slavery.

[168] Gentili (1933), Book III Ch. IX.

Jean Bodin, who was critical of slavery.[169] According to Allain, Gentili's view should be seen in the context of the growing importance of the transatlantic slave trade, which might explain his broader view of slavery.[170]

2.3.1.3 Hugo Grotius and Slavery

Whilst the previous thinkers upheld the very broad overlap between *ius naturale* and *ius gentium*, this approach would increasingly start to change with Hugo Grotius (1583–1645), the first Dutch Classic. In Grotius' thinking, law had to be divided in *ius naturale* and volitional law, "which has its origin in the will".[171] As before, the *ius naturale* remained the dictate of right reason. Volitional law had to be divided further in divine law and human law. In this last category, Grotius made yet another distinction between municipal law (the law of one state), law which was narrower than municipal law (e.g. the commands of the father) and the law of nations, his so called *ius gentium voluntarium*.[172] It is this final category which would become increasingly important in the formation of international law in the next centuries.

In his *De iure belli ac pacis*, Grotius had much to say on slavery. Whilst Grotius, having worked in the service of the Dutch East India Company himself, was certainly aware of the nascent Dutch slave trade, it was not the case that the Dutch had already become major players in the slave trade at the time of publishing in 1625.[173] Grotius' views on slavery are divided in three chapters (Book II, Cap. V; Book III, Cap VII and Cap. XIV).

Grotius acknowledged that, according to nature, no one can be a slave, thereby distancing himself from Aristotle's position.[174] At the same time, he said that it was not against nature if a man voluntarily subjected himself into complete slavery, with the underlying idea being that the slave owed lifelong service to his master in return for nourishment and other necessities of life.[175] Individuals, who have the natural right of liberty, also have the liberty of placing themselves in voluntary servitude. On the basis of consent, a master could thus derive a valid title to a slave.[176] Grotius

---

[169]"*Bodin tries to show that the law of slavery is not a part of the law of nations. But the founders of the science of law, Plato, Xenophon and Aristotle, oppose him; as who does not?*". Ibid., Book III Ch. IX.

[170]Allain (2012), p. 38. Whilst it is true that Spain and Portugal's involvement in the transatlantic slave trade had grown by this time, it does have to borne in mind that neither the English, nor the Dutch or the French were involved in the slave trade as of yet.

[171]Grotius (1925), Book I, Ch. 1, XIII. I have made use of F.W. Kelsey's 1925 translation of Grotius' On the Law of War and Peace Three Books (originally from 1646).

[172]Ibid., Book I., Ch. 1, XIV–XV.

[173]Cairns (2001), p. 201.

[174]Grotius (1925), Book III, Ch. 7, I.

[175]Ibid., Book II, Ch. 5, II.

[176]Grotius' argument is discussed in full in Cairns (2001), pp. 233–244. Although Cairns and Van Nifterik do not seem to differ as concerns Grotius' vision of slavery according to the *ius gentium*, they have a different interpretation as regards Grotius' interpretation of slavery according to the *ius*

went even further when discussing the legality of slavery under the *ius gentium voluntarium*. Here, he believed that during a formal public war, not only all those who surrendered themselves, but all without exception who were captured within enemy lines could be regarded as slaves. The same held true for the descendants of persons captured in war.[177] For legitimation, Grotius referred, among others, to Florentinus' statement on slavery as *servare* (to save) of those who would otherwise be killed.[178] As we have seen with the previous Classics, Grotius did acknowledge that this provision did not have force of law anymore during wars amongst Christian nations.[179]

All this shows Grotius' extended views on the legality of slavery. There is no proof that Grotius wrote his views with the Dutch West India Company and East India Company slave ventures in mind. But Cairns convincingly argued that, at the least, Grotius' work could and would be used later on by the maritime colonial powers as a valuable tool to support the legality of the transatlantic slave trade, as his work provided the perfect legitimation.[180]

2.3.1.4 Grotians and Hobbesians: Different Approaches, Same Belief in the Legitimacy of Slavery

Grotius' fundamental distinction in "two types of international law" would come under severe scrutiny by Thomas Hobbes (1588–1679). In *Leviathan*, the innate sociability of the human race, always closely connected to *ius naturale*, was rejected. Hobbes' worldview was one in which humanity strived towards a rational pursuit of its self-interest. His version of natural law boiled down to a fundamental right of personal security and a fundamental duty of the performance of agreements (*pacta sunt servanda*).[181] For our purposes, the most important thing to remember is that out of Hobbes' observations, the conviction grew amongst some scholars that the sole legal tie between states was provided by *ius naturale*, not *ius gentium*. That is why in the seventeenth and eighteenth century, some Classics would agree with Grotius that both *ius naturale* and *ius gentium* were valid sources of law for the conduct between states ("Grotians"), whereas the "Naturalists" would assert that it was only the *ius naturale* that was binding law of general application between states.[182]

---

naturale. Cairns believes that Grotius is dealing with slavery in the ordinary sense of the word in this part. Van Nifterik, however, believes that when Grotius is talking about *servitus* in this part of his text, he is rather dealing with a sort of unfreedom that we would translate as "perpetual service", instead of chattel slavery.

[177] Grotius (1925), Book III, Ch. VII, I–II.

[178] Ibid., Book III, Ch. VII, V.

[179] Ibid., Book III, Ch. VII, IX.

[180] Cairns (2001), p. 201.

[181] Neff (2014), pp. 167–170.

[182] The naturalists did accept that treaties between groups of states could supplement the natural law, but it had a subsidiary role in their grand scheme of thinking. Next to that, whereas Hobbes

It is in the category of the Grotians that we can find three seventeenth century Classics, namely Richard Zouche, Samuel Rachel and Johann Wolfgang Textor.

Richard Zouche (1590–1661) was a British contemporary of Hugo Grotius who also held the Regius Chair of Civil Law at the University of Oxford. His most famous treatise was the 1650 *Juris et Judicii Fecialis, sive, Juris inter Gentes et Quaestionum de Eodem Explicatio*, in which he discussed the relationship between states during war and peace.[183] His treatment of slavery was very short, part of the section "Of Ownership among Belligerents". Slavery is seen as part of the *ius inter gentes,* and Zouche made references to Aristotle (not in the context of slavery as part of the *ius naturale*) and Gaius. Once more, the fact that Christian nations had changed to the practice of ransoming, instead of enslaving fellow Christians, was mentioned.[184] Zouche thus limited himself to the European context but did not say anything directly about the nascent transatlantic slave trade.[185]

Samuel Rachel (1628–1691) and Johann Wolfgang Textor (1638–1701) were two German Classics, the former working as Chair in International Law at the University of Kiel, the latter as the Chair of Jurisprudence at the University of Heidelberg. Rachel had very little to say about slavery in his 1676 *De Jure Naturae et Gentium Dissertationes*, simply stating that "Those who surrender in such a war [a just war], or accept terms of slavery, or are captured, become the slaves of the victors by the Law of Nations". The same treatment was accorded to descendants of female slaves. Finally, Grotius was quoted on the fact that slavery had "long since fallen into desuetude" among Christians prisoners of war.[186]

Textor, in his *Synopsis Juris Gentium* of 1680, paid attention to slavery. As had become habitual by now, he noted how slavery had become a rule of the *ius gentium* after it was found harsh and brutal to kill all those who had fallen into the enemy's hands. He was more precise than some of his predecessors about the exception to enslavement in wars among Christians, observing that this exception had been

foresaw a limited substantive content for the *ius naturale*, many naturalists also diverged from this approach. Ibid., pp. 173–174.

[183] Furthermore, he is the one who first used the term *ius inter gentes* (law between nations) *instead of ius gentium* (law of nations), Ibid., p. 171.

[184] Zouche (1911), Part. I-Sect. 8–1. In the 2nd part of his work, Zouche devoted some attention to the question whether persons that had surrendered themselves after having bargained for their live could still be enslaved or detained as prisoners, a practice he condemned (Part II–Sect. 10–34). I have made use of J.L. Brierly's 1911 translation of Richard Zouche's *An Exposition of Fecial Law and Procedure, or of Law between Nations and Questions Concerning the Same* (originally published in 1650).

[185] Bush believes that by using references to Greeks and Romans, Zouche cannot have wanted to effect the domestic, English legal order. Rather, the arguments Zouche made could be extended by analogy to the issue of black slavery. Bush is convinced that this was Zouche's intent. Bush (1993), pp. 449–452.

[186] Rachel (1916), 2nd dissertation—Of the Law of Nations—XLIX and L. I have made use of John Bate's 1916 translation of Samuel Rachel's *Dissertations on the Law of Nature and Nations* (originally published in 1676).

introduced "about three hundred years ago".[187] He added that the same did not apply in wars "of the Turks and of other barbarians", on the basis of reciprocity.[188]

In stark contrast to the previous writers, we find Samuel Pufendorf (1632–1694), the seventeenth century German historian and lawyer who wrote his *De Iure Naturae et Gentium* in 1672 whilst holding the Chair of the Law of Nature and of Nations at Lund University.[189] In Pufendorf's view, only *ius naturale* could serve as a source of constraint upon states in their relations with each other. He did acknowledge the existence of treaties and customary law, but their importance was limited. The former was nothing more than a private contract between states, and ignoring custom was not seen as a breach of a binding obligation.[190] Slavery was discussed as a separate chapter "On the Power of a Master". Although Pufendorf agreed with Aristotle that "some are so stupid that they do not observe, without the lead of others, what will be of use to them" (Aristotle would call such persons natural slaves), he did reject the view that slavery was established by the *ius naturale*.[191] According to Pufendorf, the origin of slavery started in the early days of mankind, when poorer people started hiring themselves out to others ("And so the first beginnings of slavery followed upon the willing consent of men of poorer condition, and a contract of the form of "goods for work": I will always provide for you, if you will always work for me").[192] In later times, slavery would then become customary (and in Pufendorf's framework thus not binding law between states) during wars. Afterwards, slavery was also introduced for the children of the captives and for those who wanted to sell themselves. Pufendorf did mention that slavery was later restricted, and in some states entirely removed, but did not provide further clarification.[193]

---

[187]Textor (1916), Chap. 18–39–41. I have made use of J.P. Bate's 1916 translation of Johann Wolfgang Textor's Synopnis of the Law of Nations (originally published in 1680).

[188]Ibid., Chapter 18–42. He also elaborated on the question whether Turks and barbarians could legally hold Christians as slaves, which he believed they could (he considered that not all wars of the Turks were unjust and that, even if they were, the effects of slavery as a provision of the law of nations might still apply). Next to that, he clearly held that a slave should not be manumitted when he embraced Christianity, though he quoted Pope Alexander III to the effect that Christian slaves should be treated better than others (Chap. 18–43, 47–49).

[189]Note that at this point, Sweden itself also had an interest in the transatlantic slave trade, as they had a presence on the Gold Coast starting from 1650 with their Swedish Africa Company. Allain (2012), p. 46.

[190]Neff (2014), pp. 175–176.

[191]von Pufendorf (1934), Book IV-Chap. 3–2. I have made use of C.H. and W.A. Oldfather's 1934 translation of Samuel von Pufendorf's *Of the Law of Nature and Nations, Eight Books* (originally published in 1682).

[192]Ibid., Book IV–Chap. 3–4.

[193]Ibid., Book IV–Chap. 3–5.

2.3.1.5 Eighteenth Century Classics: Modest Acknowledgement of the Atlantic Slave Trade, First Moral Concerns

Our final three thinkers, Cornelius van Bynkershoek, Emmerich de Vattel and Christian von Wolff, are to be placed in the eighteenth century. By this time, the French, Dutch and English had decisively broken the Iberian monopoly in the Atlantic world and had developed extensive slave colonies themselves.[194]

In comparison with Hugo Grotius' elaborate discussions, Cornelius van Bynkershoek (1673–1743), the eighteenth century Dutch judge, had far less to say on slavery in his *Quaestionum juris publicis libri duo*.[195] His discussion on slavery started with the by now oft-discussed statement that slavery succeeded the right of slaying the captured enemy. He made a distinction between Christian nations, where slavery had fallen into disuse and where it was no longer employed against captives of war, and other cases. As for these other cases, he first discussed wars against Islamic states, with enslavement being allowed on the basis of reciprocity. Finally, he mentioned how the Dutch used slaves in Asia, Africa and America.[196] Out of this, Allain discerned that, for Bynkershoek, the law of nations precluded the enslavement of Christians and allowed for the enslavement in terms of reciprocity against Islam but was silent with respect to the situation in Asia, Africa and the New World. Interestingly, this is the first explicit acknowledgement by one of the Classics of black slavery beyond the frontiers of Europe.[197]

Christian von Wolff (1679–1754), whilst a Grotian, was one of the eighteenth century thinkers who still devoted most importance to the *ius naturale* as the law governing interstate relations.[198] Working at the University of Halle, he composed his *Jus Gentium Methodo Scientifico Pertractum* in 1749. His treatment of slavery was twofold, forming part of his chapter "Of the Law of Nations in War". Wolff acknowledged the right to capture enemies and soldiers during a just war, based on the idea that such persons were resisting the restoration of another state's legitimate

---

[194] Allain (2012), p. 48.

[195] Bynkershoek did not have much use to the *ius naturale* anymore, and pronounced that "*practice is the origin of the law of nations*". He can be seen as part of those scholars of international law who tended to tilt the balance of international law more and more towards discussions of state practice (= *ius gentium*), instead of discussing the content of the *ius naturale*. His work was unsystematic, but very useful for the day-to-day issues amongst states. Neff (2014), p. 192.

[196] Van Bynkershoek (1930), Book I-Ch. III. I have made use of Tenney Frank's 1930 translation of Cornelius van Bynkershoek's *On Questions of Public Law Two Books* (originally published in 1737).

[197] Allain (2012), pp. 48–49. Note that Bynkershoek was the only one amongst the Classics to effectively be involved in a case regarding slaves, which will be discussed later.

[198] Wolff acknowledged the existence of four categories of law. Next to the *ius naturale*, there was law that depended upon the free will of humans. This could be divided in stipulative (= treaty-based) and customary law. This did not qualify as binding between all states. Finally, he also recognised "voluntary" law, which was based on the presumed consent of all states, and universal in scope. Neff (2014), pp. 183–187.

rights, and because these persons prevented the end of the war.[199] However, by the *ius naturale*, these captives did not become slaves. He believed that there was only a right to detain the captives until the war was over, and that an individual captive could only be reduced to slavery if he had committed an offence "*worthy of that punishment*".[200] Later on, he questioned how the sovereignty of so-called slave-kingdoms, which can be understood as kingdoms beyond Europe, could be acquired.[201] Such places, where all subjects were reduced to personal servitude, could only be captured through occupation in a just war.[202]

Finally, Emmerich de Vattel's (1714–1767) *Le Droit des Gens, ou Principes de la Loi Naturelle, appliqués à la Conduite aux Affairs des Nations et des Souverains* (1757) merits our attention. Substantively, Vattel used much of Wolff's theoretical framework for his own work. However, as he explicitly intended his work to be useful for practical purposes, he ensured that Wolff's man-made law was explored more extensively.[203] Slavery was discussed in his treatment of the right to make prisoners of war. During wars, he believed that parties may lawfully capture all the subjects of the enemy state and make them prisoners. From the moment of surrender, the capturer is however faced with several limitations as to what he could do with the enemy. He could not kill the prisoner, unless he had committed a crime deserving that punishment (and, on the same account, the treatment accorded to a prisoner should be humane).[204] For slavery, the same provision applied: unless the prisoner was guilty of a crime deserving of death, he could not be enslaved. Slavery was seen as little better than taking someone's life for Vattel, who held that slavery condemned a person to a lot which was utterly at variance with man's nature. Interestingly, Vattel finished with a remark which we have not seen hitherto: a disgust of slavery itself: "As it is, that reproach to mankind has happily been banished from Europe".[205]

2.3.1.6 Conclusion: Continuity in the Legality of Slavery, Silence on the Atlantic Slave Trade

Clearly, none of the Classics denied the legitimacy of the institution of slavery. Some of them, such as Grotius and Pufendorf, even came quite close to Aristotle's theory of natural slavery. Even Emmerich de Vattel, himself clearly repulsed by slavery, did not deny its legitimacy. At the least, all Classics accorded a place to slavery in a just

---

199 von Wolff (1934), S. 811–812. I have made use of J.H. Drake's 1934 translation of Christian von Wolff's The Law of Nations Treated According to a Scientific Method (originally published in 1764).

200 Ibid., S. 814–815.

201 Allain (2012), p. 51.

202 von Wolff (1934), S. 874.

203 Neff (2014), pp. 194–198.

204 Vattel (1916), Ch. VIII, 147–151. I have made use of C.G. Fenwick's 1916 translatrion of Emmerich de Vattel's The Law of Nations or Principles of Natural law (originally published in 1758).

205 Ibid., Ch. VIII, 152.

war, though they were equally clear about the exception to this rule in wars between Christian states. Compared with the legitimation of slavery given by Aristotle or the Digest, there is a remarkable amount of continuity.

It is surprising to see that authors such as Grotius and Pufendorf had that much to say about slavery, given that the institution had already disappeared from the areas where they lived for several hundred years. This can only mean one thing: that, implicitly, the Classics were taking the transatlantic slave trade into account, and their work undeniably helped in providing a rationale for it.[206] That being said, besides allowing for slavery, the Classics did not provide any substantive rules on the conduct of states in their operations in Africa. Quite possibly, the fact that slavery as an institution was legitimised, but African slavery itself was not explicitly addressed, can be easily explained. In contrast to what the Portuguese attempted for some time, the other major European powers would not do the enslaving of Africans themselves. Instead, they were happy enough to have trade access to the continent and export Africans, who were already enslaved in Africa by fellow Africans, to their colonies. If the institution itself was legitimate, the moral burden of legitimacy of the enslavement process itself could easily be diverted towards Africa.[207]

More than one eyebrow should thus be raised when reading what the last Classic, Henry Wheaton (1785–1848), wrote about the prohibition of the slave trade in his 1836 *Elements of International Law.* He claimed that the African slave trade "had been at all times regarded by just and enlightened men as repugnant to the principles of humanity and universal morality".[208] Many of his fellow Classics would undoubtedly have begged to differ.

2.3.2 The Slave Laws of the European Colonisers

With slavery clearly legal according to international law, we must now look at the slave laws of the European colonisers themselves. This is an important question for our next chapters. Most of the discussion will try to answer what happened to the slave's personal status when he travelled from the colonies to the metropolis. This begs the question as to which laws regulated the slave's status in the colonies.

---

[206] Allain (2012), pp. 54–55. For an example of Scottish lawyers using Grotius' views to assert the legitimacy of slavery, see Cairns (2001), pp. 20–34.

[207] Bush (1993), p. 451. Bush also believes that racism might have played a role. To explain the many references to enslavement of "Saracens", Bush opines that this might have to do with the fact that the Classics of the sixteenth and seventeenth century often used medieval models as inspiration for their texts. These texts contained many references to the struggle between Muslims and Christians. Given the recent outpouring of works which have re-assessed the enslavement of Christians by the hands of the Barbary Corsairs (which postdate Bush's work), his opinion might have to be re-evaluated. Writers of that time must have been well aware of the enslavement of Christians by Muslims, and thus were not necessarily just copying from their medieval predecessors.

[208] Wheaton (1936), pp. 497. I have made use of G.G. Wilson's 1936 edition of Henry Wheaton's Elements of International Law (originally published in 1836).

For the sake of completeness, suffice it to say that for two countries, the question was relatively easily resolved. The domestic laws of the Iberian powers recognised slavery, and their laws were simply transplanted to their American colonies through the Roman law doctrine of *accessio*. This theory held that the owner of the principal thing also became the owner of the combined thing. In short, this meant that the *Siete Partidas* of Spain and the *Ordenaçoes Filipinas* of Portugal, the domestic laws governing slavery in Iberia, were also used to govern the status of their slaves in the colonies.[209] Barring domestic metropolitan legislation on slavery, next to a lack of Roman tradition in English law, the English, French and Dutch colonisers had to revert to other means.

2.3.2.1 England: Colonial-Made Slave Laws Without Metropolitan Intervention

The first British colonies were those in the West Indies (Barbados and the Leeward Islands) and North America (Virginia, Maryland and Massachusetts). Through military conquest and the subsequent spread of early colonizers, England would eventually hold an array of territories up from Canada in the North down to the Latin American coast.[210] At first, the English experimented with the use of indentured servants in their colonies. Simply said, the servant's passage to America was paid, in exchange for which he had to work a certain number of years on a colonist's estates. But a host of social and economic factors eventually led the English towards the use of slave labour.[211] Besides the Portuguese, the English were the most active slave traders, with modern estimates showing that about 3.4 million Africans were brought to the Americas by British ships up until 1807.[212] In comparison with the other powers, England was early with abolishing the slave trade and slavery itself in its colonies. The former was halted by the 1807 Slave Trade Act and the latter ended through the Slavery Abolition Act 1833.[213]

England's colonial administration, as well as the relationship between English law and colonial law, was rather peculiar. The colonies were not in the hands of two great chartered companies, as was the case for the Dutch, and neither were they as centrally administered as France's colonies. The administration of this colonial empire was instead much decentralised until the latter half of the eighteenth century.[214] The issues

[209] Watson (1989), pp. 40–62, 91–101. For Spain, this changed in 1614, when it was decided that the laws of Castile did not automatically have force of law in the Americas, unless the *Consejo de las Indias* passed the law.

[210] Morgan (2007), pp. 7–10.

[211] Ibid., pp. 18–21.

[212] For an exact breakdown of the numbers of the British slave trade, see Richardson (1998).

[213] Drescher (2009), pp. 245–267.

[214] For a comparison between the French and English colonial administration, see Taylor (2002), pp. 140–141, 373.

arising from the administration of the English colonies, and the applicable laws, has been called the question of the "Transatlantic Constitution" by some contemporary scholars.[215]

The fundamental question was whether English law (statutory and common law) applied in the colonies. This issue was first elaborated on by Chief Justice Coke (1552–1634) in Calvin's case. In this case, Coke made a distinction between several types of lands acquired by England. Under the decision, the American colonies were later categorised as "conquered infidel colonies". It was held that such colonies were personal holdings of the king and were to be governed by the royal prerogative. The applicability of English statutory and common law thus depended on what each and every royal charter said exactly.[216] This was supplemented by Chief Justice Holt in the case of *Blankard v. Galdy*. The holding of the case noted that there was also another kind of colony, namely the "previously uninhabited colonies", where English subjects carried their English law with them (and were thus not governed under the royal prerogative).[217] This distinction between conquered and previously uninhabited colonies was eventually adopted by the English Privy Council in the early 1720s.[218]

In reality, the decentralised approach of the English meant, however, that most provincial governments of the colonies had much power and made their own legislation.[219] This was subject, however, to certain limitations. The charters usually stipulated that statutes could not be "repugnant or contrary to English law", and the King's Privy Council ensured that there was some oversight to enforce this repugnancy limitation.[220]

In short, each colony thus had some private space to legislate, subject to the "repugnancy" limitation, and the applicability of English statutory and common law depended from colony to colony. This is highly relevant, because it means that the decisions of English common law courts on slavery could resonate through England's Atlantic Empire.

Both kinds of colonies, conquered and previously uninhabited, were faced with the same issue: Parliament nor English common law said much, if anything, on colonial slavery. Parliament did acknowledge the Atlantic slave trade in some acts,

---

[215]For the usage of this term, see Bilder (2008).

[216]*Calvin's case* (1608) 77 E.R. 377. The case itself dealt with the position of Scottish people under English law after the 1603 Union of the Crowns. It is also well discussed by Bilder (2008), pp. 35–40.

[217]*Blankard v. Galdy* (1693) 90 E.R. 445. The case itself dealt with Jamaica, with Chief Justice Holt deciding that Jamaica was a conquered colony. The status of colonies was often re-litigated in England, which only exacerbated the difficulty of the relationship between colonial and English law. For some examples of this re-litigation, see Bush (1993), p. 462.

[218]Van Cleve (2006), p. 619. For more literature on the relationship between colonial and domestic English law, also see Cavanagh (2017); Gould (2003).

[219]There was a distinction between royal colonies (governed more directly by the crown) and proprietary colonies (the crown granted several right to a proprietor). For an example of decentralised government in the English colonies, see Taylor (2002), pp. 140–141.

[220]Bilder (2008), pp. 40–50.

but that was basically all there was.[221] Likewise, common law courts never meddled directly with colonial slavery, besides mentioning it as a local custom ("and that negroes, by the laws and statutes of Virginia, are saleable as chattels").[222] Barring metropolitan intervention, the colonists had to erect a law of slavery by themselves. For this, they used a combination of bits of Roman slave law, English villeinage law, rules concerning chattel property and indentured servitude as sources of inspiration. In the beginning, these were mere customs, with the colonies drafting these existing practices into colonial statutes later on. Several colonies would then influence each other as various slave codes were being drawn up (the Barbados slave code of 1661 being a particularly influential example).[223] The reason the colonists could erect these laws has to do with this so-called "Transatlantic Constitution". Both conquered and previously uninhabited colonies had some sort of "private space" which allowed them to make these laws outside the existing English legal framework. By using their de facto authority (given they remained ultimately subject to the English king), the colonies created a regime of *de jure* slavery.[224] Given the fact that there was no slave law in English domestic law, one might ask himself whether the "repugnancy" limitation was not problematic for colonial slave laws. But to this question, namely whether English common law courts took the colonies into account when making decisions on slaves coming to England, we will return later.

2.3.2.2 France: Metropolitan Intervention Through the Code Noir

France started its explorations in the Atlantic in the sixteenth century, but it was only at the time of Cardinal Richelieu (Louis XIII's chief minister during the years 1624–1642) that the French developed a true appetite for colonial expansion.[225] Compared to the other European powers, France quickly tried to impose royal control over its colonies. The power of the French crown was represented by three important institutions in the colonies. There was a *gouverneur*, who represented the king's sovereign power and commanded the militias. Next to him, the *intendant* was responsible for finances, public works and the promotion of trade. *Intendants* mainly took instructions from the French *Ministre de la Marine et des Colonies*.[226] Third, to represent the interests of the chief inhabitants of the islands, several *conseils souverains* were

[221]For example, the 1698 Trade with Africa bill made reference to the African slave trade. *The Statutes of the Realm Vol. 7*, 9 Gui. 3, C. 26.

[222]Bush (1998), p. 588. Smith v Brown and Cooper, 91 E.R. 566; (1705) 2 Salk. 666, King's Bench, in Catterall and Matteson (1926), p. 11.

[223]Nicholson (1994), pp. 11–16. HeinOnline has recently created a database called "Slavery in America and the World: History, Culture & Law", which sets out the statutory provisions of every English colony's slave law (http://home.heinonline.org/slavery/).

[224]Bush (1998).

[225]Régent (2007), pp. 14, 16.

[226]Blackburn (1997), pp. 285–286.

created, comparable in function to the various French Parlements.[227] In 1674, the colonies were added to the royal domain of France.[228]

The French experiment with *engagés* (comparable to indentured servants) having failed completely, the turn towards black slave labour was quickly made. Through various *compagnies* with trade monopoly rights, most importantly the *Compagnie de Sénégal* and the *Compagnie de Guinée*, the French also actively took part in the colonial slave trade.[229] French ships, mainly leaving from the ports of Nantes, Bordeaux, La Rochelle and others, shipped approximately 1.35 million African slaves to the Americas, principally to the French Caribbean (St. Domingue, Martinique, Guadeloupe, Guyana and, until 1763, Grenada).[230] It would take two attempts to eventually abolish French slavery. Slavery was abolished a first time on 4 February 1794 during the Revolutionary Era but reinstated by Napoléon in 1802. The slave trade itself would be abolished in 1818, but it took until 1848 before the provisional government of the French Second Republic abolished slavery for good.[231]

Substantively speaking, France had to develop its own slave law. There was no equivalent *to Las Siete Partidas*, and slavery had long since disappeared from most of France. The law governing the colonists was the *Coutume de Paris*, which did not have anything to say about slavery.[232] France thus acquired slaves before it had developed a slave law, and the first regulation on slaves was through local statutes.[233]

After the colonies were formally added to the royal domain in 1674, Jean-Baptiste Colbert took the initiative. He asked the top French officials in the Antilles to draw up a *mémoire* which would summarize the "arrêts, et règlements qui ont été donné par les conseils souverains sur cette matière", given that "il n'y a dans ce royaume aucune ordonnance ou coutume qui parle des esclaves".[234] The papers made by the colonial authorities eventually served as the baseline for the famous Edict of March 1685. It was the first piece of French metropolitan legislation on the status of slaves.[235] It has to be borne in mind that this was hardly the only piece of royal legislation on the

---

[227] Rigaudière (2010), pp. 638–639.

[228] Blackburn (1997), p. 285.

[229] Régent (2007), pp. 21–27.

[230] Geggus (2001).

[231] Niort (2015), pp. 59–65.

[232] Watson (1989), pp. 83–85. References to the applicability of the *Coutume de Paris* can be found in several pieces of French colonial legislation, such as Art. 46 of the Edict of March 1685, Art. 42 of the Edict of March 1724 (the equivalent edict for Louisiana), and various edicts on the establishment of colonial *Compagnies*.

[233] In historiography, there is a persistent myth that Louis XIII officially sanctioned the French slave trade in 1642 (or even 1648 according to some authors, despite the fact that Louis XIII was already dead for 5 years then). See for example Régent (2007), p. 41; Blackburn (1997), p. 281. Very probably, this is incorrect, as has been shown by Miller (2008), pp. 18–19.

[234] Niort (2015), pp. 17–18. The work done by the colonial authorities between the letter of Colbert and the promulgation of the Edict of 1685 is excellently discerned by Palmer (1996). Usually, this contribution is read in opposition to Watson's *Slave law in the Americas*, which focuses more on the contribution of the metropolitan authorities in the creation of the Edict of 1685.

[235] The Edict of 1685 was, however, only applicable to the slaves of Saint-Christophe, Martinique and Guadeloupe, and later extended to Saint-Domingue and Guyane. Separate edicts were later

subject, and the term *Code Noir* was also used for the ensemble of royal legislation on colonial slavery, much more than just this one Edict of 1685. In the next century and a half, French slave laws would thus be further developed by a combination of (often attenuating) royal legislation and (often harsher) local regulations.[236]

2.3.2.3 The United Provinces: Reverting to Roman Law

The Dutch entered the Atlantic scene shortly after they renounced their allegiance to the King of Spain in 1581, after which the United Provinces were born. They got a toehold in the area after they captured part of Portuguese Brazil (notably Pernambuco) in 1630 and Spanish Curaçao in 1634. Although Dutch Brazil reverted to the Portuguese in 1654, the Dutch retained several colonies in the Caribbean.

The management of the Dutch colonial possessions was administered by two famous Dutch joint-stock companies, the East India Company (*Vereenigde Oost-Indische Compagnie*) in the East and the West India Company (*Geoctroyeerde Westindische Compagnie*) in the Atlantic. The governors appointed by the Dutch Republic were officers of these companies, and the Dutch state would only assert direct control over its colonies after the Batavian Revolution at the end of the eighteenth century.[237] That is not to claim that these companies had a power base independent from the States General. Quite the contrary is true. The companies were intended to serve the commerce and diplomacy of the whole of the United Provinces. Furthermore, the *Heeren* governing the company were often civic patricians with close ties to government, with the greatest influence being exerted by the province of Holland (just as Holland was dominant in the Generality).[238]

The most important Dutch plantation colony was Suriname, conquered in 1667 from the English. This colony was governed from 1683 onwards by the *Sociëteit van Suriname*, a private company led by the city of Amsterdam, a powerful Dutch family (van Aerssen van Sommelsdijck) and the West India Company.

For our purposes, it is especially the West India Company which is interesting. It was chartered by the States General on 3 June 1621 and received a trading monopoly on the slave trade, which it would hold until the early 1730s, after which private companies could enter the trade as well.[239] Overall, it is estimated that Dutch ships transported slightly more than half a million Africans to the New World. The slave

created for the Mascarenes in 1723 (Île Maurice and La Réunion) and for Louisiana in 1724. Niort (2015), pp. 21–26.

[236]Ibid., pp. 59–65.

[237]Pagden (2008), p. 2.

[238]See Israel (1995), pp. 946–951. The governing of the West and East India Company is best discussed in Gaastra (2012); den Heijer (2013).

[239]The original charter of the West India Company can be found at the website of the Avalon Project, a project by Yale Law School to collect documents relevant to the field of law, history, economics, politics, diplomacy and government (http://avalon.law.yale.edu/17th_century/westind.asp). The West India Company was also involved in procuring slaves for the Spanish colonies. Between the end of the Eighty Years' War and the beginning of the War of the Spanish succession, the

trade would, under British pressure, be abolished by King Willem I in 1814, and slavery itself in 1863.[240]

Substantively speaking, the slave law that was employed by the West India Company in the Caribbean has long remained relatively unknown. Alan Watson tried to solve this conundrum, his academic expertise in the reception of Roman law proving of immense value. Watson held that initially, the West India Company had not been given the power to legislate in the Caribbean colonies. However, a *placaet* of 13 October 1629, *Ordre van Regerienge in West-Indien*, provided that in private law actions, personal or real, the law to be applied was the common law of the United Provinces or such as it should be approved by the Heeren XIX (the West India Company's governing body).[241] This clearly referred to the Roman-Dutch law, the term given to the blended legal system of Roman law and Dutch customary law as it was applied in the United Provinces during the seventeenth and eighteenth centuries, but this did not solve the issue.[242] If there was a common denominator between the Dutch provinces with respect to slavery, it was their complete absence of slave laws. Watson believes that this conundrum was solved by a misuse or misunderstanding of Art. 61 of that same *placaet*, which stated that in other matters of contract of all kinds and trading, the common written laws ("*de gemeene beschreven Rechten*") should be followed.[243] These common written laws were a direct reference to Roman law. Although it might seem strange to consider this as the legal basis for allowing the ancient Roman laws of slavery to be used as the substantive slave laws of the Dutch colonies, Watson convincingly came to the conclusion that this is exactly what happened.[244] There is additional, and more direct proof to confirm Watson's idea. On 23th August 1636, the States General proclaimed an "instructie voor de Regeering in Brazil", which was meant to set out guidelines for the West India Company's

---

Spaniards often worked with Dutch merchants. The Dutch also launched a bid for the *Asiento* contract during the War of the Spanish Succession, but were eventually sidestepped by the English. Scelle (1906a), pp. 450–750; Scelle (1906b), pp. 576–581.

[240]On the Dutch abolition of the slave trade, see Postma (2011), pp. 289–291.

[241]Watson (1989), pp. 102–114. For the text of the *placaet*, see *Groot placaet-boeck, vervattende de placaten, ordonnantien ende edicten van de […] Staten Generael der Vereenighde Nederlanden, ende vande […] Staten van Hollandt en West-Vrieslandt, mitsgaders vande […] Staten van Zeelandt […] Vol.* 2, 1235–1248, Art. LVI. Most often, the laws of the States General were called *placaeten*, but the terms *resolutie* or *ordonnantie* (mostly for decisions of the particular States) were used as well, Gerbenzon and Algra (1972), pp. 119–122.

[242]On Roman-Dutch law, see Lee (1953).

[243]Watson (1989), p. 104. *Groot placaet-boeck, vervattende de placaten, ordonnantien ende edicten van de […] Staten Generael der Vereenighde Nederlanden, ende vande […] Staten van Hollandt en West-Vrieslandt, mitsgaders vande […] Staten van Zeelandt […] Vol.* 2, 1235–1248, Art. LXI.

[244]Watson's main proof is a reference to a case of the *Hof van Holland* and the *Hooge Raad van Holland en Zeeland* in 1736, involving a runaway slave who tried to claim his freedom before the Dutch courts. When looking at the status of slavery in Curaçao, where the slave came from, this Dutch court explicitly referred to Roman law and Art. 61 of the *placaet* of 13 October 1629. I discuss this case later. On the equation between "*gemeene beschreven Rechten*" and Roman law, see Gilissen (1981), pp. 349–352.

administration of Dutch Brazil. Article 85 and 86 dealt with the issue of slaves. Article 86 explicitly mentioned that the slaves were to be governed by the "ghemeyne Rechten", next to the statutes made by the Heeren XIX. This clearly goes further than the "re-interpreted" version of Article 61 of the 1629 placaet Watson points to.[245] Dutch substantive slave law was thus Roman slave law but supplemented by other *placaeten* and local ordinances to align it with local conditions.[246]

2.4 Conclusion: Slavery as a Sempiternal Institution

This part tried to answer two questions, one theoretical and one practical in nature.

On the theoretical sphere, we have assessed how legal thinking on slavery evolved between 1500 and 1800, having done so by discussing the views of the Classics of International Law. Starting from Spain's Francisco de Victoria and up until Emmerich De Vattel's work, we noted a great amount of continuity in the legality of slavery as an institution. Neither of these scholars doubted the legality of slavery as an institution, let alone denounce it. When it came to the issue of the African slave trade, Spanish as well as other Classics were conspicuously silent, whilst each and any of them, at the least, believed in just war as a legitimate means of enslavement. Some others, such as Grotius, also mentioned other means such as voluntary enslavement. This only applied to "the other", as all thinkers fell in line when it came to enslavement of prisoners in Christian wars, which clearly went a step too far.

In practise, each of the European colonising powers had colonies built on slave labour between the sixteenth-early nineteenth centuries. Given that, besides for Spain and Portugal, there was no metropolitan slave law, the European colonisers had to create this. The English, with their decentralised colonial structure, left the issue of regulation to the colonial assemblies themselves. The relationship between these laws and English law was very complex. Things were clearer for the French colonies. The French King had a more centralised control over them, and whilst the *Coutumes de Paris* had force of law in the colonies, legislation on slaves was made with the *Code Noir*. Meanwhile, the Dutch did not govern their colonies directly, and left this to the West India Company. Barring metropolitan laws, the Dutch had recourse to Roman slave law, supplemented by local statutes.

With these remarks in mind, we can shift our attention back to Europe. The reason why each of the colonial interlopers devised a set of slave laws for their colonies in the first place, was due to the fact that slaves had disappeared from metropolitan soil by 1200, and their national laws did not include any provisions on slavery. This begs

---

[245] Article 86 held that "*Ende sullen in haer reguard plaetse hebben alle de Wetten en de constitutien by de ghemeyne Rechten, wegen de Slaven ende onvrye Luyden gestatueert, ende de Ordonnantien die by de Vergaderinge der Negenthiene hier naer souden mogen werden gestatueert ende gepubliceert*". *Groot placaet-boeck, vervattende de placaten, ordonnantien ende edicten van de [...] Staten Generael der Vereenighde Nederlanden, ende vande [...] Staten van Hollandt en West-Vrieslandt, mitsgaders vande [...] Staten van Zeelandt [...] Vol.* 2, 1247–1264, Art. LXXXVI.

[246] As regards the case of Suriname, see Davis (2011).

the question as to how the domestic legal orders would react when slaves, coming from colonies where slavery was enacted by positive laws, arrived in a metropolis which did not have such provisions. How did England, France and the Low Countries solve this conflicts of law issue between colony and metropolis?

References

Allain J (2012) Slavery in international law: of human exploitation and trafficking. Martinus Nijhoff Publishers, Leiden-Boston

Allain J (2008) The slavery conventions: the Travaux préparatoires of the 1926 league of nations convention and the 1956 united nations convention. Brill, Nijhoff, Leiden-New York

Alves AA, Moreira JM (2010) The Salamanca school [major conservative and libertarian thinkers]. Continuum, London

Aquinas T (1274) Summa theologica. English edition: Aquinas T (1947) Summa theologica (trans: Fathers of the english dominican province). Benziger Bros, New York

Aristotle (350 BC) The politics. English edition: Aristotle (1932) The politics (trans: Rackman H). W. Heinemann, London

Ayala B (1582) De jure et officiis bellicis et disciplina militari libri III. English edition: Ayala B (1912) On the Law of War and on the Duties Connected with War and on Military Discipline, Three (trans: Bate JP) Carnegie Institution of Washington, Washington

Baker JH (2002) An introduction to english legal history. Butterworth, London

Barthélemy D (2009) The serf, the knight, and the historian. Cornell University Press, Ithaca

Belli P (1563) De re militari et de bello. English edition: Belli P (1936) A treatise on military matters and warfare (trans: Nutting HC). Clarendon Press & Humphrey Milford, London

Bély L (2010) Dictionnaire de l'Ancien Régime: royaume de France XVIe-XVIIIe siècle, 3rd edn. Presses Universitaires de France, Paris

Bilder MS (2008) The transatlantic constitution: colonial legal culture and the empire. Harvard University Press, Cambridge

Blackburn R (1997) The making of new world slavery: from the Baroque to the modern, 1492–1800. Verso, London

Bloch M (1989) Feudal society, volume I, The growth of ties of dependence [1939]. Routledge, London

Bloch M (1947) Comment et pourquoi finit l'esclavage antique. Ann Hist Sci Soc 2:30–44

Bonnassie P (1991) From slavery to feudalism in South-Western Europe. Cambridge University Press, Cambridge

Bracton H (1230) De Legibus et Consuetudinibus Angliae. English edition: Bracton H (1968) On the laws and customs of England (transl: Thorne SE) Cambridge University Press, Cambridge

Brion Davis D (2006) Inhuman bondage: the rise and fall of slavery in the new world. Oxford University Press, New York

Brion Davis D (1966) The problem of slavery in western culture. Cornell University Press, Ithaca

Brownlie I (1998) Principles of public international law, 5th edn. Clarendon Press, Oxford, New York

Brunt PA (1997) Studies in greek history and thought. Clarendon Press, Oxford

Buckland WW (2010) The roman law of slavery [1908]. Cambridge University Press, Cambridge

Bush JA (1993) Free to Enslave: The Foundations of Colonial American Slave Law. Yale J Law Humanit 5:417–470

Bush JA (1998) The british constitution and the creation of american slavery. In: Finkelman P (ed) Slavery & the Law. Rowman & Littlefield Publishers, Madison, pp 379–418

Cairns JW (2001) Stoicism, slavery, and Law—Grotian Jurisprudence and Its reception. Grotiana 22:197–231

Carlyle AJ, Carlyle RW (1916) A history of mediaeval political theory in the west, vol III, 1st edn. G.P. Putnam's Sons, New York
Carlyle RW, Carlyle AJ (1915) A history of mediaeval political theory in the west, vol I, 5th edn. Barnes & Noble, Inc., New York
Carlyle RW, Carlyle AJ (1909) A history of mediaeval political theory in the west vol II, 1st edn. G.P. Putnam's Sons, New York
Carlyle RW, Carlyle AJ (1928) A history of mediaeval political theory in the west, vol V. Barnes & Noble Inc, New York
Catterall H, Matteson D (1926) Judicial cases concerning American slavery and the negro, vol 1. Carnegie Institution of Washington, Washington DC
Cavanagh E (2017) Infidels in english legal thought: conquest, commerca and slavery in the common law from Coke to mansfield, 1603-1793. Mod Intellect Hist 1–35
Curtin PD (1969) The Atlantic slave trade. University of Wisconsin Press, Madison, A Census
da Legnano G (1390) Tractatus de bello, de represaliis et de duello. English edition: da Legnano G (1917) Treatise Concerning War, Reprisal and the Duel (transl. Brierly JL). Oxford University Press, Washington DC
Davenport F (1917) European treaties bearing on the history of the United States and its dependencies vol I. Carnegie Institution of Washington, Washington D.C
Davies W (1996) On servile status in the early middle ages. In: Bush M (ed) Serfdom and slavery: studies in legal bondage. Longman, London, pp 225–246
Davis NZ (2011) Judges, masters, diviners: slaves' experience of criminal justice in colonial suriname. Law Hist Rev 29:925–984
Davis RC (2003) Christian slaves, muslim masters: white slavery in the Mediterranean, the Barbary Coast, and Italy, 1500–1800. Palgrave Macmillan, London
Decaux E (2009) Les formes contemporaines de l'esclavage. Martinus Nijhoff Publishers, Leiden-Boston
Decock W, Birr C (2016) Recht und Moral in der Scholastik der Frühen Neuzeit 1500-1750. De Gruyter, Berlin
De Vattel E (1758) Le droit des gens ou principes de la loi naturelle. English edition: De Vattel E (1916) The Law of Nations or Principles of Natural Law (transl. Fenwick CG) Carnegie Institution of Washington, Washington DC
de Victoria F (1532) The reflections in moral theology of the very celebrated Spanish theologian, Franciscus de Victoria. English edition: de Victoria F (1917) The reflections in moral theology of the very celebrated Spanish theologian, Franciscus de Victoria (trans: Bate JP) Carnegie Institution of Washington, Washington
Drescher S (2009) Abolition: a history of slavery and antislavery. Cambridge University Press, Cambridge
Emmer PC (2007) De Nederlandse slavenhandel, 1500-1850. Arbeiderspers, Amsterdam
Epstein SA (2018) Slavery after Rome, 500–1100. Slavery Abol 39:429–430
Erpelding M (2017) Le droit international esclavagiste des nations civilisées 1815–1945. Institut Universitaire Varenne
Finkelman P, Drescher S (2017) The eternal problem of slavery in international law: killing the vampire of human culture. Michigan State Law Rev 755–803
Finley MI (1980) Ancient slavery and modern ideology. Viking Press, New York
Foviaux J (1993) De l'Empire romain à la féodalité, 2nd edn. Economica, Paris
Gaastra FS (2012) Geschiedenis van de VOC: opkomst, bloei en ondergang. Walburg Pers, Zutphen
Gallet J (2010) Servitude. In: Bély L (ed) Dictionnaire de l'Ancien Régime: royaume de France XVIe-XVIIIe siècle, 3rd edn. Presses universitaires de France, Paris, pp 1160–1163
Garnsey P (1996) Ideas of slavery from Aristotle to Augustine. Cambridge University Press, Cambridge
Geggus D (2001) The french slave trade: an overview. William Mary Q 58:119–138
Gentili A (1598) De Iure Belli Libri Tres. English edition: Gentili A (1933) Three Books on the Law of War (trans: Rolfe JC) Clarendon Press & Humphrey Milford, London

Gerbenzon P, Algra NE (1972) Voortgangh des rechtes: de ontwikkeling van het Nederlandse recht tegen de achtergrond van de Westeuropese cultuur. Tjeenk Willink, Groningen
Gilissen J (1981) Historische inleiding tot het recht. Kluwer Rechtswetenschappen, Antwerpen
Gillingham J (2008) The treatment of the defeated c. 950–c. 1350: historiography and the state or research
Gillingham J (2011) Christian warriors and the enslavement of fellow christians. In: Aurell M, Girbea C (eds) Chevalerie & christianisme aux XIIème et XIIIème siècles. Presses Universitaires de Rennes, Rennes, pp 237–256
Glanvill R (1189) Tractatus de legibus et consuetudinibus regni Anglie. English edition: Glanvill R (1965) The treatise on the laws and customs of the realm of England commonly called Glanvill (trans: Hall GDG). Nelson, London
Godding P (1991) Le droit privé dans les Pays-Bas méridionaux du 12e au 18e siècle. Palais des Académies, Brussel
Gould EH (2003) Zones of Law, Zones of Violence: The Legal Geography of the British Atlantic, circa 1772. William Mary Q 60:471–510
Grotius H (1646) De Jure Belli ac Pacis. English edition: Grotius H (1925) On the law of war and peace three books (trans: Kelsey FW) Carnegie Institution of Washington, Washington DC
Guasco M (2014) Slaves and englishmen: human bondage in the early modern Atlantic world [the early modern Americas]. University of Pennsylvania Press, Philadelphia
Hanke L (1949) The Spanish struggle for justice in the conquest of America. University of Pennsylvania Press, Philadelphia
Hanke L (1974) All mankind is one: a study of the disputation between Bartolomé de Las Casas and Juan Ginés de Sepúlveda in 1550 on the intellectual and religious capacity of the American Indians. Northern Illinois University Press, DeKalb
Hargrave F (1772) An argument in the case of James Sommersett, A Negro. W.Otridge, London
den Heijer H (2013) Geschiedenis van de WIC: Opkomst, bloei en ondergang, 4th edn. Walburg Pers, Zutphen
Hilton RH (1969) The decline of serfdom in medieval England [studies in economic history]. Macmillan, London
Holdsworth WS (1922) A history of english law, vol III. Methuen & Co., Ltd., London
Hyams P (1974) The proof of Villein status in the common law. Engl Hist Rev 89:721–749
Hyams PR (1980) King, lords, and peasants in medieval England: the common law of villeinage in the twelfth and thirteenth centuries. Clarendon Press, Oxford
Israel J (1995) The Dutch Republic: its Rise, Greatness, and Fall 1477–1806. Oxford University Press, Oxford
Jacob R (1990) Les époux, le seigneur et la cité: coutume et pratiques matrimoniales des bourgeois et paysans de France du Nord au Moyen Age. Facultés universitaires Saint-Louis, Brussels
Justinian (533) The digest of Justinian. English edition: Justinian (1985) The digest of Justinian (trans: Mommsen T, Krueger P, Watson A). University of Pennsylvania Press, Philadelphia
Keen M (1965) The laws of war in the late middle ages. Routledge & K, Paul, London
Kelly JM (1992) A short history of western legal theory. Clarendon Press, Oxford
Kosto AJ (2012) Hostages in the middle ages. Oxford University Press, Oxford
Lassen N (1988) Slavery and slavery-like practices: United Nations standards and implementation. Nord J Int Law 57:197–227
Lee RW (1953) An introduction to Roman-Dutch law. Oxford University Press, Oxford
Logan RW (1932) The attitude of the church toward slavery prior to 1500. J Negro Hist 17:466–480
Maxwell JF (1975) Slavery and the catholic church : the history of catholic teaching concerning the moral legitimacy of the institution of slavery. Rose for the anti-slavery society for the protection of human rights, Chichester
Mazel F (2010) Féodalités, 888–1180. Belin Éditeur, Paris
Miller CL (2008) The French Atlantic triangle: literature and culture of the slave trade. Duke University Press, Durham

Mirkovic M (1997) The later Roman Colonate and freedom, vol 87 [transactions of the American philosophical society]. American philosophical society, Philadelphia
Morgan K (2007) Slavery and the British empire: from Africa to America. Oxford University Press, Oxford
Morrow GR (1939) Plato's law of slavery in its relation to Greek law [Illinois studies in language and literature]. University of Illinois Press, Urbana
Neff SC (2014) Justice among nations: a history of international law. Harvard University Press, Cambridge
Neff SC (2005) War and the law of nations: a general history. Cambridge University Press, Cambridge (New York)
Nehlsen H (1972) Sklavenrecht zwischen Antike und Mittelalter: germanisches und römisches Recht in den germanischen Rechtsaufzeichnungen. Musterschmidt, Göttingen
Nicholas D (1992) Medieval Flanders. Longman, London
Nicholson BJ (1994) Legal Borrowing and the Origins of Slave Law in the British Colonies. Am J Leg Hist 38:38–54
Niort JF (2015) Le Code Noir: Idées reçues sur un texte symbolique. Editions du Cavalier Bleu, Paris
Olivier-Martin F (2010) Histoire du droit français - Des origines à la Révolution. CNRS, Paris
Pagden A (1986) The fall of natural man: the American Indian and the origins of comparative ethnology [Cambridge Iberian and Latin American studies]. Cambridge University Press, Cambridge
Pagden A (2008) Law, colonisation, legitimation and the European background. In: Grossberg M, Tomlins C (eds) The Cambridge History of Law in America-volume 1: Early America (1580–1815). Cambridge University Press, p 760
Palmer RC (2000) English Law in the Age of the Black Death, 1348–1381: A Transformation of Governance and Law. The University of North Carolina Press, Chapel Hill
Palmer VV (1996) The origins and authors of the code Noir. LA Law Rev 56:363–407
Patterson O (1982) Slavery and social death: a comparative study. Harvard University Press, Cambridge
Pelteret D (1996) Slavery in early mediaeval England from the reign of Alfred until the twelfth century. Woodbridge, Suffolk
Plato (348 BC) Laws. English edition: Plato (1984) Laws (trans: Bury RG). Harvard University Press, Cambridge
Plato (380 BC) Republic. English edition: Plato (2013) Republic (trans: Emlyn-Jones CJ, Preddy W). Harvard University Press, Cambridge
Pollock F, Maitland FW (1968) The History of English law Before the Time of Edward I, vol I, 2nd edn. Cambridge U.P
Poly J-P, Bournazel E (1980) La mutation féodale: Xe-XIIe siècles. Presses Universitaires de France, Paris
Postma JM (2011) The Dutch in the Atlantic slave trade, 1600–1815. Cambridge University Press, Cambridge
Priester LR (1987) De Nederlandse houding ten aanzien van de slavenhandel en slavernij, 1596–1863 : het gedrag van de slavenhandelaren van de Commercie Compagnie van Middelburg in de 18e eeuw. Commissie Regionale Geschiedbeoefening Zeeland, Middelburg
Rabin D (2011) 'In a Country of Liberty?': Slavery, Villeinage and the Making of Whiteness in the Somerset Case (1772). Hist Work J 72:5–29
Rachel S (1676) De jure naturae et gentium. English edition: Rachel S (1916) Dissertations on the Law of Nature and Nations (trans: Bate JP) Carnegie Institution of Washington, Washington DC
Régent F (2007) La France et ses esclaves: de la colonisation aux abolitions, 1620–1848. Grasset, Paris
Richardson D (1998) The British Empire and the Atlantic slave trade, 1660–1807. In: Marshall PJ (ed) The Oxford history of the British Empire, the eighteenth century, vol II. Oxford University Press, Oxford, p 639

Rigaudière A (2010) Histoire du droit et des institutions dans la France médiévale et moderne, 4th edn. Economica, Paris
Rio A (2017) Slavery after Rome, 500–1100. Oxford University Press, Oxford
Roberts J (2009) Routledge philosophy guidebook to Aristotle and the politics. Taylor & Francis, Hoboken
Rushforth B (2012) Bonds of alliance: Indigenous and Atlantic slaveries in New France. University of North Carolina Press, Chapel Hill
Russell FH (1975) The just war in the middle ages. Cambridge University Press, Cambridge (New York)
Saint Augustine (426) City of god, volume VI. English edition: Saint Augustine (1960) City of God (trans: Greene WC). Harvard University Press, Cambridge
Saunders AC de CM (1982) A social history of black slaves and freedmen in Portugal, 1441–1555. Cambridge University Press, Cambridge
Scelle G (1906a) Histoire politique de la traite négrière aux Indes de Castille, contrats et traités d'assiento; étude de droit public et d'histoire diplomatique puisée aux sources originales et accompagnée de plusieurs documents inédits. L. Larose et L. Tenin, Paris
Scelle G (1906b) Histoire politique de la traite négrière aux Indes de Castille, contrats et traités d'assiento, étude de droit public et d'histoire diplomatique puisée aux sources originales et accompagnée de plusieurs documents inédits, vol 2. L. Larose et L. Tenin, Paris
Schlaifer R (1960) Greek theories of slavery from Homer to Aristotle. In: Finley M (ed) Slavery in classical antiquity views and controversies. W. Heffer, Cambridge, pp 93–133
Scott JB (1934) The Spanish origin of international law [publications of the Carnegie endowment for international peace]. Clarendon Press, Oxford
Suarez F (1621) Selections from three works of Francisco Suarez. English edition: Suarez F (1944) Selections from three works of Francisco Suarez (trans: Williams GL, Brown A, Waldron J). Clarendon Press, Oxford
Taylor A (2002) American colonies: the settling of North America. Penguin Books, New York
Testart A (2002) The extent and significance of debt slavery. Rev français Sociol 43:173–204
Textor JW (1680) Synopsis iuris gentium. English edition: Textor JW (1916) Synopsis of the Law of Nations (trans: Bate JP) Carnegie Institution of Washington, Washington DC
Thompson EA (1960) Slavery in early Germany. In: Finley M (ed) Slavery in classical antiquity views and controversies. W. Heffer, Cambridge [England], pp 191–204
Van Bavel B (2010) Manors and markets: economy and society in the low countries, 500–1600. Oxford University Press, Oxford
van Bynkershoek C (1737) Quaestiones Juris Publici. English edition: van Bynkershoek C (1930) On Questions of Public Law Two Books (trans: Frank T). Clarendon Press & Humphrey Milford, London
Van Caenegem RC (2011) Historische overwegingen n.a.v. de Sachsenspiegel. In: Iuris scripta historica—Sachsenspiegel in Brüssel. Koninklijke Vlaamse academie van België voor wetenschappen en kunsten, Brussel, pp 11–15
Van Caenegem RC (1990) Galbert of Bruges on serfdom, prosecution of crime and constitutionalism. In: Lyon BD, Bachrach BS, Nicholas D (eds) Law, custom, and the social fabric in medieval Europe: essays in honor of Bryce Lyon. Western Michigan University, Kalamazoo, pp 89–112
Van Cleve G (2006) Somerset's Case and Its Antecedents in Imperial Perspective. Law Hist Rev 24:601–645
Van den Boogaart E, Emmer PC (1979) The Dutch participation in the Atlantic slave trade, 1596–1650. In: Gemery HA, Hogendorn JS (eds) The uncommon market; essays in the economic history of the Atlantic slave trade. Academic Press, New York, p 448
Van Welie R (2008) Slave trading and slavery in the Dutch colonial empire: a global comparison. New West Indian Guid West-Indische Gids 82:47–96
Verlinden C (1955) L'esclavage dans l'Europe médiévale, Tome premier: péninsule Iberique—France. De Tempel, Brugge

Verlinden C (1977) L'esclavage dans l'Europe médiévale, Tome II Italie. Colonies italiennes du Levant—Levant Latin—Empire byzantin, Faculteit van de Letteren en Wijsbegeerte, Gent

Verriest L (1946) Institutions médiévales: introduction au corpus des records de coutumes et des lois de chefs-lieux de l'ancien comté de Hainaut. Union des imprimeurs, Mons

Vink MPM (2007) Freedom and slavery: the Dutch Republic, the VOC world, and the debate over the 'world's oldest trade'. South African Hist J 59:19–46

von Pufendorf S (1682) De jure naturae et gentium. English edition: Pufendorf S (1934) Of the Law of Nature and Nations, Eight Books (trans: Oldfather CH, Oldfather WA). Clarendon Press & Humphrey Milford, London

von Wolff C (1764) Ius gentium methodo scientifica pertractum. English edition: von Wolff C (1934) The Law of Nations Treated According to a Scientific Method (trans: Drake JH). Clarendon Press & Humphrey Milford, London

Warlop E (1975) The Flemish nobility before 1300. G. Desmet-Huysman, Kortrijk

Watson A (1989) Slave Law in the Americas. University of Georgia press, Athens, GA

Watson A (1987) Roman slave law. Johns Hopkins University Press, Baltimore

Weiss G (2011) Captives and Corsairs—France and slavery in the early modern Meditteranean. Stanford University Press, Stanford

Wheaton H (1836) Elements of International Law. English edition: Wheaton H (1936) Elements of International Law (trans: Wilson GG) Clarendon Press & Humphrey Milford, London

Whittaker CR (1987) Circe's pigs: from slavery to serfdom in the later Roman world. Slavery Abol 8:88–122

Wieacker F (1995) A history of private law in Europe with particular reference to Germany. Clarendon Press, Oxford

Zeuske M (2018) Sklaverei. Eine Menschheitsgeschichte von der Steinzeit bis heute. Reclam Verlag, Ditzingen

Zouche R (1650) Juris et judicii fecialis sive juris inter gentes… explication. English edition: Zouche R (1911) An Exposition of Fecial Law and Procedure, or of Law between Nations and Questions Concerning the Same (trans: Brierly JL) Carnegie Institution of Washington, Washington DC

Chapter 3
The Development of a Legal Freedom Principle, Ca. 1500–1650

3.1 Introduction

That brings us to the crux of the issue, the central question, namely the development and evolution of a so-called freedom principle in the English, French and Dutch legal orders. To recap, the principle held that enslaved people were freed as soon as they crossed a particular state border. According to Seymour Drescher and Sue Peabody, this started as a local, popular tradition. They held that it was consolidated in legal writing in France, England and the Low Countries by the sixteenth century.[1] I will not look too much at this popular perception but will focus on the legal aspects. This means that I will assess whether the laws of these countries indeed knew of such a principle, and what its origins were. As a side note, I wish to stress that, before the end of this period, England, France and the United Provinces only had a marginal interest in the Atlantic slave trade, which was dominated by the Iberians until the second half of the seventeenth century. This was not true for the period afterwards, which will be discussed in the next chapters.

For England, Peabody pointed to legal writings in general, with Drescher mentioning the diplomat Thomas Smith (1513–1577) and the English priest William Harrison (1534–1593) as proof of a national freedom principle.[2] Respectively, they wrote *De Republica Anglorum* (first published in 1583) and the *Description of England*, two books on the social and political life of Tudor England. Smith stated that, when talking about villeins regardant and villeins in gross:

> Neither of the one sort nor of the other have we any number in England. And of the first I never knewe any in the realme in my time: of the seconde so fewe there be, that it is not almost worth the speaking. But our lawe doth acknowledge them in both those sortes.[3]

[1]In particular, see Drescher (2009), pp. 23–25, 66–67, 93–97, 100–105, Peabody and Grinberg (2011), pp. 331–339.

[2]Peabody and Grinberg (2011), p. 395, Drescher (2009), pp. 22–23.

[3]Smith (1583), Book III, Chap. 8. The book is freely consultable at http://www.constitution.org/eng/repang.htm.

F. Batselé, *Liberty, Slavery and the Law in Early Modern Western Europe*, Studies in the History of Law and Justice 17, https://doi.org/10.1007/978-3-030-36855-5_3

Harrison went further. In discussing "Degrees of People" in Elizabethan England, he claimed that:

> As for slaves and bondmen, we have none; nay, such is the privilege of our country by the especial grace of God and bounty of our princes, that if any come hither from other realms, so soon as they set foot on land they become so free of condition as their masters, whereby all note of servile bondage is utterly removed from them.[4]

Smith and Harrison were neither common law practitioners nor judges, so we will have to assess whether it was truly legally so that slaves became free upon arriving in England. To do so, we will first assess the demise of villeinage. Likewise, two interesting cases deserve our attention, namely the English Vagabonds Act of 1547 and Cartwright's case of 1569.

The same tradition purportedly existed in France. Eighteenth century slavery cases in France teach us much of the perceived origins of the French freedom principle, as some of the memorials of slaves' lawyers that pleaded for the freedom of their client in court were printed. Christianity, looking favourably to the practice of freeing slaves, was one of the sources usually given.[5] Second, an obscure 1315 *ordonnance* of King Louis X (*Le Hutin*) was sometimes cited. Third, a host of historical precedents offered additional testimony in favour of the slave's freedom. These precedents consisted of a plethora of cases, popular stories and scholarly writing from the fifteenth and sixteenth century and were often linked to the French city of Toulouse.[6]

The freedom principle tradition of the Low Countries has also been traced back to the sixteenth century, although Drescher believed that it only broke through in the Southern Netherlands, the part that remained Spanish and later Austrian after the North broke away in 1581, in the beginning of the eighteenth century.[7] Generally, scholars refer to such cases as the arrival of a slave-ship in Middelburg in 1596, in which the States of Zeeland (*Staten van Zeeland*) decided to free the Moorish slaves aboard the ship, as an expression of this tradition.[8] Likewise, writing at the end of the nineteenth century, Ernest Nys noted that the idea of slaves becoming free upon their arrival in the Low Countries had become widespread amongst scholars of the sixteenth and seventeenth century. He cited Groenewegen van der Made, Arnold Vinnius, François Zypaeus, Antoine Perez, Libert-François Christyn and Antoine Knobbaert, each of them belonging to the top-notch of sixteenth and seventeenth century legal scholarship in the Low Countries, as authorities in favour of

---

[4]Harrison (1876). I have used the 1876 translation by F. J. Furnivall (the book was originally published in 1577).

[5]de Pitaval (1750), tome quatorzième. This is the written report of the 1738 case of the black slave Jean Boucaux against his master Verdelin at the Admiralty of France. Gayot de Pitaval, the compiler of the series, has included the pleadings of Boucaux and Verdelin's lawyers, next to that of the *procureur du roi* le Clerc du Brillet. This work is invaluable to discover which legal arguments were used to establish the freedom principle. As concerns the role of the Catholic Church in the decline of slavery in the medieval era, I refer to what has been said before.

[6]Peabody (2011).

[7]Drescher (2009), pp. 23–24, Peabody and Grinberg (2011), p. 335.

[8]Peabody and Grinberg (2011). For an author using the Middelburg case of 1596 as an expression of the Dutch freedom principle, see Drescher (2009), p. 23.

this proposition.[9] Finding the origins of the freedom principle in the Low Countries from a legal perspective is more difficult and has hitherto been largely neglected by most scholars. I propose that three factors were relevant, and we will discuss all of them. As for France and England, the decline of serfdom is a factor worth discussing. Second, city charters also played a role. Finally and, for me, most importantly, a landmark case in 1532 triggered scholars to proclaim the freedom principle in the Low Countries, although the specifics of what that freedom entailed could differ.

I will make a conclusion for each country separately in this chapter but will refrain from conducting a comparative analysis until the final chapter.

3.2 England: End of Domestic Unfreedom, No Clear Freedom Principle

3.2.1 The Final End of English Villeinage and the Favor Libertatis of the Common Law

When we discussed villeinage in the previous chapter, we noted that its demise had set in by the second half of the fourteenth century. Villeinage, which was strongly linked to the manorial system of labour rents, became less relevant due to the increased labour mobility and the change towards a regime of wage labour. As a result, many villeins would gain their freedom during this era through the various means that the common law provided for this purpose.

The best-known way, the same as in Roman slave law, was through manumission of the villein by the master. This was well established by both Glanvill and Bracton, and the difference in opinion as concerns the result of a manumission between these two authors has already been discussed.[10] This was a popular means of enfranchisement, as manumitting villeins was an easy way for cash-strapped lords to make some money.[11] Next to this explicit means of manumission, the law also inferred manumission through several actions: if the lord vested ownership of land in the villein, if he received homage from him, if the villein was part of a civil jury, if an action was brought by the villein against the master before a court and the master did not plead the exception of villeinage, etc.[12] Thus, an imprudent lord was always at risk of losing his villeins.

Second, both Glanvill and Bracton (and subsequent writers) referred to exceptions that made it impossible for the lord to claim their villeins. Glanvill mentioned that

[9]Nys (1890), p. 69.

[10]Glanvill, Book V [5]; Bracton F. 4.

[11]Hilton (1969), pp. 51–55.

[12]Littleton has summed up these implicit means of manumission in his New Tenures. Littleton (1903), Chap. XI, S202–209. I have made use of Eugene Wambaugh's 1903 translation of Littleton's New Tenures (originally written ca. 1450–1460).

the villein who resided for a year and a day in a privileged town and was admitted as a citizen into its commune (the gild) became free.[13] Likewise, Bracton said that residence in a privileged city or the royal demesne for a year and a day without claim could be used as an exception against a lord who tried to claim his former villein in court.[14] Holdsworth summarised this by stating that a man who had lived in a borough or the king's demesne for a year and a day became free according to medieval common law, unless the man himself acknowledged the lord's right by paying the so-called *chevagium*.[15] The principle could also often be found in town charters, which was probably an importation from Norman practice, and which subsequently came to be known as the maxim "town air makes free".[16] However, not all town charters mentioned the principle, and some town charters would also include limitations to it, such as the fact that it would only apply during peacetime, that the villein had to become a permanent member of the local guild, had to pay a sum of money to the guild, etc. Although this exception was never extended to all cities nor to the national level, it also contributed to the decline of villeinage in late medieval England.[17]

Finally, the common law system as a whole also played its role in the disappearance of villeinage. First, English lawyers proudly asserted that the English common law had a "*favor libertatis*", meaning that in cases of doubt as concerns personal status, judges would decide in favour of the liberty of the alleged villein.[18] The principle was first asserted by Glanvill. He turned to it to explain certain anomalies in the law of villeinage, and also when he opined what a jury had to decide when faced with uncertainty as concerns the status of a purported villein.[19] That is not to say that it was proof of some innate humane tendency of the common law, as the principle was probably primarily intended to protect freemen against wrongful accusations of villein status, which would make them subject to the harsh laws of villeinage.[20] In any case, whereas Glanvill simply used the principle of "favour libertatis" to explain certain narrow legal questions, subsequent generations of lawyers would try

[13]Glanvill, Book V [5–6].

[14]Bracton, F. 190.

[15]Holdsworth (1922), p. 494. In one of the slave cases Granville Sharp was involved in (Hylas v. Newton), he also used this argument to plead for the freedom of the slave ("Hylas lived more than a Year and a day in a free State without being claimed; by which circumstance alone he is certainly enfranchised"). Sharp's Remarks on Hylas v Newton in Lyall (2017), pp. 339–343.

[16]On the origins of this maxim, generally see Mitteis (1952), Strahm (1953).

[17]Alsford (2011).

[18]For an example of the usage of the *favor libertatis* in the eighteenth century by a lawyer, see Hargrave (1772), pp. 29–32.

[19]Bracton F. 105B; F. 190. The English lawyer might be surprised to learn that the pedigree of the principle actually did not originate in the common law, but was just borrowed by Bracton from Roman law, where it was part of a broader principle of *benigniora praeferenda* (Dig. 50.17.56). This meant that in doubtful cases, the more favourable/liberal construction was to be preferred. In the case of villeinage, this was used in favour of the villein.

[20]Savine (1903), pp. 256–261.

to elevate it to a general principle of the common law of villeinage. It seems to have obtained this status by the fourteenth century.[21]

It did not end there. The aforementioned action of neifty had long been considered burdensome, with its antiquated requirement of proof by kin. Royal courts now started to allow (and later on even gave extra procedural benefits to) villeins to bring other actions against their lord as well. Examples are an action for trespass against the lord for lying in wait and threatening to seize the plaintiff as a villein, or trespass *vi et armis* in cases where the purported villein had effectively been seized in the past.[22] If this was done, the defendant (the lord) would automatically plead the exception of villeinage, lest his villein would be manumitted. Both the original action and the question concerning status would then be referred to a jury, who would decide whether the person was free or not. Jury verdicts could give effect to popular attitudes, and jury verdicts increasingly tilted in favour of liberty.[23]

The common law courts sometimes even went further in allowing a plaintiff to prove his freedom: when the defendant would plead the exception of villeinage, some plaintiffs would allege they were bastards. As villeinage passed through the male line, bastardy would bar them from villeinage. In such cases, bastardy certificates would have to be produced by the bishop of the diocese of the alleged bastard birth. It seems that certain dioceses (Norwich being a notorious example) were not disposed against producing untruthful certificates.[24]

All these reasons help to explain why, by the beginning of the Tudor era (1485–1603), villeins had disappeared as an identifiable social class. But that is not to say that there were no more villeins at all, or that the institution itself was abrogated by English law. Alexander Savine and Diarmaid MacCulloch have gathered evidence from surveys, court rolls, official correspondence and legal proceedings to conclude that, at the beginning of the Tudor era, well over 400 manors still retained villeins. At the start of the rule of Elizabeth I, about 100 or so still had them.[25] The villeins that remained were often either very poor or very rich. The former did not have any

---

[21]The best treatment of the principle can be found in Hyams (1980). He convincingly asserts that the principle did not yet break through in the 13th century. Ibid., pp. 201–219. For examples on how the procedure in villeinage cases came to be skewed in favour of liberty, see Hargrave (1772), pp. 29-32.

[22]Alleged villeins increasingly brought these actions themselves in the fifteenth century. Writs of trespass *vi et armis* and trespass on the case were concerned with the punishment and amends for past transgressions by defendants. The former encompassed wrongs committed "with force and arms" against the king's peace, whereas the latter was used for all kinds of other wrongs. Baker (2002), pp. 61–64.

[23]Baker (1995), pp. 187–191.

[24]The fact that the status of bastardy was preferred above villeinage, was called *bastardia contra villenagium* by some contemporaries. MacCulloch (1988), pp. 101–105.

[25]Ibid., p. 93. Contemporary writers such as Littleton (*New Tenures*) and Coke (first part of his *Institutes of the Laws of England*, also called *Coke on Littleton*) discussed villeinage elaborately. Savine believes that this does not necessarily teach us much more about the contemporary state of villeinage, as he believes that "the learned authors of the time made little, if any, difference between things dead and alive, and perhaps lived under the old law more than under the new one", Savine (1903), p. 243.

money to pay for their manumission; the latter were the ones the lord often preferred to extort with the financial dues that his status entitled him to, rather than manumit them.[26]

Over time, most of these villeins were freed as well, as enfranchisement remained an easy means to collect money. Quite often, the crown gave commissions to some of its courtiers to enfranchise a number of villeins on the royal demesne.[27] Although the House of Lords once discussed a bill *De manumissione servorum vulgariter dictorum bondmen,* a bill of general enfranchisement never passed Parliament.[28] The last case of villeinage that came before one of the central common law courts dates from the beginning of the seventeenth century; however, common law has always acknowledged, even up to today, the institution of villeinage. Villeinage thus theoretically still exists in English common law, and as Baker notes there are probably, theoretically speaking, quite a few "unwitting villeins breathing English air" left.[29]

However, after the Elizabethan era at the latest, this did not have any practical significance anymore, given that the few villeins left had simply ceased to be of any relevance to their masters. Villeinage thus became an empty shell, an institution without any subjects left to govern.

3.2.2 Slavery and the English Legal Order in the Sixteenth Century: Vagrants, Cartwright and the Tudor Galleys

3.2.2.1 The Promulgation and Failure of the Vagrancy Act 1547

With slavery virtually gone at the end of the sixteenth century, the old divide between free and unfree seemed to be of no more relevance in England. But the fact that legal unfreedom disappeared did not mean that English labour immediately became "free". On the contrary, the statutes and common law of apprenticeship and servants could often be very harsh, though unfreedom of labour was strictly divided from unfree status.[30] English law would have its first clash with slavery when it tried to prescribe slavery as a form of punishment for those individuals without any master or labour: the vagrant.

Poverty is a problem of all times, and "vagrant" or "vagabond" were the terms which were usually reserved for wandering beggars without a job. In principle, these

[26]Lords watched carefully over the payment of dues such as the heriot (a death duty), merchet (payment for permission for the daughter to marry), chevage (payment for permission to live outside of the manor) and fines for admittance. Savine (1903), p. 276.

[27]Ibid., pp. 270–275.

[28]Ibid., p. 243.

[29]Baker (2002), p. 472. The last case on villeinage was *Pigg v. Caley* (1617) 74 E.R. 997, in which the jury made a verdict in favour of the purported villein. In the case of *Somerset v. Stewart*, Chief Justice Mansfield held that one could still be a villein in gross, but not a villein regardant, as he believed it to have been abolished by a statute of 1660. *Somerset v. Stewart* (1772) Lofft, 12.

[30]Bush (1996), pp. 610–615. In general, see Steinfeld (1991).

persons were capable of working, which is how they were usually distinguished from "impotent beggars". During the Tudor Era, the number of these vagrants increased. Mainly, this is due to the continued warfare in this period. The Wars of the Roses and the expansionary efforts of Henry VIII left in their trail a great number of persons bereft of a place on the labour market when the war was over.[31] At the same time, the Dissolution of the Monasteries by Henry VIII in the late 1530s also meant that poor relief increasingly became subject to regulation by the state.[32]It was the underlying fear of insurrection by men with experience in battle which explains the Tudor legislation to try and deal with the issue of vagrancy, and which would eventually result in the Elizabethan Poor Law of 1601.[33] This fear is especially visible in the Vagrancy Act of 1547, which was passed when the Earl of Hertford (Edward Seymour, Protector Somerset) took the regency during the minority of Edward VI (1537–1553).[34] What made the Act so strange? It tried to introduce slavery as a punishment for vagrants.

The 1547 Act repealed all previous statutory law on the subject, and defined a vagrant as every man or woman who was not lame, impotent, aged or too ill to work and who wandered around the country and did not seek work or left it when it was offered to him.[35] A master or any other person willing to offer him work, called a "presenter", could bring the vagrant to two justices of the peace.[36] They would enquire into the case, and if they found him to be a vagrant, would brand him with a hot iron and "adjudge the said persone living so idelye to such presento' to be his slave" for a period of two years. What is more, the slave could be beaten, chained, leased, sold or bequeathed.[37] If the slave tried to flee and got caught, the runaway could again be brought before the same justices of the peace, who would now condemn him to lifelong slavery. The stubborn slave who tried to escape a second time would be seen as a felon and could be adjudged as such.[38] If no-one was interested in enlisting the services of the vagrant, the justices of the peace could act *ex officio*, apprehend the vagrant and send him to the parish where he was born. There, he would be kept as a slave to do public works.[39] Finally, other important provisions dealt with the children of the vagrants (who could be made apprentices or

[31]Pound (1971), pp. 1–3.

[32]For a short overview of the state's involvement in poor relief, see Slack (1995).

[33]Pound (1971), pp. 37–41.

[34]Ibid.

[35]*The Statutes of the Realm, Vol. 4*, 1 Edw. VI, c. 3. I will refer to the relevant articles of the statute where appropriate.

[36]The justices of the peace had their origin in the 13th century, when a number of knights were appointed by the king to "keep the peace" at the local level. The system was regularised under Edward III (1327–1377), when they received an increased number of judicial powers at the local level (e.g. enquiring into, hearing and determining several crimes). Baker (2002), p. 25.

[37]Art. I, Art. IV.

[38]In English criminal law, felonies were those crimes in which the wrongdoer could be sentenced to lose his life, his lands and his personal goods. Baker, *An Introduction to English Legal History*, 502.

[39]Art. VI.

servants until they reached a certain age),[40] impotent beggars[41] and the proclamation and continuance of the act.[42]

Two questions are interesting for our purposes. Where did slavery as a punishment, seemingly *ex nihilo*, come from, and what can the application of the act teach us about slavery and the English legal order?

For the former question, lacking any parliamentary amendments to the act, we have to suffice with the views of the one Tudor historian who has looked at the act's history. According to C.S.L. Davies, a combination of the fear of vagrants, the Christian attitude of encouraging the unwilling to work, and precedents of harsh vagrancy laws provided the foundation for the act. This was supplemented with the fact that the law was probably drafted by a small group of humanists and civil lawyers, that had much influence in government at the time, and that could find inspiration for this act in a similar provision of the Corpis Iuris Civilis.[43]

The act itself was already repealed in 1549 in favour of a new one, which reinstated the previous vagrancy act from the time of Henry VIII. Remarkably, the preambles of this law explicitly state the reason for the repeal of the previous law, claiming that the 1547 act "hath not byn putt in dewe execution, and ptelye also by reason of the multitude of the same, (thextremitie of some wherof have byn occation that they have not ben putt in ure;)".[44] That the act was indeed not well enforced, is something for which ample evidence exists.[45] But more importantly, these preambles seem to confirm to us that slavery was seen as an unacceptable institution, even for those at the lowest level of English society.

3.2.2.2 A Russian Slave in England: Cartwright's Case

The second time the English legal order came into contact with slavery before the Atlantic slave trade is even more obscure. The case has only been reported by John Rushwordt (ca. 1612–1690), who compiled a series of papers which covered the period between 1618 and 1640, just before the outbreak of the English Civil War between the Royalists and Parliamentarians.

In his work, we find a reference to a case that took place in the Court of Star Chamber. John Lilburne (1614–1657), an important Leveller[46] during the civil war era, was examined upon interrogation concerning his unlawful printing, publishing and dispersing of books, which were considered to be libellous by the infamous

[40] Art. III.

[41] Art. IX–XII.

[42] Art. XVII.

[43] Davies (1966), pp. 537–545.

[44] *The Statutes of the Realm, Vol. 4*, 3 and 4 Edw. VI, c. 16.

[45] Davies (1966), pp. 545–548.

[46] The levellers were a group of radical dissenters in the English Civil War (1642–1649) who called for the abolition of the monarchy, social and agrarian reforms, and religious freedom.

Court of Star Chamber.[47] Lilburne, well known by contemporaries for his stubbornness, refused to appear at first. When eventually taken before the Court, he likewise refused to take an oath. After having sent Lilburne to the infamous London Fleet prison, the Court of Star Chamber tried again three days later. But Lilburne remained adamant. After some additional attempts, the Court took this as contempt of court and ordered Lilburne to be whipped through the streets of London from Fleet Prison to the pillory.[48]

The whipping −500 blows with a corded-whip with a knotted end in this case, to be exact- is what interests us. Rushworth allowed himself to digress from literally recalling the Court's proceedings and discussed the punishment. Whipping, according to him, was painful and shameful, flagellation for slaves. Moreover, "in the Eleventh of Elizabeth [1569], one Cartwright brought a slave from Russia, and would scourge him, for which he was questioned; and it was resolved, That England was too pure an Air for Slaves to breath in".[49] Whereas the Vagrancy Act 1547 can be seen as a rejection of domestic slavery, this would seem to be, at first sight, a rejection by the English legal order (although which court purportedly made this judgment is unclear) of allowing slavery, imported from elsewhere, to subsist in England. The court disallowed slavery, even though the slave came from a country where that status was recognised by domestic law, as slavery was only abolished in Russia in 1723. Regrettably, things are not that easy.

First, the contentious credibility of the case can be criticised. The case cannot be found in any law report. The only time it seems to be referred to in legal proceedings before *Somerset v. Stewart* is in a House of Commons report which was made during the process of impeaching the judges of the Star Chamber right before the final abolishment of that court. One can doubt whether, in such a case, the attribution has any meaning.[50]

The problem of the credibility of the case also plagued an eighteenth century audience. In Somerset's case, Serjeant Davy, one of Somerset's lawyers, referred to the case before Chief Justice Mansfield; however, when Mansfield asked "Is there

[47] Rushwordt (1721), p. 464. Besides the royal common law courts and the Court of Chancery as an equity court, there existed (besides the many local courts) conciliar courts in England. Essentially, they were used to deal with cases that were within the residuary royal prerogative of justice. The two most important such courts were the Court of Star Chamber and the Court of Requests. For a while, Star Chamber was nothing more than the King's council meeting in a certain place. Under Cardinal Wolsey's chancellorship (1515–1529), it would increase its civil jurisdiction and eventually became a separate court by 1540. It did not have a very precise material jurisdiction, mainly serving for cases which had both a civil and criminal element. It was brought down in 1641, after a series of unpopular prosecutions had given it an association with tyrannical government. At the same time, its civil law procedures were always viewed as suspicious by the common law courts. These were quick to take over the workload of the Star Chamber after its abolishment. Baker (2002), pp. 118–121, Cheyney (1913).

[48] Rushwordt (1721), pp. 464–466.

[49] Hargrave (1772), pp. 50–52.

[50] Bush (1996), p. 610. Standards of reporting cases were generally of an inferior nature before 1750, which means that the fact that it was not reported does not conclusively establish that the case never took place Baker (2002), pp. 182–184.

any traces there existed such a Case as that of the Russian slave"? Davy could only refer to what he had found in Rushwordt.[51]

But even if we are to take the view that the case did take place, it can still be explained in a variety of ways. When John Lilburne's counsel mentioned the case before the House of Commons, they used it to assert that it was the whipping itself which had exceeded the lawful bounds, which they saw as the holding of the case. This would mean that the reference to slavery should be seen as *obiter dictum*.[52] When it was later referred to in Somerset's case, there were different views on the *ratio decidendi* of the case as well: Somerset's council evidently believed that the *ratio decidenci* was that slaves became free by their arrival in England, referring to the fact that any other reading of the case did not make sense, as scourging a villein was allowed by English law.[53] Stewart's council took another approach, with one lawyer disregarding the case, but co-counsel Dunning taking the more cunning position. He held that the case only posited that English law would not accept the Russian form of slavery when it was "exported" to England.[54]

However, it cannot be denied that the case could plausibly be constructed to say something about slavery. In fact, it was very recently found that one of John Lilburne's lawyers, John Cook (the first Sollicitor General of the English Commonwealth, who was later executed for his role in the trial of King Charles I) did just that.[55] In one of his books (the 1646 The Vindication of the Professors and Profession of the Law), he cited Cartwright to the effect that a Russian slave on English soil "was instantly a Free-man, coming upon English ground, and breathing our pure ayre".[56] Whilst one cannot discount the possibility that Cook made up this case as a justification for his defence of Lilburne, and whilst Cook's reference seems to have been forgotten when black slaves entered English soil, follow up research might still show that others saw Cartwright as confirmation of the freedom principle in England during the second half of the seventeenth century. Until such proof appears, one has to be sceptical of both the veracity of its case, and more fundamentally the question as to whether the legal community knew about the case.

3.2.2.3 The English Navy: Penal Slavery and Impressment?

For the sake of completeness, one needs to note galley slavery and impressment, neither of which seem to posit a clash between the English legal order and slavery.

Although galleys, ships propelled by rowing, were mainly used in the Mediterranean, both Henry VIII and Elizabeth I had a few galleys at their disposal: some

[51]"First Hearing in the Court of King's Bench, 7 February 1772—Arguments of Serjeants Davy and Glynn" in Lyall (2017), p. 182.

[52]Cobbett (1805), p. 1354.

[53]Hargrave (1772), 51–52.

[54]*Somerset v. Stewart* (1772) Lofft 12.

[55]Kesselring (2018).

[56]Cook (1646).

captured from the French and some domestically produced.[57] In the Mediterranean, these ships would often be manned with forced labour, consisting of convicted criminals (*forçats*) and captured Muslim slaves. Several authors have tracked references in administrative documents purporting to show that the English were also willing to man their ships with convicts, sometimes explicitly referring to slavery.[58]

Two reasons make it hard to see this as a clash between the English domestic order and slavery. Firstly, although the English government might have been willing to send convicts to the galleys, the evidence for them ever having done so is very flimsy, if not non-existent.[59]The very few times the galleys were used, they were typically filled with free labour. Second, it is very difficult to resolve whether this can be truly seen as slavery, if we refer to the previously mentioned characteristics of slavery. As Hargrave also mentioned in his argument in *Somerset v. Stewart*, this kind of slavery was usually not domestic, the convicts being sent away to serve on ships all over the British realm. It usually did not make the posterity of the offender slaves either.[60]

The same argument holds true for impressment. This was an English naval practice that was especially popular in the British Long Eighteenth Century (1688–1815). It was a practice whereby press gangs consisting of navy officers, sailors and sometimes local ruffians used violence on free English subjects to supply the British navy with adequate manpower, forcing these people to serve on their ships.[61] In popular thinking, impressment was often associated with slavery,[62] and a notable anti-slavery thinker such as Granville Sharp also staunchly opposed impressment.[63]

However, legally, this was not slavery. First, the technique of impressment itself was legal according to English courts (the most famous case being Rex v. Tubbs in 1776 under Lord Mansfield). Impressment was seen as "grounded in immemorial usage", and the technique took precedence over respect of private rights in case of matters of national security.[64] Second, despite the popular association, impressment was different from slavery. Actual slaves on British ships were clearly a different category from the impressed sailors, as the latter went free at the ends of wars and received wages for their labour (including other material benefits).[65] In fact, black slaves were sometimes not disinclined to be impressed themselves as it could offer a path to later freedom.[66]

---

[57] Adair (1920), pp. 497–512.

[58] Guasco (2014), pp. 33–38.

[59] Adair (1920), pp. 511–512.

[60] Hargrave (1772), p. 20. We will turn back to this discussion when assessing the more numerous French galleys, where we will try to make a dividing line between *forçats* and captured Turks, the latter more resembling "true slaves".

[61] Brunsman (2013), p. 2.

[62] Ibid., p. 47.

[63] Rogers (2007), p. 22.

[64] On impressment and the law, see Ibid., pp. 17–35.

[65] Brunsman (2013), p. 7.

[66] Ibid., p. 121.

3.2.2.4 English Writers: Not Much to Find

If we hope to find conclusive proof of a freedom principle in the works of the English jurists and lawyers up to 1650, we are to be disappointed as well.

The works of the great legal systemisers of seventeenth century English law, Edward Coke (1552–1634) and Matthew Hale (1609–1676) are a good place to try and find such a tradition. In the first book of his *Institutes of the Lawes of England* (also called *Coke Upon Litteton*), we find elaborate discussions on English villeinage, but nothing related to slaves coming to England.[67] In Matthew Hale's *A History and Analysis of the Common Law of England*, which was only published in 1713, we find even less. Hale simply referred to Littleton's work when mentioning villeinage, and held that it was of little practical use to devote more attention to villeinage for a person of his time.[68] Scarcely could it be claimed that England's *ius gentium* writer Richard Zouche had more to say on slavery, as his discussion was limited to a treatment of the legality of slavery according to the *ius gentium.* Apparently, even the lectures in the Inns of Court never discussed slavery, either in relation to the colonies or its status in England.[69]

For the period before 1650 then, excepting Cook's 1646 book, I have not found English jurists claiming that slaves became free upon touching the soil of England.

3.2.3 *Conclusion: The English Legal Order at the Dawn of Black Slavery: Freedom for Englishmen, or for Every Men?*

The aforementioned cases have shown us that in the period 1500–1650, the English legal order came into contact with slavery only a very few times. The discussed cases are rather casuistic. If one was expecting some clear pronouncements that slavery, as an institution, was deemed to be in conflict with the laws and customs of England, such statements are not found.

How are we to evaluate the compatibility of slavery with English law at this time then? Let us first return to the statements of Smith and Harrison. Certainly, at the time of writing, their statements were slightly overblown and did not fully reflect the truth, as bondage still existed. With respect to Smith, several authors have written that his statement did not reflect social conditions fully accurately, and that his work was mainly written as a means to impress continental lawyers with the virtues of the English institutions.[70] Likewise, Harrison's statement seems to be too far reaching as well, although one author dares to hint that Harrison's statement on slavery might

[67]Coke (1830), Section 172–212. I have made use of the 1830 translation by Thomas Coventry (*Coke on Littleton* was originally published in 1628).

[68]Hale (1713), Section XXI.

[69]Bush (1993), pp. 445–446.

[70]Davies (1966), p. 547, Savine (1903), pp. 238–242.

be an allusion to Cartwright's case.[71] Given the fact that Cartwright does not seem to have been widely known at the time, if indeed it really took place to begin with, this seems doubtful to me. In that respect, the suggestion given that the Oxford-educated Harrison might have been inspired by foreign literature he read (maybe even Jean Bodin's work) in order to proclaim the English freedom principle, looks rather more credible.[72]

With the benefit of hindsight, it could be said that Smith and Harrison had time on their side. The English common law only formally acknowledged one sort of unfreedom, villeinage, and this institution, whilst legally never abrogated, was practically dead for all purposes after the Elizabethan era. Likewise, the Vagrancy Act 1547 clearly showed that slavery was not seen as an acceptable punishment for Englishmen. This means that by the middle of the seventeenth century, it seems clear that it would be difficult to "insert" slavery in English law as a punishment for Englishmen. What remains unclear, given Cartwright's tendentious credibility and obscure meaning, is whether English law would tolerate slavery to subsist when that status had originated in the domestic laws of another country, which is a conflicts of law question. To answer this question, we must look at the reaction of the English courts when they came into contact with the issue of black slavery.

3.3 France: From a Municipal to a National Freedom Principle

3.3.1 Serfdom: Decline, Persistency and an Anachronistic Édit Royal

Starting from the 13th century, French serfs started to be individually and collectively enfranchised at a faster pace. There are many reasons for this evolution. Economic conditions slowly started to improve from the 11th century onwards as the countryside gradually became more peaceful and agricultural production increased. Likewise, the founding of cities attracted many new settlers, who were often freed from their servile bonds if they became citizens of the city or resided there for a certain duration. And even on the countryside, many serfs were freed as they succeeded in becoming wage labourers, or when the lord freed them in order to evade them from flocking to the cities.[73]

Legally speaking, serfdom did not disappear completely from France until the French Revolution. Whilst there were almost no more serfs in the area of Paris, Toulouse and Bretagne at the end of the Middle Ages, it lingered on for three more

[71] Bush (1996), p. 610. For doubts about the validity of Harrison's statement, see i.a. Holdsworth (1922), p. 507, MacCulloch (1988), p. 92, Savine (1903), p. 239, Davies (1966), p. 547.
[72] Tugendhat (2017).
[73] Olivier-Martin (2010), pp. 289–292.

centuries in other parts of the kingdom, notably in the east of France.[74] Personal servitude was only abolished by an edict of the King in 1779, and any other kind of servile dues were abolished by the French revolutionaries in 1789.[75]

It is with this context in mind that we must look at the *ordonnance* of 3 July 1315 of Louis X. In the sixteenth century, Jean Bodin (1530–1596) believed that this *ordonnance* was responsible for setting all French slaves free.[76] Likewise, it was one of the arguments used in the eighteenth century *cause célèbre* slavery case of *Jean Boucaux v. Verdelin*.[77] Even up to today, a great many scholars mention 1315 as the year in which slavery was abolished in France.[78] At first hand, one would be inclined to acknowledge this claim, as the *ordonnance*, in its preambles, said that:

> Comme selon le droit de nature chacun doit naître franc […] notre Royaume est dit & nommé le Royaume des Francs & voulant la chose en vérité soit accordant au nom.[79]

However, notwithstanding these strong terms, the *ordonnance* really only had a very limited scope. First, the *ordonnance* did not say anything about slaves, and explicitly mentioned that it was applicable to persons "*en lien de servitude*", which were serfs. Second, the king did not just give freedom out of magnanimity, reminding that enfranchisement could only happen at "bonnes et convenables conditions". Finally, by explicitly saying that he hoped that other feudal lords in the Kingdom would follow his example, it was clear that the *ordonnance* was only meant to be applicable to those areas of France which were part of the royal domain.[80]

---

[74]Gallet (2010), pp. 1160–1163.

[75]Ibid.

[76]Bodin discusses slavery as a separate topic in his *Six livres de la république*, which was first published in 1576. Whilst the first version of his book was written in French, he also made a separate Latin version in 1584 which diverged on several points from the French edition. That explains why, just as scholars Sue Peabody and Brett Rushforth have done, I turn to Knolles' English translation of the work. In this 1606 edition, Knolles tried to combine both the French and Latin versions, thus giving the best possible idea of Bodin's views. As regards the 1315 *ordonnance*, Bodin said of it that "*Lewes Hutin, who came to the crowne in the yeare 1313* [Bodin made a mistake here, as the ordonnance was made in 1315] *(the selfe same time that Bartholus liued) set at libertie all slaues for money to defray the charges of his warres; that is, as I take it, to be vnderstood of manumised men, which we call Mort-maines*" Bodin (1606).

[77]de Pitaval (1750), p. 340. I discuss this case later.

[78]I have not systematically searched for all books claiming this, but a simple search on Google books with the entry "Abolition of slavery France 1315" renders a long list of books in all fields of study still making this claim. Even very recent literature sometimes makes this assertion, see for example Tugendhat (2017), p. 4.

[79]*Lettre de Louis X le Hutin portant que les serfs du Domaine du Roi seront affranchise, moyennant finance, 3 juillet 1315* in Boulle and Peabody (2014), pp. 21–22. All great collections of French edicts mention this letter, because the original *ordonnance* has not been found in the French archives.

[80]In Medieval and Early Modern France, there was a clear distinction between the Kingdom of France and the royal domain. When the Capetian dynasty first came to power, it only controlled a small swathe of territory directly, mostly centred on Paris, which became known as the *domaine royal*. Whilst the rest of the great lords of the kingdom did acknowledge the Capetian king to be the ruler of the *regnum Francorum*, the relationship between the king and the great lords was really one of lord and vassal. This meant that the king only had limited powers over the lands of his strongest

Marc Bloch devoted a whole book to this statute (and a comparable *ordonnance* of 1318). According to Bloch, the reason for its promulgation was certainly not the principled opposition of the French king to serfdom, but rather an attempt to raise money to fund the wars between the French king and the rebellious County of Flanders. Previous appeals to raise extraordinary taxes were staunchly opposed, and as a result, the king turned towards enfranchising rich serfs to collect the necessary funds for his war effort.[81] Bloch's conclusion was equally clear. The 1315 act is not spectacular at all, since the freeing of serfs to raise revenue was a practise used by the French kings well before and after this attempt. This particular attempt only applied to a small part of the royal domain, and it was executed so unsuccessfully that a 1318 *ordonnance* was made to try and remediate this.

In short, the only remarkable thing about the act was the eloquent wordings of its preambles. This could easily lead to an overestimation of the very limited goals of the substantive clauses.[82]

Serfdom continued to be an existing though declining institution right until the end of *Ancien Régime* France, and the famous 1315 act of Louis X enfranchised hardly any serfs, and no slaves at all. Though it certainly gained a mythical meaning afterwards, as is visible from Bodin's work, it does not explain the origins of the French freedom principle.

3.3.2 Local Origins: French Municipal Freedom

Another possible origin of the French freedom principle takes us back to the municipal charters we already quickly conveyed when discussing the decline of English villeinage. Before 1200, many of the French cities north of the Loire received town charters that gave special rights to the citizens of the city.

One idea popularly associated with cities was that of "city air makes free". This maxim held that unfree persons residing in a city for a certain duration of time could not be reclaimed by their lords, and thus in effect were no more in servile condition.[83]

It needs to be borne in mind that the extinction of the lord's so-called *droit de poursuite* after a year and a day was not confined to cities. The extinctive prescription of a year and day was a more general legal principle in sway during the early Middle

vassals. One of the chief characteristics of *Ancien Régime* France would be a continued extension of the royal domain, a process which was nearly completed by the sixteenth century but continued right until the French Revolution Barbey (2010), pp. 424–426.

[81] Bloch (1920), pp. 163–172.

[82] Ibid., pp. 172–176.

[83] Hans von Strahm summarised this as "Anders als freiwillig konnte es [das Dienstverhältnis] allein nur durch die Schuld des Herrn verwirkt werden, und zwar durch länger dauernde Nichtnutzung oder durch "Verschweigung" dieses Dienstes. Säumte der Herr mit der Geltendmachung seines Anspruchs auf das Servitium länger als Jahr und Tag, so hatte er sich verschwiegen. Sein nicht genutztes Recht verfiel. Er wurde durch dessen Verlust bestraft, vorausgesetzt, daß der Servus einen Richter fand, der ihn schützte", see Strahm (1953), p. 108.

Ages, before the (often longer) Roman terms of prescription became more popular again in the late Middle Ages.[84] Cities are important though, as they were obviously in a better position to oppose a lord trying to reclaim his fugitive serf.

The origins of the "city air makes free" clause, as found in written form in town charters, can be traced back to the efforts of Spanish cities to attract settlers in the tenth and eleventh century. The provision soon found its way up north, and first appeared in Southern France in 1107.[85] This kind of privilege was not universally found in all town charters, but it became especially important in the French city of Toulouse.[86]

Although the freedom principle of Toulouse can be traced back to the beginning of the 13th century at least, the principle was written down for the first time in 1283, as the customs of the city were written down when the County of Toulouse passed into the royal domain.[87] Regarding serfdom, Art. 155b of the customs of Toulouse held that, although serfs might well exist in the city, their lords could not stop them from carrying out their business in the city of Toulouse, nor take them out of the city.[88] Strictly speaking then, Toulouse was not free, but masters were unable to exercise their seigniorial rights on serfs in the city.

The principle would start to extend in the fourteenth century, the provision being used to try and assert a slave (and not a serf, the status with which the provision originally dealt)'s freedom. Starting from this century, the historical records show a continuous, small stream of slaves from Catalonia and Roussillon fleeing from their Spanish households, where slavery was practised, towards Toulouse.[89]

The records tell about the case of a Greek slave who fled his master in Perpignan and came to Toulouse in 1373, after which the French Crown was unable to apprehend him, owing to the freedom principle of Toulouse.[90] Two other cases of 1402 and 1406 are better reported. In the 1402 case, four slaves escaped from Perpignan and took refuge in Toulouse. Their owners asked the *capitouls* of Toulouse to return the slaves,

---

[84]Ourliac and Gazzaniga (1985), Section 3.

[85]As Van Caenegem stated, "the chronology of the rise and extension of the privilege is not as well known as we would wish". He also notes how the first Spanish charters did not make mention of a term of residence, but that the year and a day requirement was found in the earliest French charters when the principle spread north Van Caenegem (1990), pp. 95–87, Nicholas (1997), pp. 155–157.

[86]For a complete, recent overview of the freedom principle in Toulouse, see Peabody (2011). An example of a town charter (Lorris) including a freedom principle clause can be found in Boulle and Peabody (2014), p. 20. Clause 18 of the charter held that a person staying in the city for a year and a day, without being reclaimed by any authority during this period, and paying taxes, would be "libre de sa personne et jouira des droits de domicile".

[87]Customary law was an important source of law in Ancient France. At the end of the Middle Ages, customs were increasingly written down and submitted to the king, as this made it easier to bring structure to the plethora of different customs in France and to effectively know the rules. This process was strengthened after the promulgation of the 1454 *ordonnance* of Montils-les-Tours, which ordered customs to be written down. Rigaudière (2010), pp. 426–442.

[88]*Titre IV (Concernant les hommages) de la Coutume de Toulouse, art. 155b, 1283* in Boulle and Peabody (2014), p. 21.

[89]Verlinden (1955), p. 814.

[90]Peabody (2011), p. 352.

but they refused.[91] The ground of their refusal was that "any sort of slave was free as soon as he had set foot in the outskirts or wider jurisdiction of the city".[92] Likewise, the *capitouls* refused a request from a master to return his female slave, who had fled Perpignan for Toulouse in 1406.[93]

However, even the freedom principle of Toulouse, as applied to slaves, could not be taken for granted in the fifteenth century, as some exchanges between the French and Aragonese authorities showed that the principle clearly had not become a general principle of French law yet. The continued stream of slaves escaping from Perpignan soon drew the ire of the King of Aragon, who started complaining to his French counterpart. In 1427, a case involving a runaway slave came before the newly established Parlement of Toulouse, the highest court in that area. The arguments made by the *procureur du roi* and the judgment of the Parlement make clear that France was not (yet) a territory of freedom, as the slave was returned to her master. However, it is unclear whether this decision refuted the freedom principle of Toulouse, or whether the slave herself had not been in Toulouse proper.[94] In 1437, the King of Aragon pressed the matter even further. Hence, after negotiations between France and Aragon, a commission was established that was responsible for reviewing claims regarding escaped slaves from Aragon who had gone to the city of Toulouse.[95] In 1440, Jean Solacii, a representative of the municipal authorities of Toulouse, defended the freedom principle of his city before this commission. Remarkably, he tried to link the freedom principle of Toulouse with the French crown, stating that the fame of the French king resided in the freedom of all the inhabitants of his kingdom.[96] The commission remained unmoved by this plea, and suppressed the privilege of Toulouse in a 1442 judgment.

In the long term, Toulouse's custom survived this temporary blow. The city appealed the case to the Parlement of Paris, which declared that the committee's decision was null and void. Likewise, when the proposed suppression of the privilege of Toulouse became part of a treaty between the French and Aragonese King,

---

[91] The *capitouls* of Toulouse were the municipal government of Toulouse during the Middle Ages and the Early Modern Era. Next to administrative functions, they also had various military and legal competences.

[92] This decision, which was first described by a seventeenth century French lawyer in the *Annales de la ville de Toulouse*, is reprinted and translated in English in Peabody (2011), p. 343. Independent Catalan sources also confirmed the existence of the case, thus enhancing the veracity of the report.

[93] Ibid.

[94] Verlinden (1955), pp. 815–817, Peabody (2011), p. 353.The *procureur du roi* was part of the King's public ministry (*ministère public*). At regular courts, one could find a *procureur du roi*, whereas at the sovereign Parlements, there would be a *procureur-général*. They were royal officers charged not only with defending the interests of the King, but also the interests of the public at large when the public interest was at stake, Rigaudière (2010), pp. 621–623. The Parlements of France were the most important courts of France. They were sovereign courts of last resort. The earliest and most important Parlement was the *Parlement de Paris*, whose jurisdiction stretched over one third of the kingdom. In the course of the fifteenth century, many other sovereign *parlements* were made, like the *Parlement de Toulouse*, created in 1443, Chaline (2010), pp. 960–965.

[95] Peabody (2011), p. 354.

[96] Ibid.

the Parlement of Toulouse accepted to register the treaty itself, but rejected the part concerning Toulouse's freedom principle custom. The custom had prevailed.[97]

By this point, Toulouse was not the only city whose records bear testimony to a tradition of the freedom principle as applied to slaves. Nearby Pamiers, for example, invoked the same principle on the basis of its 1228 city charter. In one case, a merchant from Barcelona held that the black servant of a citizen of Pamiers was actually his slave. The servant was temporarily kept as a prisoner in the castle of the city. When the case came before the municipal authorities, they refused to give the purported slave back to his master, referring to their freedom principle and various other precedents.[98]

At the end of the fifteenth century, the freedom principle thus had strong roots in the customary laws of Toulouse and various other cities. The principle was responsible for giving freedom to several Spanish slaves. However, the principle clearly had a local, not a national application, as the king of France was willing to set it aside in order to make deals with the king of Aragon. We will thus have to move on to the sixteenth century to see if the principle gained a wider territorial application at that point.

3.3.3 From Municipality to Country: The Development of a National Freedom Principle

The evolution from a municipal to a national French freedom principle probably occurred in the second part of the sixteenth century. In this era, we find Jean Bodin holding that "inso much that the slaues of strangers so soone as they set their foot within France become franke & free" in his *Six livres de la république*. Half a century later, Antoine Loisel's (1536–1617) *Institutions coutumières* claimed that "Toutes personnes sont franches en ce Royaume & si tost qu'un esclave a attaint les marches d'iceluy, se faisant baptiser, il est affrachy".[99] This sudden change begs the question how such an important principle suddenly became part of French law. First, I want to give a concise overview of the cases, popular stories and scholarly writing associated with the establishment of a national freedom principle. Second, I aim to show some

---

[97] Verlinden (1955), p. 817.

[98] Ibid., 817–818.

[99] The importance of Antoine Loisel's work cannot be overstated. After the 1454 *ordonnance* of Montils-les-Tours, a new push to write down the customs of various areas had begun in earnest. On the basis of those customs, a group of scholars ("*les commentateurs*") started writing down commentaries on the various customs. Superposed on their work, we can find *Conférences de coutumes*, which are systematic attempts to come to the biggest common denominator of the various customs of France. The most famous attempt to come to an overview of the various French customs is Antoine Loisel's 1607 *Institutions coutumières*. The fact that the freedom principle takes its place as the third principle in the title "*Des personnes*" shows that the principle was perceived to be a national French principle by this time Loisel (1607), Livre I, Tit. I, III.

of the proposed reasons for how and why the freedom principle was elevated to a national principle of French law.

3.3.3.1 Selling Slaves in Bordeaux: The 1571 Decision of the Parlement of Bordeaux

In contrast to England, we find a clear (and reliable) enunciation of France's freedom principle in a sixteenth century case. Starting from the fifteenth century, Norman seafarers, next to a sizeable community of Spanish and Portuguese merchants, had been involved in selling enslaved Guanches, the native population of the Canary Islands. One of the main ports of departure was Bordeaux. The people of Bordeaux were thus well accustomed to the slave trade, but not to what happened in February 1571. A merchant arrived with a cargo of enslaved "nègres et maures" in the city, and decided to sell the slaves on French territory.[100] One way or another, the *procureur-général* got to know of this, and appealed to the regional sovereign parliament, the Parlement of Bordeaux. According to the *procureur-général*, the slaves had to be freed, because "la France ne permettait point aucuns esclaves". The case was decided before the Parlement in the same month, which held that "la France, mère de la liberté ne permet aucuns esclaves".[101]

Some things have to be borne in mind. First, although the Parlement apparently made a sweeping judgment, this did not mean it became hard law in all of France. Sovereign parlements only had autonomous regulatory powers when acting through *arrêts de règlements*, which was not the case here. Even then, their authority was limited to the *ressort* of the Parlement.[102]

Brett Rushfordt has conducted detailed research on the case. He believes that the influence of several important sixteenth century humanists in the Parlement of Bordeaux might have influenced the case. People like the humanist Michel de Montaigne (1533–1592) were staunch protectors of French liberty and believed all people were born free, and Rushfordt believes the intellectual influence of such people was important in deciding the case.[103]

Furthermore, it is unclear whether the king himself considered France to have a freedom principle at this moment. In 1574, the French king had sent *lettres patentes* to the Parlement of Bordeaux, stating that the Spanish and Portuguese merchant community in Bordeaux was under his special protection. This measure explicitly

[100] Rushforth (2012), pp. 81–82.

[101] *Le parlement de Guyenne libère des esclaves Africans (1571), commentaires de Gabriel de Lurbe, Jean de Gaureteau et Pierre Guillebaud* in Boulle and Peabody (2014), pp. 27–28. Peabody and Boulle have mentioned the reports of three writers, with two of them being independent from each other, thus enhancing the credibility of the report.

[102] The *arrêt de règlement* can be defined as a decision with a limited scope, made by the sovereign courts with the aim to make supplementary and provisional rules within their *ressort*. This was sometimes done when the written laws, customs and jurisprudence could not offer a conclusive answer to a certain legal issue, Rigaudière (2010), pp. 678–683.

[103] Rushforth (2012), pp. 81–82.

forbade anyone to act against the "serviteurs, biens et choses quelconques" of those merchants.[104] Rushfordt opines that this decision might have been made in reaction to the 1571 ruling of the Parlement of Bordeaux, and that it might have covered the merchant's right to keep some of their slaves with them as servants whilst on French territory.[105]

Next to this landmark case, there are various other relevant court rulings, though some of them have a rather tendentious credibility.

First, Jean Bodin, who had studied at the University of Toulouse himself, pointed out several cases. One 1558 case involved the Lord of Rocheblanche in Gascony. Besides the classical feudal obligations, this lord also claimed a variety of other dues. Most importantly, he claimed the right that, if one of his serfs left the land without his permission, "hee might lead them home againe in an halter". Apparently, this was rejected by the Parlement of Toulouse "as preiudiciall unto the right of libertie".[106] Second, Bodin also recalled a case that took place when he was a law student himself (between 1550 and 1555). This time, a Genoese person passed through Toulouse with a slave he had bought in Spain. The Italian quickly noticed that it was the intention of the *capitouls* to free this slave. As a result, he freed the slave himself, but made a contract of service for life with the slave to circumvent the full application of the freedom principle. In this case, it is unclear whether the decision of the *capitouls* was made on the basis of Toulouse's freedom principle, or on the basis of a broader principle of French freedom.[107] Finally, Bodin also mentioned a third case, although we know little to nothing about it. To give extra credence to the 1558 ruling against the Lord of Rocheblanche, Bodin held that slaves of strangers became free so soon as they set their foot within France "as was by an old decree of the court of Paris [the Parlement of Paris] determined against an ambassador of Spain, who had broght a slave with him into France".[108] We know nothing more of this latest case, and in the case of *Jean Boucaux v. Verdelin* in 1738, which involved a slave claiming his freedom in France and which we will discuss later, Verdelin's lawyer rightly stated that we know "ni la date, ni les circonstances" of it.[109]

Finally, in another case on French slavery, the *Affaire Furcy* of 1843, a slave's lawyer invoked a 1538 case in favour of the freedom principle. This reference can be

---

[104] *Lettres-Patentes concernant les Portugais et Espagnols du 11 November 1574* in Moreau de Saint-Méry (1784), 9.

[105] Rushforth (2012), p. 87. It is difficult to conclusively establish that this is the case, as the *lettres patentes* use the term *serviteur* and not *esclave*.

[106] Bodin (1606), 42.

[107] The French 1576 version indicates that the *capitouls* wanted to declare the slave free on the basis of "*de la coutume générale du royaume que d'un privilege spécial que l'Empereur Théodose le grand leur donna*". The reference to Emperor Theodosius is related to a mythical, but incorrect origin of the freedom principle of Toulouse. In the Knolles edition, it is said that it was the *procureur du roi* who pointed out the free soil custom of Toulouse. In this version, there is no reference to a broader, French freedom principle. For the French 1576 version, see *Jean Bodin sur le principe du sol libre, 1576* in Boulle and Peabody (2014), pp. 22–24.

[108] See Footnote 106.

[109] de Pitaval (1750), 358.

traced back to Louis Le Caron's (1534–1613) 1593 *Pandectes ou digestes du droit françois*.[110] He mentions how he saw a case being adjudged, though he does not say which court exactly delivered this judgment. According to Le Caron, an Italian had come to France with his Greek slave. After the Greek slave's master died in France, the slave had become a paid servant, serving another lord. The Italian heirs of the deceased slave owner now tried to claim the slave back. The court refused this and declared that the Greek was free "selon le droit commun de France".[111]

3.3.3.2 Popular Histories of the Freedom Principle: Spanish Slaves on French Soil

Next to the legal cases, we also have an account of two popular histories of the French freedom principle, which were also cited during the case of *Jean Boucaux v. Verdelin*. The first one was in the context of the 1552 Siege of Metz. Historically, the Three Bishoprics of Metz, Toul and Verdun were part of the Holy Roman Empire. In the wake of the wars of the Schmalkaldic League, Emperor Charles V tried to reintegrate the protestant areas back into the catholic fold. Maurice of Saxony opposed these plans, started another revolt and managed to get the French king on his side with the 1552 Treaty of Chambord.[112] The deal also placed Metz under the protection of the French king, after which the Emperor laid siege to the city. The story of the siege (which the Emperor was eventually forced to lift) was reported by the French diplomat Bertrand de Salignac. Salignac reported how Don Luis d'Avila, the general of the Spanish cavalry, wrote a letter to François de Guise, the French commander. d'Avila asked to send back a slave, who had fled the Spanish camp, and had stolen a horse and the purse of his master. Although de Guise sent back the horse, he refused to return the slave. The reason given was that "selon l'ancienne & bonne coutume de France, qui donne liberté aux personnes, ne permettatit qu'on le pût rendre".[113]

Whilst the words of a French military commander might still be easily discarded from a legal point of view, the next case involved the King himself, the "fountain of justice" of the whole Kingdom of France. Allegedly, in 1580, a galley of the Spanish army had run aground in Calais. The governor of the city then sent a message to the King, who was in the presence of Duke Henri de Guise (the son of the aforementioned Duke of Guise) in Chartres at that moment. The ship contained about 200 to 300 Turkish, Moorish and Barbary slaves. The Spanish ambassador went to the Duke of Guise, and asked him to return the slaves to Spain. The Duke then asked King Henry III to consider the Spanish request, but the King answered that he wanted to have the issue discussed within the *Conseil du roi*. After having deliberated, the King declared

[110] Louis le Caron, also known as Charondas, was especially known for his work on the customs of Paris. See Arabeyre (2007), pp. 479–480.

[111] le Caron (1637), Livre II, Chap. II. The first edition of his work was published in 1593.

[112] Tallon (2010), pp. 48–49.

[113] *François de Guise refuse le renvoi d'un esclave au siege de Metz* in Boulle and Peabody (2014), p. 25.

that the slaves were free, on the basis that "en France, où l'on n'usait ni d'esclaves ni de forçats s'ils n'étaient malfaiteurs, il fut dit qu'ils avaient acquis leur liberté". Given that the French were allied to the Ottoman Empire at that time, and that the slaves were captured in battles between Spain and the Ottoman Empire, the king purportedly even sent these men back to Constantinople by ship. Whether this case truly happened remains subject to dispute. Boulle and Peabody have tried to track down Dom Pierre de Saint-Romuals's 1662 *Journal chronologique et historique*, which is believed to be the original source of the story. However, no one has found this story within his work, and some opine that the case might have been apocryphal. In the eighteenth century, however, it was taken seriously.[114]

3.3.3.3 Humanist Writers and the French Freedom Principle

Besides cases and popular histories, the idea of the French freedom principle as a legal principle was picked up by several jurists and lawyers in the sixteenth century as well.

Probably the most famous example is Jean Bodin, who ardently argued in favour of the French freedom principle, and showed himself to be very critical of the institution of slavery.[115] Bodin devoted a whole chapter of his *Six livres de la République* to slavery. After having discussed the origins of the institution, he questioned whether slavery was natural and profitable to a Commonwealth, or whether it was contrary to nature and unprofitable. Bodin answered this question by summarising the arguments for and against slavery, asking himself which of the two was the better, before coming to the conclusion that slavery was unnatural and unprofitable.[116] Bodin (after many references to Greco-Roman slavery) then continued to look at the decline of slavery in Europe. He believed that it started when Muslims had decided not to enslave one another, an idea that was then picked up by Christians around 1250.[117] On France specifically, he said that slaves had already disappeared for more than four centuries, and that Louis X had freed all slaves who were willing to pay for this (which is an incorrect view of the content of the 1315 *ordonnance*). Referring to the several aforementioned cases that Bodin, a native of Toulouse, knew of, he came to the conclusion that France's soil automatically conferred liberty to slaves.[118]

[114] *Henri III libère des forçats "Turcs, Maures et Barbares" sortis d'une galère espagnole échouée à Calais, env. 1580* in Boulle and Peabody (2014), pp. 26–27.

[115] Arabeyre (2007), pp. 92–94. As we noted before, Bodin's antislavery attitude was heavily criticised by Alberico Gentili.

[116] Bodin (1606), pp. 32–36.

[117] Ibid., 40. Bodin also wrote that the Christian world had been cleared of slaves since the year 1250, which can easily be discarded as a gross mistake.

[118] Ibid., 42. One qualification might be that, as regards the mysterious case of the ambassador in the Parlement of Paris, it only applied to "*slaves of strangers*" coming to France. It is unclear whether Bodin would believe that it was possible for Frenchmen to come with their slaves to France without the slaves being freed. Given that France was not yet involved in the Atlantic slave trade, it is little surprising that Bodin did not foresee this hypothesis. I would tend to believe that Bodin's mind-set

Bodin was an influential writer, but hardly the only one to come to the conclusion that France's freedom principle had become a fundamental principle of its law governing persons. Nys, for example, mentioned two other French *jurisconsultes* who believed that France's soil conferred freedom to slaves, namely Charles de Grassaille (1495–1582) and Louis le Caron.[119] Likewise, François Ragueau (15??–1605), Jacques Cujas' successor at the University of Bourges, referred directly to the decision of the Parlement of Bordeaux in his 1600 *Indice des droits royaux et seigneuriaux* to assert that slaves became free upon touching French soil.[120]

Eventually, even Hugo Grotius picked up the idea in his *De iure belli ac pacis*, which was published whilst he resided in Paris. According to Grotius, the law of nations regarding captives had not always been observed amongst all nations. As an example, he cited how the ancient Jews had the habit of freeing slaves who came into their territory if the slave had not come into the condition of slavery due to a fault of his own (e.g. as is the case with penal enslavement). Grotius opined that this might be the origin of the then current practice in France, where freedom was also given to slaves entering the French territory. In contrast to the ancient Jews, however, Grotius asserted that freedom "is now granted not only to those captured in war, but also to other slaves of any sort".[121]

All this helps to explain why, at the beginning of the seventeenth century, Antoine Loisel believed the freedom principle of France to be one of the fundamental maxims of the French law of persons. In fact, he was just affirming what seems to have by then become a growing consensus amongst French writers.[122] Unfortunately, we do not know which source or legal precedent convinced Loisel of the principle, a question with which successive editors of his work struggled as well.[123] Somewhat more obscure is his reference that the freedom principle of France only counted for baptised slaves. The origins of this precondition date back to the fifteenth century Italian writers Giovanni d'Anagni and Ange de Gambiglioni. Their works were quite influential at the time, and probably served as the inspiration for Loisel's requirement

---

would also have foreseen that slaves coming with a French master to France would have been freed, as Brion Davis stated that Bodin's concept of an organic state would not have permitted the dualism of slavery and freedom Brion Davis (1966), pp. 111–112.

[119] Nys (1890), p. 69, Arabeyre (2007), pp. 383, 479. Nys also referred to the historiographer Jean du Bouchet (1599–1684).

[120] *François Ragueau affirme le principe du sol libre, 1600* in Boulle and Peabody (2014), p. 28. Cujas himself does not seem to have written anything on the French freedom principle, see Prevost (2015).

[121] Grotius (1925), Book III, Chaps. VII and VIII. Grotius cites Jean Bodin as an authority to validate his point.

[122] Boulle and Peabody (2014), p. 18, Arabeyre (2007), pp. 514–516.

[123] Peabody discusses the great variety in explanation (references to Thomas Aquinas, Jean Bodin, Church sources, …) that Loisel's successive editors tried to give to the principle in Peabody (1996), p. 31.

of baptism to receive freedom.[124] That being said, one should downplay the importance of the exception, as it was no necessary precondition in the works of several other writers, and slowly disappeared over time.[125]

3.3.3.4 Explaining the Change: Franco-Habsburg Rivalry and Barbary Encounters

Discussing all these expressions of the French freedom principle is one thing. It is more difficult to explain how a principle that was shared by some cities in the fifteenth century, was suddenly elevated to the national sphere.

One explanation for this change focuses on the rivalries between France and the Habsburg Empire in the sixteenth century. When France and Aragon had good relations, the French king was clearly willing to do away with municipal freedom traditions. So the argument goes that the inverse makes sense as well. When relations were bad, the French king had no incentive to act against the freedom principle, if the primary result would be Spanish slaves fleeing to France. One argument in favour of this thesis points to a 1553 prohibition of Emperor Charles V in Spain to export slaves from his territories to France under penalty of a lifetime sentence to the galleys.[126] Likewise, one has to remember that Spain and Portugal were already heavily engaged in the Atlantic slave trade, whilst France still had to make its first inroads into the Atlantic at the end of the sixteenth century. Writers such as Bodin thus cannot have had much to lose when they indirectly exposed the Iberian barbarity of the slave trade, by criticising the institution of slavery.[127]

Besides the French-Habsburg rivalries, recent historians have looked to the other side of the Mediterranean to explain the national French freedom tradition. During the sixteenth century, the Ottoman Empire conquered much of North Africa. Located far from Constantinople, these areas nominally became regencies of the Sublime Porte, but retained some autonomy in practice. This area would become known as "Barbary". Just as had happened in the *Reconquista*, Muslims and Christians often enslaved each other in this area, as Barbary pirates seized Christians both on sea and on land (going as far as Iceland).[128] For the majority of Frenchmen, the "face" of slavery in the sixteenth century must have been that of French Christians being captured as slaves in one of the Barbary ports, thus explaining the antislavery sentiment. In this view, the French freedom principle was more about self-preservation than about protecting others.[129] That being said, the Barbary encounters went both ways and there was a small presence of Barbary slaves in Southern France as well.

---

[124] Nys (1890), p. 62.
[125] Ibid.
[126] Peabody (2011), pp. 355–356.
[127] Brion Davis (1966), p. 112.
[128] Weiss (2011), pp. 7–19.
[129] Rushforth (2012), pp. 83–84.

The freedom principle clearly seems not to have counted for them, as we will discuss in the next chapter.

3.3.4 *Conclusion: The French Legal Order at the Dawn of Black Slavery: French Freedom as a National Principle*

Between 1500 and 1650, the French legal order came into contact with slavery various times, and it developed a tradition of a French freedom principle over time.

One origin of the French freedom principle can easily be discarded: Louis X was talking about serfs, not slaves, in his 1315 *ordonnance*, and he was not even planning to free all of them.

The true roots of the French freedom principle can be found in the transformation of municipal town charters which reiterated principles of extinctive prescription for serfs after one year and one day, and which were subsequently used to declare slaves free. This was most relevant in French cities close to the Spanish border such as Toulouse, as these cities were on the fault line between a Spanish government which tolerated and regulated slavery, and France, where the institution had simply perished away without ever being formally abolished. However, the principle's roots were only as strong as the cities' leverage would allow, as the French king had no qualms to abolish it temporarily for the purpose of good relations with the rulers of Aragon.

During the course of the sixteenth century, the principle was picked up by scholars, courts and the public at large, and elevated to a national principle of French law. Be it because of the Spanish-Habsburg rivalry or due to Barbary encounters, the municipal principle of the fifteenth century had become well entrenched in the sixteenth century, solidified by the influential works of writers such as Bodin and Loisel.

Two things do have to be borne in mind. First, we have been able to find the French freedom idea expressed in a variety of settings, but not in any royal legislation. Though writers and sovereign courts might have had much influence, confirmation from the highest authority in French law, the King, was lacking.[130] Second, it is clear that the idea of the freedom principle was gradually built up over time. Whilst Loisel still posited a link between slavery and baptism, this qualification would disappear towards the end of the seventeenth century. The various discussed cases and even Louis X's 1315 ordinance were slowly moulded to create a coherent idea of an unconditional freedom principle, as the idea that France conferred freedom to everyone entering her territory became an essential feature of French thought.[131]

---

[130] Nys (1890), p. 63. At most, one could refer to the 1580 case in which Henry III freed the slaves of the grounded Spanish ship in Calais, but this is a dangerous conclusion given its tendentious credibility.

[131] Peabody (1996), p. 32. More poetically, Peabody said that "*Like a seashell tossed by the tides, the maxim's barnacle like accretions and collisions with opposing forces eventually distorted its original form*".

3.4 Low Countries: Developing the Freedom Principle Along French Lines: From Antwerp to the XVII Provinces

3.4.1 *The Decline of Serfdom in the Low Countries*

As everywhere else in North-Western Europe, serfdom fell into decline in the Low Countries in the second half of the Middle Ages. In comparison with neighbouring regions, its breakdown already started in the twelfth century in some areas. Many reasons could once more be given: demographic changes, the progress of agriculture and the clearance movement, territorial lords and cities trying to increase their power to the detriment of manorial lords, etc.[132] Likewise, many of the territorial lords, such as the Counts of Flanders, Hainaut and Holland sometimes enfranchised whole groups of serfs at once, or made legislation to attenuate some of the characteristics of serfdom (for example, by changing the right of *mainmorte* to a right of *meilleur catel* for the serf's lord).[133]

In some regions such as Flanders and Brabant, the decline was almost completed by the end of the twelfth century. In others, it would take longer.[134] It is safe to say that whereas serfdom had thus ceased to be an institutional reality in most of the provinces of the Low Countries at the end of the Middle Ages, it remained present in some areas and was not legally abolished until the end of the *Ancien Régime*. As concerns those last vestiges of serfdom, we can note that the written customs of three areas in the Southern Netherlands (Hainaut, Aalst and Luxemburg) still contained references to the institution in the sixteenth and seventeenth century, although it became less relevant over time there as well.[135] Likewise, in the North, remains of serfdom could be found in the provinces of Gelderland and Overrijsel up until the Batavian Revolution at the end of the eighteenth century.[136]

We do not find general decrees of emancipation in the Low Countries either. We already noted how the *ordonnance* of Louis X in 1315 did not at all free all slaves or serfs, which would have been relevant for the territories subject to the French crown, such as the County of Flanders—which, in any case, was not a part of the royal domain. Though the influential eighteenth century Flemish jurist Georges de Ghewiet (1651–1745) tried to trace back the disappearance of slavery in the Southern

[132]See, i.a. Godding (1991), p. 49, Van Bavel (2010), pp. 83–93, Nicholas (1992), pp. 124–129, Verriest (1946), p. 163.

[133]The right of *meilleur catel* was comparable to the heriot in the English law of villeinage. It allowed the lord to take the serf's "best" moveable good or most valuable chattel after his death.

[134]Van Bavel (2010), p. 86.

[135]Godding (1991), p. 49.

[136]Andreae (1906), p. 20.

Netherlands by pointing at a decree of the Flemish Countess Marguerite of 1232,[137] this is most certainly also incorrect. In fact, that ordonnance only abolished the right of *meilleur catel* for free people in a small part of the County of Flanders.[138]

Likewise, there was no general emancipation decree made by the Flemish, Burgundian or Spanish lords of the Low Countries. In law, serfdom thus continued to exist until the end of the *Ancien Régime*, but in fact, the number of serfs had become small by the end of the Middle Ages and further declined between 1500–1650. The great majority of the population of the Low Countries was certainly free in the sixteenth century, but this alone does not explain the origins of the freedom principle in these areas.

3.4.2 "City Air Makes Free": Cities and the Decline of Serfdom

One of the reasons that is usually given for the decline of serfdom in the Low Countries has to do with the vigorousness of the cities in the Low Countries, with urban development being especially important in Flanders in the early middle ages. By the end of the fifteenth century, Flanders, Brabant and Holland (the three most important provinces of the Low Countries) had all become highly urbanised. This begs the question as to the role cities might have played in the eventual enunciation of a nationwide freedom principle for slaves.[139]

The same proviso as elsewhere is in place. The idea of "one year and one day" as a form of extinctive prescription existed long before the appearance of city charters.[140] That being said, "*the waning of serfdom was related to the rise of the towns*", as the eminent Belgian legal historian Van Caenegem stated.[141]

As noted by that same author, there is no indication that a general principle of *Stadtluft macht frei* was in sway in Flanders in the first half of the twelfth century[142] (or elsewhere for that reason, as the work of Léo Verriest for the County of Hainaut can attest for example[143]). Yet clearly, personal freedom was connected to urban areas in one way or another. One famous example involves a case reported by Galbert of Bruges, a twelfth century chronicler from Bruges.[144] When the Flemish count William Clito (1102–1128) arrived in the city of Lille with his retinue in August

[137] De Ghewiet actually mentioned 1132, but given that Countess Marguerite lived between 1202 and 1280, we can safely assume this must have reflected a small typographical error from De Ghewiet's part.

[138] See de Ghewiet (1736), Partie prémiére, Tit. II, XXXV, Godding (1991), p. 48.

[139] Nicholas (1997), Israel (1995), pp. 9–20.

[140] Heirbaut (2013), p. 283.

[141] Van Caenegem (1995), p. 152.

[142] Ibid., p. 153.

[143] Verriest (1910), pp. 90–100.

[144] On Galbert of Bruges, see i.a. Van Caenegem (1990).

1128, he spotted one of his runaway serfs. After arresting him in order to be sent back, the city went into an uproar. It is a bit unclear what the townsmen were asserting. It could be that they wanted to preserve the freedom of the runaway serf, or that they were defending the special peace that protected their market, or that they wanted the Count to resort to a judicial process.[145] Whichever of these was the case, this case shows that urban municipalities were in a better position to assert the personal freedom of their citizens.

The principle of "city air makes free" as applied to serfs itself, was also to be found in municipal city charters of the later Middle Ages. It was not to be found in municipal charters before the second half of the twelfth century. In fact, the principle had only just appeared in Southern France in the early twelfth century, and it took another half-century before it first appeared in a Flemish charter, namely that of the city of Nieuwpoort in 1163. Art. 10 of this charter held that "whoever remains here for one year and one day will be free".[146] There are no systematic overviews of which city had and which city did not have freedom provisions, but the provision was far from general in the Low Countries, and the exact terms could vary quite a bit.[147] Before the sixteenth century, there are no indications that a slave tried to make use of this principle, but this should not be surprising. Slavery had perished in these areas early on, and societies with slaves, such as Spain and Italy, were geographically distant from the Low Countries, so that it is clear that the original principle simply referred to serfs.

For our purposes, it is interesting to see what the city charters of the two cities that would be most important in the colonial trade had to say on this issue. By 1500, Antwerp had become the most important trading centre of the Low Countries, and it became a major centre of Portuguese and Spanish trading in the sixteenth century. During the Eighty Years' War, the city was suffocated by the Duke of Parma's siege in 1584–1585, and more than half of its population fled to the north in the ensuing years.[148] That moment marked the ascendancy of Amsterdam, which then became the trading capital for the Dutch colonial ventures.

Although both Antwerp (1221) and Amsterdam (1301) already received their own city laws early on (rights which were subsequently sometimes changed), their customs were only officially written down in the sixteenth century for Antwerp and in 1644 for Amsterdam.[149] In the case of Antwerp for this period, besides for the

[145] Van Caenegem (1995), p. 153.

[146] Van Caenegem (1990), pp. 96–99.

[147] Nicholas (1992), p. 105, Van Caenegem (1990), pp. 96–99, van Schevichaven (1924), pp. 51–54. For an example of how the principle exactly applied in concrete cases (Mons and Valenciennes), see Verriest (1910), pp. 94–100.

[148] Denucé et al. (1937), pp. 77–84, Israel (1995), p. 219.

[149] In 1531, Emperor Charles V ordered that all customs had to be written down. There was much opposition in the Low Countries to do this, and the order had to be repeated several times in the ensuing decades. Antwerp's customs were written down in 1547–1548, 1570, 1582 and 1608. I have made use of the 1582 version, which was printed. In the future United Provinces, Charles V's order was less adhered to in general. This also explains why Roman law could penetrate so easily in the legal system of the Dutch Republic in the seventeenth century. Rooseboom, the *stadssecretaris*

fourteenth century *Keurboeck metten doppen*, there existed the *Antiquissimae* of 1570–1571, the *Impressae* of 1582 and the *Compilatae* of 1602. Our focus here will be on the *Impressae*, because it was the only version of these that was brought to print.[150]

Interestingly, both the city rights of Antwerp and Amsterdam include provisions related to slavery. In the case of Antwerp, article 36, I-II of its city rights, which dealt with the state and condition of persons ("*Vanden Staet ende Conditie van Persoonen*") mentioned that:

> I. Within the city and surroundings of Antwerp, all people are free and no slaves.
>
> II. The same holds true for all slaves that have come to the city and its surroundings, who are free and outside of the power of their Masters or [their masters'] Wives: and as far as they try to keep them as slaves or have them serve them against their will may proclaim *ad libertatem patriae*; and can have their Masters or [their Masters'] Wives brought before court and can have themselves proclaimed free there.[151]

For Amsterdam, almost exactly the same provision could be found in Chapter 39 of its municipal laws.[152] This is scarcely surprising, as the city rights of Amsterdam were heavily influenced by Antwerp, in many ways its predecessor as the most vibrant city of the Low Countries. This can be seen from the fact that the *Impressae* were reprinted several times in Amsterdam. What is more, Gerard Rooseboom, the compiler of Amsterdam's city rights in 1644, used the *Impressae* as his model, and it has been asserted that the freedom principle of Antwerp was amongst those provisions copied almost *verbatim*.[153]

One thing does have to be borne in mind. Whereas the application of the fifteenth century Toulousian freedom principle held that a slave became free as soon as he set foot on the soil of the city, the provisions of Amsterdam and Antwerp are slightly different. In fact, taken on their face value, they require an action from the slave himself. Slaves coming to the city were held to be free, but if their masters disagreed and kept them as slaves against their will, the slave needed to take matters into his own hands, by having recourse to the courts. These would then declare him free.

In any case, suffice it to say that some cities in the Low Countries also had their own municipal freedom traditions. This brings us to two questions which we still ought to consider. First, how did the municipal tradition become a national principle

---

of Amsterdam, made a compilation of the municipal laws of Amsterdam in 1644 (I have used the second edition of 1656).

150 Jacobs (2000), pp. 61–62.

151 The translation is my own. The Dutch version reads that "*Binnen den stadt ende vryheyt van Antwerpen syn alle menschen vry ende gheen slaven. Item alle slaven binnen de stadt oft vryheyt ghecomen wesende, syn vry ende buyten de macht van heurlieder Meesters oft Vrouwen: ende soo verre men die wilde als slaven houden en de teghens heuren danck doen dienen moghen proclamaeren ad libertatem patriae, ende heurlieder Meesters oft Vrouwen voor de Weth doen daghen ende hen aldaar rechtelyk vry doen verclaeren*". *Rechten, ende costumen van Antwerpen* (I have used the 1582 edition), Art. XXXVI.

152 Rooseboom (1656), Caput XXXIX.

153 Bosch (1951), pp. 143–146.

(and in which of the sources of law could it be found), and how did these traditions fare when faced with genuine slaves?

3.4.3 The Low Countries: The Development of a National Freedom Tradition: Theoretically Created, Practically Ignored

3.4.3.1 The Case of the Slave Simon

Whilst the road for the introduction of a nationwide freedom principle was paved by the decline and virtual disappearance of unfreedom in the Low Countries, as well as municipal town charters, it is my contention that it was a 1532 case that triggered the idea that slaves became free upon their arrival in the Low Countries. The ties between the remaining French possessions in the Low Countries (e.g. Flanders, Artois, etc.) had been cut through by the 1526 Treaty of Madrid, meaning that French precedents were, strictly speaking, of no legal relevance to the establishment of the freedom principle in this region.

In 1532, the governor (*landvoogd*) of the XVII Provinces, Mary of Austria, asked the Great Council of Malines (*Grand Conseil de Malines*) for advice regarding a request that was received by the central authorities. This court was the "supreme court" of the Low Countries. It had been created in the fifteenth century to bring about a certain degree of centralisation in the areas under the control of first the Burgundian dukes and then the Habsburg monarchs.[154] What did Mary ask for exactly?

The Portuguese ambassador in Antwerp, where Portugal had strong commercial interests, apparently owned a slave named Simon. The slave had accompanied his master when travelling to the German city of Mainz but suddenly escaped and remained at large somewhere in the XVII Provinces. A representative of the Portuguese embassy sent a letter to the Emperor (Charles V), and asked him to make *lettres patentes* which would order all his officers in the Low Countries to capture the slave as soon as they would see him, and deliver him back to the embassy. The Portuguese representative legitimised his request by referring to Spanish customs, noting that the slave belonged to the ambassador, as he had bought him at the time.[155]

[154]Its authority as supreme court, with the possibility to receive appeals from the highest court of the particular counties and duchies of the XVII Provinces was partially eroded, as the Northern provinces (except Holland and Zeeland) largely ignored it and the Councils of Brabant (which included Antwerp) and Hainaut remained sovereign Coppens et al. (1994), pp. 448–461, Fruin and Colenbrander (1922), pp. 140–143. When all provinces of the Low Countries had come into the hands of Charles V, this region was often referred to as the XVII Provinces.

[155]The case was first brought to my attention by Ernest Nys' work, although he does make a small mistake by asserting that the case took place in 1531, Nys (1890), pp. 65–66.There are three relevant "parts" in this case. First, there is the request of the Portuguese representative. Second, there is Mary of Austria's letter of 6 March 1532 to the Great Council of Malines, asking for their advice. Finally, there is the answer of the Great Council of Malines, dated 7 March 1532. The *Recueil des*

The request was picked up by Mary of Austria. The governess, probably surprised by such a request, decided to ask for advice on this matter to the Great Council of Malines, instead of immediately complying with the demand. The reason she declined to instantly help the Portuguese ambassador does not seem to be related to any tensions between Portugal and the Habsburgs.[156] If we read Mary's request to the Great Council of Malines, dated 6 March 1532, we see that she was probably hesitating for domestic socio-political reasons. Mary indicated that this matter seemed to be of importance for the personal freedoms that had always been upheld in the XVII Provinces, which is why she wanted the advice of the Great Council of Malines.[157]

She already received an answer from the Council one day later. It gave a very short advice in which it recommended that Mary deny the request of the Portuguese representative. The councillors held that the nature and liberties of the XVII Provinces had to be taken into account. In this region, slavery was unknown, and therefore, the request should be denied.[158] Unfortunately, we do not know how the Great Council of Malines exactly came to this decision. Of course, unfreedom must have mostly seemed like a thing of the past for the Council. Slavery had long since been gone from the XVII Provinces, and at most, an occasional serf could still be found. Maybe they had taken the customs of Antwerp into account. Although these customs did not provide for it explicitly, one could well deduce from Art. 36 I–II that the Antwerp authorities ought not to help masters to enforce their rights against slaves. Or maybe the council did not want to make a precedent that would seem to recognise slavery in the XVII Provinces.

One does have to bear in mind that this advice was no blanket enunciation of the freedom principle. The Great Council of Malines did not say that a slave became free as soon as he touched the soil of the XVII Provinces. The advice only implied two things, namely (1) that slavery was not recognised by the domestic laws of the XVII Provinces and (2) that the authorities of the Habsburg Netherlands ought not to render assistance to a slave-owner who has lost his slave in these countries and tried to reclaim him. But the decision quickly got a life of its own, as it was picked up and slowly transformed by scholars.[159]

---

ordonnances des Pays-Bas autrichiens contains a reprint of the first part of the case (see Gachard and Verhaegen (1877), pp. 504–506). All the materials related to the case can be found in the State Archives of Belgium. *Grand Conseil de Justice des Pays-Bas à Malines, T. III, 376–379.* Many thanks to the staff of the State Archives of Belgium for helping me with transcribing the relevant parts of this case. An abbreviated report can be found in Gaillard (1900), p. 41.

[156] I have not found any indication of tensions between the Portuguese and the Habsburg authorities in 1532 in the following works: Pirenne (1908), Disney (2009).

[157] The relevant part reads that "Et pour ce que la matière semble être de poids et de consequence pour la liberté qui les toujours entretenu des pays de par deça". *Grand Conseil de Justice des Pays-Bas à Malines, T. III, 376–379.*

[158] The relevant part reads that "Eu regard à la nature et liberté des pays de par-deça, ou l'on ne use de servile condition, quant à la personne". Ibid.

[159] Seymour Drescher asserts that the Southern Netherlands only aligned themselves with the freedom principle of their neighbours in the early eighteenth century. Drescher quoted an eighteenth century source which mentioned this advice of the Great Council of Malines, but apparently did not

3.4.3.2 Developing the Tradition in Scholarly Writing

The decision of the Great Council of Malines was one thing. It being known by people was another thing as there were no collections made of the case law of the Great Council of Malines until Paulus Christinaeus (1553–1631) published one in 1626.[160]

On the basis of the references that were made by Simon Groenewegen van der Made (1613–1652), a Dutch jurist who cited many authorities on the question of what happened to slaves arriving in the Low Countries, I have tried to reconstruct the spread of the case, and its transformation into a clear affirmation of the freedom principle.

The decision of the Great Council of Malines seems to have spread quickly. The first reference I found to it was by Nicolas Clenardus (1495–1542), a Flemish grammarian with an ardent interest in the Islamic world, and who lived for a while in Fez. In 1541, he wrote a letter to the abbot of Tongerlo, in the Duchy of Brabant. Clenardus was well acquainted with slavery (a slave had learned him Arabic), and he decried that he had heard about a decision of the Great Council of Malines, which decided that slaves became free upon touching the soil of these territories.[161] Clearly, this was a very broad interpretation of the actual content of the Council's advice.

Possibly interested by Clenardus' reference, the next person to mention the freedom principle was Johannes Molanus (1533–1585). A theologian studying and living in Leuven, Molanus wrote a book on canon law (*De Canonicis. Libri Tres*) in 1572. In this book, a separate chapter was devoted to the question of what happened when slaves came to the Low Countries ("Quando inter Belgas servi & libertine esse desierint"). As part of this chapter, Molanus referred to the case that had come before the Great Council of Malines, noting some details of the case and its exact date. On the basis of that case, he also came to the conclusion that in those (European, one can assume) regions belonging to the Spanish Emperor but outside the Iberian Peninsula, it was impossible to have slaves. And if these slaves came here, they immediately became free, even against the will of their masters ("Caeteris illis regionibus Caesaris extra Hispaniam, non posse haberi servos, sed statim eos liberos fieri, invito Domino").[162] Again, whether the Great Council of Malines intended its decision to be interpreted this broadly is doubtful. But at least this is what both Clenardus and Molanus made of it.

say that it had already occurred in 1532. Quite to the opposite of Drescher's assertion, the Southern Netherlands seem to be the first area in which a sovereign court decided that slavery was not recognized by the domestic laws of its territory, even sooner than in England or in France Drescher (2009), p. 23.

160 Gilissen (1981), p. 389.

161 Clenardus (1566), p. 81–90. I wish to thank Prof. Dr. Dirk Heirbaut for his help in translating some parts of the Latin texts made reference to in this chapter.

162 Molanus (1587), Liber III, Cap. XXXIV. I have not been able to consult the 1572 edition which was printed in Leuven. Molanus referred to Clenardus, so he might have picked up the idea from him.

This reference was then picked up by Petrus Gudelinus (1550–1619), a jurist from Leuven who wrote *De iure novissimo* (posthumously published in 1620). In this book, he tried to compare the private law of the Low Countries with Roman law.[163] He also asked what happened to slaves who came from the Iberian Peninsula to his region. After noting that they became immediately free upon arrival in France (referring to Charondas, the writer who mentioned the 1538 case of the Greek slave), he duly followed what Molanus said. On the basis of the precedent that the Great Council had set, he also believed slaves to become free upon arrival in the Low Countries.[164]

From that moment onwards, a plethora of scholars started to refer to this freedom principle as a fundamental maxim of the law in the XVII Provinces. It has to be borne in mind that the decisions of the Great Council of Malines did not have precedential value, nor was the court recognised as being sovereign in several of the XVII Provinces. Scholars did not seem to bother too much about this, and various variants of the idea of freedom spread in sixteenth and seventeenth century works both in the Spanish Netherlands and the United Provinces.[165]

In the Spanish Netherlands, we find the same expression of the freedom principle mentioned in for example Franciscus Zypaeus' (1580–1650) *Notitia iuris Belgici*, Paulus Christinaeus' *Practicarum questionum rerumque in supremis Belgarum curiis actarum et observatarum decisiones,* and Jean-Antoine Knobbaert's (d. 1677) *Ius civile Gandensium.*[166] The web of cross-referencing increased over time. Where Zypaeus and Christinaeus stuck close to referencing the original case of the Great Council of Malines, Knobbaert more generally claimed that slaves coming to Flanders immediately became free. After noticing the "perfect freedom" which the citizens of his own city of Ghent enjoyed, he mentioned how "Quod plus est, si Servus aliunde adductus, Flandricum solum attigerit: hoc ipso liber est". To assert his claim, he referred to scholars from various countries.[167] Next to these writers, Ernest Nys also mentioned Libert-François Cristyn (1639–1717) and Antoine Perez (1584–1672) as scholars who made reference to the freedom principle.[168]

In the United Provinces, we find various writers giving credence to the idea of the freedom principle as well. For example, we find similar pronouncements in Simon Groenewegen van der Made's (1613–1652) *Tractatus de legibus abrogatis*

---

[163]Gilissen (1981), p. 359.

[164]Gudelinus (1620), Liber I, Cap. IV. Although Clenardus and Molanus did not refer to French precedents, Gudelinus and many others did. The references to such writers as Bodin and Charondas might also have inspired enunciations in favour of immediate freedom for slaves coming to this region, as opposed to the requirement of having to petition the authorities.

[165]During the Eighty Years War, the XVII Provinces were torn apart, giving rise to the United Provinces in the North and the Spanish Netherlands in the South.

[166]Zypaeus (1635), Liber VI, De Servis, Christinaeus (1626), Vol. 4, Decis LXXX.

[167]Knobbaert (1677), Art. X, Observatio Quinta. Knobbaert referred to Gudelinus, Christinaeus, Hugo Grotius, Bodin and the customs of Antwerp.

[168]Nys (1890), p. 69.

in Hollandia and Arnold Vinnius' (1588–1657) *Institutionem imperialium commentarius in quatuor libros.*[169] Interestingly, Groenewegen van der Made (and in his wake Vinnius) made reference to the customs of Antwerp. Possibly due to that factor, Groenewegen van der Made came to a slightly different pronouncement of the Dutch freedom principle, as he held that:

> And its name at this time hath grown out of use among us. So much so indeed that slaves who are brought from hither from elsewhere, so soon as they shall have entered the limits of our government, even against the will of their masters, can appeal to the judiciary [ad libertatem proclamare possint], in behalf of their freedom.[170]

That is not to say that we do not find blanket enunciations of the freedom principle, which did not require recourse to the courts, in the United Provinces. For example, in Simon van Leeuwen's (1626–1682) *Het Rooms-Hollandsch Recht*, we find another scholar arguing in favour of instant freedom for slaves coming to the territory of the Republic ("de Slaaven ende Lijf-eygnen, die van andre Wijken hier gebragt warden, so haast als sy de Grensen van onze Landen genaakten, metter data, in weer-wil van hare Heeren ende Meesters, voor vrye lyden verklaart werden").[171] The freedom principle was thus widespread in scholarly writing in the seventeenth century, both in the United Provinces and the Spanish Netherlands.[172]

3.4.4 Ignoring the Precedent: Antwerp and Middelburg

The best way to test whether these precedents were effectively lived up to is to look to those areas where slaves were most likely to appear.

---

[169]Groenewegen van der Made (1649), Liber I, Tit. VIII, Vinnius (1659), Liber I, Tit. III. On the life of Groenewegen van der Made and Vinnius, see Gerbenzon and Algra (1972), pp. 134–142. To prove how widespread the idea of the freedom principle had become in the Low Countries at this point, one can simply point at the references that are used by Groenewegen van der Made. He mentioned the Customs of Antwerp and the works of Grotius, Gudelinus, Perez, Zypaeus, Christinaeus, Jean Papon, Charondas, Bernard Automne, Denique, and Boer.

[170]This English translation can be found in Cobb (1858), pp. 371–372.

[171]van Leeuwen (1664), Boek I, Deel V.

[172]The reader might ask himself why I am not mentioning the greatest Dutch lawyer of the seventeenth century, Hugo Grotius. The reason is that I believe that he did not really pronounce himself on this issue in the *Inleidinge tot de Hollandsche rechts-geleerdheid*. What Grotius did mention was that he believed that, although some marks of unfreedom were left in Holland (referring to servile dues), all people in Holland were free. Likewise, he mentioned how it was impossible for someone to completely relinquish his own liberty ("*maer niemandt en ma by ons door handeling hem zelve sijns vrijheids in 't gheheel weerloos maecken*"). To me, this sounds as an acknowledgement that the people of Holland could no longer become slaves. However, that is not the same as claiming that other people arriving in Holland (which is a conflicts of law issue, not an issue of domestic law) could not remain slaves Grotius (1952), I. 4 (2), II. 1 (47). I have made use of the 1952 translation of *Inleidinge tot de Hollandsche rechts-geleerdheid* by Folke Dovring (the work was originally published in 1631).

For once, we know that the first sizeable "black presence" in the Low Countries was in Antwerp. This can be connected to the presence of Iberian merchants, coming from countries where slavery was legal. In Spain and Portugal, amidst rising anti-Jewish sentiment, decrees of expulsion in 1492 and 1497 had ordered the Jews to either convert, or to leave the kingdom. We know that many of those Jews, both the ones who kept their religion and the *christianos nuevos,* left their homeland, some of them coming to the Low Countries. They sometimes travelled together with their slaves.[173] In the North, they could primarily be found in Amsterdam (to which we will return later), but in the South, they came to Antwerp, as an outgrowth of the city's place in the Portuguese trading empire. Unfortunately, we do not know much about the presence of slaves in Antwerp. Some twentieth century Belgian scholars claimed that Antwerp had the second-largest black presence in Europa, right after Lisbon. Others have tried to refute this and believe their presence to have been minimal.[174] No one seems to have conducted a thorough analysis of the Antwerp municipal archives to measure the presence of slaves in Antwerp, and this is a fruitful area for further research.

The little evidence we do have from the municipal records indicates two things. A link between baptism and slavery was made here as well, and the Antwerp authorities did not consider a slave to be free upon touching the soil of their city (to know whether they effectively freed slaves who petitioned them, we lack data).[175]

In a 1516 municipal order, the city of Antwerp promised to give a reward to those persons who would bring back two unbaptised Moors to their masters ("*twee Mooren nog niet kerstende wesende*"). The slaves belonged to a Portuguese merchant and had disappeared.[176] Likewise, in 1563, a Moorish slave petitioned the Antwerp authorities to recognise his freedom. Whilst his master claimed that he had fled, the Moor claimed that he was freed by his master before. Next to that, he held that he was born a Christian and considered this to be a relevant element in favour of his freedom.[177] Other evidence confirms that slavery existed in the city. For example, historians have found two notarial deeds of manumission in 1544 and 1556.[178] Likewise, in 1540, we find proof of the sale of a slave in the city.[179] Clearly, municipal authorities and

[173]Schorsch (2004), pp. 50–53.

[174]The few articles on this issue in Belgian historiography are all nearly a century old. For the discussion concerning the amount of slaves, compare Denucé and Goemaere (who claim there were many slaves) with Saunders (who claims their presence was negligible) Denucé et al. (1937), pp. 27–36, de Saunders (1982), p. 188.

[175]Anyhow, such a case would have never made it to the Great Council of Malines, given that the Council of Brabant (*Raad van Brabant*) remained sovereign in the Duchy of Brabant. The first collections of decisions of the Council of Brabant were only made in the seventeenth century, so we will probably not find proof of any cases there either, as the black presence in Antwerp faded away after the Spanish siege of 1584–1585. Municipal court records and *Requestboeken* might hopefully shed some light on this issue in the future.

[176]Goris (1923), pp. 541–544.

[177]Ibid.

[178]Goemaere (1963), p. 30, Goris (1923), p. 544.

[179]Goris (1923), p. 544.

notaries were unconcerned with the pronouncement of the Great Council of Malines, or the nascent freedom tradition.

In the North, we find one curious case before the seventeenth century. In 1596, a ship with 130 Moors aboard arrived in the port of Middelburg.[180] The ship was captured from the Portuguese and apparently, captain Melchior van den Kerckhoven wanted to sell the slaves in Middelburg. This was disallowed by the burgomaster of the city and the States of Zeeland. They decided that the slaves, who were all baptised Christian slaves, had to be set at liberty ("gestelt in heure vrye liberteyt").[181] If the case had ended here, this would have been a clear confirmation of the Dutch freedom principle, and some scholars do only mention this part of the case.[182]

However, the merchant Pieter van der Haegen, who was the owner of the captured ship, took the case to the States General. There, he filed a request to be allowed to bring the Portuguese crew of the ship to Portugal, and the Moors to the West Indies. At first, the States General refused, but the merchant filed a new request. This time, things ended badly for the slaves. The States General decided that the merchant could do with the slaves as he wished ("soe hy 't verstaet"), and that they were not planning to interfere in this matter any further.[183] If this decision is taken into account, the States General clearly did not consider the soil of its provinces to have given freedom to slaves (even when baptised) upon arrival.

Given the fact that many of the Middelburg protagonists were to become involved in the Dutch slave trade later on, Hondius has concluded that the episode shows that the Dutch authorities wanted to send a multi-layered message. To the individual ship owner and the wider community of merchants and captains, the idea was that whereas the slave trade itself was not deemed to be problematic, slaves ought not to be sold in the metropolis. At the same time, the general population was presented with a more positive message, as the Zeeland authorities tried to keep the myth that there was no slavery in Zeeland, and that Christians could not be treated as slaves.[184]

[180]The case has been retold almost endlessly in historiography. I have taken most of the facts and the interpretation of the case from Dienke Hondius' recent assessment of it Hondius (2009).

[181]Ibid., pp. 33–34. The decisions of the States of Zeeland of 15 November 1596 are quoted *verbatim* by Hondius.

[182]Blakely (1993), p. 4, Drescher (2009), p. 23. Drescher notes how Pieter Emmer believed that the slaves were probably taken to a slave market in Antwerp. I have found no proof of the existence of such a market.

[183]*Resolutiën der Staten Generaal, deel 9, 1596/1597*, 333–334.

[184]Hondius (2009), p. 39.

3.4.5 Conclusion: The Legal Order of the XVII Provinces at the Dawn of Black Slavery: Limited Precedent, Extended Freedom Principle

Between 1500 and 1650, the Low Countries had encounters with slavery at several points in time, and scholars developed a freedom principle in these countries.

To the people of the Low Countries, unfreedom must have seemed something from the distant past, as the great majority of the population was free in the sixteenth and seventeenth century. That being said, there was no general emancipation in the Low Countries, and an ever-declining number of serfs could still be found there.

One of the reasons for the decline of serfdom in the Low Countries can be found in the vigorousness of its cities. They were in a position of power to assert the personal freedom of their citizens, and the idea of *Stadtluft macht frei* was to be found in some city charters as well. Antwerp and Amsterdam, those cities that became most involved with the colonial ventures had freedom provisions in their city laws. However, the enunciation was not a blanket conferral of the freedom principle, as the slave had to be aware of the provision in the first place, and then had to petition the authorities to gain his freedom.

A national freedom principle tradition was created in the Low Countries thanks to an accidental case which made it to the Great Council of Malines. When the Portuguese ambassador tried to get help in reclaiming his slave Simon, the Council rejected this request by holding that slavery did not exist in the Low Countries. Soon afterwards, this case was moulded by scholars to construct a tradition of the freedom principle. An ever-increasing web of cross-references to both domestic and foreign writers served as a means to solidify the idea of the freedom principle in legal thinking. The exact preconditions of the freedom principle could differ and were influenced by the customary provisions of cities such as Antwerp.

In practice, the freedom principle had a mixed record in the sixteenth century. Early cases from the United Provinces and Antwerp indicated that slavery could well be allowed to exist here, as slaves who came to these areas did not receive their freedom automatically and were sometimes sold and manumitted.[185]

[185]For the sake of completeness, I might add that Grotius also talked about galley service (without using the term slavery). He noted that whereas no-one in the Dutch Republic could abrogate his freedom, one could lose his liberty because of a crime, if he was sentenced to the galleys or a house of correction ("*Iemand kan oock de selve* [de vrijheid] *door misdaed verbeuren, als die tot de roei-schepen ofte in tucht-huizen warden verbannen*"). I have not found secondary literature on the use of galley convicts by the Dutch (which is also explained by the fact that they only had one galley around 1600). Even if convicts were used in the galleys, it does not seem likely that the Dutch considered this to be an exception to their freedom principle or that it ever caused them to write much about it Grotius (1952), II. 1 (47).

References

Adair ER (1920) English galleys in the sixteenth century. Engl Hist Rev 35:497–512

Alsford S (2011) Urban safe havens for the unfree in medieval England: a reconsideration. Slavery Abol 32:363–375

Andreae SF (1906) Het Oud-Nederlandsch burgerlijk recht, 1ste bundel. Bohn, Haarlem

Arabeyre P (2007) Dictionnaire historique des juristes français (XIIe–XXe siècle). Presses Universitaires de France, Paris

Baker JH (2002) An introduction to English legal history. Butterworth, London

Baker JH (1995) Personal liberty under the common law of England, 1200–1600. In: The Origins of Modern Freedom in the West. Stanford University Press, Stanford, p 384

Barbey J (2010) Domaine royal. In: Bély L (ed) Dictionnaire de l'Ancien Régime: royaume de France XVIe–XVIIIe siècle, 3rd edn. Presses universitaires de France, Paris, pp 424–426

Blakely A (1993) Blacks in the dutch world: the evolution of racial imagery in a modern society. Indiana University Press, Bloomington

Bloch M (1920) Rois et Serfs. Un chapitre d'histoire capétienne, Champion, Paris

Bodin J (1576) Les six Livres de la République. English edition: Bodin J (1606) The six books of a common-weale (transl. Knolles R). Adam Islip, London

Bosch JW (1951) Remarques sur quelques influences, exercées en matière de droit, par les provinces méridionales sur les provinces septentrionales des Pays-Bas jusqu'en 1795. Leg Hist Rev 19:133–157

Boulle P, Peabody S (2014) Le droit des noirs en France au temps de l'esclavage: textes choisis et commentés. L'Harmattan, Paris

Brion Davis D (1966) The problem of slavery in western culture. Cornell University Press, Ithaca

Brunsman DA (2013) The evil necessity: British naval impressment in the eighteenth-century atlantic world. University of Virginia Press, Charlottesville

Bush JA (1996) The first slave (and why he matters). Cardozo Law Rev 18:599–629

Bush JA (1993) Free to enslave: the foundations of colonial American slave law. Yale J Law Humanit 5:417–470

Chaline O (2010) Parlements. In: Bély L (ed) Dictionnaire de l'Ancien Régime: royaume de France XVIe–XVIIIe siècle, 3rd edn. Presses universitaires de France, Paris, pp 960–965

Cheyney EP (1913) The court of star chamber. Am Hist Rev 18:727–750

Christinaeus P (1626) Practicarum quaestionum rerumque in supremis Belgarum curiis actarum et observatarum decisiones. Hieronimy Verdussi, Antwerpen

Clenardus N (1566) Epistolarum libri duo. Christophori Planti, Antwerpen

Cobb TRR (1858) An inquiry into the law of negro slavery in the united states of America. T. & J. W. Johnson & Co—W. T, Williams, Philadelphia

Cobbett W (1805) Cobbett's complete collection of state trials, vol 3, pp 1627–1640. R. Ragshaw, London

Coke E (1628) Coke upon littleton. English edition: Coke E (1830) A readable edition of coke upon littleton (transl. Coventry T). Saunders and Benning, London

Cook J (1646) The vindication of the professors and profession of the law. For Matthew Walbancke, and are to be sold at his shop at Graies Inne gate, London

Coppens H, Aerts E, Baelde M (1994) De centrale overheidsinstellingen van de Habsburgse Nederlanden 1482–1795. I. Algemeen rijksarchief, Brussel

Davies CSL (1966) Slavery and protector somerset; the vagrancy act of 1547. Econ Hist Rev New Ser 19:533–549

de Ghewiet G (1736) Institutions du droit Belgique. Charles-Maurice Cramé, Lille

de Pitaval G (1750) *Causes célèbres et intéressantes, avec les jugemens qui les ont décidées, Tome quatorzième*. Jean Neaulme, The Hague

Denucé J, Blaeu WJ, Verbist P (1937) Afrika in de XVIde eeuw en de handel van Antwerpen. De Sikkel, Antwerpen

Disney AR (2009) A history of Portugal and the Portuguese empire: from beginnings to 1807, vol I. Cambridge University Press, Cambridge: Portugal
Drescher S (2009) Abolition: a history of slavery and antislavery. Cambridge University Press, Cambridge
Fruin R, Colenbrander HT (1922) Geschiedenis der staatsinstellingen in Nederland tot den val der Republiek. Nijhoff,'s-Gravenhage
Gaillard A (1900) Inventaire des mémoriaux du Grand Conseil de Malines. XIVe, XVe et XVIe siècles. P. Weissenbruch, Brussel, Tome I
Gallet J (2010) Servitude. In: Bély L (ed) Dictionnaire de l'Ancien Régime: royaume de France XVIe–XVIIIe siècle, 3rd edn. Presses universitaires de France, Paris, pp 1160–1163
Gerbenzon P, Algra NE (1972) Voortgangh des rechtes: de ontwikkeling van het Nederlandse recht tegen de achtergrond van de Westeuropese cultuur. Tjeenk Willink, Groningen
Gilissen J (1981) Historische inleiding tot het recht. Kluwer Rechtswetenschappen, Antwerpen
Godding P (1991) Le droit privé dans les Pays-Bas méridionaux du 12e au 18e siècle. Palais des Académies, Brussel
Goemaere P (1963) Anvers et ses esclaves noirs. Rev générale belge 99:27–36
Goris JA (1923) Uit de Geschiedenis der vorming van het Antwerpsch stadsrecht: Slavernij te Antwerpen in de XVIde eeuw. Bijdr Geschied 15:541–544
Groenewegen van der Made S (1649) Tractatus de legibus abrogatis et inusitatis in Hollandia vicinisque regionibus. Franciscum Moyardum, Davidem Lopez de Haro, Leiden
Grotius H (1631) Inleidinge tot de Hollandsche rechts-geleerdheid. Dutch edition: Grotius H (1952) Inleidinge tot de Hollandsche rechts-geleerdheid (transl. Dovring F). Universitaire Pers Leiden, Leiden
Grotius H (1646) De Jure Belli ac Pacis. English edition: Grotius H (1925) On the law of war and peace three books (trans: Kelsey FW) Carnegie Institution of Washington, Washington DC
Guasco M (2014) Slaves and englishmen: human bondage in the early modern atlantic world [the early modern Americas]. University of Pennsylvania Press, Philadelphia
Gudelinus P (1620) Commentariorum de iure novissimo libri sex. Hieronymi Verdussi, Antwerpen.
Heirbaut D (2013) Privaatrechtsgeschiedenis van de Romeinen tot heden. Academia Press, Gent
Hale M (1713) The history and analysis of the common law of England. Nutt J, Stafford
Hargrave F (1772) An argument in the case of James Sommersett, A Negro. W. Otridge, London
Harrison W (1588) Description of Elisabethan England. English edition: Harrison W (1876) (transl. Scott W). Walter Scott, London
Hilton RH (1969) The decline of serfdom in medieval England [studies in economic history]. Macmillan, London
Holdsworth WS (1922) A history of english law, vol III. Methuen & Co., Ltd., London
Hondius D (2009) Blacks in early modern Europe: new research from the Netherlands. In: Clark Hine D, Keaton TD, Small S (eds) Black Europe and the African diaspora. Blackness in Europe. University of Illinois Press, Champaign, pp 29–47
Hyams PR (1980) King, lords, and peasants in medieval England: the common law of villeinage in the twelfth and thirteenth centuries. Clarendon Press, Oxford
Israel J (1995) The dutch republic: its rise, greatness, and fall 1477–1806. Oxford University Press, Oxford
Jacobs BCM (2000) Rechtsculturen in Brabant en Brabantse rechtscultuur. zeventiende eeuw 16:55–64
Kesselring K (2018) Slavery and Cartwright's Case before Somerset. Leg Hist Misc
Knobbaert J (1677) Jus civile Gandensium. Michael Knobbaert, Antwerpen
le Caron L (1637) Pandectes ou digestes du droit français. Estienne Richer, Paris
Lyall A (2017) Granville Sharp's Cases on Slavery. Hart Publishing, Oxford
Littleton (1460) New Tenures. English edition: Littleton (1903) (transl. Wambaugh E). John Byrne & Co., Washington DC
Loisel A (1607) Institutes coustumiéres. Abel l'Angelier, Paris

MacCulloch D (1988) Bondmen under the Tudors. In: Cross C, Loades D, Scarisbrick JJ (eds) Law and government under the Tudors. Cambridge University Press, Cambridge, pp 91–110
Mitteis H (1952) Über den Rechtsgrund des Satzes "Stadtluft macht frei". In: Festschrift Edmund E. Stengel zum 70. Geburtstag am 24. Dezember 1949 dargebracht von Freunden, Fachgenossen und Schülern. Böhlau, Münster
Molanus J (1587) De canonicis. Libri tres. Arnold Mylius, Cologne
Moreau de Saint-Méry M (1784) Loix et constitutions des colonies Françoises de l'Amérique sous le vent. Quillau, Paris
Nicholas D (1997) The growth of the medieval city: from late antiquity to the early fourteenth century. Routledge, London
Nicholas D (1992) Medieval flanders. Longman, London
Nys E (1890) L'esclavage noir devant les jurisconsultes et les cours de justice (première partie). Rev droit Int législation comparée 22:57–69
Olivier-Martin F (2010) Histoire du droit français - Des origines à la Révolution. CNRS, Paris
Ourliac P, Gazzaniga J-L (1985) Histoire du droit privé français - de l'An mil au code civil. Albin Michel, Paris
Peabody S (2011) An alternative genealogy of the origins of French free soil: medieval Toulouse. Slavery Abol 32:341–362
Peabody S (1996) There are no slaves in France: the political culture of race and slavery in the ancien régime. Oxford University Press, New York
Peabody S, Grinberg K (2011) Free soil: the generation and circulation of an Atlantic legal principle. Slavery Abol 32:331–339
Pirenne H (1908) Geschiedenis van België. Deel 3. Van den dood van Karel den Stoute tot de komst van den hertog van Alva in de Nederlanden. Volksdrukkerij, Gent
Pound J (1971) Poverty and vagrancy in Tudor England [seminar studies in history], 2nd edn. Longman, Harlow
Prevost X (2015) Jacques Cujas (1522–1590). Jurisconsulte humaniste [Travaux d'Humanisme et Renaissance]. Librairie Droz SA, Genève
Rigaudière A (2010) Histoire du droit et des institutions dans la France médiévale et moderne, 4th edn. Economica, Paris
Rogers N (2007) The press gang: naval impressment and its opponents in Georgian Britain. Bloomsbury Academic, London
Rooseboom G (1656) Recueil van verscheyde keuren en costumen midtsgaders maniere van procederen binnen de stadt Amsterdam. Jan Hendricks, Amsterdam
Rushforth B (2012) Bonds of alliance: indigenous and Atlantic slaveries in New France. University of North Carolina Press, Chapel Hill
Rushwordt J (1721) Historical collections of private passages of state, vol. 2. Browne D, London
de Saunders AC (1982) A social history of black slaves and freedmen in Portugal, 1441–1555. Cambridge University Press, Cambridge
Savine A (1903) Bondmen under the Tudors. Trans R Hist Soc 17:235–289
Schorsch J (2004) Jews and blacks in the early modern world. Cambridge University Press, Cambridge
Slack P (1995) The English poor law, 1531–1782 [new studies in economic and social history]. Cambridge University Press, Cambridge
Smith T (1583) De Republica Anglorum. Henrie Midleton, London
Steinfeld RJ (1991) The invention of free labor: the employment relation in english and American law and culture, 1350–1870 [studies in legal history]. University of North Carolina Press, Chapel Hill
Strahm H (1953) Stadtluft macht frei. In: Das Problem der Freiheit in der deutschen und schweizerischen Geschichte. Jan Thorbecke Verlag, Ostfildern
Tallon A (2010) L'Europe au XVIe siècle. Presses Universitaires de France, Paris, États et relations internationales

Tugendhat M (2017) Slavery and comparative law in eighteenth century England, University of Leicester Research Paper No. 17–08
Van Bavel B (2010) Manors and markets: economy and society in the low countries, 500–1600. Oxford University Press, Oxford
Van Caenegem R (1995) Law and century Flanders. In: Cultures of Power. Lordship, Status and Process in Twelfth-Century Europe. University of Pennsylvania Press, Philadelphia
Van Caenegem RC (1990) Galbert of Bruges on serfdom, prosecution of crime and constitutionalism. In: Lyon BD, Bachrach BS, Nicholas D (eds) Law, custom, and the social fabric in medieval Europe: essays in honor of Bryce Lyon. Western Michigan University, Kalamazoo, pp 89–112
van Schevichaven HDJ (1924) Slavernij en dienstbaarheid, hoofdzakelijk in de vroege middeleeuwen [Werken uitgegeven door Gelre, Vereeniging tot beoefening van Geldersche geschiedenis, oudheidkunde en recht]. Gouda Quint, Arnhem
van Leeuwen S (1664) Het Rooms-Hollands-Regt. Hackens, Leiden
Verlinden C (1955) L'esclavage dans l'Europe médiévale, Tome premier: péninsule Iberique - France. De Tempel, Brugge
Verhaegen P, Gachard LP (1877). Recueil des ordonnances des Pays-Bas autrichiens. 3ième série, IV. Goemaere, Bruxelles
Verriest L (1946) Institutions médiévales: introduction au corpus des records de coutumes et des lois de chefs-lieux de l'ancien comté de Hainaut. Union des imprimeurs, Mons
Verriest L (1910) Le servage dans le Comté de Hainaut. Les sainteurs. Le meilleur catel, Hayez, Bruxelles
Vinnius A (1659) Institutionum imperialium commentarius in quatuor libros. Ludovicum & Danielem Elzevirios, Amsterdam
Weiss G (2011) Captives and corsairs—France and slavery in the early modern meditteranean. Stanford University Press, Stanford
Zypaeus F (1635) Notitia iuris Belgici. Hieronymym Verdussium, Antwerpen

Chapter 4
England Ca. 1650–1800: Neither Emancipated nor Fully Enslaved

4.1 Introduction

After having looked at the origins of this freedom principle, we now move to the next century and a half. In contrast with the period before, one thing changed. England, France and the United Provinces increasingly succeeded in breaking the Iberian monopoly in the Americas, and started acquiring colonies of their own. As mentioned before, each of these countries turned to the Atlantic slave trade to fuel their colonial economy. As an outgrowth of this turn to African slave labour, at times African slaves started ending up in England, France and the Low Countries. How did the legal order of these countries react to this black presence?

4.2 England: Neither Emancipated nor Fully Enslaved

4.2.1 The Historiography of Black Slavery in England

Popular history has it that the first black settlers in England were taken there in 1555 by John Lok, who brought five Africans to Britain that were to serve as translators.[1] In their wake came the first Africans who were victims of the Atlantic slave trade, their numbers increasing due to the Elizabethan wars against Spain. It is often claimed that Queen Elizabeth I was the first to point at a "black problem" in England. She proclaimed several "Edicts of Expulsion" (two Acts of the Privy Council and one Tudor Royal Proclamation) in this period to remove the so-called *blackamoores* from

[1]There are several books on the history of black people in England, most of them written in the seventies. The best known are the works of F. O. Shyllon, James Walvin and Peter Fryer, on which I have drawn heavily to decipher the historiography of black people in England.

F. Batselé, *Liberty, Slavery and the Law in Early Modern Western Europe*, Studies in the History of Law and Justice 17, https://doi.org/10.1007/978-3-030-36855-5_4

England.[2] But whether Elizabeth deliberately tried to remove Africans or not, which is subject to debate, the venture was unsuccessful.

The African presence in England increased after the takeover of Jamaica in 1655, and more so after the *Asiento* contract was given to England at the 1713 Treaty of Utrecht.[3] It probably reached its apex in the years after 1763, as the number of absentee West Indian planters that preferred to live in England increased.[4] Most blacks came to Britain in two ways. First, it was customary for captains of slaving vessels to be allowed the transporting of a few slaves in each cargo for their personal profit, whom they would bring with them to Britain. Second, West India planters often took some of their slaves with them when they came to the metropolis. For both categories, blacks could serve as cheap labour and as a means to promote their social status in England.[5]

A great many historians have tried to measure the black presence in England in the period of the British involvement in the African slave trade. One genealogist recently made a database on Africans in Britain. She believes that there were between 10.000 and 20.000 blacks in England during this period, but pointed out that many of them were not necessarily enslaved.[6] All in all, Drescher estimates that blacks represented between 0.09 and 0.2 percent of the population of Great Britain in 1771, right before Somerset's case.[7] Although this does not seem much, black persons were concentrated in the trading ports, and one assessment even claims that they represented 2 to 3 percent of the population of London by 1771.[8]

Primarily, it is the condition of these black persons which is to our interest. Some of them, just like in the New World, were obviously personally free, and in that sense

[2]Shyllon, Walvin and Fryer believed that Queen Elizabeth I tried to expel the Africans from England because they threatened the purity of English blood, would take away the employment opportunities of English servants and were consuming food which would otherwise go to English subjects Shyllon (1974), pp. 1–2, Walvin (1973), pp. 8–10, Fryer (1984), pp. 10–12. Recent historiography has tended to view these "Edicts of Expulsion" from another perspective, believing that the two Acts of the Privy Council (dated 11 July 1596 and 18 July 1596) were some sort of "reward" that allowed a loyal subject to sell a certain number of *blackamoores* abroad. The same author contends that the royal proclamation (undated, but probably made in 1601) which wanted to expel all blacks from the kingdom was never actually promulgated and remained in draft form Weissbourd (2015). The two acts and royal proclamation are reprinted in Weissbourd's article. For another recent account which largely concurs with Weissbourd, see Kaufmann (2008).

[3]Shyllon (1974), pp. 1–2.

[4]Rabin (2011), p. 9.

[5]Ibid., 3–5.

[6]Chater (2007), pp. 66–83. To give some examples of the uncertainty: Wise mentions how contemporaries in 1772, during Somerset's case, gave a number for the slave population of England that was between 3.000 and 40.000, whilst Lord Mansfield referred to a number of 14.000–15.000 slaves. Drescher has also made a broad assessment of the number of black people in Britain, and settles on a number of 10.000 at the time of Somerset Wise (2006), p. 8, Drescher (1987), pp. 27–30.

[7]Ibid., 27–30.

[8]Wise (2006), p. 8. Given that London had a population of approximately 750.000 citizens at that time, that number does seem to be substantially too high. Likewise, Rabin's assessment that "England in the eighteenth century and London in particular was racially diverse" seems to be a bit of an overestimation Rabin (2011), p. 7.

not much different from regular Englishmen in that period. But as Lord Mansfield himself stated in Somerset's case, many black people were unfree. There is quite some evidence which suggests that there was a limited public traffic of black people in England. In particular, there are some reports on the existence of small slave markets in cities such as Liverpool, Bristol and London at times. Likewise, newspapers included advertisements to sell or recover a runaway slave every now and then.[9] But, as Van Cleve has asserted, it is a good practice to talk about "near slavery" in many of these cases, as there is little evidence to suggest that black people in England were treated in the same way as in the Atlantic colonies, areas which were economically much more dependent on slave labour. In that sense, whereas there is proof of sales, imprisonment, wageless compelled service and forcible shipment abroad of English blacks, the harshest practices of the Atlantic (e.g. dismembering or scourging a slave) were probably not practiced in England. What is more, it is unclear whether slave status was seen as heritable for black slaves in England.[10]

This immediately brings us to the thorny questions: what was the status of those black people that served as slaves in England's Atlantic colonies, when they arrived with their masters in Bristol, London or Liverpool? Did they remain slaves *de jure*? Could villeinage be used to define their status? Would the opposition to slavery in the wake of the Vagrancy Act 1547 be repeated, and slavery be deemed to be "too extreme" to gain recognition by the English legal order?

For the answer to those questions, we will have to look to Westminster and the common law and equity judges. Parliament's proceedings, however, will not help us much in our enquiry. Although there was apparently an attempt to insert a clause regulating the use of slaves in England into a master and servant bill in the House of Lords, Parliament eventually never made legislation on the issue. However, this proposal does suggest that parts of Parliament, at the least, considered slavery to be legal in England, though we cannot infer much more from these documents.[11] Thus, the recognition of slavery in England has to be traced by looking at what the common law and equity courts said of the subject, before, during and after the *cause célèbre* of Somerset v. Stewart.[12]

---

[9]I should point here in particular to the impressive "Runaway Slaves in Britain: bondage, freedom and race in the eighteenth century" project. By mid-2019, the project had been able to trace 835 advertisements concerning runaways in British newspapers dating from 1700 to 1773.

[10]Van Cleve (2006a), pp. 607–611.

[11]There was also another proposal for an Act encouraging the conversion of African slaves, which was to be applicable to slaves in England as well. Likewise, we noted how Parliament considered the African slave trade to be legal, but did not make substantive slave regulation for the Americas, leaving a void that could be filled by the local American governments. Paley addresses the various parliamentary proposals to create a legislative framework for slavery, most of them addressing the colonial situation, but also these two mentioned and aborted proposals that seemed to be applicable to slaves in England as well Paley (2010).

[12]Our focus will be on cases from central courts, as those cases can usually be found in the English Reports. There definitely were some local cases, but in general, less research has been devoted to them, and this remains a fruitful avenue for future research. See, for example George (1965), pp. 140–144.

4.2.2 *Early Encounters: A (not so) Confused State of Slavery Before Somerset?*

Before 1772, English courts had the opportunity to evaluate disputes concerning slavery in a dozen or so cases. Some preconditions have to be borne in mind. First, although some of the cases resulted in seemingly sweeping judgments, the reader always has to bear in mind that the clear distinction between the *ratio decidendi* and the *obiter dictum* of a case implies that the precedential value of some statements was severely curtailed. This is especially true for a topic such as slavery, in which the personal feelings of judges can more easily be inferred from judgments. Second, some of the cases were poorly reported and not always well known to contemporaries, as judgments were sometimes published long after they were delivered.[13] We also do not know to what extent manuscript versions of some of these decisions circulated amongst judges and barristers, a common practice in the eighteenth century.[14] Third, before Somerset, it seems that there has not been a single case in which the state of slavery itself was directly at issue. Cases that reached the royal courts were concerned with actions of trespass, trover and *indebitatus assumpsit*.[15] In other terms, we are dealing with cases of what we would now call contract law or tort law, in which

[13]Wiecek (1974), pp. 89–95. This is a very important issue. Thanks to the *Judicial cases concerning American slavery and the negro* collection, we now have a good overview of the reported cases on the issue. However, it seems that only some of them were well-known at the time, and were sometimes equally badly known by nineteenth century judges. For example, in 1876, an English commission was created to enquire what ships of the Royal Navy had to do when they were in the territorial waters of another country and faced with fugitive slaves who came aboard. As part of his advice on this matter, then Chief Justice Cockburn (1802–1880) included an overview of what he believed to have been the relevant cases related to slavery in England. For the period before Somerset, he only knew of *Smith v. Brown and Cooper*, the Yorke-Talbot opinion, *Pearne v. Lisle* and *Shanley v. Harvey*, but did not mention some of the other cases mentioned in this chapter. See *Royal Commission on Fugitive Slaves: Report of the Commissioners*, XXVIII-LVI.

[14]Oldham (2012).

[15]As noted before, trespass writs are a group of writs that were used to make a claim for civil wrongs. Originally, trespass writs could only be issued in respect of wrongs that were committed "with force and arms", the so called trespass *vi et armis*. Starting from the 1350s, the necessity of *vi et armis* was abandoned and general writs of trespass were issued, with the plaintiff being required to set out his special cause (which was basically a question about the alleged wrongdoing of the plaintiff. For example, trespass *de bonis asportatis* was used in cases of trespass to a person's goods). These actions were called trespass on the case or actions on the case. Trover is a specialised form of the action on the case which only emerged during the sixteenth century. An action of trover can be brought by the plaintiff to recover the value of personal chattels that have been wrongfully converted by another for his own use. The difference with trespass is rather technical. In trespass, the gist of the action is that there is a wrongful violation or disturbance of one's possession. In trover, the gist of the action was not the manner or the wrongfulness of the taking, but the idea that personal property belonging to the plaintiff had been taken possession of by the defendant, and that this defendant wrongfully withheld ("converted") this personal property from the plaintiff (= denial of title is the central issue, not the wrongdoing itself). In an action in trover, the property itself cannot be recovered, but only the value of what is being taken. The action of *assumpsit* can be seen as the forerunner of modern English contract law. Starting from the sixteenth century, but especially after Slade's Case in 1602, it was established that *indebitatus assumpsit* (assumpsit in

claims arose concerning an African slave, who was seen as personal property by at least one of the parties. As a result, we only get to know more about the state of slavery by looking whether these courts went behind the alleged property interest and effectively said something related to the slave, the kind of merchandise at hand.[16]

4.2.2.1 Unsound Footing: The Infidel Rationale

The earliest reported case at the Court of King's Bench was *Butts v. Penny* in 1677. The plaintiff brought an action of trover for 100 *negroes* who were in Southeast Asia and were taken by the defendant.[17] The defendant made an analogy with the law of villeinage, using it to assert that there could be no property in the person of a man sufficient to maintain trover. But the court held otherwise. As *negroes* were treated as merchandise amongst merchants, and also because they were infidels, the King's Bench said that there "might be" a property in them sufficient to maintain trover. The precedential value of the case should be doubted; a judgment was given for the plaintiff *nisi causa*.[18]

A second case, *Gelly v. Cleve*, was adjudged in 1694 at the Court of Common Pleas and came to the same conclusion as *Butts v. Penny*, namely that "Trover will lie for a Negro boy, for they are heathens".[19]

For the sake of completeness, Sir Thomas Grantham's case of 1687 in King's Bench also involved a slave. In this rather strange case, Sir Thomas Grantham, an English tobacco trader, took a "monster" with him from the East Indies, which he exposed to the sight of Englishmen for profit.[20] The case report mentions we were

---

lieu of debt) could be used as a means to recover debts arising from breach of contract Baker (2002), pp. 59–64, 341–346, 397–400.

[16]In cases related to the slave trade, we know that common law judges did not go behind the property interest at stake, as slaves were simply classified as "cargo" Bush (1998), pp. 388–389.

[17]*Butts v. Penny* (1677), 2 Levinz 201 in Catterall and Matteson (1926), p. 9. Rabin used another report (1 Freem. 452), which asserted that the court was dealing with a trover claim for 10 *negroes* (the Levinz report mentions 100 *negroes*). We also know that the *negroes* were in Southeast Asia thanks to this report (this, by the way, also serves to show that in the eighteenth century, there was a tendency to use the term *negroe* both for people from African descent as well as for people tracing their descent to the Indian sub-continent). Interestingly, this report mentions that "*although by the law with us a man cannot have an absolute property in the body of another*", a statement not to be found in Levinz Rabin (2014), p. 206. The reason why these actions, originating outside England, can be found in the reports is that personal actions could be laid in English courts even if the cause of action arose abroad Baker (2002), p. 475.

[18]*Nisi causa* means that there was no final judgment, as the case was held over at the request of the attorney general. The record for the subsequent final judgment has not been found. That being said, the case would sometimes be cited in subsequent cases Wiecek (1974), pp. 89–90.

[19]*Gelly v. Cleve* (1694), 1 Ld. Raym. 147 in Catterall and Matteson (1926), p. 10. In *Somerset's case*, Hargrave opined that this slave was also in the Americas instead of England, but we cannot know this conclusively from the report. A third early case, *Noel v. Robinson*, also allowed an action of trover for a slave, but the reasoning of the judge cannot be inferred from the report. *Noel v. Robinson*, (1682), 1 Vernon 453 in Catterall and Matteson (1926), p. 10.

[20]*Sir Thomas Grantham's Case* (1682), 3 Mod. 120 in Catterall and Matteson (1926), p. 9.

dealing with a man "who had the perfect shape of a child growing out of his breast as an excrescency, all but the head". An educated guess would say that we are dealing with a Siamese twin of which one died at birth, and that Sir Grantham decided to use this slave for the purposes of hosting a "freak show", a sort of exhibition which had become popular in England starting from the sixteenth century. The report mentions that the slave was baptised and taken away from Sir Thomas Grantham. Grantham, undeterred, brought a writ *de homine replegiando* against the person who had detained his "monster", and the Indian was eventually returned to Sir Thomas Grantham. Given we have no information on any proceedings or arguments at the King's Bench, it seems impossible to infer clear principles from this case.

At first sight, the fact that trover was allowed for slaves, seems to indicate that English common law gave some recognition to slavery arising in one of the English colonies. Otherwise, the English courts could have decided to disallow the action, based on the fact that there could not be personal property in a man according to common law. But given that in both of the cases, the slaves themselves were abroad, the question remained whether English courts would act the same if the slave had been in England. Second, the cases were also decided on a very unstable footing, as both *Butts v. Penny* and *Gelly v. Cleve* seemed to be decided on the basis that the slaves were not baptised Christians. Instead of wholeheartedly embracing chattel slavery in England, such reasoning would create legal uncertainty for colonial slaveholders, as a slave might well be baptised.[21]

4.2.2.2 Chief Justice Holt and Slavery—Emancipation or "Slavish Servants"?

In the period 1689–1710, England's most important judge was Sir John Holt (1642–1710), who presided the Court of King's Bench. During this period, three better reported cases concerning slavery were decided before the English courts.

In *Chamberline v. Harvey* (Court of King's Bench, 1696/1697), a plantation slave was brought to England, where, after some endeavours, he started working for one Robert Harvey as a servant, receiving wages. The plaintiff (one Willoughby Chamberline) alleged that the *negro* was his slave, and brought an action of trespass *de bonis asportatis* against the defendant for the loss of value and services of this slave. The report includes an overview of the arguments of counsel, with plaintiff's counsel trying to erect an English law of slavery derived from the laws of villeinage. In addition, the plaintiff's counsel also remarked that a broad judgment against slavery would disrupt the slave trade. Defendant's counsel countered this with references to slavery as contrary to the *ius naturale*, the *favor libertatis* of English law and the fact that the slave's legal status, acquired under the *lex loci* of an American plantation, should be disregarded in England. Furthermore, given that the slave was baptised, the defendant's counsel pleaded that this could serve as a manumission. Next to that,

[21] Note that the reporter of *Sir Thomas Grantham's case* found it relevant to mention that the "monster" was baptised Van Cleve (2006a), p. 615.

the defendant's counsel also explicitly repudiated the analogy between villeinage and slavery, arguing that the slave could neither be seen as a villein regardant nor as a villein in gross.[22] Holt decided to deliver a narrow judgment. The issue of baptism conferring manumission was ignored, but Holt decided that neither a general action of trespass, nor an action for trover, thus directly contravening *Butts v. Penny*, would lie for taking away the *negro*, because "a negro cannot be demanded as a chattel". Holt did offer some solace to slaveholders, by suggesting that "a special action of trespass for taking his servant, per quod servitium amisit" might be possible. In such an action, the master could not recover the value of the slave himself, or damage done to the servant, but only sue for recovery of the loss of service. In allowing this, Holt tried to equate the slave with what he called a "slavish servant". In short, the court's decision seemed to be a first (slight) blow to the rights of slaveholders but did not declare slaves emancipated.[23]

At first sight, Holt seemed to have gone further in the next case, *Smith v. Brown and Cooper* (Court of King's Bench, 1705). In this case, the plaintiff declared an *indebitatus assumpsit* for a *negro* which he had sold to the defendant in Cheap, one of the wards of the City of London. Although the jury verdict went in favour of the plaintiff, defendant asked for a motion in arrest of judgment, which was granted.[24] Holt made a sweeping statement that "as soon as negro comes into England, he becomes free. One may be a villein in England, but not a slave". At the same time, he told the plaintiff that he should have said that the sale of the slave had happened in Virginia, and not England. According to Holt, the laws of that country, being a conquered territory subject to the King, allowed for slavery ("by the laws of that country, negroes are saleable"). There are two ways to read this judgment. Either this showed that slavery did not exist at all in England, or it just showed that "pure chattel slavery" did not exist in England, which would make the case consonant with *Chamberline v. Harvey*.[25] It is also little unclear whether Holt was encouraging litigants in this case to use a pleading fiction (namely saying that the sale of a sale in England took place in Virginia) in order to allow slavery actions before English courts. Furthermore, the case did not have precedential value either, as the report mentions that the attorney-general intervened during judgment to indicate a certain technicality to the Chief Justice. After this intervention, in the words of the report, "nothing was done".[26]

---

[22] *Chamberline v. Harvey* (1696/1697), 3 Ld. Raym. 129 in Catterall and Matteson (1926), pp. 10–11. A more thorough account, including the arguments of counsel, can be found in 87 E.R. 596 Rabin (2014), pp. 208–209. There is also a second (slightly different) report for this case where the case is referred to as *Chamberlain v. Harvey*, see Lyall (2017), p. 31.

[23] Van Cleve (2006a), pp. 616–617.

[24] *Smith v. Brown and Cooper* (1705), 2 Salkeld 666. Motion in arrest of judgment was a common law procedure whereby questions could be raised in banc after the trial. It allowed the defendant to ask the court that although the facts alleged by the plaintiff were found to be true by a jury, they disclosed no cause of action on which plaintiff could succeed Baker (2002), pp. 82–85.

[25] Van Cleve (2006a), pp. 617–618.

[26] Wiecek (1974), p. 92.

The third case in which Holt dealt with slavery, *Smith v. Gould* (Court of King's Bench, 1706) can serve as an argument in favour of construing *Smith v. Brown and Cooper* narrowly. This case dealt with an action of trover for a *negro* (of whom it is unclear whether he was in England or abroad), which the court declined in a motion in arrest of judgment. Holt declared that trover was not possible, given the owner did not have an absolute property right in the slave. However, he reiterated his support for an action *per quod servitium amisit*, and added an alternative possible action, trespass *quare captivum suum cepit*. The latter would allow the plaintiff to show that the *negro* was his and that he had bought him. This made it easier for a master to claim damages for the loss of the services of his slave.[27]

In conclusion, Holt imposed murky limits on which incidents of slavery were to be allowed in England. Clearly, he held that classical chattel slavery, the state in which the slave would find himself in the colonies, could not be allowed under principles of English common law. However, unless one broadly interprets the meaning of *Smith v. Brown and Cooper*, he also held that at least some incidents of slavery would be allowed under English common law, equating the slave with a "slavish servant". Furthermore, it is apparent that Holt believed that the English common law and the law of the colonies were two separate legal systems. Accordingly, in his view, judgments based on English common law would not create awkward issues for English colonies that clearly allowed for slavery.[28]

4.2.2.3 The Era of Yorke-Talbot: The Nadir of the English Freedom Principle

In the early 1720s, the Privy Council adopted the previously discussed theory of "conquered" versus "discovered" colonies, which, according to Van Cleve, meant that Holt's decisions might render slavery unlawful in those colonies which were governed by English common law. These were primarily the discovered colonies, but also those conquered colonies which would have received the relevant part of the common law by royal assent.[29]

The legal uncertainty thus created was not beneficial for slave-owners. Historiography believed for a long time that this is why slave-owners went to Sir Philip Yorke (1690–1764), at that time the attorney-general, and Sir Charles Talbot (1685–1737), the solicitor-general, to find a listening ear for their grievances.[30] The two of them drafted ("upon a petition in Lincoln's Inn Hall, after dinner", according to

[27] *Smith v. Gould* (1706), 2 Salkeld 666 and 2 Ld. Raym. 1274 in Catterall and Matteson (1926), pp. 11–12.

[28] Van Cleve (2006a), pp. 623–624.

[29] Ibid., pp. 619–620.

[30] The attorney-general, solicitor-general and king's serjeants together were the King's Counsel in ordinary, tasked with advising the crown in litigation Baker (2002), pp. 164–165. Traditionally, historiography believed that it were the plantation owners who pressed Yorke and Talbot to deliver this opinion. For example, see Wiecek (1974), pp. 31–32, Van Cleve (2006a), pp. 619–620, Drescher (1987), pp. 31–32.

Lord Mansfield[31]) the infamous Yorke-Talbot opinion on the status of slavery in England. In that opinion, Yorke and Talbot determined four points: (1) A slave coming from the West Indies, with or without his master, did not become free by arriving in England; (2) the master's property or right in the slave was not at all varied or determined by this arrival; (3) baptising the slave did not change his legal status; and (4) masters could compel their slaves to return together with them to the colonies.[32] Although this statement could, technically, not overrule judgments by common law courts, the position of these legal heavyweights led contemporaries to conclude that the opinion had little less authority than settled law.[33] More recent historiography has partially revised this understanding of the Yorke-Talbot opinion. In a recent article, Travis Glasson has convincingly argued that the opinion was primarily solicited by Anglican missionaries seeking the means to allow for easier conversion of the slaves to Christianity (given that the idea that "baptism bestows freedom" had been present in English thought for a long time). The slave owners only started using this opinion afterwards, when they found out the potential benefits it offered them.[34] In any case, given the benefits to slaveholders, they were quick to try and ensure that the opinion became well known.[35]

Things did not end there. A 1732 Act of Parliament ("For the more easy Recovery of Debts in his Majesty's Plantations and Colonies in America") gave rich Englishmen with an interest in the slave trade even more reason for joy. This act, made in the wake of an economic slump in the colonies (and the accompanying defaults), allowed English merchants to prove their debts and obtain judgments against colonial debtors in English courts. More importantly, for the purpose of settling debts, slaves were to be treated as personal property.[36]

The Yorke-Talbot opinion would only become more important in the ensuing years, as Talbot became Lord Chancellor in 1733, and Yorke (now known as Lord Hardwicke) became Chief Justice of the King's Bench. Upon Talbot's passing in 1737, Hardwicke succeeded him as Lord Chancellor. Whilst in this position, Hardwicke got the opportunity to give his opinion sound footing in law (or more exactly, equity[37]) in the case of *Pearne v. Lisle* in 1749. In this case, the plaintiff, the owner

---

[31] *Somerset v. Stewart* (1772), Lofft 1.

[32] *Opinion of Sir Philip York[e], then Attorney-General, and Mr. Talbot, Solicitor-General*, 33 Dict. Of Dec. 14,547, 1720 in Catterall and Matteson (1926), p. 12.

[33] Wise (2006), pp. 30, 46.

[34] Glasson (2010).

[35] Drescher (1987), p. 32.

[36] *The Statutes at Large, from Magna Charta to the End of the Eleventh Parliament of Great Britain, Anno 1761, Vol. 16*, 5 Geo. II, C. 7; Priest (2006), pp. 421–427. Because of the acknowledgement of slaves as personal property in this specific situation, Van Cleve and Glasson have called this the "commercial law analogy" of the Yorke-Talbot opinion Van Cleve (2006a), p. 620, Glasson (2010), p. 284.

[37] As Lord Chancellor, Hardwicke would hear cases in the Court of Chancery. Technically speaking (and unlike today), the common law as it was created by the courts of King's Bench and Common Pleas was separate from the equity developed at the Court of Chancery. However, the parties in *Somerset v. Stewart*, and indeed Lord Mansfield himself, did not seem to make a big distinction

of fourteen slaves in Antigua, had an agent over there who had hired the slaves out to the defendant. The defendant refused to pay the sum due for the use of these slaves. As the defendant, who was in England at that point, was planning to leave England for Antigua, the plaintiff asked for an order of *ne exeat regno*.[38] Hardwicke refused to grant this. He first expounded on the nature of the demand (all *obiter dictum*). He claimed that trover would lie for a *negroe*, that *Smith v. Gould* was determined on a technicality (thus refuting its value), and that the idea of English freedom carried no weight. Furthermore, he equated villeinage with slavery ("There were formerly villains or slaves in England") and denied that this institution was abrogated. As to the reason for discharging the order (the *ratio decidendi*), Hardwicke believed that the laws of the colonies and the laws of England were broadly the same ("All our colonies are subject to the laws of England, although as to some purposes they have laws of their own"), which meant that the plaintiff could ask for justice to the courts of Antigua. This made rendering the order *ne exeat regno* unnecessary.

This position can be well contrasted with Holt's words in *Smith v. Brown and Cooper*. Clearly, Lord Hardwicke believed in a uniform view of the laws of the colonies and the laws of England. With such a vision, Hardwicke obviously had to come to the conclusion that slavery, which was clearly recognised by positive law in the colonies, would have to be legal according to English law as well. Otherwise there would seem to be an irreconcilable conflict between an English common law not allowing slavery on the one hand and, on the other hand, Englishmen taking their common law with them to the colonies and allowing for slavery.[39] Such a contradiction could not be allowed to exist in Hardwicke's framework. Scholars do disagree on the practical importance of this case, and whether it was well known.[40]

Apparently though, even Lord Chancellors could disagree on the topic. The final case on slavery before *Somerset v. Stewart*, Shanley *v. Harvey*, was decided in 1762 at the Court of Chancery of Hardwicke's successor, the Earl of Northington. In this case, the Court had to deal with a bill for an account of personal estate by the administrator of a deceased person against that person's *negro* slave (according to the report, an hour before dying, the deceased person gave a large amount of money to her slave).[41] It is unclear how the status of the slave became an issue in the litigation, but the Earl of Northington dismissed the bill and mentioned that "As soon as a negro sets foot

between precedents from common law cases and equity cases, which is why the distinction should not be taken too strict here. Baker (2002), pp. 97–99.

[38] *Pearne v. Lisle* (1749) Ambler 75 in Catterall and Matteson (1926), p. 12. This was an equitable writ, with the purpose of restraining a person from leaving the jurisdiction of the court or the state.

[39] It was during this period that the idea that "Englishmen carry their English law with them" became popular. Hulsebosch (2006), pp. 654–655, Van Cleve (2006a), pp. 620–621.

[40] Wiecek believes the case was not so important, given that it was only published long afterwards, whereas Van Cleve believes it was the most important case Lord Mansfield had to grapple with in *Somerset v. Stewart*. Wiecek (1974), pp. 94–95, Van Cleve (2006a), pp. 620–621.

[41] *Shanley v. Harvey* (1762), 2 Eden in Catterall and Matteson (1926), p. 13. An account of personal estate was a means to discover what, if anything, one party was owing to another. Baker (2002), pp. 363–365.

on English ground, he is free".[42] Scholars believe the case to have been little known and to have had little effect on subsequent cases.[43]

Undoubtedly, there are other instances on which the issue of slavery according to English law arose, though they did not play a major role in Somerset v. Stewart.

For example, Granville Sharp himself referred to two other cases that allegedly argued in favour of the illegality of slavery on English soil. In the case of *Gallway v. Caddee,* decided in Guildhall, it was ostensibly declared that the plaintiff could not claim the defendant, a *negro,* because the court declared defendant to be "free on his first setting foot on English ground". Likewise, in the case of *De Pinna v. Henriques* (also decided in Guildhall), verdict was apparently given for the defendant, who protected "a poor Negro woman, claimed by the plaintiffs as their slave".[44] These local cases are most certainly fruitful avenues for further research, as our current knowledge of their importance or unimportance is limited (Sharp learned of *Gallway v. Caddee* because "[he] accidentally met with a gentleman, who was present at this trial"[45]).[46]

Other instances also confirm a growing interest in the issue in the 1760s, when the black presence was at its apex. For example, Rabin points at the existence of a letter in The Gentleman's Magazine in 1764 which protested against the importation of "Negroe servants" into England. Likewise, she also pointed at the work of a local justice of the peace, John Fielding (1721–1780), who likewise complained about West Indian slave owners bringing their slaves to England to serve them.[47] Finally, another legal official spoke out on the issue: Lord De Grey (1719–1781), who was Attorney-General in 1766–1770 before being appointed as Lord Chief Justice of the Common Pleas in 1770. In a private case that Sharp knew about, but De Grey prohibited him from publishing (or so Sharp claimed), De Grey held that there could be "an Interest by Contract in the Service of this Female Slave. But no property in her person by the Law of this Country".[48]

---

[42]Chief Justice Cockburn opined what the exact facts of the case were. The slave had been given by his master to his niece, who made the gift of money to the slave just before she died. Probably, the master then instituted a suit to have an account of this money, on the basis that the recipient, a slave, could not acquire anything for himself. *Royal Commission on Fugitive Saves: Report of the Commissioners*, XLVII.

[43]Van Cleve (2006a), p. 621, Wiecek (1974), p. 95.

[44]Sharp (2014), p. 4–5. I have made use of the 2014 edition of Granville Sharp's A Representation of the Injustice and Dangerous Tendency of Tolerating Slavery (originally published in 1769).

[45]Ibid.

[46]For an example of some local London cases, see George (1965), pp. 140–144.

[47]Rabin (2011), p. 8.

[48]De Grey Opinion, in Lyall (2017), p. 335. Also see Wise (2006), p. 123.

4.2.2.4 Scholars and Slavery: Confirmation of Near Slavery?

Given that we have now seen some case law seemingly going "pro and against" allowing slavery in England in both the courts of common law and equity, one might hope that contemporary jurists would shed some light on the status of slavery.

First, whilst there are no apparent traces of lawyers and jurists upholding the idea of the freedom principle in England before the second half of the seventeenth century, there are clearly some pronouncements on the issue shortly afterwards. Second, by far the best writer to turn to for the eighteenth century would be William Blackstone (1723–1780), the Vinerian Professor at Oxford University. His Commentaries on the Laws of England, besides arguably being the first comprehensive survey of English law since Bracton, were also written between 1765–1769, right after *Shanley v. Harvey* but before *Somerset v. Stewart.*

As concerns the latter part of the seventeenth century, Van Cleve found some scholars referring to the situation of slaves coming to England. The first one was Edward Chamberlayne (1616–1703), a famous English writer who wrote his *Angliæ notitia, or The present state of England* in 1669, to give an overview of the social-political conditions of seventeenth century England. In a chapter on servants, Chamberlayne wrote that a slave in England "is upon landing ipso facto free from Slavery, but not from ordinary service". We do not know where Chambelayne got this idea from, but it does have to be borne in mind that he was well-versed in the civil law, having received law degrees from Oxford and Cambridge.[49]

This civilian influence is even clearer in Thomas Wood's (1661–1722) *A New Institute of the Imperial or, Civil Law*, which was the standard treatise on the civil law in the eighteenth century Anglo-American world. When discussing Book I of the Institutes, Wood also touched upon the subject of slavery. It is clear that he had read the works of Dutch lawyers, as he referred to Vinnius and Groenewegen to assert that slaves might claim their freedom in various European countries. Although neither of these two lawyers referred to England when discussing the freedom principle in their own work, Woods added his own country as one where slaves could claim their freedom before the courts.[50] Given the lack of English sources to which Wood refers, it seems rather unrealistic that Wood actually conveyed the state of English common law in order to assert that slaves could claim their freedom in England. More realistically, it must have seemed impossible to him that England would not boast the same freedom tradition as could be found on the continent, which would explain his addition of England.

One scholar more versed in the common law was Charles Molloy (1640–1690). He wrote *De Jure Maritimo et Navali,* the most popular book on the English law of naval trade in the eighteenth century. Given the importance of the slave trade in eighteenth century naval trade, it is not so surprising to find Molloy discussing slavery. Interestingly, Molloy mentioned that "[as regards slaves] Trover is not maintainable by the Laws of England". This is all the more interesting, given that no (known)

---

[49] Van Cleve (2006a), p. 612, Chamberlayne (1669), 514.

[50] Wood (1704), 31.

common law court had yet pronounced itself on this issue! However, he immediately qualified this statement by adding that "There may be a servitude which may amount to a labour or suffering equal to that of Captives".[51] This cannot be equated with a full freedom principle pronouncement, as Molloy simply stated that there cannot be an absolute property interest in slaves in England.

These works are interesting because they seem to infer that the issue of slavery in England might have been discussed more than we currently believe, although it is tempting to note the influence of a civil law background in two of these works. Likewise, two of them assert that while pure chattel slavery did not exist in England, the right of service might continue. This seems very much like a confirmation of "near slavery".

What did William Blackstone, arguably the most important eighteenth century English jurist, think? It is in the first book of his Commentaries on the Laws of England that we find his views on slavery. They are stretched out between two parts of that book (Chap. 1: Of the Absolute Rights of Individuals and Chap. 14: Of Master and Servant). In the first chapter, Blackstone lauded the political and civil liberties of England. He believed that the English spirit of liberty was so deeply implanted in the English "constitution" that the moment a slave landed in England, he fell under the protection of the laws and became *eo instanti* a freeman with regard to all natural rights.[52] To substantiate his point, he gave *Smith v. Brown and Cooper* as an authority. However, this far going statement must be contrasted with what is subsequently said in Chap. 14. Here, Blackstone repeated that pure and proper slavery cannot subsist in England. But he continued by adding a qualifying clause: "with regard to any right which the master may have acquired, by contract or the like, to the perpetual service of John or Thomas, this will remain exactly in the same state as before".[53] English soil did not seem to be fully liberating then, although the extent to which a master's right in the "slavish servant" still existed remained unclear.

Granville Sharp was incensed by what he found in Blackstone and used him as an argument to assert the illegality of slavery in England. However, Blackstone himself was clearly ambivalent on the issue. In correspondence between him and Sharp, he even clarified that "I only desired not to have a Passage cited from my first Edition as decisive in favour of your Doctrine (Book 1. Chap. 1 which I thought I had sufficiently explained and guarded by what followed in Chap. 14 [...]".[54]

Much has been made in historiography of what occurred next. In the next edition of Blackstone's Commentaries (the first book already moving to its second edition in 1766), the content of the statement of Chap. I had changed. England still had its "spirit of liberty", but this time, a slave only "so far becomes a freeman [as he

[51]Molloy (1682).

[52]Blackstone (1765), 123.

[53]Ibid., 411–413.

[54]Letter from Blackstone to Sharp, 20 February 1769 in Lyall (2017), p. 359.

falls under the protection of the laws]; though the master's right to his service may probably continue".[55]

Though this apparent change of heart was already noted by contemporaries during Somerset's case, F. O. Shyllon has gathered a host of evidence to show that the change of the sentence in Chap. I was probably made at the advice of Lord Mansfield, the judge who would have to decide the case of *Somerset v. Stewart* (and a long-time friend of Blackstone).[56] Although Shyllon focused on the intention of Mansfield, Oldham believes that one could equally well adopt a neutral reading of Lord Mansfield's role. The inconsistency between Chaps. I and XIV would have been quite clear to any good lawyer, and pointing this out did not necessarily reflect Mansfield's own intentions.[57] What is clear, however, is that Blackstone's epoch does not bring us much closer to a clear statement of the law of slavery in England.

4.2.2.5 Slavery and English Law at the Eve of *Somerset's Case*: Ambiguity or Consistency?

What can we make of this dozen or so cases by English royal courts before 1772? Basically, two approaches seem possible, and both have some merits.

The first one seems to be followed by a majority of recent scholars on the state of slavery in England, and they posit quite a pessimistic vision of what these cases can teach us. Whereas some commentators still cautiously held that English law was "unsettled"[58] or "suggesting several directions in which the law of slavery might evolve",[59] others deemed the state of slavery to be "confused and uncertain",[60] "a determined attempt [by the courts] to avoid the issue",[61] "producing considerable ambiguity",[62] "far from coherent",[63] "piecemeal and contradictory"[64] or even "in hopeless disagreement",[65] to cite but a few.

---

[55]Blackstone (1766). In the fourth and subsequent editions that were made during Blackstone's life, "possibly" replaced "probably". For an overview of all the change, during the lifetime of Blackstone, of the Commentaries on the Laws of England, see Blackstone's Commentaries in Lyall (2017), pp. 356–357.

[56]Shyllon's evidence is based on the postscript of the second edition of Blackstone's work, which mentioned that the new edition was made so soon partially because some of Blackstone's "learned friends" pointed out some of his errors; a confrontation between Granville Sharp and William Blackstone; accusations by Prince Hoare (Granville Sharp's biographer) and other circumstantial evidence Shyllon (1974), pp. 55–76.

[57]Oldham (2004), pp. 316–317.

[58]Oldham (1988), p. 48.

[59]Wiecek (1974), p. 89.

[60]Paley (2002), p. 180.

[61]Paley (2006), p. 662.

[62]Glasson (2010), p. 282.

[63]Lyall (2017), p. 29.

[64]Peabody (1996), p. 5.

[65]Fiddes (1934), p. 499.

Against this viewpoint, it is remarkable how George Van Cleve seems to be the first scholar to offer a different narrative, arguing in favour of a two-pronged framework for the state of slavery in England before Somerset. One part of his work focused on the exact contours of slavery in England. The other part concerned the relationship between English laws and colonial slavery laws. As concerns the former part, Van Cleve proposed to look at English law, not by asking whether slavery was legal in England, but by looking at the issue from a conflict of laws perspective.[66] His approach leads to a conclusion that the English courts seemed to create "near slavery" (or "slavish servitude", to quote Holt) for slaves coming to England. The idea of Van Cleve is that, whilst common law courts did not recognize classical chattel slavery, and that the status of slaves who came to England was governed by English law, they were not fully emancipated either.[67] Second, to explain for the cases diverging from these broad principles, such as *Pearne v. Lisle*, Van Cleve asserts that such cases stem from the views of individual judges on the relationship between English law and colonial law. As Holt believed in strict independence between the laws of England and the laws of the colonies, curtailing slavery in England would not have negative effects for the laws of the colonies.[68] Such a dualistic vision was impossible in Hardwicke's view as he believed in broad legal uniformity between England and the colonies. As a result, he must have felt that his decision could reverberate in the colonies. Consequently, *Pearne v. Lisle* had to decide that slavery was also legal in England, as it would be easy to claim, in Hardwicke's view, that, if held otherwise, colonial statutes on slavery were "repugnant" to English law and thus liable to be declared void.[69]

I believe Van Cleve's two ideas help to explain many of the above-discussed slave cases. However, I am in doubt whether these concepts are able to adequately explain everything. For once, it should be noted that it was Chief Justice Holt who, in the case of *Blankard v. Galdy* of 1693, spoke about the distinction of conquered colonies and discovered colonies and the different application of English laws in them. It seems difficult to reconcile this with the idea that Holt might have rendered his judgments because he knew that they would not apply to the colonies. Clearly, if his reasoning in *Blankard v. Galdy* was to be followed, these judgments would have had practical effects for the discovered colonies. Likewise, if the vision of broad interdependence between colonial laws and English laws became increasingly popular after 1720, it

---

[66]Watson adopts a similar conflicts of law analysis, this time centred on Mansfield in Somerset v.Stewart itself, in Watson (2006).

[67]Van Cleve (2006a), pp. 604,613–614. This is clearly reminiscent of our current manner of reasoning in private international law. In general, the courts of the forum recognise the validity of a status created under the law of the jurisdiction where the legal relation at issue arose (*lex loci*), unless the results would be considered inconvenient in the jurisdiction of the forum.

[68]For example, see his views on the laws of the colony of Virginia, as referred to in *Smith v. Brown and Cooper*.

[69]Van Cleve (2006a), p. 624.

is more difficult to explain the case of *Shanley v. Harvey*, where this interdependence was seemingly not taken into account.[70]

4.2.3 Somerset's Case: *High Expectations, Limited Judgment*

We now come to an assessment of what is by far the most famous case of an enslaved person in Europe, *Somerset v. Stewart*. Although I will defend the proposition that the result of the case was far from decisive, both plantation owners and the early abolitionist movement saw it as a test-case for the legality of slavery in England. Books have been written on this case, and it still resonates in popular English thinking.[71] A wide discussion of abolitionism would lead us too far and is not the purpose of this work, so suffice it to mention Sir Granville Sharp's pivotal role. An early abolitionist, it was Sharp who tried to persuade his fellow Englishmen to make an end to the Atlantic slave trade, and who litigated several cases involving English slaves in the royal courts.[72] The man he would have to convince, was the Scottish Lord Mansfield. Mansfield was one of the most important justices of the eighteenth century as Chief Justice of the Court of King's Bench from 1756 to 1788. Moreover, he is lauded as one of the most distinguished judges of the English common law system as a whole.[73] We will briefly look at the precedents of Somerset, Somerset itself and the meaning of Mansfield's holding in the case.[74]

[70]Because gaining a full understanding of the complex relationship between English law and colonial clearly fell outside the scope of this work, I have not explored this point much further. Professor Van Cleve was so kind to point out that the analysis of the relationship between colonial law and English law is very complex and also dependent on specific types of claims and circumstances. Private correspondence with Professor George Van Cleve, 1/05/2017. Also, "ambiguity" and "consistency" do not have to be diametrically opposed to each other. The case law was consistent in the sense that it can be explained by looking at the views of a certain judge on the legal relationship between the colonies and the metropolis, and that there was neither full emancipation nor (except for Hardwicke) full recognition of slavery. However, between the incidents of slavery which one judge allowed and another did not, there was some uncertainty.

[71]One recent book on *Somerset's case* is Wise (2006). For the importance of *Somerset's case* in current English thinking, see for example judge Tom Bingham's popularized pocketbook The Rule of Law Bingham (2010), pp. 56–58.

[72]For an introduction to Sharp's life, see Wise (2006), pp. 31–45.

[73]An introduction to Mansfield's life can be found in Oldham (2004), pp. 3–11. In theory, the Court of King's Bench and the Court of Common Pleas hierarchically stood next to one another, but Mansfield did all he could to make his court the "most attractive" for litigants. Ibid., 48.

[74]Ever since Mansfield's holding in *Somerset v. Stewart* in 1772, the case has been meticulously discussed by successive generations of scholars, creating a sheer endless amount of material. To assess the case, I have made use of the following works: Wise (2006), Van Cleve (2006a), Van Cleve (2006b), Shyllon (1974), Walvin (1973), Davis (1975), Hulsebosch (2006), Paley (2006), Oldham (2004), Wiecek (1974), Fiddes (1934), Drescher (1987), Rabin (2014), Nadelhaft (1966), Cotter (1994), Lorimer (1984), Jackman (2018), Watson (2006).

4.2.3.1 Somerset's Antecedents: Avoiding the Issue (Again)

Granville Sharp's involvement with enslaved African persons in England started with the case of the slave Jonathan Strong.[75] Strong had been repeatedly struck by his master David Lisle on the head with a revolver, after which his master had cast him into the street to die. Strong recovered, but Lisle discovered he was still alive, kidnapped him and sold him to a Jamaican planter. Granville Sharp heard of this, and through an intervention of the Lord Mayor of London, Strong was freed. The planter, James Kerr, filed a charge of trespass *de bonis asportatis* against Sharp, but failed because of procedural mistakes with his writs.[76]

Incensed by this early success, Sharp soon had a new slavery case to deal with. John Hylas, a freedman, saw how his wife Mary, a slave, was kidnapped in England and shipped back to the West Indies by her master. The case was brought before the Court of Common Pleas, but dispirited by the Yorke-Talbot opinion, which held that masters could forcibly return their slaves, Hylas' lawyers only asked for monetary damages. Though one of Newton's lawyers told Lord Wilmot, the Chief Justice of the Court of Common Pleas, that the case involved the difficult question of the legality of slavery in England, Wilmot neglected the issue and kept to a narrow ruling awarding damages and ordering the return of Mary.[77]

In 1771, Mansfield himself could no longer avoid confronting slavery in the case of Thomas Lewis. Lewis was a slave who had tried to escape his London master, Mr. Stapylton, several times. Stapylton, seemingly irritated by this behaviour, lured Lewis into a trap at a wharf. There, hired captors were waiting to kidnap Lewis and put him on a ship bound for Jamaica. By a stroke of luck, a passerby heard what was happening and warned Granville Sharp. Sharp managed to have the slave freed from the ship, but decided to go further and started criminal proceedings against Stapylton. The case was initially brought to a local court (the Middlesex Quarter Sessions), but after the grand jury had indicted Stapylton his lawyer decided to lift the case to the level of the Court of King's Bench.[78] Mansfield was disinclined to decide the issue. He tasked the jury with either finding the defendant Stapylton guilty or returning a special verdict if the jury thought that Stapylton had property ownership in Lewis. In the event of the latter, Mansfield might have had to decide on the legality of slavery in England; however, his instructions to the jury were clearly drafted in a way to

[75] The source texts for all these cases can be found in Lyall (2017). Obviously, one needs to treat these manuscripts with due criticism. The case of Jonathan Strong, for example, was written down few years after the facts by Sharp himself. Likewise, for the case of *Hylas v. Newton*, we have to trust a short report made by Sharp himself, given that the original has not (yet?) been found. The manuscript for *The King (Lewis) v. Stapylton* is clearly the most credible, as it is a (very rare) verbatim account of the proceeding in the King's Bench.

[76] Wise (2006), pp. 21–30. For the text, see Jonathan Strong in Lyall (2017), pp. 91–98.

[77] Wise (2006), pp. 45–58. For the manuscript, see Hylas v Newton in Lyall (2017), pp. 337–338.

[78] Wise (2006), pp. 59–67.

encourage it to choose for a verdict of guilty, which the jury did.[79] That way, the larger question was avoided again.[80]

During and after the case was decided, it became clear that Mansfield was doubtful on the issue, and rather not be faced with it at all. First, when one of the lawyers showed Mansfield the Yorke-Talbot opinion after the jury had made its decision, Mansfield stated that "perhaps it [the right of property in Negroes] is much better it never should be finally Discussed or Settled", and that "I hope it never will be finally discussed [,] For I would have all Masters think they were Free and all Negroes think they were not because they would both behave better".[81] Second, when Lewis' lawyers moved to have Stapylton sentenced a little while after the case, Mansfield refused to do so. It looked like Mansfield had had second thoughts and was doubting whether the fact that he allowed Lewis to witness to attest his own freedom was actually possible. Though Lewis' lawyers pressed more than once, they let the issue pass when it became clear Mansfield would not be moved.[82]

This solution would no longer be available to Mansfield when Somerset's case was brought before him.

4.2.3.2 Somerset v. Stewart: Testing the Law

Facts and Arguments of Counsel

The facts of Somerset's case are straightforward. James Somerset was the slave of Mr. Charles Stewart, a customs officer in the Massachusetts Bay Colony, where slavery was legal. Stewart came over from the Americas and brought Somerset with him. Whilst in England, Somerset tried to flee his master but was eventually caught. Stewart then consigned his slave to a certain Captain Knowles, who was to sell Somerset in Jamaica. Granville Sharp managed to intervene and secured a writ of habeas corpus on Somerset's behalf.[83]

---

[79]Oldham (2004), pp. 310–312.

[80]For the manuscript, see King (Lewis) v Stapylton—Proceedings in the Court of King's Bench in Lyall (2017), pp. 99–129.

[81]Ibid., 128–129.

[82]Motions for Judgment—The King (Lewis) v. Stapylton in Lyall (2017), pp. 130–132. Also see Wise (2006), pp. 107–110.

[83]The facts of the case can be found in *Somerset v. Stewart* (1772) Lofft 1, next to the abundant secondary literature. A writ of habeas corpus was one of the prerogative writs, and it became the principal safeguard of personal liberty in the English common law. The function of the writ is to question the lawfulness of an imprisonment, and the writ ensured that the English courts could protect a wide range of personal liberties Baker (2002), pp. 146–147. As we are dealing with a case of habeas corpus, the correct way to refer to the case is actually *R. v. Knowles, ex parte Somerset*. As the case is best known under the name *Somerset v. Stewart*, I have and will continue to use this way of referencing to it. Scholars have been grappling for decades with choosing the "most correct" report of the case, and "Exactly what Lord Mansfield said […] has been the subject of microscopic examination", Oldham (1988), pp. 45, 54. In contrast to the aforementioned cases, *Somerset v. Stewart* was widely discussed in both the English and the American press. Four versions of the case have gained some popularity (though more exist), namely the Lofft version, an account in

As the writ was returned, the case had to be discussed at the Court of King's Bench. As with previous cases, Mansfield tried to get the case settled without having to pronounce judgment. But as both the planters and Sharp's team wished to receive legal clarity, all these efforts failed, prompting Mansfield to say "fiat justitia, ruat caelum".[84]

For his legal defence, Somerset could count on the experienced serjeants William Davy and John Glynn, next to junior counsel Francis Hargrave and Alleyne. Stewart's team consisted of the well-known former solicitor-general John Dunning, supplemented by James Wallace.[85]

It was Francis Hargrave who gave the gist of Somerset's argument. Hargrave started by articulating the facts, tried to define slavery, and traced the institution's history, its decline in Europe and its revival in the Americas.[86] Next, Hargrave went far and wide to discuss how English law only knew of one kind of slavery, namely villeinage, and how English law could not admit the return of a new kind of slavery. Given that, according to Hargrave, it was not legally permissible to enslave captives in war anymore in England shortly after the Norman takeover (which was a broadly correct assessment historically speaking), there could only be villeins remaining in case of servile birth ("time out of memory") and by confession. Clearly, Somerset fit neither of these two cases.

Next, Hargrave contended that the *favor libertatis* of the English common law had progressively depleted the ranks of the class of villeins. English villeinage had thus become an empty shell, but it was also the only means of allowing "slavery"

the *Gentleman's Magazine*, an account in the *Scots Magazine* and a handwritten document in the Granville Sharp manuscripts. Given that Lofft was the only reporter of the Court of King's Bench at that moment, and was also present at the case, I will treat his version as being "holy" for the purpose of coherence (it is also my impression that many recent scholars, such as for example Steven Wise, tend to follow either this report or the Scots Magazine report). For a primer to the discussion on the various versions of *Somerset v. Stewart*, see Wiecek (1974), pp. 141–146. One's choice of the "most correct version" can clearly affect one's views on the breath of the case. For example, Nadelhaft prefers the Gentleman's Magazine version. Because that version nowhere mentions Mansfield referencing to "positive law" in his decision, Nadelhaft puts stress on some other nuances of the case than other writers preferring other versions. See Nadelhaft (1966), pp. 200–201.

[84]Oldham (2004), p. 313.

[85]For the manuscript of the case (including the various versions of the decision), see Lyall (2017), pp. 144–216. The setup of the case is excellently explained in Lyall as well (pp. 17–18). The hearings continued over five separate days, nl. (1) Arguments of Serjeants Davy and Glynn on 7 February 1772, (2) Arguments of Mansfield (counsel for Somerset) on 9 May 1772, (3) Arguments of Hargrave and Alleyne on 14 May 1772, (4) Arguments of Dunning and Davy om 21 May 1772 and (5) Judgment by Lord Mansfield on 22 June 1772. Only the final three parts are included in the Lofft report (the first part can be found in Lyall (p. 144–182), the second part is assembled on the basis of newspaper reports in Shyllon (1974), pp. 94–95). Many of the arguments are repeated by the lawyers, and my focus here is on the argument made by Hargrave. In the same year as the case, his memorial was printed as *An Argument in the Case of James Sommersett, A Negro*. Although the argument presented there does not fully match with what Hargrave must have exactly said in court, the general structure of the argument is closely similar to the Lofft report, and given that it is more structured than the notes Lofft took during trial, I have primarily made use of the pamphlet to reconstruct Hargrave's argument.

[86]Hargrave, *An Argument in the Case of James Sommersett, A Negro*, 1–25.

in English law. Slavery as professed in the American colonies, then, could only be legal in England if Parliament made it legal.[87] He also believed that the English law of contract for services might at most allow a contract to serve for life (in return for wages), but not voluntary enslavement. He was even doubtful about the validity of such life contracts.[88]

Hargrave continued his argument by construing the existing slave cases in England to the benefit of Somerset, although a disadvantageous case such as *Pearne v. Lisle* was craftily omitted from his considerations.[89] He then finished his argument by responding to several objections that his opponents might give. For example, he acknowledged that several English statutes, implicitly at least, seemed to allow slavery in the Americas. However, he contended that they were only applicable there.[90] Likewise, to counter the objection that the *lex loci* of the slave ought to be respected, he argued that this would create great inconvenience, and that it might eventually lead to a complete revival of domestic slavery in England. Interestingly, to give some added strength to the argument, he referred to other European states, mentioning examples of cases and scholarly writing in Scotland, the United Provinces and France that ought to show that these countries reacted to this issue by rejecting slavery.[91]

Finally, perhaps anticipating a recourse to Blackstone's ideas, Hargrave did not believe that a theory to change the slave's status to servant whilst in England held sway. At what time did such a contract between the master and his servant start? What were the terms of this contract? Simply said, such a contention posed more questions than it could solve.[92] In short, Hargrave was convinced that the laws of England ought to set Somerset free on his arrival in the country, and that this had to be an entire and unencumbered form of freedom.[93]

It was up to Wallace and Dunning to answer these claims.[94] Wallace's argument was the more extreme. Slavery was still found in "three quarters of the globe", and even in Europe it had not completely disappeared, as he mentioned Poland and Russia. When West Indian regulations allowed for slavery, it was not up to the King's Bench, or any other court, to see if these regulations were the best possible. As long as the regulations had force of law, they needed to be adhered to, even in English courts.

---

[87] Ibid., 25–45.

[88] Ibid., 47–50.

[89] Ibid., 51–59.

[90] Ibid., 67.

[91] Ibid., 68–75.

[92] Ibid., 75–77.

[93] In the Lofft report, the arguments in favour of Somerset by Alleyne and serjeant Davy are also given. Their considerations broadly align with the ones mentioned by Hargrave.

[94] Just like Hargrave, the plantation owners were also engaged in the "pamphlet war" surrounding the case. The best known pamphlet in favour of the slavers' position is Samuel Estwick's *Considerations on the Negroe cause*.

Second, he tried to turn Hargrave's argument. There might well be no statutory law allowing slavery in England, he admitted, but neither was there a law against it. What is more, villeinage had "all but the name [of slavery]". And as far as the precedents were concerned, they could well be used against Hargrave as well, as Wallace laid much stress on his biggest asset, the Yorke-Talbot opinion. He finished by warning the court with a public policy argument. If the King's Bench was going to make a broad decision, mass financial losses for the colonial proprietors would be the result. Surely the King's Bench did not want to be involved in such an enterprise?[95]

Dunning's argument was a bit more cunning and revealed the real desires of the slave owners. Dunning believed that Mansfield should use this case, not necessarily to "legalise" full-fledged chattel slavery in England, which was not the planters' main concern anyway, but rather to enforce a service for life in Somerset. The continuance of the slave's services was the most important issue for slave masters, and the fact that not all the incidents of villeinage or chattel slavery were transplanted to African slaves in England was of lesser concern. This, in turn, is very much in accordance with a wish to uphold the status quo of the "slavish servant" status alluded to by Van Cleve.[96]

Mansfield's Judgment

This left the case in the hands of Lord Mansfield. He was not happy with this in the first place as he mentioned once more how he had urged the parties to come to a mutual agreement. As this did not work, there was no choice but judgment. Mansfield started by setting out the terms of his decision. We were not dealing with a contract for sale of slave (which, he considered "*is good here*"), but with the person of the slave himself as the object of enquiry. He acknowledged that many of the consequences of slavery clearly went against the laws of England. Equally, he had to confess that setting 14,000 or 15,000 men free (Mansfield's assessment of the number of black slaves in England), was not a palatable choice either. He did not even believe that the issue could be conclusively settled and encouraged the merchants to ask to Parliament to make legislation to govern the status of black slaves in the metropolis.

The slave owners actually (finally) heeded his call and appealed to Parliament; however, Parliament rejected this call and the slave owners did not press the matter much further, as they were probably convinced that the case would go in their favour.[97]

---

[95] Wallace's argument can be found at Lofft, 8–9.

[96] Dunning's argument can be found at Lofft, 12–14.

[97] Lofft, 17–19. In the past, the West Indian planters had proved to be a powerful interest group, capable of influencing Parliament's legislation Taylor (2002), pp. 216, 438. Van Cleve mentions two reasons why Parliament did not act. First, it seems that it was already internally divided on the issue of slavery at the time of Somerset, and declined to make legislation in favour of either abolitionists or the planters. Second, the planters were apparently convinced that they were going to win this case. The plantation owners had thought that *Somerset's case* would be decided after the so called "twelve judges procedure" had been followed, an informal procedure in which the 12 common law judges (4 from King's Bench, Common Pleas and the Exchequer) collectively deliberated on a difficult legal question. They were convinced the twelve judges would agree with their view, on the basis that colonial property, recognised by English statutes, would also be deemed property in the metropolis Van Cleve (2006a), p. 631, Baker (2002), pp. 522–523.

Mansfield was finally ready to deliver his judgment on 22 June 1772. After repeating the facts, the content of the Yorke-Talbot opinion and the precedent of *Pearne v. Lisle* allowing trover for the sale of *negroes*, Mansfield made clear that his judgment was essentially about one thing only: "whether the cause on the return [of the writ of habeas corpus] is sufficient". Here again, we see Mansfield's reluctance to come to a sweeping judgment on the status of slavery itself. His conclusion remains all the more famous, and deserves to be quoted in full:

> So high an act of dominion must be recognized by the law of the country where it is used...The state of slavery is of such a nature, that it is incapable of being introduced on any reasons, moral or political; but only positive law, [...]. Whatever inconveniences may follow from a decision, I cannot say this case is allowed or approved by the law of England, and therefore the black must be discharged.[98]

As a result, Somerset was allowed to stay in England, and disappeared from the historical records soon after the case.

Evaluating Mansfield's Decision: A Very Narrow Holding

Having discussed *Somerset v. Stewart* in full, the question remains what was decided in the case concerning the status of slavery in England, and what was not.

One thing that was decided, and which is not disputed by any scholar, is that a master could not take hold of his slave and compel him to leave for the colonies. If the master did so, a slave could secure a writ of habeas corpus.[99] But was there more to Mansfield's ruling?

First, did Mansfield emancipate all the slaves in England, and did he decide that slavery could not exist there? Frankly, I believe the answer is no. Although this is clearly what the popular understanding of the case became, the debate on the holding in the case was re-opened by the Manchester historian Edward Fiddes (1864–1942) in 1932. Since then, the consensus in the scholarly community seems to be in favour of a more limited holding.[100]

Amongst the recent scholars to examine *Somerset v. Stewart*, one notable exception is W.R. Cotter. He does hold that Mansfield ended *de jure* slavery in England, referring amongst others to how American courts immediately after the Revolution understood Somerset to stand for the proposition that slavery was unknown under the common law, prompting the need for positive law (colonial statutes) on the issue.[101]

---

[98]Lofft, 19.

[99]This proves, once more, that whatever the status of a person is under foreign law, questions of personal status in the English courts must be determined by using English common law, not colonial law. Van Cleve, "Somerset's Case and Its Antecedents in Imperial Perspective," 634.

Lofft, 19.

[100]Fiddes (1934). Amongst the secondary literature I have cited, i.a. Watson, Van Cleve, Walvin, Davis, Hulsebosch, Paley, Oldham, Wiecek, Drescher, Nadelhaft, Lorimer, Jackman and Rabin all argue in favour of a limited holding of the case. One author who goes for a "middle of the road" position is Steven Wise. His understanding seems to be that it was Mansfield's intention to declare the slaves personally free with his Somerset judgment, but that he might have gotten second thoughts later on, after which he tried to limit the reach of his judgment *ex post facto* Wise (2006), pp. 205–215.

[101]Cotter (1994).

I personally side with the majority in holding that Mansfield's case actually did not decide the status of black slaves taken to England itself, besides the fact that such slaves could not be taken back to the colonies against their own will. Although his reference to "so high an act of dominion" could well be stretched (e.g. is the sale of a slave not "so high an act of dominion" as well?), Mansfield did mention, though not as part of the ratio decidendi, that "Contract for sale of a slave is good here".[102] Given Mansfield's refusal to declare the slaves emancipated, the status of "near slavery" for English blacks seemed to be upheld.[103] For plantation owners, the case could serve as a reminder that they should not try to "cross the line" of what one was allowed to do to another person in England. In that sense, Mansfield's judgment seems to be more of a case of individual justice being done to a particular person, rather than a pronouncement on broad principles of English law.[104]

A novelty in *Somerset v. Stewart* was Mansfield's idea that slavery had to be instituted by positive law in each and every country.[105] The fact that Mansfield preferred to use positive law, instead of holding that slavery was against English common law, might find its explanation in the relationship between the colonies and the metropolis. Mansfield was well acquainted with issues of conflicts of law, and, for example, had in previous decisions referred to the conflicts of law theory of the Dutch law professor Ulrich Huber (1634–1694).[106] If Mansfield had explicitly found that slavery went against the common law, this would have either meant that it was technically illegal in several of the British colonies (if Lord Hardwicke's reasoning was followed), or, if one did not want this outcome, that the colonies had to be treated as conquests outside of the common law framework (if Holt's reasoning was used).[107] Other scholars however believe the reference to positive law to be rather insignificant, and more of a rhetorical choice.[108]

In conclusion, Mansfield's decision in *Somerset v. Stewart* broadly left us where we were. His opinion created more uncertainty than certainty, but maybe this is what Mansfield wished in the first place.[109]

---

[102]This can be construed as referring to the sale of slaves outside of England, or out- and inside England.

[103]Van Cleve (2006a), p. 637, Davis (1975), p. 498.

[104]Oldham (2004), p. 306.

[105]Through those words, we can also ascertain that Mansfield was not a proponent of Aristotle's natural slavery thesis.

[106]Watson (2006).

[107]Van Cleve believes that this was a deliberate effort to demolish the legal justification for slavery on any other basis but positive law, but this is heavily doubted by Hulsebosch. Van Cleve (2006a), pp. 638–640, Hulsebosch (2006).

[108]Hulsebosch (2006), p. 651.

[109]Mansfield's remarks in *R. v. Stapylton* point to the fact that he was in favour of upholding the status quo. See Van Cleve (2006a), pp. 637–638, Paley (2006), p. 664.

4.2.4 After Somerset: The End of de Facto *and* de Jure Slavery *in England*

Given the lack of clear outcome in Somerset's case, it is useful to look at the cases that happened between 1772 and 1834, the year in which slavery, with some minor and temporary exceptions, was abolished in the British Empire. Doing so can shed some more light on the way in which the English legal order reacted to English slavery in the wake of *Somerset v. Stewart.*

4.2.4.1 The End of de Facto Slavery in England

Whereas slaves were still to be found in England in the immediate years after Somerset, one should be mindful that discussions on cases post-1790 are often more of a theoretical nature, as by all purposes, there is proof that de facto slavery had died out in Britain by the early 1790s. In that sense, if there ever were a law of slavery in England, it had grown close to villeinage in one aspect, namely that it had become an institution without any subjects to regulate.

To substantiate this belief, several scholars have pointed to the differences between this period and the rest of the eighteenth century. For example, there were only few instances of offer of sale of slaves in newspapers after Somerset.[110] The last reported instance of deportation is dated 1792. Even those few cases were often dubious examples, and the historical records are mostly silent afterwards.[111]

How did this change come about? For once, the number of black persons coming to England sharply declined in the post-Somerset era. Although several contemporary English newspapers mostly correctly reported Mansfield's decision, many slave owners and slaves interpreted the case as meaning that slaves became free upon coming to England. Masters would thus have an interest in taking slaves out of the country, and in limiting the entry of new ones. That is not to say that masters did not use other tricks to enjoy the continued service of their slaves, as can be seen through the example of indentured servitude.[112]

---

[110]The Runaway slaves in Britain-database still contains several entries in the aftermath of Somerset's case, but the last advertisements found were in 1780.

[111]Drescher (1987), pp. 41–42. Cotter makes a very strong case when he discusses the evidence for the end of the de facto existence of slavery in England post-Somerset. His conclusion however, which claims that incidents of slavery had already been barred from England almost right after *Somerset's case*, is too far reaching Cotter (1994). Paley refers to one example of 1812, but that case was more related to the limits of the Habeas Corpus Act 1679 rather than the freedom principle per se Paley (2002), p. 175.

[112]Cairns shows how the popular meaning of *Somerset's case* resonated amongst Scottish slaves, masters and the broader public in Scotland in Cairns (2012). Although not discussed exhaustively in this monograph, a few words on Scotland are in order. First, it has to be borne in mind that Scots law and the Scottish law courts were preserved after the Union with England in 1707. The legality of slavery was also a hotly debated issue in eighteenth century Scotland. There, the case for freedom was conclusively (and less ambiguously than in England) settled in 1778 in the case of

Professor Douglas Lorimer focuses on the black servants' own agency to explain for the change by the 1790s. He proposes to look at slavery not as a legal institution, but rather as a social institution. In so doing, he sees the importance of Somerset's case in the fact that it made it easier for slaves to make good on their escapes from their masters, and in how the case influenced popular opinion on the legality of slavery in England.[113]

The decline also has much to do with the changed atmosphere in England. Abolitionism had become a popular movement by the 1780s, and mobilisation and enforcement of the rights of black Africans had become a popular cause.[114] If the courts still had reason to pronounce judgment on a case involving English law and slaves after the 1790s, it was mostly due to a particular set of coincidental circumstances.

4.2.4.2 Continuity in the English "Law of Slavery"

But what was the *de jure* situation of slavery in England? Courts started wrestling with the ambiguities of Somerset from the outset of the judgment. In a local court case (*Cay v. Crichton*) in 1773, which again involved the inventory of a deceased person who had owned a black slave, the judge reached the conclusion that Somerset had indeed abolished slavery in England, and that this grant of freedom had retroactive effect for slaves in England.[115]

This case was quite predictive for the decisions of the lower courts. Our focus has been on the common law courts of King's Bench and Common Pleas. However, it must not be forgotten that, even at the end of the eighteenth century, the majority of criminal cases and a great deal of the administrative business was left not to the central courts, but to the local justices of the peace in England, meeting in Quarter

Knight v. Wedderburn. In that year, the Scottish Court of Session, Scotland's supreme civil court, affirmed a local 1774 decision which held that "*the State of Slavery is not recognised by the Laws of this Kingdom and is inconsistent with the principles thereof and Found that the Regulations in Jamaica concerning Slaves do not extend to this Kingdom*". It is very noteworthy that in the lawyers' memorials, we again find references to foreign law on the freedom principle (the memorials being filled with references to England, France, the Low Countries and Germany). The issue had also arisen earlier in Scotland, for example in the case of Sheddan v. Montgomery in 1756. However, because the slave died before the Court reached a conclusion, we only have the memorials of both parties in that case. The Sheddan case can also serve as an example of how the 1532 case that came before the Great Council of Malines was subsequently misconstrued by scholars. The lawyer of the slave Montgomery based the freedom tradition of the United Provinces upon "gives a memorable instance of a judgment to that purpose, where some Spanish slaves had made their escape, and claimed their liberty, and by a solemn decision were declared free". Besides for the fact that the case involved a slave owned by a Portuguese person, not a Spaniard, this is also an overly extensive reading of what was decided by the Great Council of Malines. On the case, also see Cairns (2001), pp. 222–224.I thank Professor John Finlay of the University of Glasgow for having shared with me his photographs of the written memorials in Sheddan's case.

113 Lorimer (1984).

114 Cotter (1994), p. 45.

115 Wiecek (1974), p. 108.

sessions.[116] Often, they represented the county elite, and were people chosen more for their status in society than for their knowledge of the law. In such a setting, and mindful of the fact that abolitionist thought became more and more popular, it is scarcely surprising to see how local magistrates would accord a meaning to Somerset that diverged from what Mansfield actually meant.[117]

Clearly, this was not what Lord Mansfield had in mind, and on the basis of subsequent judgments, there is ample evidence to show that Mansfield really only had a limited judgment in mind during *Somerset v. Stewart*.[118] For example, *Gregson v. Gilbert* and *Jones v. Schmoll* were two insurance cases, in which the dispute that was dealt with involved claims for the loss of slave cargo. In both cases, Mansfield declined to look at the property which was insured, namely slaves, and simply used customary principles of insurance law.[119]

Sales of slaves were not problematic for Mansfield either. In 1773, one Thomas Jones, a slave merchant, sought a writ of habeas corpus for the Robin John brothers. They were two African brothers who had tried to flee from their enslaver in America and hoped to return to Africa via a ship that was to pass Bristol first. When the captain of the ship discovered they were slaves, he kept them imprisoned in irons onboard. Thomas Jones knew the two brothers, as they were part of the elite of their African tribe and had been forcibly sold into slavery after a dispute with another tribe.[120] This case was even more threatening than *Somerset v. Stewart*. In Somerset's case, no one doubted that Somerset had been a slave in the Americas. Here, the Africans asserted that the manner in which they were made slaves was illegal. They believed their enslavement was open to challenge under the African laws and could not be condoned by an English court. They contended that it was Englishmen in English ships and in contravention of English law who had brought them from Africa and carried them into slavery in America. Mansfield himself clearly saw that this risked posing questions about the legitimacy of enslavement by war, and again studiously avoided to reach a decision.[121] This time, he had more success, as all parties recognised it was in their interest if English courts avoided pronouncing on the issue. The captain who had removed the Africans from their hometown agreed to pay money to their alleged

---

[116]Paley (2002), p. 179.

[117]Paley stresses that this new "mythology" of *Somerset's case* was created over time. It is very difficult to generalise the views of lower judges, although it is apparent that, with the memory of the protagonists of *Somerset v. Stewart* gradually fading away, it became easier to misconstrue the case. Ibid., 179–181.

[118]Or, alternatively, if we are to follow Wise, that Mansfield had "second thoughts", Wise (2006), pp. 205–215.

[119]*Gregson v. Gilbert* (1783) 99 E.R. 629 and *Jones v. Schmoll* (1785) 1 Term R. 130 n. in Catterall and Matteson (1926), pp. 19–20. The first case also dealt with a *cause célèbre*, as the insurance claim was for slaves who had been thrown overboard the slave-ship Zong, which had a lack of drinking water on board. This became known as the "Zong Massacre" Oldham (2004), p. 318. For all primary sources related to the Zong case, see Lyall (2017), pp. 217–334.

[120]The case is unreported but well documented, and is treated in full by Ruth Paley Paley (2002), pp. 166–175.

[121]Ibid., pp. 168–172.

owners, and the Robin John brothers were returned home. The compromise between the parties was formally accepted by the King's Bench and clearly mentioned that the money paid was "for the purpose money or value of the said two Africans". Although the term slave was not explicitly mentioned, the King's Bench clearly had no problem with transactions involving humans.[122]

Likewise, in the 1782 case of *Cook v. Kelly*, the plaintiff sued Kelly because he had delivered Kelly a slave to sell in England, but Kelly had not paid for this. The plaintiff won the case, and Mansfield did not believe the sale of slaves to be problematic, it was probably not even argued.[123]

Another opportunity to reiterate his limited views arose in the 1785 case of *The King v. The Inhabitants of Thomas Ditton*. This case involved a black slave brought to England by her colonial master. In England, she continued to work for him, and when he died, the black person lived with her former master's widow, before eventually leaving her. The slave then decided to apply for poor relief but needed a parish of settlement to be covered. For this, the black person would need to show that she was hired by her master.[124] Especially revealing are Mansfield's remarks during the plea of the black persons' lawyers. When one of them remarked that the court had never decided before that *negros* brought to England were under an obligation to serve there, Mansfield quickly intervened to say that "The determinations go no further than that the master cannot by force compel him to go out of the kingdom", which is a clear reference to *Somerset v. Stewart*. A little further, Mansfield remarked that "The case of Somerset is the only one on this subject. Where slaves have been brought here, and have commenced actions for their wages, I have always nonsuited the plaintiff". The lawyers pleaded that although, strictly speaking, there was no contract for wages, the Poor Relief Act could not be construed to exclude this situation. Mansfield again simply evaded the issue. Without asking whether the person *could* be hired, he simply used a strict interpretation of the text of the Poor Relief Act 1662 and held that she *was* not hired.[125] This proved, once more, that Mansfield did not believe that slave status fully disappeared upon a slave's arrival in England, although Cotter—considering his stance that Somerset's case had ended *de iure* slavery— tries to construe the case as only meaning that the legal relationship between a master and a former slave would have to be decided on a case-by-case basis.[126]

A non-legal argument against a broad view of *Somerset v. Stewart* can be derived from Mansfield's own life. Sir John Lindsay, Mansfield's nephew, had slept with a black slave, who became pregnant. The child, Dido, was taken care of by Lord Mansfield, who treated her with great compassion. Although she was no slave, in his

[122]Ibid., pp. 172–175.

[123]*Cook v. Kelly* is unreported, but discussed by James Oldham Oldham (2004), p. 319.

[124]*The King v. The Inhabitants of Thames Ditton* (1785), 99 E.R. 891.The Poor Relief Act 1662 was one of the successors of the Vagrancy Act of 1547. For the purposes of deciding which parish was responsible for someone in need of poor relief, a "settlement certificate" was needed to clarify the parish to which a person belonged. In order to receive such a settlement, a person had to proof he or she was continually hired by a settled resident for more than a year and a day.

[125]Paley (2002), p. 177.

[126]Davis (1975), p. 496, Paley (2002), p. 177, Walvin (1973), p. 134, Cotter (1994), p. 39.

own will, Mansfield "confirmed her freedom". Cotter believes that this was either a precautionary measure because "the various legal relationships between a former master and slave in England had not been fully articulated in cases subsequent to Somerset" or alternatively to protect her, if she was to travel to territories where slavery was still recognised. The latter reason requires quite a stretch of the mind. And if the former reason holds true, this seems to speak, in my opinion, more in favour of Van Cleve's idea of "near slavery", rather than full-fledged emancipation because of Somerset's case.[127]

Furthermore, some masters found a means to evade what was really decided in *Somerset's case*, namely that a master could not compel his slave to return to the colonies. The trick was to let the slave sign an indenture, in which s/he promised to work for his master under specified conditions whilst in England. That way, the slave was technically free in England but could be shipped back to the Indies without an application of *habeas corpus* being open to him, as the indentured servant had technically agreed to follow his master wherever he went.[128] As the 1799 case of *Alfred v. Marquis of Fitzjames* shows, where an indentured servant who had formerly been a slave, sued for his wages, "near slavery" remained the legal norm. The court held that, barring an original contract of service for wages with an explicit wages clause, Alfred had no title to recover wages.[129]

4.2.4.3 Somerset Expanded: The Full (Though Non-universal) Freedom Principle of England

Up to 1800, whereas lower courts seem to have been more inclined towards enforcing the freedom principle of England, the higher common law courts of Mansfield and his immediate successors were more reluctant and kept the idea of near slavery alive. However, I do not believe that slavery was only legally abolished in England itself by the Slavery Abolition Act 1833, as one group of scholars holds.[130] Three cases make

---

[127]Cotter (1994), p. 51.

[128]To prove that English courts allowed this practise, Walvin cited the case of *Keane v. Boycott*. This involved a case where a slave had signed an indenture prior to coming to England with his master. Upon arrival in England, a third party enticed the indentured servant to enlist in the armed forces. The third party was sentenced because he wilfully enticed an indentured servant away from his master. As Cotter notes, this cannot be equated with disallowing a writ of habeas corpus if the indentured servant would be forced back to the colonies., and it is therefore no good example *Keane v. Boycott* (1795), 2 H. Bl. 511 in Catterall and Matteson (1926), p. 21. Ruth Paley discusses another unreported case concerning the indentured servant John Hamlet, in which the court does condone the indentured servants' forced return to the colonies, and this does seem to be a valid example of the practice Walvin (1973), p. 135, Paley (2002), p. 178, Cotter (1994), p. 42. This trick was apparently used in Scotland as well, see Cairns (2012), pp. 308–310.

[129]*Alfred v. Marquis of Fitzjames* (1799) 170 E.R. 518.

[130]Cotter has made a list of scholars, dividing them into three categories depending on whether they believed *Somerset v. Stewart* ended *de jure* slavery in England, whether *de jure* slavery in England only ended through general emancipation in 1834, or whether it happened in the 1790 s (he seems to confound the de facto and *de jure* end of slavery in this third category) Cotter (1994), pp. 32–33.

clear that in the early nineteenth century, the Court of Common Pleas, the Court of King's Bench and the High Court of Admiralty, a specialised jurisdiction,[131] all believed that the English soil conferred freedom. I would contend that the freedom principle was the *ratio decidendi* in at least one of these cases under common law. One nuance is needed though. England's own air seems to have been too pure to allow for slaves at this point, but two of the cases also held that the slave's freedom could disappear if they returned to the colonies.

In *Williams v. Brown* (Court of Common Pleas, 1802), Williams, a runaway slave who had come to England, contracted to become a seaman at Brown's ship in England. When the ship arrived in Grenada, then a British colony, Williams was claimed as a runaway slave by his former master and delivered to him. He was then manumitted by his former master in return for some money, paid by Brown. In exchange, Williams had to sign an indenture with Brown, promising to serve him for three years at a lower wage than was agreed before. Back in England, Williams considered the agreement to be null and void and claimed wages from Brown. In this case, the court did not allow him to claim these wages. Two things were of interest. First, the court held that the plaintiff had indeed become free when he came to England ("Being as free as any of us while in England"), but upon return to Grenada, the status of slavery had "reverted" to him. This is the first indication, albeit *obiter dictum*, that the air of England had full purifying effect for slaves, even though this air did not follow the slave when he went back to the colonies.[132]

Twenty-two years later, the King's Bench was asked to deliver judgment in the case of *John Forbes v. Cochrane and Cockburn*. The plaintiff, a British merchant in the Spanish provinces of East Florida, sued Cochrane and Cockburn, two knights. The merchant had a cotton plantation. One day, some of his slaves had managed to escape to the ship of the defendants. The knights harboured the slaves, and after Forbes failed in persuading his slaves to return to him, they were brought to Bermuda to live as free persons. Forbes alleged that the knights had enticed the slaves away, and had wrongfully harboured, detained and kept them even after he had noticed the knights that the slaves were his property. The Court of King's Bench decided that the ship was to be seen as some kind of "floating island", in which the laws of England applied. Forbes' action was disallowed, and two of the three judges came to this decision by holding that English soil had conferred full freedom to the slaves. For the first time, one of the high courts of England made its decision based on the fact

[131] Originally, the High Court of Admiralty was, like the Conciliar Courts, another court that was influenced by civilian influence and stood outside of the common law system. This was due to the fact that courts of common law originally could not entertain causes of action that arose abroad, as it would be impossible to summon a jury from the place where the case was "laid" (One could however solve the trick by a pleading fiction, such as claiming the case was laid in "Ghent in the county of Kent"). As common law courts were ever superstitious to assert their dominance, they slowly encroached on the admiralty's jurisdiction, in the process absorbing this specialised law into the common law. Whilst the Court was at its nadir in the seventeenth century, it would regain some of its jurisdiction in the nineteenth century. This resulted in some interesting slave cases, though most of them were related to admiralty's jurisdiction as a prize court Baker (2002), pp. 122–124.

[132] *Williams v. Brown* (1802), 3 Bos. And Pul. 69.

that slavery was completely illegal in England. As this was the *ratio decidendi* of two judges, the freedom principle finally was clearly recognized in English common law.[133]

The final important case on slavery in England, *The Slave Grace* (High Court of Admiralty, 1827) confirmed the English freedom principle. The case itself is quite comparable to *Williams v. Brown*. It concerned a slave who had stayed in England, subsequently returned to the colonies, and whose status was now in question. Lord Stowell held that *Somerset's case* had decided that "the air of our island is too pure for slavery to breathe in", and that slavery had become extinct in England as it was unsuitable to the "genius of the country". However, it clearly was not too genius yet for the English colonies, as Stowell believed that another maxim, "Once free for an hour, free for ever", only applied to villeins, and that Grace had reverted into a state of slavery by returning to Antigua.[134] The impact of the case was limited, as slavery was abolished by Parliament all over the British Empire six years later.[135]

Thus, in the early 1800s, even the high British courts believed that slavery was abolished by *Somerset v. Stewart*, and they confirmed this in their own decisions. As for the reason for this change of heart, abolitionist thought probably had much to do with it. It is well known that the abolitionists were very crafty when it came to spreading ideas not on what a decision necessarily really held, but what they could make the decision to mean.[136] As Lord Mansfield slowly became a shadow of the past, so did the idea that black slavery, for a very long time at least, had led a life at the fringes of the English law, neither fully accepted nor rejected. The belief that English law had always protected human liberty became a living illusion.

4.3 Conclusion

In the period 1650–1833, the English legal order was faced with slavery as a result of the Atlantic slave trade. The courts had to deal with this conflicts of law issue

133 *Forbes v. Cochrane and Cockburn* (1824), 107 E.R. 450. Judge Bayley's decision was not made on the basis of the status of the purported slaves. Justice Holroyd held that "*They were not slaves by the law which prevailed on board the British ship of war*", and his decision was made on the basis that "*The moment they got on board the English ship there was an end of any right which the plaintiff had by the English laws acquired over them as slaves*". Judge Best held that "*It is an antichristian law, and one which violates the rights of nature, and therefore ought not to be recognized here. For these reasons I am of opinion that our judgment must be for defendant*" and believed that "*I say there is not any decided case in which the power to maintain an action arising out of the relation of master and slave had been recognized in this country*". When it came to the continuing right of the service of the slave that Blackstone had alluded to, Judge Best believed that this was a "*service to our country, service to our relations for the protection they have offered us, and service by compact*", which obviously cannot be equated with a mandatory right to service for life.

134 *The Slave, Grace* (1827), 166 E.R. 179.

135 Wiecek (1974), pp. 111–112.

136 Paley (2002), pp. 181–184.

that arose when colonial masters took one or more plantation slaves with them as a status symbol, or as a cheap means of labour. Their status was recognised by colonial statutes, but what happened to their status when they came to England was an unsettled legal question before the Atlantic slave trade began.

Before *Somerset's case* in 1772, English courts only had the possibility to address this issue in an indirect way, as the few conflicts that did arise were usually related to the right of property in the slave, but never concerned the slave, seen as a person, himself. Undoubtedly, the Yorke-Talbot opinion had dissuaded many from pleading in favour of the slave's freedom, and up until some years before Somerset, abolitionism was a marginal current of thought. When the courts addressed the issue, they seemed to allow for some form of "near slavery" in England. Full chattel slavery was not acknowledged, but neither were the slaves fully emancipated. England's air, at this time, was clearly impure.

At one point in time, it does seem reasonable to say that English law fully recognised the status of slavery, conferred in an English colony, in England. Chancellor Hardwicke, in the Yorke-Talbot opinion and *Pearne v. Lisle*, clearly conceived of an idea of a uniform imperial law, which had to be able to account for slavery. Parliament did not make any statutes on the issue, but given the fact that the case law allowed for "near slavery", and maybe even "real slavery" during the tenure of Hardwicke, the need for planters to file requests to Parliament must have been more limited anyway. At the same time, these theoretical hassles have to be placed in their perspective. Only a mere trickle of the slaves present in England were the subject (or the object) of a court ruling, and most masters did not seem to have bothered too much about the questionable legality of this peculiar kind of property in England.

The landmark case of *Somerset v. Stewart* did not usher in a revolution. Rather, it should be seen as a return to the idea of "near slavery" that had been developed by English courts in the first half of the eighteenth century. Mansfield did not emancipate the English slaves, but his decision was a warning. Clearly, the boundaries of what was to be allowed in England went less far than what the Yorke-Talbot opinion had delineated half a century earlier. The holding of the case was open to interpretation, but given Mansfield's earlier comments, he must have been well aware of the confusion he created, and willing to allow the case to mean different things in different contexts.

In the period after Somerset, the abolitionists managed to seize control of one of those possible meanings of *Somerset v. Stewart*, and as public opinion slowly shifted in favour of abolitionism, English law followed its lead. At first, the lower courts, filled by laymen construed a broad meaning of *Somerset v. Stewart*. They were to be followed by the higher courts after the cloud of Mansfield himself had disappeared, although touching the English soil would still not protect the slave upon his return to the colonies.

In conclusion, from the seventeenth to the early nineteenth century, English courts were only to a very limited extent responsible for giving a measure of protection to black slaves arriving in England, and Parliament played no role at all. The English legal order reacted to the issue of black slavery by respecting the master's property rights whilst in England, and only imposed some limitations. "Near slavery" became the legal condition for blacks in England, as judges were possibly also wary of the impact of their decisions in the colonies. When the English common law courts finally affirmed the freedom principle of England, an idea which had been touted by Harrison long before but seemingly forgotten during the era of black slavery, they did so not as legal revolutionaries, but rather by confirming an abolitionist consensus that had already come in place.

References

Baker JH (2002) An introduction to English legal history. Butterworth, London

Bingham T (2010) The rule of law. Penguin Books, London

Blackstone W (1765) Commentaries on the laws of England. Book the First, 1st edn. Clarendon Press, Oxford

Blackstone W (1766) Commentaries on the laws of England. Book the First, 2nd edn. Clarendon Press, Oxford

Bush JA (1998) The British constitution and the creation of American slavery. In: Finkelman P (ed) Slavery and the law. Rowman and Littlefield Publishers, Madison, pp 379–418

Cairns JW (2012) After somerset: the scottish experience. J Legal Hist 33:291–312

Cairns JW (2001) Stoicism, slavery, and law—grotian jurisprudence and its reception. Grotiana 22:197–231

Catterall H, Matteson D (1926) Judicial cases concerning American slavery and the negro, vol 1. Carnegie Institution of Washington, Washington DC

Chamberlayne E (1669) Angliae Notitia, or, the present state of England: T. N., London in the Savoy

Chater K (2007) Black people in England, 1660–1807. Parliam Hist 26:66–83

Cotter W (1994) The somerset case and the abolition of slavery in England. J Hist Assoc 79:31–56

Davis DB (1975) The problem of slavery in the age of revolution, 1770–1823. Cornell University Press, Ithaca

Drescher S (1987) Capitalism and antislavery: British mobilisation in comparative perspective. Oxford University Press, New York

Fiddes E (1934) Lord mansfield and the sommersett case. Law Q Rev 50:499–511

Fryer P (1984) Staying power: the history of black people in Britain. Pluto Press, London

George MD (1965) London life in the eighteenth century. Penguin Books, London

Glasson T (2010) Baptism doth not bestow freedom: missionary Anglicanism, slavery, and the Yorke-Talbot opinion, 1701–1730. William Mary Q 67:279–318

Hulsebosch DJ (2006) Nothing but liberty: somerset's case and the British empire. Law Hist Rev 24:647–657

Jackman A (2018) Judging a judge: a reappraisal of lord mansfield and somerset's case. J Legal Hist 39:140–156

Kaufmann M (2008) Caspar Van Senden, Sir Thomas Sherley and the 'blackamoor' project. Hist Res 81:366–371

Lorimer DA (1984) Black slaves and English liberty: a re-examination of racial slavery in England. Immigr Minor 3:121–150

Lyall A (2017) Granville sharp's cases on slavery. Hart Publishing, Oxford

Molloy C (1682) De jure maritimi et navali, or, a treatise of affairs maritime and of commerce in three books, 3rd edn. London

Nadelhaft J (1966) The somersett case and slavery: myth, reality, and repercussions. J Negro Hist 51:193–208

Oldham J (2012) The indispensability of manuscript case notes to eighteenth-century barristers and judges. In: Musson A, Stebbings C (eds) Making legal history. Cambridge University Press, Cambridge, pp 30–52

Oldham J (2004) English common law in the age of mansfield [studies in legal history]. University of North Carolina Press, Chapel Hill

Oldham J (1988) New light on mansfield and slavery. J Br Stud 27:45–68

Paley R (2010) Parliament and slavery, 1660–c.1710. Slavery Abol 31:257–281

Paley R (2002) After somerset: mansfield, slavery and the law in England 1772–1830. In: Landau N (ed) Law, crime and English society 1660–1830. Cambridge University Press, Cambridge, p 264

Paley R (2006) Imperial politics and English law: the many contexts of somerset. Law Hist Rev 24:659–664

Peabody S (1996) There are no slaves in France: the political culture of race and slavery in the ancien régime. Oxford University Press, New York

Priest C (2006) Creating an American property law: alienability and its limits in American history. Harvard Law Rev 120:385–459

Rabin D (2011) 'In a country of liberty?': slavery, villeinage and the making of whiteness in the somerset case (1772). Hist Work J 72:5–29

Rabin D (2014) Empire on trial: slavery, villeinage and law in imperial Britain. In: Dorsett S, McLaren J (eds) Legal histories of the British empire—laws, engagements and legacies. Routledge, Abingdon, pp 203–217

Sharp G (1769) A representation of the injustice and dangerous tendency of tolerating slavery. English edition: Sharp G (2014) A representation of the injustice and dangerous tendency of tolerating slavery. Cambridge University Press, Cambridge

Shyllon FO (1974) Black slaves in Britain. Oxford University Press, London

Taylor A (2002) American colonies: the settling of North America. Penguin Books, New York

Van Cleve G (2006a) Somerset's case and its antecedents in imperial perspective. Law Hist Rev 24:601–645

Van Cleve G (2006b) Mansfield's decision: toward human freedom. Law Hist Rev 24:665–671

Walvin J (1973) Black and white: the negro and English society 1555–1945. Penguin press, London

Watson A (2006) Lord mansfield; judicial integrity or its lack; somerset's case. J Comp Law 2:225–234

Weissbourd E (2015) Those in their possession": race, slavery, and queen elizabeth's "edicts of expulsion. Huntingt Libr Q 78:1–19

Wiecek WM (1974) Somerset: lord mansfield and the legitimacy of slavery in the anglo-American world. Univ Chicago Law Rev 42:86–146

Wise SM (2006) Though the heavens may fall: the landmark trial that led to the end of human slavery. Pimlico, London

Wood T (1704) A new institute of the imperial or civil law. W. B., London

Chapter 5
Strains on French Freedom: Turks and Nègres in Metropolitan France

5.1 French Galley Slavery: An Unexplored Exception to the French Freedom Principle?

5.1.1 Louis XIV's Galley Fleet

Previously, the English experiment with galleys has already been noted. However, in the North Sea, galleys always remained very much peripheral, given that they were not very useful in those waters. Not so for France. Although the defects of galleys had become clear by the end of the sixteenth century, they were still in sway in the Mediterranean.[1] The expansion of France's galley fleet had started when Richelieu was in power. The cause was taken up by Louis XIV (France's *Roi Soleil* between 1643 and 1715). Under his rule, the galley fleet expanded until it reached a number of about 50 ships in 1690. In the eighteenth century, the disadvantages of galleys became ever clearer, and they fell into decline until the *Corps des galères* was abolished in 1748.[2]

Galleys were useful as coastal patrols and could serve as an expression of Louis' power, but they also offered symbolic value. Whilst the French King was not disinclined against making peace treaties with the Barbary States when necessary, conducting just wars against Muslims also helped to convey the impression of Louis as "the most Christian King". And there most certainly was an almost continuous state of war between the Barbary States and the European Mediterranean powers, as many ships were subject to this *guerre de course* (commercial raiding). Between the sixteenth and the nineteenth century, almost one million Christians were enslaved by the Barbary pirates, some of them to be kept in Barbary and some of them to

[1]Bamford (1973), pp. 10–30.

[2]Boyer (1969), p. 73.

F. Batselé, *Liberty, Slavery and the Law in Early Modern Western Europe*, Studies in the History of Law and Justice 17, https://doi.org/10.1007/978-3-030-36855-5_5

be ransomed. But capturing "the other" also went the other way round, and we are primarily interested in the state of those Muslims captured by the French.[3]

We want to consider the condition of the persons who were rowing in these galleys, the *chiourme des galères*. In fact, three categories of rowers have to be distinguished: *benevoglies*, *forçats* and *Turcs*.[4]

The *benevoglies* were considered to be voluntary rowers. The French idea was to have "*les miséraux*" of their society, such as the vagabonds, put into the galleys as a means of being employed. The system did not have much success, and the vocabulary soon changed to call these voluntary oarsmen "*mariniers de rame*". Although life at the galleys was hard for them, they were not chained, did not have to wear the infamous clothing of the other oarsmen and received a small wage.[5] Clearly, they do not legally classify as slaves.

Things become more difficult with the second category, the *forçats*. Generally, this term was used for those persons who were condemned to the galleys because of a crime they had committed. Being sentenced to the galleys as a punishment was already known in fifteenth century France, but the condemnations soared during the time of Louis XIV. It was Colbert, Louis XIV's long-time chief minister, who sent letters to the French courts to encourage them to condemn people to the galleys to fill Louis' ships with unpaid labour.[6] In the period 1680–1748, approximately 60.000 persons were sentenced to the galleys for a temporary or permanent time for crimes such as murder, theft or desertion (and in some cases even because of Protestant beliefs).[7] Classifying these persons becomes more difficult. If slavery is to be defined by factual conditions, then one could easily claim that they were slaves, as they were chained, received no wages and could be whipped in the galleys. If slavery is defined by legal status, things become more difficult. Although it is clear that by current standards, *forçats* would be classified as slaves, I would dare say that most seventeenth century Frenchmen did not perceive them as such. There are various reasons for this: condemnations to the galleys were usually only for a certain duration of time, and the progeny of the convicts did not become slaves. But the most important reason to vie in favour of the proposition that *forçats* were no slaves, is

[3]An introduction to Mediterannean slavery, both from the viewpoint of the Barbary States and France, can be found in Fontenay (2010), pp. 500–502. Unfortunately, there is no single book solely devoted to the issue of Muslims enslaved by the French during this era. When mention is being made of these slaves, this is usually done as chapters in books that are concerned with the French galleys themselves (some of the scholars who have written most extensively on French galleys being Paul Masson, Michel Fontenay, Paul Bamford and André Zysberg).

[4]Various authors, both contemporary and recent, tend to confound these categories. Things are made worse because of the fact that the term *forçat* or *benevoglie* is not commonly used in the English language, and the three categories tend to be simply translated as galley slaves. Next to that, it is difficult to determine whether the *forçats* were "true slaves" or not, making the issue of translation only more difficult. For an author who notes this difficulty, see Stanziani (2014), p. 34.

[5]Zysberg (1987), pp. 62–63.

[6]Ibid., p. 63.

[7]Ibid., pp. 59–116.

just because there was a third category of oarsmen who could be safely classified as genuine slaves, namely the "Turks".

There were about 12.000 Muslims in the galleys of France. Generally, this category was simply called "Turk", which was used as a quasi-synonym for *esclave* in France by the mid-sixteenth century.[8] There are various reasons to classify the Turks as a separate category, and to see them as "real slaves". First, the means of procurement of the Turks. This was done in three ways. First, many were purchased on slave markets across the Mediterranean (chiefly Livorno and Malta, but also French port-cities such as Marseille). Modern estimates even hold that during the second half of the seventeenth century, the expenditures for buying slaves represented more than two percent of the overall budget for the galleys.[9] Second, they could be captured at sea (and on land) during the various raids that were held by the warring parties.[10] Third, *forçats* trying to escape their condemnation to the galleys had the possibility to exchange their own labour for that of a Turk (except if they were Protestants), bought by themselves or their family and friends.[11] Next to this, royal *ordonnances* made a distinction between *forçats* and Turks. For example the *ordonnance* of 11 February 1687 set administrative rules on the galleys and decided that Turks had to comprise one-quarter of the oarsmen of a galley, whereas *forçats* had to count for the remaining three-quarters.[12] Finally, the religion of this category also bears testimony to the fact that we are dealing with slaves. Although "Turk" was used as a lump category and many captives were not actually ethnic Turks, nearly all of them were Muslims. The occasional orthodox Greek or Russian could be found amongst them, but administrative correspondence shows that attention was paid to ensure that Christians were usually not to be found amongst this category.[13]

As Louis XIV made several peace agreements with the Barbary States at the end of the seventeenth century, this resulted in a decline of the number of Turks in the galleys. Louis XIV then experimented with putting black and Iroquois slaves in these ships. Those experiments failed, and the number of Turks would slowly

[8]Weiss (2011), p. 399. I will simply use the word Turk here, but the reader should bear in mind that it is a synonym of "slave" in this context.

[9]Boyer (1969), pp. 59–60; Weiss (2011), p. 400.

[10]Boyer (1969), pp. 61–63.

[11]Ibid., p. 60. This in itself clearly shows the distinction between *forçats* and Turks.

[12]Ibid., p. 55. It does not appear in the *Recueil général des anciennes lois françaises.* The distinction between *forçats* and Turks is also made clear in several other *ordonnances* (do note that the term "*esclave*" is not used in any of them). In book 19 and book 20 of the *recueil général*, which cover the period of 1672 until 1715 (this coincides with the time when the French galleys were at the zenith of their importance), there are several acts that mention a distinction between Turks and *forçats*. To name but a few: *Ordonnance portant défenses aux gardiens conduisant des turcs ou des forçats, d'entrer dans aucun cabaret ou autre lieu public, ni de sortir la ville* of 9 December 1682; *Ordonnance portant que les forçats et Turcs trouvés saisis de choses volées seront punis du fouet* of 21 October 1695; *Ordonnance portant que les forçats qui frapperont et blesseront avec ferremens les pertuisaniers, seront condamnés a mort* of 20 December 1713 (p. 614, Tome 20). See *Recueil général des anciennes lois Françaises Vol. XIX*, 409; *Recueil général des anciennes lois Françaises Vol. XX*, 259, 614.

[13]Masson (1938), p. 281; Weiss (2011), pp. 403–405; Boyer (1969), pp. 63–66.

dwindle, until there were fewer than 200 left right before the abolition of the *Corps des Galères*.[14] In all of these elements, one can see a clear application of what the Classics of International Law said. The exception not to enslave the opponent only counted in just wars between Christian nations, but the infidels were fair game.

5.1.2 Turks and the Freedom Principle: An Unspoken Exception?

All this is relevant for one simple reason that, except for one recent article, has almost been fully neglected by scholars. How did this issue intersect with the freedom principle of France? We know that slaves were on the galleys, and we also know that most of them must have touched the soil of France at various moments. The oarsmen spent spring and summer at sea, but during fall and winter, the galleys remained docked in several French ports, most importantly Marseille. During this period, the Turks slept in docked galleys or, by the eighteenth century, in barracks. Many of them worked in local factories during the day or had small shops.[15] If we were to follow the logic of the sixteenth century freedom principle precedents, one would presume that these Turks became free upon setting foot on French soil. However, this was not the case. There were no acts regulating their status whilst in France, and no author has reported a case involving one of these slaves so far. No scholar has attempted to systematically evaluate whether and what seventeenth century jurists had to say about this issue. The few references in secondary literature that do mention the thoughts of scholars on this issue often refer to eighteenth century sources, and are mostly derived from articles in the great *encyclopédies* of that era.[16]

[14]Zysberg (1987), pp. 60–61; Bamford (1973), pp. 170–171.

[15]Weiss (2011), pp. 398–399.

[16]The only determined attempt to explain this anomaly between the freedom principle and slavery has been made by Gillian Weiss. She only discusses the works of several eighteenth century writers. When it comes to the seventeenth century, she notes that "*only after colonial slaves began claiming liberty in the metropole did questions about the lawfulness of keeping esclaves turcs arise*". It would be interesting to see whether this is truly the case, if one were to systematically check whether the great jurists from the time of Louis XIV really did not write anything about this issue. It seems little surprising that many scholars refer to eighteenth century encyclopaedia, as they would often include separate articles on "*galères*" or "*galériens*". Besides Weiss (2011)., the only articles which I have found giving examples of the views of some jurists on this issue are Vigie (1985); Stanziani (2014). Weiss refers to the eighteenth century historian Jean-Baptiste Durival and the jurist François Bourjon. Vigie mentions the jurists Joseph-Nicolas Guyot, Claude-Joseph de Ferrière and Boucher d'Argis. Stanziani likewise refers to Ferrière and Boucher d'Argis. All of them, besides Durival le Jeune, can be found in Arabeyre (2007), pp. 113–115, 126–127, 326–327, 394. I have mostly limited myself to giving an overview (and commenting) on the views of the authors mentioned by those sources. Additionally, I have found the issue of Turkish slaves in France discussed by the author known as Chambron. He was a citizen of Marseille who wrote a *Traité général du commerce de l'Amérique,* a popular eighteenth century book on the commerce of the Americas. Given he was from Marseille, where the Turkish presence was most visible, and given his interesting views on this issue, I have taken note of his remarks as well.

The administration's views on the issue are visible in a 1694 letter of then Minister of the Marine Louis Phélypeaux, the Count of Maurepas.[17] He asserted that "Tout homme qui a une fois touché les terres du royaume est libre". However, there was one exception, namely for "Turcs et mores qui sont envoyés à Marseille pour le service des galères, parce que, avant d'y arriver, ils sont achetés dans les pays estrangers où cette espèce de commerce est establ*i*".[18] As we will see, the Count of Maurepas came to a different conclusion when he discussed whether blacks who arrived in France became free upon touching the French soil, notwithstanding the fact that black people were also bought in countries where this kind of trade was established. Next to that, the Count of Maurepas' statement also does not take note of those Turks who were captured during war, and thus not bought. The letter can best be understood as a means of trying to explain away the anomaly between the freedom principle and Turkish slavery for the sake of the importance that the galleys had to Louis XIV, but it did not succeed in offering an adequate legal explanation for the enslavement of Turks.[19]

Another way to explain the anomaly could be to give it a religious spin. As noted, Antoine Loisel held that France's soil only rendered freedom to slaves who were baptised.[20] This requirement can be supported by a 1698 decision of the *Cour de Conscience*. This was not a regular court, but part of the faculty of theology of the Sorbonne, and moral issues could be discussed with its theologians.[21] In 1698, such a question was posed regarding the legality of the Atlantic slave trade. The *Cour de Conscience* decided that, under certain conditions, the Atlantic slave trade did not go against Christian conscience. One sentence in the decision mentioned that the French king "*ne fait point difficulté d'acheter des Esclaves Turcs, quoiqu'il y' en ait très peu qui embrassent le Christianisme*".[22] Again, this might show that the idea of baptism giving freedom was also more widespread in France and subsequently explains the lack of debate concerning these Muslim slaves. We know that baptism as a precondition for freedom eventually withered away, certainly so after the Edict of 1685 required black slaves to be baptised. However, we need more research on seventeenth century legal tracts to conclusively prove this hypothesis.

---

[17]The *secrétaires d'état* were important actors in the central government of France during the *Ancien Régime*. The institution already had predecessors in the fourteenth century, but was created in its then current form by Henri II in the middle of the sixteenth century. They were the highest administrative officials, but the king could always remove them from office. There were four *secrétaires d'état*, one being responsible for interior matters, another for foreign matters, one for the marine and one for war. Rigaudière (2010), pp. 553–554.

[18]The Maurepas letter is mentioned by Zysberg (1987), p. 59.

[19]Weiss (2011), pp. 402–403.

[20]Loisel (1607), Livre I, Tit I, III.

[21]At this time, references to the Sorbonne either denoted the *collège universitaire* or the faculty of theology of Paris. The reference here is to the latter. Compère (2010), pp. 1172–1173.

[22]Fromageau and de Bussy de Lamet (1745), 1080–1084. Weiss also believes that, in this one sentence, we find an implicit referral to Louis XIII's authorisation of enslavement as an effective means of evangelising pagans. As noted before, it is highly unlikely that Louis XIII made this pronouncement. Whether this myth had already become part of the mind-set of lawyers and theologians at this point is unknown to me. Weiss (2011), pp. 403–405.

In the eighteenth century, when the galleys were already a thing of the past, we also find some scholars expounding on this exception to the freedom principle. How did they respond? In some *encyclopédies*, the issue was simply ignored. Only *forçats* were discussed, and these were not equated with slaves.[23] Others did equate *forçats* with slaves and believed this showed that penal enslavement was an exception to the French freedom principle. Again, this ignored the question of the Turks.[24] Some scholars did make the distinction between the *forçats* and the Turks. Several means were then used to explain the anomaly between the freedom principle and the presence of slaves. Some seem to have found their legitimation in the right of reprisal. The idea was that the Turks were the ones who had committed some kind of "first fault" by capturing French subjects. In return, the French were then allowed to enslave the Turks as well, even if some would hold that they could only be kept as prisoners rather than slaves.[25] Another means of legitimation solved the conundrum by claiming the Turks were no "real slaves". The idea was that the French did not have the right of life and death over them, and that their children were considered as being personally free as well. Consequently, one could claim that this was no "real exception" to the French freedom principle.[26]

What is clear, is that we cannot explain this anomaly by solely looking at the legal side of the story. That is why Weiss has also looked at other factors to explain why this issue did not arouse much suspicion in France. Besides the aforementioned legal explanations, she points at various factors: the rise of France's naval ambitions in the Mediterranean, the propaganda value of Muslim slaves for a "most Christian king" such as Louis XIV, and the fact that the Turks' unfreedom must have come less to the fore in a multi-ethnic city such as Marseille, to name but a few.[27]

Given the foregoing, I believe any conclusion on the issue of galley slavery is rather tentative. Until the latter part of the eighteenth century, part of the oarsmen of the French galleys were Turkish slaves, and most of these Turks must have reached the French soil at some moment. There is no indication that any of them were successful in appealing to the freedom principle of France, and they thus remained in a condition of slavery.

---

[23] Guyot (1779), pp. 486–490; Boucher d'Argis (1782), pp. 690–697.

[24] de Ferrière (1769), pp. 558–559.

[25] Durival (1757), "Galérien". The encyclopedia of Diderot & d'Alembert was first published between 1751 and 1766 and can be found online at http://xn--encyclopdie-ibb.eu/index.php/morale/2009024668-jurisprudence-marine/858967454-GAL%C3%89RIEN. de Bourjon (1770), Livre I, Ch. I. Weiss' reading of Bourjon can also be interpreted differently. Bourjon confirms that all persons in France are free, but then gives two exceptions to this rule. According to Weiss, these two exceptions are (1) black persons taken to France from the colonies by their masters and (2) the right of reprisal against nations who enslave Frenchman. This is a possible reading of Bourjon's text, but another reading is equally possible. It could also be said that the exceptions are (1) the still-existing *gens de main-morte* in certain parts of France and (2) the black persons taken to France from the colonies. The right of reprisal is then linked to black slavery, not to Mediterranean slavery.

[26] Chambron (1783), 208.

[27] Weiss (2011).

How do we explain the anomaly? Socio-politically speaking, there were arguments why the issue did not arise much suspicion. However, we are still faced with the legal anomaly between the freedom principle and Turkish enslavement. Pending further research, I would dare say the problem was approached by lawyers and administrative officials in various ways.

One way to solve the problem was to simply ignore it. Broadly speaking, this seems to have been the approach of the administration. When a double standard started to appear at the end of the seventeenth century, with freedom for black slaves but slavery for the Turks, the administration engaged in weak sophistry to try and explain the difference. Given that the number of Turkish galley slaves went down just when the number of black slaves went up, the administration did not have to deal with the issue later on. Another means to explain the anomaly would be by pointing out that the French soil was only regarded to be "free" for Christians, not the infidel in the seventeenth century. This extra condition to acquire liberty disappeared soon after the promulgation of the Edict of 1685 and could help to explain why there was no reaction from lawyers and scholars to Turkish enslavement. This hypothesis also helps to understand why eighteenth century scholars did feel the need to explain the anomaly, as by their time, baptism was much less linked to attaining freedom. Those scholars could then choose to ignore the issue when discussing the *galères*, could posit penal enslavement as an exception to the French freedom principle, make vague references to a right of reprisal, or claim that the Turks were simply "no real slaves".

5.2 Black Slaves in France: The Freedom Principle Versus Slavery, Paris Versus the Atlantic

5.2.1 The Historiography of Black Slavery in France

Because of commercial contacts with the Mediterranean world, it is clear that some black persons, usually Muslim slaves, were already to be found in France during the Middle Ages.[28] This exposure, still very much limited to the Mediterranean provinces, would start to increase in the fifteenth and sixteenth century. We noted the example of the Parlement of Bordeaux in 1571, and it is sure that the influx of blacks only increased after this incident. For the seventeenth century, we know of examples of black slaves in the galleys, African states dispatching "ambassadors" to the French court and even a (quite probably fictional) anecdote which claimed that the French ambassador to the peace negotiations at Münster in 1644 had a retinue of 140 blacks.[29] As France became increasingly embroiled in the Atlantic slave trade, numbers continued to rise, especially so after France lost part of its colonial empire

[28] Verlinden (1955), pp. 762–765.

[29] McCloy (1961), pp. 11–13.

in the wake of the Seven Years War. Just as in England, some French proprietors wished to take one or more slaves with them during their stay in France.

In contrast to England, the French tried to measure the size of the black presence in their kingdom several times. For example, an edict in 1716 and a declaration in 1738, which we will discuss, ordered some form of registration for black slaves who arrived in France. Additionally, an admiralty ordinance of 1762, a 1777 declaration and a ministerial request of 1807 tried to come to a general census of colored people, free and enslaved, in France.[30]

Various historians have tried to bring structure to all those registrations in order to chart the black population of France. These documents show us that most blacks arrived in Nantes (608 blacks declared between 1740 and 1777), La Rochelle (660 blacks declared between 1719 and 1777) and Bordeaux (1028 blacks declared between 1720 and 1770).[31] At the same time, we have to take these numbers with a grain of salt. For example, in Bordeaux, whilst we know of a little more than 1000 declarations of arrival, we also know of 2735 departures. This discrepancy proves that, for various reasons, masters did not always declare their slaves upon arrival.[32] Likewise, registration requirements were primarily met in the years immediately following legislation that asked to register blacks, again pointing at possible underestimation of the numbers by focusing on these records.[33] A recent, very complete overview of the presence of people of colour (both enslaved and personally free) is provided in the three-volume *Dictionnaire des gens de couleur dans la France moderne*, which has been able to trace some form of recording for 19.015 people of colour that touched France's soil at one point between the start of French colonisation and 1792.[34]

The census of 1777, for which we probably have the best details and analysis, suffers from the same issue. Given that this census was made with the aim of expelling (mostly black) slaves from France, whilst free blacks often did not realise that the measure also asked them to register themselves, one ought to scarcely be surprised that it underestimates the number of black people in the kingdom.[35] A reconstruction of this census comes to a number of 2031 blacks in France. Taking into account the degree of underestimation, between 4000 and 5000 black people (which was also what contemporaries gave as their measure of the black presence in France) seems to be our best assessment for the final quarter of the eighteenth century.[36]

Though black people could be found all over the kingdom, two rules of thumb are relevant. First, the black presence was concentrated in Bordeaux, Nantes and Paris,

---

[30] More precisely, the declaration of 1777 asked for the registration of "*aucun noir, mulâtre ou autres gens de couleur*".

[31] The great majority of these arrivals were slaves, and Koufinkana only counted 13 free blacks in these registers. Koufinkana (2008), pp. 46–49.

[32] Saugera (1995), pp. 290–291.

[33] Boulle (2009).

[34] See Noël (2011), (2013), (2017).

[35] Boulle (2007), pp. 170–171.

[36] Ibid., p. 170.

the three of them accounting for almost 60% of all blacks in France. Second, the further a region was located from the sea, the lower the number of black persons generally was.[37] All in all, this shows, just like in England, a marginal presence of black persons, strongly concentrated in a few cities. The black presence in France did not comprise more than 0.02% of the French population in the eighteenth century, though their presence was obviously more visible in Paris, Bordeaux and Nantes (representing about 0.16, 1.04 and 0.99% of the population there).[38] The number fell afterwards, and whilst the 1807 census came to an (underestimated) population of 1295 blacks, estimates of a real population of 1600–1700 blacks show the decline.[39]

As concerns status, Koufinkana's research has shown that, whereas until the end of the *Ancien Régime* the great majority of black people arriving in France were slaves, there had always been some free blacks in France as well.[40] Several black persons were also (legally or illegally) enfranchised in France, and the *table des requêtes* of the Parisian admiralty court, for example, shows that 93 acts of enfranchisement were registered by that court between 1750 and 1790.[41] Likewise, we know of a regiment of about 100 free black soldiers in the French army of Maurice de Saxe in the middle of the eighteenth century, an experiment which was repeated during the Revolutionary and Napoleonic Era.[42]

When it comes to those persons counted as slaves, one has to bear in mind that, as in England, there is no proof that the most horrible practises of the French colonies were repeated in France. Many cases show how black people were mistreated and held in low esteem by their masters, but much of this is also applicable to French domestic (and personally free) servants.[43] In this sense, whilst I have found no scholar using this term in the French context, one could claim that the idea of "near slavery" held true for the factual condition of most slaves in France as well. However, the danger of re-shipment to the Antilles and elsewhere was a sword of Damocles hanging above the slave's head.

This brings us to the crux of the question, namely the legal status of those black persons who were enslaved in French colonies and who were brought to the metropolis by their masters. On the one hand, taking the seemingly strong roots of the French freedom principle into account, one would expect that they became free upon arrival. On the other hand, the example of the Turks already showed that the French were willing to neglect their freedom principle. Again, to find answers, we will have to look at royal legislation and case law. In contrast to England, legislation can tell us much.

---

37 Ibid., pp. 181–182.

38 Ibid., pp. 196–197.

39 Sibalis (2003), pp. 95–106.

40 Koufinkana (2008), pp. 46–49.

41 *Table des requêtes présentées à l'amirauté de France, 1730–1790* in Boulle and Peabody (2014), p. 73.

42 Ibid., pp. 73–85; Corvisier (1968), pp. 367–413. The most famous example during Napoléon's time was obviously Thomas-Alexandre Dumas (1762–1802), a general in Napoléon's revolutionary army, who was of African descent.

43 Boulle (2006b), pp. 38–40.

The French King made an edict in 1718, a declaration in 1738 and a declaration in 1777, all of them solely dealing with the issue of black persons in France. Likewise, various *Arrêts du Conseil*, *ordres du roi*, ministerial *ordonnances* and administrative correspondence also shed light on the condition of black people in France.[44] Next to these legislative initiatives, we also need to look at how courts dealt with the issue. Again, there is a stark contrast with England, as there are many more cases dealing with the status of purported slaves in France. All of the reviewed cases were first heard at the 50 Admiralty Courts of France. Cases emanating from such a court could still be appealed to various other courts, depending on the location of the Admiralty. The most important Admiralty Court was the *Siège général de l'Amirauté de France à la Table de Marbre* (the Admiralty of France) in Paris, which could sometimes hear cases on first instance and sometimes on appeal, after which another appeal to the Parlement of Paris was possible.[45]

[44]In *Ancien Régime* France, we find quite some variety in the forms of royal legislation. *Lettres patentes* were the most important form. Depending whether the act was meant to be general and perpetual, or whether it was meant to deal with a particular and temporary issue, these could be divided in *grandes lettres patentes* and *petites lettres patentes*. The former could be divided in three categories (although the distinction only became truly settled in the eighteenth century): *ordonnances*, *édits* and *déclarations*. The term *ordonnance* was used when dealing with legislation of a rather general nature, wheras *édit* was used for measures which were limited to a certain subject (e.g. black slaves in France). The *déclaration*, finally, was meant to explain, complete or restrain one of the aforementioned legislative acts. The *petites lettres patentes* dealt with a particular situation, and could be obtained on request of an individual, a city, a region or a community or persons. *Arrêts du conseil* had become a separate form of royal legislation by the end of the Middle Ages. In essence, they were the decisions that the king took while he was in his council, although his actual presence was more often than not a fiction. Next to those two forms, there were also the *ordonnances sans adresse ni sceau*, which were legislative acts in the domains where the king's powers were the most unconstrained, and the *lettres closes*, which was a general term used to signify many kinds of royal decisions that did not fall under any of the other categories. Whereas the *arrêts du conseil* were usually immediately sent to the persons that had to execute them, *lettres patentes* were first sent to the chancellor and then to the Parlements. The chancellor analysed whether the act was in conformity with the customs and laws of the kingdom, after which he would seal the document. The next step would be to send the act to the sovereign Parlements. If the Parlement believed that the act was not legally sound, it could send formal objections or *remonstrances* to the king. The king might then agree to change the law, or he could come to the Parlement himself and force it to register the law by the *lit de justice* procedure. The effectiveness of these *remonstrances* heavily depended on the balance of power between the Parlements and the King, as various French kings (most notably Louis XIV) tried to curtail the possibilities of the Parlements to refuse to register acts. What the exact consequences of non-registration were, was also a matter of debate. The extreme parliamentarian position held that acts which were not registered could not be executed, whereas the extreme royalist position professed that registration added nothing to the validity of a law. Rigaudière (2010), pp. 657–678; Olivier-Martin (2010), pp. 389–400; Shennan (1968), pp. 50–86.

[45]The jurisdiction of the admiralty courts is complex, but well explained in Mousnier (1974), pp. 293–295. As regards jurisdiction, this was quite different for the main "slave cities" of France (Paris, Nantes and Bordeaux). Many northern cities would have their own admiralty seat (e.g. Calais and La Rochelle), from where recourse lay to the Admiralty of France and from there on to the Parlement of Paris, although for Dunkerque, for example, appeals from its admiralty were to be sent

5.2.2 *The Earliest Cases: Upholding the French Freedom Principle*

The earliest instances of black slaves arriving in France all point to the same direction, namely a widely shared, but sometimes qualified, respect for the French freedom principle.[46]

In 1691, two *nègres* from Martinique arrived in France after having hidden themselves on the ship *l'Oyseau*.[47] In an instruction sent by the Count of Maurepas to the governor-general of the French Antilles, Louis XIV had decided to grant freedom to these slaves ("La liberté étant acquise par les lois du Royaume aux esclaves aussitôt qu'ils touchent la terre"). At the same time, the inattentive captain of the ship had to pay 300 livres for each of those slaves to their former master.[48] The king eventually decided to formalise the decisions in stowaway cases, reiterating in a 1694 *ordonnance* that captains who took slaves to France by accident had to pay 400 livres for each of them to their former masters.[49]

With the issue of stowaways settled, the question soon arose as to whether colonial proprietors could bring their slaves with them to France and keep them. Again, the proprietors were to be disappointed. In a 1696 letter to the intendant of Martinique, Maurepas said that *nègres* brought to France gained their freedom, and this was repeated in correspondence of 1698 and 1710.[50]

---

to the Parlement of Paris immediately. For Nantes, cases from its admiralty court could be appealed to the Parlement of Bretagne. The Parlement of Bordeaux had jurisdiction for appeals emanating from three admiralty courts in Guyenne. I have not checked all the judgments made by these courts myself, but have focused on the cases for which written *mémoires* were published (the cases of Jean Boucaux, Francisque, Roc, Pampy and Julienne v. Isaac Mèndes France and Furcy). All of the cases that came before the Admiralty of France have been analysed by Sue Peabody in her landmark study *There Are No Slaves in France* (154 cases in which the slave was freed every single time). Given that all of those published *mémoires* are related to proceedings at Parisian courts, this method bears the risk of neglecting the fact that the king himself might still intervene in these cases; and minimising the importance of decisions made by admiralty courts in other cities besides Paris. This is also pointed out by Dwain C. Pruitt, whose PhD thesis dealt with the situation in Nantes, see Pruitt (2005). However, Peabody seems to be the only one who engaged in exhaustive analysis of court records. For areas outside of Paris, there will thus primarily be reference to secondary literature. The reader will note that many of the references in this chapter refer to Peabody's landmark study, which has significanty improved upon much earlier work (primarily by Lucien Peytraud, Jules Mathorez, Léon Vignols and Shelby McCloy).

[46]In general, see Peabody (1996), pp. 13–15.

[47]As for England, I will sometimes use the words "*nègre*", "*noir*", "*mulâtre*" or "*gens de couleur*", but only when the primary materials themselves used this term.

[48]*Le roi punit un officier de marine pour avoir introduit des esclaves en France* in Boulle and Peabody (2014), p. 29.

[49]*Ordonnance de Sa Majesté, rendue au sujet des nègres venant des îles de l'Amérique*, 28 avril 1694 in Ibid., p. 30.

[50]*Les esclaves venus en France seront affranchi, même s'ils retournent aux colonies, 1698* in Ibid., p. 31. The correspondence of 1696 is quoted verbatim in Koufinkana (2008), p. 33. The ministerial order of 1710 can be found in Boulle (2014), p. 22. This correspondence also proves the sophistry of the Count of Maurepas in relation to Turkish slaves. Just like Turks, *nègres* were acquired from

Yet the government did allow for some partial exceptions. For example, the king ordered that some *nègres* who had participated and were captured by the enemy in a French military expedition in Cartagena, after which they were brought to France, would only be enfranchised if their part of the booty was given to their masters.[51] Likewise, there was a case of an enslaved woman from the Antilles who had travelled to France in 1677, before returning voluntarily to the Antilles without having claimed her freedom. When her many children and grandchildren found out that their predecessor had been in France and tried to claim their freedom on the basis of this stay in 1707, the French administration made an exception to its freedom principle for slaves who had voluntarily returned to the colonies.[52]

5.2.3 The Edict of 1716: First Limitations to the French Freedom Principle

Things would soon change. In 1715, the Admiralty Court of Nantes heard the case of Pauline Villeneuve, a young slave who sued for her freedom against her master, as she refused to go back with him to the colonies. Lawyers and judges in the case found no existing law on the issue and, on the basis of a technicality, the judges declared her free.[53]

The year after, a *mémoire* concerning the issue of black slaves in France was circulating at the French Ministry of Marine. Gérard Mellier (1674–1729), later mayor of Nantes and at the time a subdelegate of the *intendant* of Bretagne, seized this moment to respond to the *mémoire*, which questioned whether slaves coming to France ought to be declared free or not. Mellier clearly drafted his answers with the interests of Nantes, which was heavily dependent on the slave trade, in mind. First, he noted how Nantes already had a custom contrary to the freedom principle, as masters were allowed to keep their slaves in Nantes if they registered them with the Admiralty Court of Nantes (due to the lack of registration, Villeneuve was declared free). Mellier searched for positive law on the issue, but only came across the Edict of 1685 (the "Code Noir"), which dealt with colonial slaves. Lacking any substantive legislation on the situation of blacks coming to France, Mellier urged the government to take action. Evidently, Mellier suggested the King to choose for an option that would make an exception to the French freedom principle. To legitimise the exception, he used several arguments: the French slave traders were actually saving Africans from their overpopulated continent and instructing them in the catholic faith, it would be

---

countries in which slavery was allowed, yet black slaves could make use of the French freedom principle whereas Muslim slaves apparently could not.

[51] *Le principe du sol libre n'empêche pas les anciens propriétaires de bénéficier du service de leurs esclaves avant leur affranchissement*, 1699 in Boulle and Peabody (2014), p. 31.

[52] Peabody (1996), pp. 14–15; *Lettre du ministre de la marine, Jérôme de Pontchartrain, sur les nègres amenés en France, 10 juin 1707* in Boulle and Peabody (2014), p. 39.

[53] Pruitt (2007), p. 152; Peabody (1996), pp. 15–16.

bad for the development of the colonies if rich proprietors had to take French servants with them instead of black slaves, and black slaves coming to France could learn a useful craft whilst they were here. Mellier finalised his work by proposing a tentative edict which set out the conditions of this exception to the French freedom principle.[54]

Alhough Mellier's *mémoire* was not completely copied by the government (they omitted some provisions on fugitive slaves), the crux of Mellier's argument was retained in the first great piece of royal legislation, the Edict of 1716 "Concernant les esclaves Nègres des colonies".[55] This change of heart in comparison with the confirmations of the freedom principle during Louis XIV's reign has been linked with an emphasis on pursuing policies in accordance with France's economic best interests during the regency period.[56] The edict allowed inhabitants and officers who were employed in the colonies (but only them) to take slaves with them, but only if this was done to instruct slaves in the catholic faith, or to teach them a craft ("pour leur apprendre en même temps quelque art and metier").[57] Furthermore, the colonists needed to obtain a written permission (containing several details) from the relevant colonial governor or commander and had to register this permission both at the *greffe* of the court of the French colonial district where they resided and the Admiralty Court where they disembarked in France (within 8 days of arrival).[58] If these conditions were met, the slave did not acquire his liberty whilst in France and could be compelled to return to the colonies. If the procedural conditions were not met, or in case the slave married in France with the permission of his master, the slave was deemed to be free.[59] Furthermore, sales of slaves were explicitly prohibited in France, and the law also provided for an exception to the freedom principle for stowaways.[60] Finally, to ensure that the stay of *nègres* in France would be temporary, it was stated that colonists wishing to settle in France for good had one year, as from the moment of their decision to stay, to send their slaves back. If this was not adhered to, these slaves were to be deemed free as well.[61]

This law created the first explicit limitation on the French freedom principle, but it still had to be registered by the Parlements. And here, things went wrong. Although scholars still disagree as to which Parlements exactly registered the Edict of 1716, some things are certain: the edict was registered by the Atlantic Parlements of Bretagne, Bordeaux and Normandy, but not by the important Parlement of Paris.[62] The

---

[54] *[Gérard Mellier], Réponses au Mémoire présenté à Nosseigneurs du Conseil Royal de la Marine concernant les nègres esclaves que les officiers et habitants des colonies françaises de l'Amérique amènent en France pour leur service* in Boulle and Peabody (2014), pp. 40–43.

[55] Pruitt (2007), p. 155.

[56] See Abanime (1979), p. 22; Pruitt (2005), pp. 62–63.

[57] Art. 2, Edict of 1716.

[58] Art. 2–3, Edict of 1716.

[59] Art. 5 and 7, Edict of 1716.

[60] Art. 11 and 14, Edict of 1716.

[61] Art. 15, Edict of 1716.

[62] The discussion concerning the registration of the Edict is summarized in Peabody (1996), p. 18. Peabody has found primary material confirming registration by the Parlements of Dijon and Bretagne. The registration by the Parlement of Bretagne is also confirmed by Pruitt, "The Opposition of

reason for the Parisian refusal has been linked by Sue Peabody to the strong presence of Jansenist thought in the Parisian Parlement. This was a Catholic theological movement which was especially important in France, but eventually denounced by the Vatican in 1713 through the papal bull Ubigenitus. Apparently, Jansenist thinkers believed that this edict touched on a matter of religion. When a Jansenist scholar called Pierre Lemerre was consulted on the matter by Joly de Fleury, the *avocat général* of the Parlement of Paris, he argued against registering this edict, on the basis that it would be in violation of an indigenous French tradition of liberty and freedom. The Parlement seems to have followed this advice and did not register the edict. As the presence of slaves cannot have been but marginal in Paris at this time, the royal authorities did not press the matter any further. [63]

5.2.3.1 Jean Boucaux V. Verdelin: A Judgment in Favour of Liberty

The Parisian refusal to register the Edict of 1716 only came to the fore when the first case on slavery was heard by the Admiralty of France: that of Jean Boucaux against his master Monsieur Verdelin.[64] The case was so important because it was well-documented and published in the *causes célèbres*, provided ample ammunition for lawyers in subsequent cases, and because it set the Admiralty of France's first precedent to free slaves that petitioned it.[65] The facts of the case were quite straightforward. Jean Boucaux was the slave of the Governor of Cap Français and his wife in the French colony of Saint Domingue (present-day Haiti). After the governor died, his wife, Madame de Beaumanoir, remarried Monsieur Verdelin, a sergeant in the king's army in France. The new couple went to Saint Domingue for dealings regarding the inheritance of the first husband of Beaumanoir. When the couple was set to return for France, they decided to take Boucaux with them, after having received permission from the new governor of Cap Français. They disembarked in La Rochelle,

the Law to the Law: Race, Slavery, and the Law in Nantes, 1715–1778," 156. In a more recent article, Erick Noël also held that the edict was registered in the Parlements of Bordeaux and Normandy, Érick Noël, "L'esclavage dans la france moderne," *Dix-huitième siècle* 39, no. 1 (2007): 367. Various scholars have claimed registration in several other Parlements, but they have not provided primary references to ascertain this. Whilst I have not been in the position to verify any registrations myself, I could point out one extra Parlement which most probably did registered the Edict of 1716. As is clear from George de Ghewiet's 1736 *Institutions du droit belgique*, the *Parlement de Flandres* was amongst those registering it. It was Alan Watson who noted this reference, although he believed it was an exception to the freedom principle of Belgium. It has to be borne in mind though that, ever since the 1668 Treaty of Aix-la-Chapelle, the areas under the *ressort* of the Parlement of Flanders, merely a very small part of territory that formerly belonged to the Spanish Netherlands, had been French territory, de Ghewiet (1736), pp. 78–79; Bély (2007), p. 230; Watson (1989), p. 107.

[63] Peabody (1996), pp. 19–22. Although it was up to the Parlement itself to decide whether or not to register a royal law, the *parquet* would also make its own report indicating whether it was in favour of registration or not. This would be reported to the Parlement. Mousnier (1974), pp. 375–378.

[64] Excerpts of the case before the Admiralty of France can be found in Boulle and Peabody (2014), pp. 51–54. I have made use of the full report, which can be found in de Pitaval (1750), pp. 333–416.

[65] Peabody (1996), pp. 23–24.

registered him at the admiralty, and took him to their home, where he served as a cook for almost 10 years. However, Boucaux married in secret, and this raised the ire of his master. Relations between the two soured, and when Verdelin feared that Boucaux would flee from his house, he had Boucaux imprisoned in Paris. Boucaux applied to the Admiralty of France to receive his freedom and also claimed back wages, and the court set a hearing.[66]

Mallet, Boucaux's lawyer, opened his plea by referring to slavery as against nature but instituted by the laws of war, and by going over what he perceived as the history of slavery in France. Crediting Christianity for the decline of slavery, Mallet subsequently referred to many of the historic precedents to establish the French freedom principle. He skilfully connected the various instances to give the idea of one seamless story of the French freedom principle. The 1315 *ordonnance* of Louis X, an example from Toulouse, the history of the Siege of Metz and references to Bodin and Loisel were all used to establish the French freedom principle. The Edict of 1685 was acknowledged, but its functioning limited to the French colonies. When it came to the Edict of 1716, Mallet pointed at the many provisions which were not met: one could doubt whether "cooking" qualified as a *métier* (thus contravening Art. 2); the permission which Verdelin received from the governor of Cap François lacked details such as the name, age and appearance of Boucaux (thus also contravening Art. 2); and Verdelin had seemingly settled in France for good (contravening Art. 15). Mallet concluded that Boucaux thus had to be declared free.[67]

Tribard, Verdelin's lawyer, disagreed. Interestingly, he did acknowledge the validity of the French freedom principle, seeing it as a *prérogative éminente* of the French kingdom. However, he believed that the Edict of 1685 and the Edict of 1716 had created clear exceptions to the principle. The first claim is remarkable, as it argues in favour of some kind of "one imperial law" for both metropolitan and colonial France. Tribard analyzed various provisions of the Edict of 1685, showing how these were all meant to restrict the slave in his everyday life. According to Tribard, it was inconceivable that this law would not apply anymore if a black slave would cross from one part of the French realm to another part. "N'est ce pas toujours la même loi qui les fuit partout", Mallet asked. Because of the Edict of 1685, the French freedom principle only applied to foreigners, but not Frenchman, arriving in France with their slaves. Tribard tried to bend the examples to his benefit, noting that they all preceded the Edict of 1685 and all dealt with foreigners coming to France with their slaves. Though this was the main point, he (rather unconvincingly) also asserted that the formalities of the Edict of 1716 were met. He ended with a public order argument, duly noting that a decision in favour of the slave might well cause uproar in the colonies.[68]

Next, Le Clerc du Brillet, the *procureur du roi* in the Admiralty of France, offered his views and clearly sided with Boucaux. He also acknowledged the French freedom principle, made the same misconstruction of the *ordonnance* of 1315 as Mallet and

[66]de Pitaval (1750), pp. 333–336.
[67]Ibid., pp. 336–345.
[68]Ibid., pp. 345–363.

added some other references to assert the freedom principle. He referred to the 1571 decision of the Parlement of Bordeaux, the case involving King Henry III, and Grotius' views on the French freedom principle. Brillet is the only one of the three who mentioned that neither the Edict of 1685 nor the Edict of 1716 had been registered by the Parlement of Paris. Given his own position as a representative of the king, he did not believe this to be a conclusive element to settle the case. He quoted the Edict of 1685 verbatim and limited its sphere of action to the colonies. He did acknowledge the validity of the Edict of 1716 in France. To dispose with this argument, Brillet reviewed whether the conditions of the Edict had been met. He came to the same conclusions as Mallet, even adding that Verdelin's registration at the Admiralty of La Rochelle had not happened within eight days of disembarking (thus contravening Art. 3). Brillet finished by referring to Tribard's "public order" argument, asserting that the court ought not to take this into consideration.[69]

The Admiralty of France then made a decision, holding that Boucaux was free as from his entry in France ("libre de sa personne and biens dès son arrive en France"). They also awarded him back wages for all his previous work. Unfortunately, as with almost all French court cases up until the end of the *Ancien Régime*, we have no idea on which grounds the court made its judgment, as French courts usually did not provide their rationale.[70] It might be that the court considered the non-registration to be the most important matter, but the case might as well have been decided on the merits of the Edict of 1716. The case did not end there, as Verdelin succeeded in appealing the case to the *Conseil du Roi*.[71] The *Conseil* decided that Boucaux remained free, but cancelled the award of back wages, banned Boucaux from Paris and prohibited him from returning to the colonies.[72]

5.2.3.2 Tightening the Reins: The Declaration of 1738

Three months after this case, the king issued the Declaration of 1738 "*Concernant les nègres esclaves des colonies*" in order to modify the Edict of 1716. Quite possibly, the case of Jean Boucaux might have had something to do with it, as the preambles of the declaration certainly point to some of the procedural conditions that were

[69] Ibid., pp. 363–391.

[70] French *Ancien Régime* courts (especially the Parlements) would normally not motivate their judgments. For the Parlements, this was partially related to the fact that they wanted to stress their sovereign status and felt they did not need to explain themselves. It also had to do with the formal lack of precedential value of judgments, and the fear of many courts that motivating their judgments would encourage appeals. Courts were only obliged to motivate their judgment after the French Revolution. Rigaudière (2010), p. 685.

[71] As the King was the highest and ultimate source of law, the *Conseil du Roi* could make *arrets d'évocation* and *arrêts de cassation,* revoking sentences of any other French court. Evocation could happen on the initiative of the council itself, but a party could always ask the council whether it would consider its case. Ibid., pp. 624–625.

[72] *La Couronne intervient dans l'Affaire Boucaux, 1738–1739* in Boulle and Peabody (2014), p. 55. Peabody opines that the council's decision not to allow Boucaux to return to the colonies might show that Tribard's public order rationale did touch a nerve. Peabody (1996), p. 40.

breached by Verdelin. Equally, reference was made to the "bad habits" that slaves learned in France, and a fear of a mixture of French and black blood inspired the legislation as well.[73]

In terms of content, the Declaration of 1738 kept the Edict of 1716 intact but tightened the conditions to bring black slaves to France. Procedurally speaking, newly arrived slaves also had to be registered at the admiralty of the place where they would live in France, besides the admiralty of the port of arrival.[74] Second, the freedom principle was limited even more. When the procedural conditions (registration, permission, etc.) were not met, the slave would not gain his freedom, but would be confiscated *au profit du roi* and sent back to the colonies.[75] The same punishment was meted out for masters who currently held slaves in France, but did not register them within three months of the publication of the declaration. These slaves also had to be sent back to the colonies within one year.[76] For the first time, the period during which colonial inhabitants could keep their slaves in France was restricted as well, as the period was capped at three years.[77] One exception was allowed: colonists planning to keep their slaves for a longer period in France could pay 1000 *livres* to the colonial authorities in advance.[78] Finally, the declaration opted for a blanket marriage ban for any *esclave nègre* in France and ordered that slaves could only be enfranchised through their master's testament.[79]

Registration was problematic again, as the Parlement of Paris, probably as the only Parlement this time, refused to register the declaration. The link between Paris' refusal to register the law and the declaration's references to slavery was made explicitly by later French authorities.[80] As before, all of the Parlements in regions with ties

[73]Peabody (1996), p. 37; Boulle (2014), p. 25; *Déclaration du roi, concernant les nègres esclaves des colonies, 15 décembre 1738* in Boulle and Peabody (2014), pp. 64–67.

[74]Art. 3, Declaration of 1738.

[75]Art. 4, Declaration of 1738.

[76]Art. 9, Declaration of 1738.

[77]Art. 6, Declaration of 1738.

[78]Art. 8, Declaration of 1738.

[79]Art. 10 and 11, Declaration of 1738.

[80]See, for example, the *Rapport de Sartine au Conseil des dépêches, proposant la nouvelle loi sur les noirs, [9 août 1777]* in Boulle and Peabody (2014), pp. 95–99.

to the Atlantic slave trade did register the law.[81] Despite Paris' refusal, it did acknowledge the Declaration of 1738 in one respect, as records were kept of slaves who were brought to the capital.[82] Registration or not, the Count of Maurepas, then Marine minister, did try to enforce the law in 1741, when the first period of three years was about to end. Administrative correspondence between the Count and the authorities of La Rochelle (within the *ressort* of the Parlement of Paris) shows how he wanted warnings to be issued to all those not in conformity with the law. Some local research proved that neglect of the law was widespread in La Rochelle, as almost all slaves there belonged to non-colonists, and almost no-one was planning to send the slaves back. Although the authorities did try to enforce the law every now and then in this early period, they soon neglected the issue, certainly so after the Count of Maurepas fell in disgrace in 1749.[83] Because of this neglect by the highest authorities, it is necessary to look to the situation "on the ground" in both Paris and the Atlantic port cities.

In the Admiralty of France, where the Edict of 1716 and Declaration of 1738 remained unregistered, a flurry of lawsuits asking for freedom started to pour in. Whilst the court did not hear any cases in the years 1740–1749, it heard 11 freedom suits in the next decade and 71 in the ensuing one.[84] In all of these cases, the slave won his freedom.[85]Given the slaves were not confiscated *au profit du roi,* one can safely opine that the court must have been making its decisions on the basis of non-registration, and combined this with an acknowledgement of the French freedom principle.

Peabody opines that there might have been various reasons it took so long before slaves started using the Parisian courts to ask for their freedom: a slave would only go to court if he was unhappy in his circumstances; he would need to have access to legal representation and the means to afford it; and few of the lawyers themselves

[81]Again, there is some divergence amongst scholars. Peabody has found a printed copy of the Declaration of 1738 which specifically refers to its registration by all the Parlements, the sovereign councils and *conseils supérieurs* of the colonies, except for Paris. Boulle and Pruitt concur in this opinion. Erick Noël agrees that it was not registered by the Parlement of Paris, but adds Toulouse, Pau, Aix, Nancy, Metz, Arras and Douai to this list. He makes use of the *Rapport de Sartine au Conseil des dépêches, proposant la nouvelle loi sur les noirs, [9 août 1777]*. This report, however, just mentions Dijon, Grenoble, Besançon and Metz as having registered "*Ces lois*", meaning both the Edict of 1716 and the Declaration of 1738 (Noël asserts they only registered the Declaration of 1738), but does not seem to exclude registration by other Parlements (given the report mentions "*tels que*"). Koufinkana believes it was not registered by Paris and Toulouse, but does not mention a primary source for Toulouse's apparent refusal. Peabody (1996), p. 38; Boulle (2014), p. 26; Pruitt (2007), p. 159; Koufinkana (2008), p. 106; Noël (2007), p. 369.

[82]According to Peabody, this can be explained by the fact that the admiralty clerk could charge a fee for registering these declarations, and because a refusal would be seen as a political statement of a lower administrative clerk. Peabody (1996), p. 39.

[83]Boulle (2014), p. 28.

[84]*Tableau des requêtes présentées à l'amirauté de France, 1730–1790* in Boulle and Peabody (2014), p. 73.

[85]Peabody (1996), p. 55.

probably initially realized the opening that was created by Paris' non-registration of the slave legislation.[86]

When the number of slaves asking for their freedom strongly rose after 1760, there were various reasons: another highly published case in 1759, plus a 1762 ordinance of the Admiralty of France ordering blacks to be registered, probably increased attention to the issue of personal status. Likewise, Peabody believes that lawyers might have been tempted to take these cases because of the remuneration, and the experience and chance of winning they offered. Personal sympathy for the cause of the client could have come into play as well.[87] The pay argument is an interesting one, given that the one Parisian lawyer who defended 52 slaves did not seem to have been driven by abolitionist sentiment. In some cases, there is evidence of an informal network of free blacks helping slaves, but another source of remuneration could have been the fact that Parisian courts would sometimes grant back-wages to former slaves. However, as this was apparently quite rare, the arguments of legal experience and personal sympathy might have come more into play.[88]

The slave's quest for freedom did not necessarily end in the Admiralty of France. Of the 6 slaves who were declared free in this court in 1755, at least four where shipped back to the colonies by an *arrêt* of the *Conseil du Roi*.[89] Although no-one has traced the exact number of cases in which the King intervened, one scholar opines that these few instances were not isolated.[90] Moreover, the records show that in various cases, slaves were put under the protection of the Admiralty of France, which requested more information before it would deliver a judgment. As there was no final decision in several of these cases, one can presume that these slaves were sent back on special order of the King to the colonies.[91]

In one instance, the Parlement of Paris itself got the opportunity to assess a freedom request of a slave. Francisque, a slave from Pondicherry, India, had been declared free by the Admiralty of France. His master decided to appeal the case to the Parlement of Paris. The case is interesting because the *mémoire* for the slave was published by his lawyer and showed some marked differences in the arguments being used vis-à-vis

---

[86]Ibid., pp. 51–52.

[87]Again, this is a very interesting argument that still needs to be further explored. The fact that so many blacks appealed for their liberty in Paris, could mean that there was a network systematically informing black slaves of the possibility of freedom. Clearly, some lawyers were involved in this network. Professor Pierre Boulle hints that some lawyers were motivated to take slavery cases because of grievances against the absolutist tendencies of the crown. I wish to thank Professor Boulle for sharing some of his thoughts regarding the reasons Parisian lawyers took on these cases with me. Private correspondence with Professor Pierre Boulle, 13/05/2017.

[88]Peabody (1996), pp. 92–94. There is no exact data on the number of slaves who asked and received back wages from the Admiralty of France. It is Professor Sue Peabody's understanding that many petitioners asked for them, but that few of these requests were probably granted. Private correspondence with Professor Sue Peabody, 27/04/2017.

[89]Ibid., p. 56.

[90]Koufinkana (2008), pp. 102–104. In Professor Peabody's understanding, this did not happen in the majority of the cases, though the issue is still subject to further research. Private correspondence with Professor Sue Peabody, 27/04/2017.

[91]Boulle and Peabody (2014), p. 81.

the case of Jean Boucaux. Whilst the second argument of Francisque's lawyers was still based on the non-respect of the formalities of the Edict of 1716 and Declaration of 1738, the main argument used this time was that the provisions of these laws did not apply to people from the Indian subcontinent.[92] The Indian subcontinent was seen as fertile and governed by legitimate monarchs, whereas Africans needed to be disciplined by the Europeans. And though it was true that the skin colour of Indians resembled those of blacks, surely their nose, lips, and hairs were different ("Qu'ils n'ont point le nez si écrasé, si aplati, les lèvres si épaisses, si saillantes, en ce que, au lieu de ce duvet cotonneux & crêpé qui couvre la tête des Africains, ils portent de longues et belles chevelures"). In short, Francisque resembled more of a European than an African and had to be declared free according to his lawyer.[93] Eventually, Parlement granted him his freedom, but it is unclear whether this was done on the basis of non-registration, or on the basis of Francisque's Indian heritage.[94] The importance of this case, was that it showed that a more race based ideology had set in within the French elite by the second half of the eighteenth century. This has been linked to an increase in social stratification in the colonies, and the fact that the influence of colonists on the highest echelons of French metropolitan society was on the rise.[95]

One should bear in mind that the quality of Peabody's work on Paris tends to obscure one element: both the Edict of 1716 and the Declaration of 1738 were registered by the Parlement of Bordeaux and the Parlement of Bretagne, which included the principal port cities of Bordeaux and Nantes. In those cities, it does not seem that the soil was free.[96]

More than one-third of the French slave voyages originated in Nantes, the city was economically dependent of the slave trade and the black presence was very much visible in contemporary reports.[97] One inhabitant of the city also wrote a *mémoire* in 1738 advocating in favour of the position of Monsieur Verdelin, Jean Boucaux's

---

[92]One reason for the relative neglect of the Declaration of 1738 is obviously that the slave would be confiscated instead of declared free if the formalities were not met. Peabody (1996), p. 59.

[93]*Mémoire signifié pour le nommé Francisque, Indien de nation, 1759* in Boulle and Peabody (2014), pp. 75–78.

[94]Peabody (1996), pp. 69–70. Erick Noël has also noted the existence of a similar case in Southern France, where an enslaved Indian woman named Ketna was declared free by the Parlement of Aix, see Noël (2019).

[95]Peabody (1996), p. 68.

[96]Between 1730 and 1790, Peabody discovered 154 cases in which the Admiralty of France gave freedom to the slave, next to 93 acts of enfranchisement registered by the court. This means we have a total of 247 freed slaves in Paris. The fact that we also know that more than 600 slaves were registered in Nantes, more than 600 in La Rochelle and more than 1000 in Bordeaux, gives reason to put the number of 247 liberated slaves into perspective. Koufinkana (2008), pp. 47–48.

[97]The black presence in Nantes is discussed in de Wismes (1992), pp. 147–173; Pruitt (2005). de Wismes' work is of more limited use as concerns the legal position of slaves in Nantes, and contains some legal errors (e.g. asserting that the Edict of 1685 stipulated that every slave coming to France became free, which it did not). Pétré-Grenouilleau likewise discusses the impact of the slave trade in Nantes, but only mentions the issue of black slaves in the city in passing, Pétré-Grenouilleau (1998), pp. 132–133.

owner.[98] We also know of one case involving the slave Catherine Morgan in Nantes in 1746. After she was beaten by her master, she fled him, and the case eventually came before the Admiralty Court of Nantes. In this case, the Admiralty found that the slave had not been registered by her master upon arrival, and confiscated her *au profit du roi*. We lack a thorough analysis of the judgments of the Admiralty of Nantes, but given that the Declaration of 1738 was registered by the Parlement of Bretagne, there is no reason to assume that this was no standard judgment.[99] In fact, Dwain C. Pruitt, who wrote extensively on the situation in Nantes, went as far as to say that the Nantais did not embrace the "freedom principle", but rather advocated for an "unfreedom principle" which protected the property rights of slave owners.[100]

The scarce evidence from Bordeaux points in the same direction. Despite the lack of judgments, we do know that the number of slaves leaving Bordeaux surged in the immediate aftermath of the Declaration of 1738 but returned to normal levels soon after. Likewise, we know of cases of slaves who stayed for 12, 16, 24, 42 and even 49 years in Bordeaux. These are all flagrant breaches of the Declaration of 1738.[101] All this should lead us to conclude that in France, two opposing forces were at work: freedom for those slaves that were able to petition the courts in Paris, but respect for the rights of proprietors elsewhere.

5.2.3.3 From Status to Race: The Police Des Noirs

The Change to Racial Bias

If the case of Francisque served as a first example to make distinctions not so much on the basis of status (slave vs. free) but on the basis of race (African vs. Europeans/Indians), more was to come. In the wake of the Seven Years War, the colonial planters increased their sway over the Marine Department. The two next Marine Ministers, the Duke of Choiseul and the Duke of Praslin, who respectively led the ministry in 1761–1766 and 1766–1770, were well connected to the colonial *haute société*. After the war was over, the Duke of Choiseul even drafted a circular letter ordering all black slaves to leave the kingdom. He rescinded his order several months after, probably swayed by the fact that the colonists themselves were not too happy to see black slaves return from France (as they believed those slaves to have become insolent by their stay in the metropolis).[102]

[98] Pruitt (2007), p. 156.

[99] Peabody (1996), pp. 41–48; Boulle (2014), p. 27.

[100] Pruitt (2005), p. 51.

[101] One chapter in André Saugera's work is concerned with "*Les Noirs en Guyenne*", but he does not discuss any judgments of the Admiralty of Bordeaux. Dominique Rogers surveys much of the previous historical research on the black presence in Bordeaux, does not discuss court cases, but points to the many flagrant breaches of the Declaration of 1738 in Aquitaine. Saugera (1995), pp. 287–310; Rogers (2001), pp. 103–121.

[102] Boulle (2006b), pp. 23–25.

This measure still made a distinction between free and enslaved blacks, but this was soon to change. Remarkably, the racial bias also became a live force in the Admiralty of France. In the wake of yet another case in which a slave was freed, Guillaume Poncet de la Grave (1725–1803), the new *procureur du roi*, started denouncing the presence of blacks in France.[103] Though he agreed that slaves coming before the court had to be freed in accordance with the law, he also believed that blacks committed many crimes and that they had turned Paris into a public market in which blacks were freely sold.[104] In any case, his lament was the occasion for the Admiral of France, the Duke of Penthièvre, to make an ordinance in 1762 ordering all blacks, both free and slave, to register themselves at the admiralty court, in order to get an assessment of the size of the "black problem".[105] This blurring of the lines of status in favour of race was not limited to this instance. Choiseul's successor, Praslin, made clear in administrative correspondence that it was his intention to limit the possibilities of the mixture of blood between black and white in France ("*sang-mêlés*") and believed that there was a clear distinction between the *race nègre* and the *race indienne*.[106]

In the short term though, not much changed. Slaves were still freed by the Admiralty of France, and the court even started to register unconditional manumissions of slaves by their masters at the end of the 1750s. This contradicted the Declaration of 1738, which only allowed manumissions by will.[107] One case drew most attention, namely that of the slave Roc in 1770, because the *mémoire* of his lawyer, Henrion de Pansey, was published again. Substantively, the lawyer recounted the familiar arguments in favour of the slave, but also showed himself as an abolitionist. Next to this, he laid much stress on the necessity of the registration of the law ("Mépriser la formalité de l'enrégistrement, citer dans les tribunaux une loi qui n'en est point revêtue, c'est choquer la constitution"), and also seemed to be making the link between slavery and political domination.[108]

All this occurred just when France was embroiled in a standoff between Louis XV and his Chancellor Maupeou on the one hand and the Parlement of Paris on the other hand. The direct cause of the conflict was a case in which the Parlement of Paris took sides with the Parlement of Bretagne regarding an unpopular provincial governor, but the king's authority vis-à-vis the Parlements had been in decline for far longer. Maupeou eventually chose for an unprecedented move, abolishing the Parlement of Paris, and with it the Admiralty of France, between 1771 and 1774.[109]

---

[103] For a short overview of Poncet de la Grave's views on the black presence in France, see Rachel Tolin Schultz (2017).

[104] *Guillaume Poncet de la Grave dénonce les abus causes par la presence de noirs à Paris. Réquisitoire à l'Amirauté de France, 1762* in Boulle and Peabody (2014), pp. 79–80. This was clearly exaggerated, given the very limited presence of blacks in France. Peabody (1996), p. 87.

[105] Peabody (1996), pp. 73–85.

[106] Boulle and Peabody (2014), p. 63.

[107] Peabody (1996), p. 91.

[108] *Pierre Paul Nicolas Henrion de Pensey [i.e. Pensey], Mémoire pour le nommé Roc, nègre, contre le sieur Poupet négociant, 1770* in Boulle and Peabody (2014), pp. 88–90.

[109] Shennan (1968), pp. 316–320; Peabody (1996), p. 105.

The Declaration of 1777

After Maupeou fell out of grace in 1774, the Parlement of Paris and the Admiralty of France were re-established. Soon after, the Admiralty came to a new standoff against measures taken by Versailles. So far, the Admiralty of France had always acquiesced with the occasional *arrêts* of the *Conseil du Roi* annulling one of its sentences, or with the explicit orders of the King to have a slave sent back to the colonies. The Admiralty of France now decided it did not admit this disrespect for its authority any longer. In a 1775 case, the court gave freedom to a slave called Jean-Louis and placed him under the protection of the court whilst they were deciding on his request for back wages. When the slave's master came back with an *ordre du Roi* to arrest Jean-Louis and ship him back to the colonies notwithstanding this protection, the Admiralty of France had enough. His jailer had to appear before the court, and the Admiralty threatened him not to release Jean-Louis to his master or anyone else, under the threat of severe penalties.[110] Nor was this the only instance when the two authorities came into conflict, as the same thing happened when the Admiralty wanted to free the slave of the well-connected Count of Choiseul-Gouffier. Likewise, in the published case of P*ampy* and *Julienne v. Mèndes France*, the Jewish slave-owner Mèndes France openly boasted that he would ensure that his freed slaves were arrested by the king.[111]

Something had to be done. Whilst Pierre-Joseph De La Haye, the *lieutenant général* of the Admiralty of France sent a request to then Minister of the Marine Antoine de Sartine, who was in office between 1774 and 1780, to change this state of affairs, Poncet de la Grave also sent a proposal to the minister with his own views on possible new legislation.[112] Though nothing came of the latter proposal, Sartine did intervene. In September 1776, *lettres patentes* asking for a suspension of all cases regarding the personal status ("*état*") of blacks, pending new royal legislation, were published and registered in the Parlement of Paris.[113] A legislative committee was created a few days after, and the law was drafted by August 1777. When Sartine presented it to the *Conseil des dépêches* in 1777, the gist of the law was clear. Sartine acknowledged the problems with the previous laws, which had not been registered by the Parlement of Paris. This had created a situation in which the Parisian Courts freed slaves on the basis of the French freedom principle ("L'inconvénient de l'opposition de la loi à la loi", as Sartine called it). In addition, a race related argument played a role. Sartine believed that the presence of *nègres* (and other coloured people) was multiplying in the kingdom, and that the French blood and skin colour was slowly

---

[110]Boulle (2006b), p. 20.

[111]Whereas Boulle puts most stress on this conflict between the Admiralty of France and the contrary *ordres du roi*, Peabody, Abanime and Pruitt focus on the case of *Pampy* and *Julienne v. Mèndes France* as the trigger for new royal legislation. Erick Noël gives attention to the governmental connections of the Count of Choisseul-Gouffier. Boulle (2006a), pp. 19–21; Peabody (1996), pp. 107–111; Pruitt (2005), p. 82; Abanime (1979), p. 24; Noël (2007), p. 374.

[112]The *lieutenant général* was the most important subordinate of the Admiral of France. One of Poncet de la Grave's proposals was to create a special court with competence for questions of the personal status of blacks in France. Boulle and Peabody (2014), pp. 83–84.

[113]The *lettres patentes* are partially reprinted in Koufinkana (2008), p. 89.

being altered because of this importation. The previous motives to bring blacks into the kingdom, namely to teach them a craft or to instruct them in the Catholic faith, had become less important by now. As a result, whilst acknowledging the status quo for blacks that were already in France, Sartine wanted to close the gates of France for new blacks trying to enter the country, both those that were free and enslaved. To counter any opposition from the Parlement of Paris, he had consulted with the Parlement's president before and ensured that the law did not include references to *libres* or *esclaves*. Henceforth, black people were to be legally defined as *domestiques noirs*, whilst free became "qui ne sont point en service" and enslaved "en leur service".[114]

When the declaration of 1777 *pour la Police des noirs* was presented at 9 August 1777, the goal was clear: France had to get rid of its black presence. When it came to "noir, mulâtre, ou autres gens de couleur" in someone's service (the slaves), a blanket ban for their introduction in France was instituted.[115] Likewise, people of colour that were personally free were banned from entering the kingdom.[116] Only one concession towards the colonists was kept: they could take one slave to serve them whilst travelling to France, but upon arrival, the slaves had to be put in *dépôts* which were to be established at the major French port cities. They were kept and fed there (for which the master had to consign 1000 livres) and taken back to the colonies by the first available ship. Whilst they were in a *dépôt* on French soil, their personal status could not change.[117] All people of colour currently in France, both the enslaved and the free, had to be registered at the seat of the admiralty court of their domicile within one month.[118] With respect to the enslaved, the article seemed to imply that, after this delay of one month, people of colour could only remain in the service of their masters if they did so out of their own consent, hinting at manumission ("Voulons que, passé le délai, il ne puisse retenir à leur service lesdits noirs, que de leur consentement").[119] Abanime opines that this article was necessary to ensure the support of the Parlement de Paris.[120] All this was supplemented by two *arrêts* of the *Conseil du Roi*, which granted an extra delay of two months to masters wishing to send their slaves back to the colonies, and also ordered a blanket intermarriage ban between *blancs* and *noirs*.[121] Sartine took special care to ensure

[114] *Rapport de Sartine au Conseil des dépêches, proposant la nouvelle loi sur les noirs [9 août 1777]* in Boulle and Peabody (2014), pp. 95–99.

[115] *Déclaration du Roi pour la Police des noirs, donnée à Versailles le 9 août 1777, enregistrée en parlement [de Paris] le 27 desdits mois et an* in Peabody and Boulle (2014), pp. 99–102.

Art. 1 declaration of 1777. For the sake of consistency, I will still refer to slaves when dealing with this category.

[116] Art. 2, Declaration of 1777.

[117] Art. 4, 5 and 13, declaration of 1777.

[118] Art. 9 and 10, declaration of 1777.

[119] Art. 9, declaration of 1777.

[120] Abanime (1979), pp. 26–27.

[121] *Arrêt du Conseil d'État du Roi, concernant le retour des noirs, mulâtres [etc.] aux colonies, du 7 septembre 1777* and *Arrêt du Conseil d'État du Roi, du 5 avril 1778, concernant les mariages des noirs, mulâtres, ou autres gens de couleur* in Boulle and Peabody (2014), pp. 102–103, 121.

the declaration's registration, which happened in all the Parlements, including Paris, and the West Indian *Conseils Souverains* over the next months.[122]

Paris Versus the Atlantic: The Rift Remains

At first, the declaration of 1777 seemed to be well respected, as 125 new declarations were made in Paris during the first month of the enforcement of the Police des Noirs.[123] Over time, Poncet de la Grave even swayed the minister of the Marine to start a *cartouche* system in Paris. All coloured people had to register with the Admiralty of France, after which they would receive a certificate. If blacks were found without bearing a certificate, they could be arrested.[124]

This relative ease did not endure for long. In fact, despite the fact that one would expect there to be no more slaves in France (given no new slaves would have been allowed in, and all the slaves that lived in France before the declaration would have had to leave the country), this simply was not so. Starting from the spring of 1778, the Admiralty of France started entertaining petitions for freedom again. Between 1780 and 1789, they freed 43 slaves and registered 58 acts of manumission.[125] What is more, in a slave case from 1786, the Admiralty and an *ordre du roi* again came to loggerheads for the same reasons as in 1775. In Paris, things did not really change much then.[126]

One of the reasons that Paris could entertain new freedom lawsuits undoubtedly had to do with the Atlantic port cities. Although all Parlements duly recorded the declaration of 1777, colonists in Nantes, Bordeaux and other ports in France were obviously not amused by the fact that they could no longer bring slaves with them or had to send their old slaves back. This opposition is visible in many ways. For example, certain provincial intendants were very reluctant to provide Versailles with information on blacks resident in their city, and had to be warned by special letters from the royal administration.[127] Likewise, the head of the Admiralty Court of Bordeaux sent a lengthy rebuffal on the quality of the declaration's provisions to Minister Sartine, only to be ignored.[128] In the same way, Bordeaux had to be pressed by the royal authorities to establish a *dépôt*, after the authorities had initially said that they did not have a suitable place for this in the city.[129] Other evidence points to instances of fraud, non-registration and special requests for additional time to retain slaves.[130]

The picture from Nantes is largely the same. First, the Parlement of Bretagne only registered the Declaration after it received clarification from Versailles concerning

[122] Boulle (2006a), pp. 27–30.
[123] Peabody (1996), p. 123.
[124] *Arrêt du Conseil d'État pour la Police des noirs, mulâtres [*etc.*] qui sont dans la ville de Paris, du 11 janvier 1778* in Boulle and Peabody (2014), pp. 116–117.
[125] *Tableau des requêtes présentées à l'amirauté de France, 1730–1790* in Ibid., p. 73.
[126] Ibid., p. 113.
[127] McCloy (1961), pp. 50–51.
[128] Boulle and Peabody (2014), pp. 87–88.
[129] Peytraud (1897), p. 392.
[130] Rogers (2001), pp. 104–110.

article 9 of the Declaration of 1777. They wanted confirmation that if a master did register his slave, the slave was not automatically freed after the delay of one month. Versailles allowed this (although this was contradicted by the language of the *Arrêt du Conseil* of 7 September 1777), which shows the duplicity of Sartine in trying to both please the Parlement of Paris and the slave trade interests.[131] Despite this victory, Nantes' opposition to the police des noirs quickly became clear. For example, the *procureur du roi* of the Nantes Admiralty Court was temporarily dismissed from his duties because he was working against the wishes of the central administration in enforcing the declaration of 1777. Although the official had asserted in the summer of 1777 that Nantes was home to 700 blacks, and that black people arrived almost daily, he seemed to be unable to find any of them when the new law came into effect. Likewise, when a group of officials were sent to the city on an inspection tour, they encountered resistance to enforcing the terms of the declaration of 1777 everywhere.[132] It seems quite clear that in this context, slaves still entered the country every now and then.

The Breakdown of the Police Des Noirs

Although the law did have its effect in the short term, and a substantial number of slaves left France, it unravelled few years after it was made. The problems were many: it was difficult to find adequate *dépôts*, and paying for their upkeep proved to be an issue as well. Admiralties were loath to register slaves because the declaration of 1777 required them to do this for free (*gratis*). Furthermore, exceptions were quickly made to the *dépôt* regime. Humanitarian grounds might come into play, exemplified by a case in which a black slave serving as the nurse of the babies of a colonial proprietor and breastfeeding them could not be kept in the *dépôt*. Likewise, some slaveholders were highly connected and undoubtedly could fetch exceptions for themselves. Blacks who were already in the kingdom and belonged to a powerful lord could thus afford to ignore the declaration.[133]

The subsequent *Arrêts du Conseils* also helped to obfuscate the issue. They contradicted previous clarifications to Nantes, and the *arrêt* that had started the cartouche system also mentioned that it had to be given to both free and enslaved ("s'ils sont en service") blacks, though the latter category could technically speaking no longer exist in France.[134]

Although the government realised that its efforts had failed, it did not try to make any other all-encompassing legislation on this issue during the remainder of the *Ancien Régime*. Although a new legislative committee proposed a second attempt to send all coloured people out of the kingdom, the Marine Minister was happy enough with prolonging the Parisian cartouche system in 1783.[135] Finally, in 1789, amidst

---

[131] Pruitt (2007), pp. 164–165; Abanime (1979), pp. 26–27.

[132] Ibid., pp. 164–174.

[133] Boulle (2006b), pp. 33–37.

[134] Ibid.

[135] *Arrêt du Conseil d'État du Roi, Pour le renouvellement des cartouches des noirs qui sont à Paris, du 23 mars 1783* in Boulle and Peabody (2014), pp. 129–130.

revolutionary fervour in France, a new embargo disallowing travel of coloured people in between France and the colonies was established. The rationale was that it would be for the best if these persons did not take cognisance of the Revolutionary ideas taking France in their grip.[136]

5.2.3.4 The Revolution: Disappearance, Return and Decline of Slavery in France

At the end of the *Ancien Régime*, some abolitionist thought had set in metropolitan France, though it remained more of an elite phenomenon in comparison with the mass English movement.[137] Attacks were made against the legitimacy of black slavery, though the idea of the intellectual inferiority of black people did remain in sway. In 1788, this led to the foundation of the *Société des Amis des Noirs*, which tried to sway electors for the States General to include requests for the abolition of the French slave trade and slavery.[138] However, despite references to human liberty in the *Déclaration des Droits de l'Homme et du Citoyen*, slavery was not discussed initially.[139]

Slavery finally got addressed in the period of the *Assemblée Constituante*. Abolitionism was not evident, because there were five interest groups at work. The first one was the *Société des Amis des Noirs*. Second, there were the *Commission des colons résidant à Paris*, alongside the *Société de correspondants des colons*. Both defended the interests of the white planters, but the latter (better known as the *Club Massiac*) supported more autonomy for the colonies. Next came the *Députés extraordinaires des manufactures et du commerce*, defending the interests of the ports associated with the slave trade, who usually sided with the white colonists. Finally, there was a group of *Colons Américains* representing the interests of the *libres gens de couleur*, who wanted true equality between them and the white elite, though they failed at securing representation in the *Assemblée*.[140] Given these strong lobbies in favour of preserving the status quo for colonial slaves, the result reached was not surprising. In 1791, two decrees were made. The most socio-politically important one of 24 September 1791 decided that the status of colonial slaves had to be decided by the colonial assemblies themselves, thus essentially preserving slavery in the colonies. However, when it came to metropolitan France, the opposite solution was chosen. For the first time, the French freedom principle became unequivocally part of the

---

[136] *Le ministre de la Marine declare un embargo sur les voyages des gens de couleur entre les colonies et la metropole, automne 1789* in Ibid., 130.

[137] In general, the somewhat lukewarm attitude of the Continent towards the abolitionist movement has often been contrasted with the vigorousness of this movement in the United Kingdom at the end of the eighteenth century. Drescher (1994), p. 65.

[138] Koufinkana (2008), pp. 121–125.

[139] Boulle and Peabody (2014), p. 133.

[140] Ibid, pp. 134–136.

written law, as the Decree of September 28, 1791 stated that: "Tout individu est libre aussitôt qu'il est entré en France".[141]

Colonial slavery was eventually dealt with few years later, during the period of the *Convention Nationale*. Although the official report indicated that there was a general consensus to abolish slavery, this was certainly not the case. In fact, when slavery was abolished all over the French realm at 4 February 1794, this was a panic measure intended to get the black population on the side of the French as their colonies were invaded by England and Spain.[142]

The question of the relationship between the French legal order and slavery did not end here.[143] Napoléon re-established slavery in the French colonies in 1802 and 1803. At the same time, regulations concerning blacks coming to France were made. Inspired by the Declaration of 1777, the consuls made an *arrêté* in 1802, which was supplemented by a ministerial *arrêté* in 1807. Using the same terms as the Declaration of 1777 (thus avoiding references to slaves), the former ordered a blanket ban for all foreigners to brings *noirs, mulâtres, ou autres gens de couleur* into the country. However, free blacks and blacks coming with their masters (slaves) could enter the kingdom if they had the requisite permission. [144] The second law went further and decided that any black individual still arriving in France had to be kept at a *dépôt* and sent back.[145] Strictly speaking, the law of 1791 was not abolished, but the French authorities at least did not seem keen to enforce it anymore.

During the period of the Restoration (1815–1830), the government started to revert back to a policy of making a distinction between *libres de couleur* and slaves. The slave trade had already been officially banned by both Napoléon and Louis XVIII, but the government was not austere in enforcing this ban.[146] As concerns free blacks, an exception was made to this reinstated *Police des Noirs*-like regime. Henceforth,

[141]*Décret du 28 September 1791 (loi du 16 oct. 1791)* in Ibid., 149. Boulle believes that the fact that the two decisions were made so close to one another, might prove that the colonists won the major battle, whilst the codification of the French freedom principle could serve as a sweetener for the interests of the *libres hommes du couleur* and the *Société des Amis des Noirs*. Boulle (2014), p. 37.

[142]Bénot (1993), pp. 349–361.

[143]I am only offering a "*coup d'oeil*" on the status of slavery in France after the first abolition of slavery. This is due to several reasons. First, a thorough review of the nineteenth century freedom principle goes beyond the scope of this work. Second, much work remains to be done on this issue by scholars in comparison with the eighteenth century. Third, in contrast to England, the institutional setup of France changed drastically vis-à-vis the *Ancien Régime*, as Admiralty Courts and Parlements were amongst the first victims of the Revolution. Many primary materials for the nineteenth century are collected in Peabody and Boulle, *Le droit des noirs en France au temps de l'esclavage*, 131–243, to which I would refer the reader for a more ample treatment. Pruitt also discusses the situation in Nantes after the Revolution, which shows much continuity until the black presence in the city had almost completely disappeared in the 1840s. Pruitt (2005), pp. 103–148.

[144]*Arrêté du 13 messidor an X (2 juil. 1802) portant défense aux noirs [*etc.*] d'entrer sans authorisation sur le territoire continental de la République* in Boulle and Peabody (2014), p. 178.

[145]*Arrêté ministériel de juillet 1807, extrait de la lettre du préfet de Loire-Inférieure au maire de Nantes, 3 aôut 1807* in Ibid., 179.

[146]Ibid., 184.

colonial administrators could make discretionary exceptions to the travel bans, in order for (rich) *libres de couleur* to be able to come to France.[147] As concerns slaves, the government continued the *dépôt* policy (70 slaves were in one between 1817 and 1819). However, they also decided that, if a master did not take care to place his slave in a *dépôt* and the slave subsequently fled, they could do nothing.[148] After some such cases, the government tried to impose a blanket ban on slaves coming to France in place once more.[149] In short, the Restoration showed a slow change of once more using status, namely free or enslaved, instead of race, namely white versus coloured, as a benchmark for policy.

Eventually, it took another revolution for the French freedom principle to be codified in law for good. After the July Revolution, the government started to effectively enforce its ban on the slave trade. But some slaves still came to France in the early years after the revolution.[150] The government decided to solidify the French freedom principle in law once and for all during one final *cause célèbre*.

The case dealt with a former slave called Furcy. He had lived for most of his life as a slave on *Île de la Réunion* (known as Île Bourbon before 1793, and also between the English invasion of 1810 and the end of the restored Bourbon dynasty in 1848) and *Île de France* (Mauritius). After a conflict with his master, he tried to assert his freedom. His lawyers used two arguments, namely that his mother had once been on French soil and thus free and that he was of Indian descent, and that the laws of slavery were not applicable to him (an argument also used by Francisque). Given that some of the judges of the colonial courts in *Île de la Réunion* were well known to Furcy's master, the court judged against him. When the English invaded *Île de la Réunion*, they freed Furcy, but given that the French authorities in *Île Bourbon* made clear that they would not protect Furcy from confiscation if he returned to that island, he took his case to the courts in metropolitan France. There, he succeeded in bringing the case before the French *Cour de Cassation* in 1835, which would eventually annul the judgment in 1840. The slave-owner's widow and heirs followed up by taking the case to the *Cour royale de Paris*.[151]

The government did not wait for the outcome of the *Affaire Furcy* to take action. In 1836, it made a new *ordonnance* on French free soil, which restated the ideas of 1791. Henceforth, colonists wishing to take a slave to France had to enfranchise him or her before departure. If they did not do so, the slave was free as from the moment of him or her disembarking in France. Finally, all slaves currently residing in France were freed as well.[152]

---

[147] *Circulaire ministérielle confidentiele aux administrateurs des colonies "sur le passage en France des personnes de couleur", 5 août 1818* in Ibid., 199

[148] Ibid., 212.

[149] *Circulaire du ministre de la Marine aux administrateurs des colonies, 3 mars 1824, et des ports, 6 mars 1824* in Ibid., 205.

[150] Ibid., pp. 211–216.

[151] On the *affaire Furcy*, see Peabody (2009), (2015), (2017).

[152] *Ordonnance du Roi relative aux esclaves des colonies amenés ou envoyés en France par leurs maîtres, 29 April 1836* in Boulle and Peabody (2014), p. 226.

Whilst this would have been enough to ensure Furcy's freedom, the *Cour royale* had the last word on slavery in France in 1843, five years before slavery was abolished in France's colonies once more:

> La Cour […] considérant que c'était une maxime de droit public en France que tout esclave qui touchait le sol français devenait libre […] dit que Furcy est né en état de liberté et d'ingénuité.

Furcy was free, and France's soil has remained free ever since.[153]

5.2.4 Conclusion

By 1650, French law had developed a clear freedom principle, which could be found in a loose collection of rulings based on customary principles of French law, popular tales and scholarly writing. When black slaves from the colonies first arrived in the metropolis, this principle was acknowledged by the French government. However, as the influx of slaves increased and colonial interests pressed for a solution, the government intervened to limit and eventually abrogate the French freedom principle.

Three great pieces of legislation were made to solve the issue, namely the edict of 1716, the declaration of 1738 and the declaration of 1777. There are three points of interest concerning this legislation. First, the legislation became progressively more prohibitive on the introduction of slaves in France. The first legislation left many inroads for masters, the second started to restrict the time of stay in France and the third measure simply banned the entrance of people of colour in France. Second, the legislation showed the development of an evolution from status to race as a basis for policy. Whereas the first two acts were based on the distinction between free and enslaved, the third piece of legislation tried to contain the two categories in the term *domestique*. Third, none of the three pieces of legislation ever fully succeeded, as all of them partially unravelled soon after they were made.

Barring enforcement from above, it is the situation on the ground which can teach us the most about the French freedom principle. And here we see a bifurcated France. In Paris, less dependent on the colonies for its economic development and influenced by Jansenist thought, the idea of the French freedom principle reigned. The Admiralty of France and the Parlement of Paris consistently ruled in favour of freedom, and even the successful registration of the Declaration of 1777 did not stop this. This did not happen in cities such as Bordeaux and Nantes. Though we lack an analysis of the judgments of their Admiralty Courts, the fact that they registered the first two pieces of royal legislation without any problems, but opposed the enforcement of the *police des noirs*, gives us reason to believe that a case such as Catherine Morgan's was standard procedure in this part of France. Throughout the *Ancien Régime* then, France was divided in a part which recognised the freedom principle, and a part where the soil had become unfree. That being said, the slave himself had to petition

[153] *Arrêt de la Cour royale de Paris dans l'affaire Furcy, 23 décembre 1843* in Ibid., pp. 232–233.

for his freedom in Paris, an avenue which was clearly only open to a small minority of slaves, as masters were clearly not restricted in any other way in their use of slaves serving them in France.

Eventually, it took two Revolutions to rid France of slavery. The French Revolution succeeded in eradicating it from French soil a first time, but abolitionism had not gained full strength in France at that point, and it was re-established by Napoléon soon afterwards. Though the number of blacks in France was smaller than before, the freedom principle had been abrogated again. It was only after the July Revolution and right before French colonial slavery itself was permanently abolished in 1848 that the government chose to reassert the French freedom principle for once and for all.

References

Abanime EP (1979) The Anti-Negro French Law of 1777. J Negro Hist 64:21–29

Arabeyre P (2007) Dictionnaire historique des juristes français (XIIe-XXe siècle). Presses Universitaires de France, Paris

Bamford P (1973) Fighting ships and prisons: Mediterranean galleys in France in the age of Louis XIV. University of Minnesota Press, Minneapolis

Bély L (2007) Les relations internationales en Europe (XVIIe-XVIIIe siècles). Presses Universitaires de France, Paris

Bénot Y (1993) Comment la convention a-t-elle voté l'abolition de l'esclavage en l'an II? Ann Hist Revolut Fr 293:349–361

Boucher d'Argis A (1782) "Galérien" in Encyclopédie Méthodique. Jurisprudence. Pancoucke, Paris

Boulle P-H (2014) Élaboration et pratique de la législation sur les Noirs en France au cours du XVIIIe siècle. In: Niort J-F, Régent F (eds) Les colonies, la Révolution française, la loi. Presses Universitaires de Rennes, Rennes, pp 21–40

Boulle P-H (2006) Racial purity or legal clarity? The status of black residents in eighteenth-century France. J Hist Soc 6:19–46

Boulle PH (2009) Les déclarations parisiennes de non-blancs entre 1738 et 1790 : permanence des catégories et interchangeabilité des statuts. Nuevo Mundo

Boulle PH (2007) Race et Esclavage dans la France de l'Ancien Régime. Perrin, Paris

Boulle PH, Peabody S (2014) Le droit des noirs en France au temps de l'esclavage: textes choisis et commentés. L'Harmattan, Paris

Boyer P (1969) La chiourme turque des galères de France de 1685 à 1687. Rev Occident Musulman Mediterr 6:53–74

Chambron M (1783) Traité général du commerce de l'Amérique. Tome second. Marc-Michel Rey, Amsterdam

Compère M-M (2010) Sorbonne. Dictionnaire de l'Ancien Régime: royaume de France XVIe-XVIIIe siècle, 3rd edn. Presses Universitaires de France, Paris, pp 1172–1173

Corvisier A (1968) Les soldats noirs du maréchal de Saxe. Le problème des Antillais et Africains sous les armes en France au XVIIIe siècle. Rev française d'histoire d'outre-mer 55:367–413

de Bourjon F (1770) Le droit commun de la France et la coutume de Paris réduits en principes, Tome premier. Grangé & Cellot, Paris

de Ferrière C (1769) Dictionnaire de droit et de pratique. Tôme premier. V. Brunet, Paris

de Ghewiet G (1736) Institutions du droit belgique. C.-M. Cramé, Lille

de Wismes A (1992) Nantes et le temps des négriers. France Empire, Paris

Durival M (1757) "Galérien". In: Encyclopédie ou dictionnaire raisonné des Sciences, des Arts et des métiers, tome septième
Drescher S (1994) The long goodbye: Dutch capitalism and antislavery in comparative perspective. Am Hist Rev 99:44–69
Fontenay M (2010) Esclavage méditerranéen. In: Bély L (ed) Dictionnaire de l'Ancien Régime: royaume de France XVIe-XVIIIe siècle, 3rd edn. Presses universitaires de France, Paris, pp 500–502
Fromageau G, de Bussy de Lamet A (1745) Le dictionnaire des cas de conscience T. 1. Paris
Guyot JN (1779) "Galères" in Répertoire universel et raisonné de jurisprudence civile, criminelle, canonique et bénéficiale, tome vingt-sixième. Pancoucke, Paris
Koufinkana M (2008) Les esclaves noirs en France sous l'Ancien régime: XVIe-XVIIIe siècles. L'Harmattan, Paris
Loisel A (1607) Institutes coustumières. Abel l'Angelier, Paris
Masson P (1938) Les galères de France (1481–1781): Marseille, port de guerre. Hachette, Paris
McCloy S (1961) The Negro in France. University of Kentucky Press, Lexington
Mousnier R (1974) Les institutions de la France sous la monarchie absolue: 1598–1789. Presses Universitaires de France, Paris, Tome II
Noël E (ed) (2011) Dictionnaire des gens de couleur dans la France moderne (fin XVe s. - 1792) Paris et son bassin. Librarie Droz, Paris
Noël E (ed) (2013) Dictionnaire des gens de couleur dans la France moderne. Volume II. La Bretagne Entrée par année (début XVIe siècle - 1792). Librarie Droz, Paris
Noël E (ed) (2017) Dictionnaire des gens de couleur dans la France moderne. Volume III. Le midi Entrée par année (fin XVIe siècle - 1792). Librarie Droz, Paris
Noël É (2007) L'esclavage dans la france moderne. Dix Huit Siecle 39:361–383
Noël É (2019) Les gens de couleur de l'océan Indien en France à la veille de la révolution. Ann Hist Revolut Fr 395:103–117
Olivier-Martin F (2010) Histoire du droit français - Des origines à la Révolution. CNRS, Paris
Peabody S (1996) There are no slaves in France: the political culture of race and slavery in the Ancien Régime. Oxford University Press, New York
Peabody S (2009) La question raciale et le «sol libre de France»: l'affaire Furcy. Ann Hist Sci Soc 64:1305–1334
Peabody S (2015) Freedom papers hidden in his shoe: navigating emancipation across imperial boundaries. French Polit Cult Soc 33:11–32
Peabody S (2017) Madeleine's children: family, freedom, secrets, and lies in France's Indian Ocean colonies. Oxford University Press, Oxford
Pétré-Grenouilleau O (1998) Nantes au temps de la traite des Noirs [La vie quotidienne]. Paris
Peytraud L (1897) L'esclavage aux Antilles françaises avant 1789: d'après des documents inédits des archives coloniales. Hachette, Paris
Pruitt DC (2005) Nantes Noir. Living race in the city of slavers. Emory University
Pruitt DC (2007) The opposition of the law to the law: race, slavery, and the law in nantes, 1715–1778. Fr Hist Stud 30:147–174
Rachel Tolin Schultz A (2017) 'The purity of the blood': poncet de la grave, pronatalism and empire. Mod Contemp Fr 25:1–13
Rigaudière A (2010) Histoire du droit et des institutions dans la France médiévale et moderne, 4th edn. Economica, Paris
Rogers D (2001) Présences noires en Aquitaine au XVIIIe siècle, une question à redécouvrir. Bull l'Institut Aquitain d'Études Soc 76:103–121
Saugera E (1995) Bordeaux port négrier. XVIIIe-XIXe siècles. Chronologie, économie, idéologie. Karthala, Paris
Shennan JH (1968) The parlement of Paris. Cornell University Press, Ithaca
Sibalis MD (2003) Les noirs en France sous Napoléon: l'enquête de 1807. Rétablissement de l'esclavage dans les colonies françaises, 1802. Maisonneuve & Larose, Paris, pp 95–106

Stanziani A (2014) Sailors, slaves and immigrants. Bondage in the Indian Ocean world, 1750–1914 [Palgrave series in Indian Ocean world studies]. Palgrave, New York

Verlinden C (1955) L'esclavage dans l'Europe médiévale, Tome premier: péninsule Iberique - France. De Tempel, Brugge

Vigie M (1985) Justice et criminalité au XVIIIème siècle : le cas de la peine des galères. Hist économie société 345–368

Watson A (1989) Slave law in the Americas. University of Georgia press, Athens, GA

Weiss G (2011) Infidels at the Oar: a Mediterranean exception to France's free soil principle. Slavery Abol 32:397–412

Zysberg A (1987) Les galériens: vies et destins de 60 000 forçats sur les galères de France 1680–1748. Seuil, Paris

Chapter 6
The United Provinces: Abandoning the Freedom Principle Sub Silentio(?)

6.1 The Historiography of Black Slavery in the United Provinces

We noted how the first sizeable proportion of blacks in the Low Countries was to be found in Antwerp. In the seventeenth and eighteenth centuries, the bulk of the black presence shifted to the Northern part of the Low Countries.

In the early seventeenth century, the largest proportion of slaves lived amongst the Sephardic Jewish community and those ethnic Jews who had come from Antwerp to the North after that city had fallen into decline.[1] These Iberians were accustomed to using slaves in their own country. Given that legislation had prohibited Jews to have Christian slaves from early on, the obvious choice for them fell to black pagan slaves.[2] Recent research has also shown the existence of a very small black community in 17th century Amsterdam, which can be linked to the rise of the Dutch Empire, especially so after the conquest of Recife in 1630.[3]

The second wave, which was more numerous, arrived in the eighteenth century, again mostly in the second half of that century. Here as elsewhere, masters took their slaves from the West Indies (mainly Surinam, secondarily Curaçao) with them to the United Provinces.[4] Next to them and comparable to what we saw for England as well, some slaves also arrived when ship captains were allowed to take one or more with them that were subsequently sold or given to someone (so-called *presentslaven*).[5]

[1] Hondius (2008), pp. 91–93; Oostindie and Maduro (1986), pp. 143–144. As mentioned before, I will normally use the term "black" to refer to Africans coming to the United Provinces. Only where the sources themselves use the contemporary terms "Swert", "noir", "Moor" or "Neger" will I sometimes make use of those terms. Blakely (1993), pp. 31–37.

[2] Schorsch (2004), p. 94.

[3] Ponte (2019).

[4] Hondius (2008), pp. 95–97.

[5] Schreuder (2017), pp. 26–27.

F. Batselé, *Liberty, Slavery and the Law in Early Modern Western Europe*, Studies in the History of Law and Justice 17, https://doi.org/10.1007/978-3-030-36855-5_6

During the seventeenth-eighteenth century, slaves were occasionally taken from the East Indies to the United Provinces as well, but far less is known of them.[6]

Lacking a census, the numbers of black people in the United Provinces cannot be exactly measured. Over time, several scholars have tried to give a measure of the black population primarily using ship records.[7] Two scholars have made assessments for this period, and the most recent one, that of Oostindie, comes to a number of 749 black people and native Americans going to the Netherlands from Surinam between 1729 and 1781 (with 672 of them returning in the same period).[8] We do not know the numbers for the Antilles but can safely presume that they were far lower. The Antilles served more as trading centres than as plantation colonies and were tied stronger to the Caribbean economy than to the metropolis. Furthermore, slaves who wanted to flee their masters from this area had the opportunity to try and reach the Spanish mainland colonies, as the Spaniards often granted freedom to those slaves.[9] We are faced with the same problem for the Dutch East Indies, where we lack any numbers.[10]

That being said, we do know that the issue of taking blacks to the metropolis was perceived to be an issue at times by different Dutch colonial governments. One author has traced immigration restrictions for slaves in the *Placaetboeken* of the WIC colonies, and another one has traced the regulations made by the EIC. The EIC was most stringent, enacting several blanket bans on taking slaves to the metropolis in the seventeenth century.[11]

As concerns their regional spread, the great majority of black people lived in the Province of Holland, more specifically in the bustling trade metropolis of Amsterdam. Next came the Province of Zeeland, where Vlissingen and Middelburg were the cities economically most involved in the slave trade in all of the Dutch Republic, particularly with the rise of the Middelburgse Commercie Compagnie in the eighteenth century. However, the amount of black people in Zeeland must have been fairly small in comparison with Holland, as return goods from Surinam mostly arrived in markets in Amsterdam. Besides for those two provinces, we know of the occasional appearance of black people in cities such as Groningen or Hoorn as well, although the numbers must have been minimal.[12] In comparison with France and England, the black presence was rather small.[13]

---

[6] Fatah-Black and van Rossum (2014), pp. 65–69.

[7] The obvious disadvantage here is that only those blacks which were declared for are counted, with the real numbers probably being quite a bit higher.

[8] Oostindie and Maduro (1986), pp. 6–9; Buve (1963), pp. 10–11.

[9] Jordaan (2012), pp. 115–117; Oostindie and Maduro (1986), p. 137.

[10] Fatah-Black and van Rossum (2014), pp. 65–69.

[11] Hondius (2011), pp. 384–385; Fatah-Black and van Rossum (2014), pp. 65–69. For examples from the Cape Colony, which fell under overall East India Company command, see Schoeman (2012), pp. 1017–1018.

[12] In general, see Blakely (1993), pp. 227–228; Oostindie and Maduro (1986), pp. 6–9. More specifically for Zeeland, see Priester (1987), pp. 15–21.

[13] Oostindie (2005), pp. 137–139. Barring better statistics, it is somewhat difficult to compare with France and England. The population of the United Provinces was approximately 2 million in 1784.

What was the legal status of those coming from the colonies? Again, we find the presence of few free blacks amongst those going to the metropolis (for Surinam, 74 between 1729 and 1781 according to Oostindie), and a majority of these free black people stayed in the metropolis. But the great majority of the arrivals were clearly slaves (87/101 between 1729 and 1749 and 569/648 between 1749 and 1781 for the Surinam-Amsterdam sea route according to the same data).[14] Again, the colonial practices were not fully repeated in the United Provinces. The slaves who came were seen as novelties, and often, it was the master's "favourite" who would accompany him to the metropolis.[15]

The question as to their personal status in the United Provinces is much harder to answer. In the previous chapter, we have seen how there was a strong freedom tradition in the Low Countries. Unfortunately, we have very few cases that tell us something about the slave's legal status in the Dutch Republic. As for France and England, this partially has to do with the relative well-being of the slave's situation in the United Provinces vis-à-vis the lot of most plantation slaves, as well as the enslaver's obvious position of power. This, together with the fear many must have had for a forced return to the Dutch Indies, limited the slave's incentives to petition the courts. In contrast to France and England, there were also fewer slaves coming to the metropolis and little evidence of networks of free blacks in the eighteenth century who could help their enslaved colleagues. Next to that, much research on blacks in court cases is still in the making. As a result, recent scholars still turn to a combination of notarial deeds and inventories, passenger lists, incidental court cases and even paintings and drawings to learn more about black people in the United Provinces during the eighteenth century.[16] In that sense, conclusions from this part are more tentative than they are for England or France. For the period before 1734, I have not been able to find any court cases myself, and I will draw on secondary sources to try and explain the slave's legal status in the United Provinces up to that point. After that date, we do know something about the way in which courts dealt with stowaways. Next to that, the Dutch followed the French example by making legislation on the issue through a *Placaet* in 1776. This allowed masters to send their slaves to the metropolis, albeit under certain conditions.[17] Likewise, scarce material from the nineteenth century gives an indication of the relationship between the freedom principle and black slavery.

The city of Amsterdam was home to about 200.000 people at the end of the eighteenth century. If we take into consideration that only 87 slaves came to The Netherlands between 1729 and 1749 and 569 between 1749 and 1781 (with the great majority of them returning), the black population does indeed seem small in comparison with England (with its population of approximately 9 million by the middle of the eighteenth century). The difference with France, which had a population of about 20 million at that point, seems less stark.

[14]Oostindie and Maduro (1986), pp. 6–9.

[15]Blakely (1993), p. 230.

[16]Fatah-Black and van Rossum (2014), p. 61.

[17]The terminology of these acts could differ. Most often, the laws of the States General were called *placaeten*, but the terms *resolutie* or *ordonnantie* (the latter mostly for decisions of the particular States) were used as well. Gerbenzon and Algra (1972), pp. 119–122.

6.2 Pre-1776: Mixed Outcomes(?)

Especially for the seventeenth and early eighteenth century, it is very difficult to trace the relationship between these slaves and the law. Theoretically, not much seems to have changed. If we look at Johannes Voet's 1707 *Commentarius ad pandectas*, we find the same enunciation of the freedom principle as before. Voet was amongst those mentioning that the slave had to take action himself to have his liberty confirmed ("invito domino possit confestim ad libertatem proclamare").[18] Did slaves ever try to assert this right? There are only few indications.

In 1656, the slave Juliana, who had come with her master to Amsterdam from Brazil, refused to return to the colonies and asserted her freedom. This was purportedly because some persons had made her believe that she was free and not obliged to serve her master in the Dutch Republic. We have no idea whether Juliana ever went to court to assert this right, or whether her master succeeded in taking her back.[19]

In 1661, we find another case. The Jewish merchant Moses Netto, who had fled Brazil together with his slave after the Portuguese takeover, wanted to take his *morinneke* to the Dutch colony Essequibo. The church council (*Kerkeraad*) of Middelburg opposed this, noting that the slave was baptised and that slaves became free upon arrival in the Republic ("in haere vryheit te laeten na de wetten van onse landen"). That being said, the case seemed to be immersed with anti-Jewish sentiment. Also, the church councils were local bodies of the Dutch Reformed Church who regulated the affairs of the Church within the community, no real courts.[20]

The best indication that at least some authorities attached weight to the freedom principle, comes from the Dutch Cape Colony. The late Karel Schoeman, a renowned historian of South Africa, found evidence of an instruction that was sent by the Heeren XVII, the governing board of the East India Company, to Batavia (current day Jakarta) and from there to the Cape in 1714. Though the original instruction seems to have been lost, it was referred to in other documents. According to the sources, the instruction mentioned that slaves returning from the colonies could not "without new and legitimate cause, against their will, […] be enslaved anew", and another 1790 source mentioned it as containing the principle that "such slaves, having touched on the soil of the Fatherland, were no longer subject to slavery and thus unsellable". Whilst these instructions remained internal matters that technically only affected EIC employees, it does show us that the freedom principle was not completely forgotten in the early eighteenth century.[21]

Finally, some slaves seem to have also known of the idea. Making use of archives in Surinam, Buve noted the story of a former Surinam slave who considered himself to be free once he had arrived in Amsterdam in 1742. Subsequently, the person

---

[18] Voet (1707), Liber I, Tit. V.

[19] The case is discussed by Hondius (2011), p. 381.

[20] This case can be found in Oostindie and Maduro (1986), p. 155; Israel (1995), p. 368.

[21] Schoeman (2012), pp. 1017–1018.

remained in the city and worked there in the service of the Prussian representative, apparently as a freeman.[22]

Besides those few cases, indications are that slaves who did not effectively try to assert their freedom, never gained it for simply having been in the United Provinces. First, Oostindie's numbers indicate this. From the 656 slaves that travelled to the United Provinces between 1729 and 1781, 627 returned to the colonies as slaves.[23] Second, many local officials did not seem to have made much trouble over the status of slavery. Again, we find examples of various manumissions,[24] references to slaves in notarial deeds[25] and sales of slaves.[26] We lack cases in which the argument of baptism was used, but the idea of baptism bestowing freedom was present in the Dutch colonies as well. In 1747, the *Classis* of Amsterdam declared that "the acceptance of Christianity…does not make servants, male and female slaves, free persons". It is unclear whether this message was only meant for a colonial audience, or whether it was intended to be of relevance to the metropolis as well.[27]

We know more about the situation of stowaways because they were more likely to be mentioned in administrative correspondence or court proceedings. In the early eighteenth century, there were various cases of stowaways from Curaçao who had arrived in the United Provinces. The few slaves who did so believed they would have been considered free upon arrival in Holland. In reality, the *kamer Amsterdam* (an administrative body which was responsible for day-to-day correspondence with the government of Curaçao) routinely had the slaves sent back.[28] Despite the fact that the origins of Dutch free looked quite strong, there does not seem to have been much hesitance amongst governmental organs to neglect this tradition.

The issue of stowaways was clearly an enduring problem, and one case came before a local court in 1736. We know of this case thanks to the notes that Cornelius van Bynkershoek made in his *Observationes tumultuariae*. In this work, Bynkershoek took notes of the court cases that came before the Supreme Court of Holland and Zeeland (*Hooge Raad van Holland en Zeeland*), which was the highest court in the provinces of Holland and Zeeland. Normally, a case that came before this court originated in a local court, and was then appealed to either the Court of Holland (*Hof van Holland*) or the Court of Zeeland (*Hof van Zeeland*). After obtaining leave, it was possible to lodge an appeal with the Supreme Court of Holland and Zeeland. Although the ten judges did discuss the merits of cases with each other, the public at large only knew whether the appeal was allowed or rejected, as the judgments were

[22]Buve (1963), p. 12.

[23]Oostindie and Maduro (1986), p. 7.

[24]Schorsch (2004), p. 95; Beyerman (1977), pp. 566–568.

[25]Hondius (2011), p. 380.

[26]Oostindie and Maduro (1986), p. 144.

[27]De Jong (1971), pp. 431–432. *Classes* were gatherings of preachers. Within the structure of the Dutch Reformed Church, they stood below general synods and provincial synods, but above the church councils. Israel (1995), pp. 367–368. Until 1772, the Dutch Reformed Church in the colonies was subject to the jurisdiction of the *Classis* of Amsterdam.

[28]Jordaan (2012), pp. 109–110.

not motivated. This also explains why Bynkershoek's collection is so important, as he gives us some insight in the court's reasoning.[29]

A slave called Nicolaus (Bynkershoek uses fictional names in his *Observationes tumultuariae*, and calls the slave Pamphilus[30]) fled from his Curaçaon master and arrived in Amsterdam in 1734. Seemingly, he had heard about the freedom principle of the United Provinces, as he asked for his freedom at a local Amsterdam court ("ad libertatem proclamat"). The local court agreed,and freed him. His master appealed the case to the Court of Holland. This court decided that Nicolaus remained a slave and had to return to Curaçao, referring to a precedent of October 29, 1734 in which it had made the same decision regarding a stowaway. This decision was then appealed to the Supreme Court of Holland and Zeeland.

The slave's lawyer referred to the example of the Great Council of Malines in order to have Nicolaus declared free. However, Bynkershoek's court decided to reject the appeal. Bynkershoek's notes indicate that two reasons swayed the judges. To dispose with the precedent of 1532, the judges held that this situation was different. The slave came from Curaçao, which belonged to the Dutch realm, and not from another kingdom, as was the case in 1532 (namely, from Portugal). In Curaçao, Roman law regulated slavery on the basis of the *placaet* of 13 October 1629. As a result, the court decided to apply Roman law and not domestic Dutch law in this case, referring to the title "*De servus fugitivus*" of the Corpus Iuris Civilis. Second, another motive was clearly present, as Bynkershoek mentioned that slaves were necessary to run the colonies. For that reason, slaves fleeing to Holland could not be allowed to become free upon their arrival.[31]

We currently know of no further cases, but in a 1776 report of the *Staten van Holland* (hereafter: States of Holland), we do find a statement that the courts of that province did not believe that stowaways became free upon arriving in Holland. They referred to precedents that had come before the various courts of Holland but did not give any specifics ("dat zulks ook in dier voegen een en andermaal by de Hoven van Justitie in deese Provincie verstaan was").[32]

[29] Sirks (2012).

[30] The real name of the slave can be found in van der Linden (1793), Liber I, Tit. V—De Statu Hominum. As Bynkershoek's observations were only published in the twentieth century, and the case was not referred to by Bynkershoek in his *Quaestiones juris privati*, van der Linden, who lived between 1756 and 1835, must have heard of it by another scholar or outside source.

[31] van Bynkershoek (1926), IV, 2966. I have made use of the 1926 translation by Eduard Maurits Meijers. On the case, also see van Kralingen (2014); Van Oosten (1962).

[32] *Rapport op de Missive van Gouverneur en Raaden van Suriname, concerneerende de vryheid der Slaaven die in het Vaderland zyn geweest, 19 juli 1775,* 4.

6.3 Regulating Slavery in the Metropolis: The Placaet of 1776

6.3.1 Jan Nepveu's Request: Does the Metropolitan Soil Render Free?

The only time when the States General considered the difficulties related to the status of slaves who had come to the Republic seems to have been created by its own imprudence. In February 1775, the governor of Surinam, Jan Nepveu, sent a request for clarification to the States General. In the past few months, he had been faced with two similar cases. In the first one, the Surinam slave Andries had claimed that he was free after having travelled to the metropolis. He had left his master and had already become a wage labourer for another citizen of the colony. The widow of his former master was flabbergasted by this claim and asked the governor whether it was truly so that slaves who had travelled to the metropolis became free, as she had never heard this claim before. The second case explained where the idea came from. The creditors, the money lending company Valckenier and Du Quesne, of a deceased plantation owner called Thomas Wybrand van Rees wanted to sequestrate several slaves who belonged to the deceased owner's mortgaged plantation. However, the widow of the plantation holder refused to turn over two slaves, known as Blondin and Sabina. These two were probably amongst her favourites. She justified her refusal by referring to the fact that the two slaves fell under the scope of a resolution of the States General, which had purportedly declared that slaves who had come to the United Provinces became free upon arrival.[33] This case must have been typical for its time, as the Amsterdam stock exchange had suffered a dramatic crash in 1773, which led to a string of bankruptcy and sequestrations in Surinam.[34]

The governor said that two resolutions of the States General, dated 9 August 1771 and 23 June 1773 were the source of this confusion.[35] In both cases, some individual slaves were declared free, after they had been in the metropolis with the consent of

[33] Ibid., pp. 15–30. This document seems to have slipped through the mazes of the net of most Dutch historians and legal historians, as I have only found it discussed in short in Jordaan (2012), pp. 87–93. Jordaan mostly limits his explanation to this document and the *Placaet* itself. Priester learned of the Nepveu document by consulting sources from the province of Zeeland, more in particular the Verzameling Van de Perre-Schorer, 1641–1795 (Van de Perre being the representative of the nobility of Zeeland in the province's assembly as well as in the States General). By focusing on Zeeland, Priester missed some of the documents that emanated from Holland (though Van de Perre did take note of some of them). As such, he could not see what I believe is pivotal to understand the background of the placaet, namely the fact that the placaet seems to have been almost completely pushed through by Holland, without much independent input from the States General. The documents made reference to in this chapter are from the States of Holland and of the States General.

[34] For background on the Dutch West Indies plantations and the crisis of 1773, see Van de Voort (1973), pp. 153–196.

[35] As these were decisions given in particular cases, we cannot find them referred to in the *Placaetboeken*.

their masters. As this was obviously causing troubles in Surinam, Nepveu wanted to know whether it was truly the case that all slaves who had once travelled to the Republic became free. If so, were these blacks to be treated as being fully free ("*vrye Lieden*") or solely as manumitted persons (*Gemanumitteerden*), against whom some legal obligations could still be imposed?

What were these two resolutions about? Both of them can be found in the archives of the States General, as they were both discussed during one of its meetings.

The first resolution, dated 9 August 1771, related to a woman called Marytje Criool and her daughter Jacoba Leilad (who, the source indicates, was a *mulatto)*.[36] Both of them were originally slaves of Willem Hendrik van Steenberg, who was active in one of the most important organs of state of the Surinam colony, the *Raad van Politie*. Criool asked the States General to send her letters confirming her freedom, in order for her to be able to enjoy the same freedoms in Surinam as freeborn persons, and in order for Steenberg not to be able to claim her back. We do not know what the source of her apparent conflict with her former owner was, but we do know why she claimed her freedom: she had set foot in the Dutch republic with her master before. The States General had decided to hand over this case to its lawyers, who subsequently seem to have given a positive advice in favour of the slave's freedom, most likely on the basis of Criool having been in the Netherlands.[37] As a result, we find the States General confirming that Criool and her daughter immediately and legally received their freedom ("daar door haar vrijheid dadelijk en wetteglijk verkreegen hebben") because they had been on the soil of the republic with permission of their master ("met kennis en bewilliging van haren toenmaligen Heer en Eigenaar den voorn. Willem Hendrik van Steenberg"). As a result, the two of them did not need letters to confirm their freedom, they had been free from the moment they had set foot in the Republic and had to be legally considered as manumitted persons back in Surinam. This is a rather general confirmation of the freedom principle, with an exception for stowaways who obviously did not get permission from their masters.[38]

The second resolution of 23 June 1773 reads as a variation on the first one. This time, the case related to Jan Nepveu's predecessor as governor of Surinam until 1770, Wigbold Crommelin. He had taken two of his slaves, called Christiaan Africaanus and

[36]See NL-HaNA, Staten-Generaal, 1.01.02, inv.nr 1437 and NL-HaNA, Staten-Generaal, 1.01.02, inv.nr 2800. I will refer to both the *eerste minuten* (the former reference) and the *geresumeerde minuten* (the latter reference) for each of the archival documents discussed. The difference between the two is that the eerste minuten show what was written down at the meeting itself. After the meeting, the responsible clerk would then re-write and expand upon the *eerste minuten*, if needed, to make the *geresumeerde minuten*.

[37]Ibid. The source mentions that the lawyers gave their advice on 30 July 1771. Unfortunately, this advice was not to be found in the *eerste* or *geresumeerde minuten* of the meetings of that month.

[38]Buve mentions a 1772 resolution of the States General, which declared that a slave and her daughter who had travelled to Amsterdam were declared free. This has since been restated by many scholars. I have not been able to verify Buve's source (to be found in a local Suriname archive). I am tempted to believe that Buve's source might have made a small mistake and was actually referring to the 1771 resolution of the States General mentioned here. Given the similarities between this case and Buve's source, it seems reasonable to imply that we are dealing with one and the same decision, which was made in 1771, not 1772. Buve (1963), p. 15.

Anna Elisabeth van Chattillon, with him to the Republic in 1770. Back in Surinam, the by then ex-governor decided to give freedom to his slaves. Therefore, he asked the States General to send him letters confirming the freedom of these two slaves. The text learns us that the Sociëteit van Suriname, whose opinion was asked by the States General, clearly had some misgivings ("*bedenkelijkheeden*") with doing so. However, the States General decided to stick with the 1771 precedent, reiterating that freedom letters were not needed for slaves that had set foot in the Republic with the permission of their masters.[39]

Although Nepveu's request was sent to the States General, we find it discussed by the States of Holland. This should not surprise us too much. Holland paid for more than half of the national finances, and was the pre-eminent power in the States General. Therefore, many affairs were discussed concurrently by the States of Holland and the Generality, or even first by the States of Holland. In the latter case, the issue would only be referred to the Generality after it (mostly informally) became clear what the views of Holland were.[40]

When the States of Holland learned of Nepveu's request early in 1775, they decided to send this issue to its *Gecommitteerde Raad*, after which *pensionaris* Bosschaert reported his findings to the States of Holland on 19 July 1775.[41]

Bosschaert started by pointing out that the two aforementioned resolutions of the States General were given in particular cases, and definitely not intended to serve as general policy. This despite the fact that on their face value, the lawyers of the States General did seem to believe they were proceeding upon general principles, namely that a slave coming to the Republic with the permission of his master was deemed to be free. That being said, Bosschaert considered that it would be a good idea to make guidelines, so that the status of slaves who had been to the motherland became clear once and for all. For the moment, there was no legislation on the issue, although even Bosschaert acknowledged that there was a clear legal tradition in the United Provinces which held that all persons in his country were free ("volgens de seeden, maximes en constitutie deeser Landen"). Slaves enjoyed the same freedom as everyone else whilst they were here, and they could have themselves declared free in court if the master opposed this.[42]

At the same time, he also held that if these slaves returned to the colonies, their residence in the Republic had not made them *eo ipso* free forever. In fact, the idea

[39]The key phrase reads "als met kennis en bewilliging van haaren heer en Eygenaert Wigbolt Crommelin hier te lande gekomen zijnde, en daar door haare vrijheijd dadelijk en wettiglijk verkreegen hebbende, geene brieven van vrijdom uyt haare slavernije nodig hebben, en dat gen[oemnde] twee personen dienvolgende in Suriname retournerende als vrijgelaten personen sullen worden geconsidereert". See NL-HaNA, Staten-Generaal, 1.01.02, inv.nr 1459 (eerste minuten), NL-HaNA, Staten-Generaal, 1.01.02, inv.nr. 2822 (geresumeerde minuten).

[40]Israel (1995), pp. 291–297.

[41]The *Gecommiteerde Raden* were standing committees of the particular States. They supervised the routine administration of each province and helped to develop the particular States into genuine provincial governments. Ibid., pp. 276–284.

[42]*Rapport op de Missive van Gouverneur en Raaden van Suriname, concerneerende de vryheid der Slaaven die in het Vaderland zyn geweest, 19 juli 1775*, 1–3.

of freedom was trumped here by another interest, namely the property rights of masters. Bosschaert's theory was that, whereas the rights attached to slavery could not be exercised in the Republic, the slave did not permanently "lose" his status because of a stay in the metropolis, and the rights of the master were "re-attached" to the slave when he returned to the colonies. This stood in contrast to the views of the Generality lawyers, who in their two resolutions had clearly argued in favour of full and permanent liberty for slaves who had come to the Republic with the permission of their masters. Bosschaert stated that this was a clear misuse of the authorities (quoting Voet, Groenewegen van der Made and the customs of Antwerp and Amsterdam). He believed that these scholars did not actually pronounce themselves on the issue of colonial slaves coming to the metropolis and were simply referring to each other as an authority for their statements. He proposed that the 1636 *Instructie voor de Reegering in Brazil*, which referred to Roman law as the substantive provisions of slave law, was of much more relevance here. Bosschaert did agree that the rights attached to slavery could not be exercised in the Republic but he had an important proviso: a judge could decide to have a slave sent back to the colonies, notwithstanding the idea of the freedom principle, and he did not believe this to be in conflict with the idea of Dutch liberty.[43]

Bosschaert then proposed a concept-*Placaet* to solve all these issues. In his opinion, it had to take four factors into consideration: whether slaves came here with or without the knowledge of their masters, whether those who had permission intended to stay here or not, whether their masters had liberated them before sending them to the motherland or not, and whether the slaves were mortgaged or not.[44] Finally, to answer the governor's request, he advised that the slaves referred to were only to be treated as manumitted persons.

We can only make educated guesses why Holland wanted to make severe modifications to the pre-existing freedom principle. It is very possible that the interests of the Sociëteit van Suriname, which already grumbled in 1773 upon the release of ex-governor Crommelin's two slaves, might have been pivotal. As pointed out, one of the three shareholders of the Sociëteit was the city of Amsterdam itself. If they were particularly annoyed by the possibility of slaves asserting their freedom simply for having been in the Republic, this could well explain why they pushed for the placaet. Likewise, many of the Surinam slaveholders had outstanding debts with Amsterdam banks. The reference to mortgaged slaves might thus have been directly inspired by the case of the creditors hoping to sequestrate the slaves of the mortgaged plantation. Theoretically speaking, in the wake of the banking crisis of 1773, masters could try to avoid sequestration of slaves by sending them to the motherland and claiming that they had become free, as the widow Nepveu seems to have attempted. Given that a whopping 81% of loans committed to Surinam planters between 1766 and 1775 came from Amsterdam, and the second biggest lender was also a Holland city (Rotterdam),[45] the States of Holland clearly had an interest in limiting the freedom principle.

---

[43] Ibid., pp. 3–5

[44] Ibid., 6.

[45] Van de Voort (1973), p. 103.

6.3.2 *Liberty Is Good, but Property Rights Are Better: The Placaet of 1776*

In the *Resolutiën van Holland*, we find that the States of Holland deliberated on the issue on 8 February 1776. They agreed with Bosschaert's report, and only made some very small changes in his concept-*Placaet*.[46] At the same time, they decided to send the *Placaet* to the States General, where it could then be discussed.[47]

When we read the relevant Generality documents of 23 May 1776, one can easily see how the process was fully guided by Holland. When we take a look at the *eerste minuten*, one notes that the proceedings of the States of Holland were simply copied *verbatim*, although this copying is obviously not to be seen anymore in the *geresumeerde minuten*.[48] The only changes made were those that were necessary to show that the deliberations related to the States General, which is why for example the phrase "that the affair shall be brought before the Generality" is deleted by the scribe.[49] The Generality approved the proposed placaet without much ado, and ordered it to be sent to the West India Company, the Sociëteit van Suriname and the directors of the Dutch Berbice colony (a small Dutch colony around the Berbice river which later became part of British Guyana). Interestingly, the document does not mention anything about the East India Company, which shows again that the Placaet might have been conceived as a means to stop the specific problem of slaves claiming their freedom in Surinam.[50]

We should not be surprised to see little intervention by the other provinces, given that both their financial interests, as well as the number of black people on their soil, must have been very limited. However, that one other province with a stake made a remarkable intervention, the consequences of which are very unclear. In the margin of the decision by the States General, we find written that "The Lords Deputies of the Province of Zeeland have declared, for the time being, to not be encumbered by this".[51] This qualification by Zeeland was not discussed by L.R. Priester, who had access to the archival files for Zeeland, and I am likewise unsure what the intentions of Zeeland were. It could mean several things, namely that Zeeland preferred the continued application of the freedom principle, or that it considered the restrictions

[46] *Resolutien van de Heeren Staaten van Holland en Westvriesland in haar Edele Groot Mogende Vergadering genomen in den jaare 1776, Eerste* deel, 70–76. There were some small changes made in Art. 5, Art. 6 and Art. 7.

[47] Technically speaking, the Union of Utrecht certainly did not consider that an issue such as this belonged to the competence of the States General, but if all Provinces agreed, basically any matter could be tabled there. Israel (1995), pp. 291–297; Fruin and Colenbrander (1922), p. 188.

[48] NL-HaNA, Staten-Generaal, 1.01.02, inv.nr 1498 (eerste minuten), NL-HaNA, Staten-Generaal, 1.01.02, inv.nr 2861 (geresumeerde minuten).

[49] The original remark reads "*dat de zaak ter Generaliteit daar heenen zal worden gedirigeerd*", the translation is my own.

[50] Schoeman confirms that there was no official notice given to the Cape Colony by the Heeren XVII about this placaet, see Schoeman (2012), p. 1020.

[51] The original remark reads "De Heeren Gedeputeerden van de Provincie van Zeeland hebben verklaart hierop vooralsnog ongelast te zijn"; the translation is my own.

on the freedom principle by the placaet, discussed below, as either too far-ranging or not far-ranging enough. Given Zeeland's financial interest in the slave trade and the practice of some of its captains to give away *presentslaven*, it seems rather unlikely that their reflex was made in order to protect the freedom principle. Unfortunately, I have not found any clarification to the declaration of Zeeland in the documents of the States General nor of Holland.

Finally, what did the resolution itself say?

The preamble shows how property rights clearly trumped the natural liberty of the metropolis. It acknowledged that all people who were in the Republic were recognised as free. However, this could not be fully allowed for blacks and other slaves who came from the colonies. Allowing this would ensure they could never be sent back to the colonies against their will, and that slavery would not "re-attach" if they eventually returned to the colonies. Such a proposition would go against the property rights and the freedoms of the Dutch citizens and had to be remediated.

For the category of slaves who were freed by their masters before they came to the Republic, things were clear. They were to be considered as fully free in the metropolis, but only as manumitted persons if they returned to the colonies.[52]

The Republic was less permissive of runaways. Even if they reached the metropolis, they remained slaves. Their masters could ask permission from the courts in the place where the slaves had hidden themselves to have them sent back to the colonies. For this category, the soil became completely unfree.[53]

The third category consisted of those slaves who were sent by their masters to the United Provinces to conduct some business for them. If they did not return voluntarily, they could be constrained by the court, and they remained slaves in the meantime. However, their stay was limited to six months, which could be extended on request for a maximum of another six months. If these time constraints were not met, the slave was considered to be free. If he returned to the colonies later, he would only be counted as a manumitted person there.[54]

The interests of creditors were considered as more important than the interests of the colonial proprietors in one case. If slaves were mortgaged, they could only be taken to the metropolis if sufficient caution money was paid, and if there had been written permission by the colonial government. If these conditions were not met, the proprietor was fined and the creditor could still have the slaves sent back to the colonies (except if their owner had already granted them their freedom before).[55]

The *placaet* ended with a non-retroactivity clause, and an order for the *placaet* to be published and made known. As said, it was sent to the directors of the WIC, the

[52]The *Placaet* can be found in the *Groot placaet-boeck, vervattende de placaten, ordonnantien ende edicten van de [...] Staten Generael der Vereenighde Nederlanden, ende vande [...] Staten van Hollandt en West-Vrieslandt, mitsgaders vande [...] Staten van Zeelandt [...] Vol. 9*, pp. 526–526. Art. 1 and 3 Placaet of 1776.

[53]Art. 2 placaet of 1776.

[54]Art. 4–6 placaet of 1776. It is interesting that, just like the French Declaration of 1738, a time limit was imposed on the slave's visit to the metropolis. Bosschaert did not refer to the situation in France, so this could be coincidental.

[55]Art. 7, placaet of 1776.

directors of the *Sociëteit van Suriname* and the directors of the small Berbice colony. However, we only find it published in the *Placaetboeken* of Surinam, which further confirms the idea that it were especially Surinam slaves travelling to the metropolis.[56]

6.3.3 Enforcing the Placaet of 1776

If we are to follow the lead of the *Resolutiën van Holland*, one gets the impression that, on the short term at least, the issue of black slaves who had come to the metropolis further caught the attention of the States of Holland.[57]

On 12 August 1776, Sir Aron Jacobs Polak, a Surinamese planter, had sent a request to the Generality.[58] Polak had come to the Republic in 1769, and had apparently decided to make his stay more comfortable by taking four slaves with him. After his return to Surinam, someone must have told his four slaves about the resolution of 9 August 1771 ("door instigatie van andere Kwaadwilligen", the resolution mentions). He asked for an explicit confirmation from the States General that the resolution did not apply to those four slaves, who considered themselves as being free for the moment. The case made it to the meeting of the States of Holland again. They advised that the four ought to be confirmed as being slaves and referred the case back to the Generality.[59]

The pattern of the previous acts was duly followed here as well. In a meeting of 30 September 1776, the records of the States of Holland were once more mostly copied verbatim. The States General clarified (or post facto changed the scope of, depending on one's interpretation) that the resolution of 9 August 1771, with which it had declared that Marytje Criool and her daughter were free upon having entered the Netherlands, was of no use here. It was made in a particular case, and as a result, Sir Aron Jacobs Polak's four slaves who had been in the Republic remained enslaved as well.[60]

---

[56]The content of the *placaet* was known in Curaçao as well, as Hondius reports that several cases in Curaçao courts referred to it between 1776 and 1852. Hondius (2011), pp. 385–386. For the Suriname publication on 1 September 1776, see de Smidt and van der Lee (1973), pp. 897–898.

[57]For the period 1524–1791, the *Resolutiën van Holland* have been digitized. One starts finding references to slaves starting from the 1653–1668 index. However, all of these references, except the index for the period 1771–1780, only refer to either citizens from the Republic who have been enslaved in North Africa, or issues involving colonial slavery. It is only in this 10 year period that we find some references to slaves who have visited the Republic, and even then, all of them are clustered in the period between Jan Nepveu's request and 1777. After that case, there are no more references to be found.

[58]In contrast to the previous cases, we know very little about this man, though Van de Voort found his name amongst records of debtors in 1757. Van de Voort (1973), p. 285.

[59]For the case at the States of Holland level, see *Resolutien van de Heeren Staaten van Holland en Westvriesland in haar Edele Groot Mogende Vergadering genomen in den jaare 1776, Tweede* deel, 1286–1287

[60]NL-HaNA, Staten-Generaal, 1.01.02, inv.nr 1498 (eerste minuten), NL-HaNA, Staten-Generaal, 1.01.02, inv.nr 2861 (geresumeerde minuten).

A second, more elaborate case, soon came before the States General. One way or another, Blondin and Sabina, the two slaves who were partially responsible for the enactment of the Placaet of 1776, had travelled to the Republic in 1775 together with their child Cicero. Blondin had even found a job there.

Unfortunately, when the case came before them on 30 December 1776, this did not seem to matter a great deal to the States General. It were the creditors that had sequestered the plantation where Blondin's family originally came from who asked for intervention by the States General. They asked for another confirmation that the resolution of 9 August 1771 freeing Marytje Criool was given in a particular case and had no precedential value, which the States General duly confirmed. The family would have to go back to Surinam.[61]

Unexpectedly, the case did not end there. In the private papers of Pieter van Bleiswijk (1724–1790), the *raadspensionaris* (Grand Pensionary, the most important civil servant[62]) of Holland between 1772 and 1787, we find a request for reconsideration of the States General's decision of the previous year.[63] In this rare document, we hear the Blondin family's version of the events.

According to them, when their deceased owner Thomas Wybrand van Rees had taken them with him to the Republic in 1763, he intended that they had thereby gained their freedom. The family pleaded that they had returned to Surinam voluntarily, and had lived there as free persons in the years after. Things apparently started going wrong in 1774, when the widow of van Rees got into financial difficulties, and Blondin and Sabina were included on an inventory of the estate. The property being sequestered a little while later, the new owners Valckeniers and Du Quesne quickly wanted to lay their hands on the Blondin family, who by then lived with the widow in Panamaribo, the capital of the colony. Eventually, they left her, and Blondin ended up in the service of a high-ranking soldier named Jan Willem van Oldenbarnevelt (named Witte Tullingh), in the Republic. However, Du Quesne and Valckenier were not to be deterred. They had already petitioned the Court of Holland and had asked permission to send a *deurwaarder* (enforcement officer) in order to bring the family back into slavery. The family now asked support from the States General to free them on the basis of their purported free status as from 1763, or, even if they did not agree, to make an equitable decision.

Holland took a particular interest in the case again, and wanted the request examined by the deputies of the city of Dordrecht and the *Gecommitteerde Raad* of Holland.[64] A few months later, Bosschaert reported his findings to the States of Holland, and they agreed with him in rejecting the slaves' request. Bosschaert pointed to the fact that the placaet of 1776 had confirmed in writing that slaves did not become free solely by having resided in the Republic. He did confer that the placaet of 1776

[61] NL-HaNA, Staten-Generaal, 1.01.02, inv.nr 1501 (eerste minuten), NL-HaNA, Staten-Generaal, 1.01.02, inv.nr 2864 (geresumeerde minuten).

[62] On this office, see Israel (1995), pp. 454–455.

[63] NL-HaNA, Raadpensionaris Van Bleiswijk, 3.01.25, inv.nr. 342.

[64] *Resolutien van de Heeren Staaten van Holland en Westvriesland in haar Edele Groot Mogende Vergadering genomen in den jaare 1777, Eerste deel,* 111–112.

had a non-retroactivity clause, which stated that for cases predating its enactment, the *status quo* would apply. But were Blondin and Sabina free before that period, or not? Bosschaert discussed the results of his enquiry as to their status in Surinam. He came to the conclusion that they had always remained slaves and had simply tried to make the resolutions of 1771 and 1773 applicable to themselves. What is more, he held that, the resolutions of 1771 and 1773 aside, there had never been recognition of the maxim that coming to the Republic meant that a slave remained free when he returned to the colonies. Although this was Bosschaert's main legal argument, another consideration influenced him. It was duly noted that if all slaves who had been here before the Placaet of 1776 were as "insolent" as Blondin and Sabina, and started claiming their freedom, the banks and creditors which kept many of the Surinam plantations afloat would be in trouble, as the value of mortgaged slaves disappeared through enfranchisement.[65]

Clearly, this sealed the fate of the family, and the Generality followed the advice of Holland on 4 April 1777, condemning Blondin and his family to slavery again.[66] We hear of the family one final time in May 1777. In the meantime, the plantation's creditors had pushed their case in the Court of Holland. Their case seems to have stalled there (the record is unclear as to exactly why). On the creditors' request, the States of Holland eventually decided to send a letter to the Court of Holland, stating that the court had to render its assistance to the petitioners in order to have the slaves sent back. [67]

We do not know what eventually happened with Blondin and his family, but should assume that all did not end well. After this episode, both the records of the States of Holland and the States General become silent on slavery in the metropolis again.

If we look at Johannes van der Linden's popular 1793 abridgments to Voet's *Commentarius ad Pandectas*, he only took note of the same cases which we just discussed. Whereas Voet himself believed that slaves coming to the metropolis could have themselves declared free by a court ruling, van der Linden nuanced this. He noted the exception for runaways on the basis of the 1736 ruling, the exception that was created by the Placaet of 1776, and he also referred to the case of Aron Jacobs Polak.[68]

So far, one can only wonder whether any more cases came before the court, or whether the States General bothered to studiously enforce the Placaet of 1776 in the long term. We have reason to be sceptical about the latter question.[69] Indeed,

---

[65]Ibid., pp. 328–332.

[66]NL-HaNA, Staten-Generaal, 1.01.02, inv.nr 1505 (eerste minuten), NL-HaNA, Staten-Generaal, 1.01.02, inv.nr 2868 (geresumeerde minuten)

[67]*Resolutien van de Heeren Staaten van Holland en Westvriesland in haar Edele Groot Mogende Vergadering genomen in den jaare 1777, Eerste deel,* 776–777.

[68]van der Linden (1793), Liber I, Tit. V—De statu hominum; Gane (1955)., Book I, Tit. 5, Sect. 3. I have made use of Gane's 1955 translation of Voet's work. Another author who has discussed the Placaet of 1776 is H.J. Arntzenius (1734–1797), a professor of Roman law at Utrecht University. Arntzenius (1783), Tit. VIII.

[69]It is likely that there were other cases, but municipal archives need to be researched more thoroughly on this issue to convey a fuller image of the Dutch freedom principle.

circumstantial evidence suggests that the unclarity about the legal status of slaves who had been in the Republic remained as great as ever.

First, there are two curious cases that seem to point at a modification of the placaet of 1776, though this is not to be found in the records of the States General or the States of Holland. A former slave called Caatje sent a request to the States of Holland in 1778. She had been in the Republic with her master, who had provided her with freedom letters during that stay. However, back in Surinam, the man who she stayed with, a vicar called Du Pasquier, had taken away her freedom letters "for safe-keeping". As she feared for her freedom, she asked the city to send her a copy of those letters. It is the answer by the Amsterdam authorities which is interesting. Freher, the clerk dealing with the case, confirmed that she was obviously free, because "she had lived far longer than a year and six weeks in the Republic, before the Resolution of the States concerning the slaves of the colony; and before the latest Resolution living undisturbed in this country for a year and six weeks was enough to be freed forever from all marks of slavery".[70]

The case is rather strange. In neither of the previous sources does the requirement to have lived in the Republic for "a year and six weeks" come to the fore. And yet, it appears in a second case. This case involved John Gabriel Stedman (1744–1797), a Dutch colonial soldier known as the author of a work called *The Narrative of a Five Years Expedition against the Revolted Negroes of Surinam*. In this work, a prominent role was played by Quassie van Timotibo, a slave who took the side of the Dutch in the revolt. Interestingly for our purposes, Stedman both knew of the *placaet* of 1776, and reported how Quassie went to the Republic. One scholar has looked at the diary of Stedman, which stated that Quassie was declared free on 10 July 1778. Exactly one year and six weeks after he arrived in the Republic.[71] Again, it is unclear where this idea originated.

Moreover, the *placaet* even caused considerable confusion outside of the Republic. Schoeman has traced some cases that arose in the Cape Colony in 1790, again involving the legal status of some slaves who had been in the Republic. The local Council of Policy was unsure how to proceed. There was reference to the instruction of 1714 which argued that slaves having touched the soil of the fatherland became free, others averred that this instruction had been repealed and replaced by a rule that stated that the slave only became free after having stayed in the motherland for three years, and yet other colonisers believed that the placaet of 1776, although not promulgated by the EIC, was also good law in the Cape Colony. Unfortunately, the

[70]The translation is my own. The original reads "Dunkt Freher, dat zij egter natuurlijk vrij is, als hebbende hier te lande veel langer als een jaar en zes weeken gewoond alvoorens de laatste Resolutie van H.H.M. aangaande de slaaven der colonien; En voor die laatste Resolutie was een jaar en zes weeken hier te lande ongestoord woonende genoeg om altijd van alle slavernij bevrijd te blijven". The document can be found at Vrije neegerin Caatje - Amsterdam en Slavernij. In: Stadsarchief Amsterdam. http://www.amsterdam-slavernij.nl/item/vrije-neegerin-caatje/. Accessed 22 September 2018. There are small mistakes in the transcription provided there, as the "alvoorens" is translated by "zoals" instead of "before".

[71]Mok (2017)

clarifications that the Cape colonists might have received from the Heeren XVII back in the Republic has not been found in the records.[72]

In retrospect, the *placaet* of 1776 seems like an emergency measure, which was made after some Resolutions of the States General had created the impression that slaves who had ever touched Dutch soil, were free. Obviously, this idea was dangerous to both the *Sociëteit van Suriname* and metropolitan creditors. Holland must have felt that its interests were threatened by these decisions, and forced a limitation on the freedom tradition upon the Generality, for whom this issue must have been less important. To further limit the damage of the 1771 and 1773 resolutions, the decisions in the cases of Polak and Blondin were made. As the immediate danger of financial loss retracted, the attitude of casual neglect returned.

6.4 Black Slavery in the United Provinces After the Batavian Revolution: Unexplored and Unproblematic?

6.4.1 The Batavian Republic and the Kingdom of Holland: Unclear Situation

The Dutch Republic did not escape the Revolutionary fervour of the end of the eighteenth century either. In 1795, with assistance from France, the Batavian Republic was proclaimed. Mimicking the French, the Dutch promulgated their own version of the Declaration of the Rights of Man and of the Citizen, which held in its first article that all people were born free and with equal rights. Would this be the precursor of a French-style confirmation of the freedom principle?[73]

Abolitionist philosophy had also spread in the Netherlands during the second half of the eighteenth century. Although older historiography has tended to believe that abolitionism was never very important, more recent research has brought some new perspectives. For example, between 1755 and 1807, 144 publications related to slavery and the slave trade appeared in the Republic, with 131 of them being critical about slavery and/or the slave trade. Whilst there was still a difference with the situation in England, where abolitionism had become a mass social movement, the Dutch debate clearly was not that muted as has been thought before.[74]

Arend Huussen has asked the question whether this abolitionist fervour actually resulted to anything when three drafts for a new constitution (to replace the 1579 Union of Utrecht as the "constitution" of the United Provinces) were drawn up: the 1796 *Plan van Constitutie*, the 1797 *Ontwerp van Constitutie* and the 1798 *Staatsregeling voor het Bataafsche Volk*. The results were sobering. Where some

[72]Schoeman (2012), pp. 1020–1023.

[73]Gerbenzon and Algra (1972), pp. 169–174.

[74]Huussen (1999); Drescher (1994); Jansz (2005).

representatives initially still wanted slavery to be discussed, this soon broke down to requests to discuss the slave trade, but not slavery itself. And by the time the 1798 *Staatsregeling* was created, after the 1797 *Ontwerp* had failed to receive popular support, there was widespread agreement in the National Assembly to mention neither slavery nor the slave trade in the new Dutch constitution. The situation was not altered by the next constitutions, nor after the French annexation in 1810.[75]

On a cursory note, one could ask whether the French law of 28 September 1791, France's codification of the freedom principle, also became part of the Dutch laws during the period of the French annexation between 1810 and 1815. Whilst this transplantation of the French freedom principle happened in the Southern Netherlands, I have not found proof to establish the same for The Netherlands. Two decrees, one of 8 November 1810 and another of 6 January 1811, included long lists of French laws which were to be applied in the areas of the former Dutch Republic. The law of 28 September 1791 was not amongst them (and neither were the later decisions inspired on the Declaration of 1777).[76]

Not much thus seems to have changed concerning the treatment which black slaves could expect whilst in the Netherlands. There were probably not many of them in the metropolis at this point, given that Surinam was taken over by British forces between 1799 and 1816. That being said, we simply lack cases to ascertain conclusively what would have happened to a slave claiming his freedom at this point.[77]

6.4.2 Codifying the Dutch Freedom Principle: The Dutch Civil Code of 1838

The Dutch freedom principle was only codified for the first time in 1838. Although Napoléon's civil code continued to be used even after his downfall, the United Kingdom of the Netherlands, uniting the North and the South once more, soon set to develop a new civil code. Eventually, this code was only promulgated in 1838, after the South had already seceded to become newly independent Belgium.[78] The Dutch freedom principle was finally confirmed at this point, as Art. 2, 2nd part of the new Dutch civil code now held that:

---

[75] Huussen (1999).

[76] Kunst (1967), p. 108. For the French laws that were applied in the Netherlands, see the three volume series *Verzameling van wetten, besluiten en andere regtsbronnen van Franschen oorsprong in zooverre deze, ook sedert de invoering der nieuwe wetgeving, in Nederland van toepassing zijn* (ed. C.J. Fortuijn). On this period in Dutch legal history, generally see Berkvens et al. (2012).

[77] Interestingly, in his 1806 *Regtsgeleerd practicaal en Koopmansboek*, Johannes van der Linden proclaimed a broad vision of the freedom principle. According to this work, every slave became free upon arrival in the metropolis, besides for runaways. This could prove that the 1776 *Placaet* was indeed considered defunct, or it might have been the case that van der Linden simply added less nuance to this work in comparison with his abridgements to the *Commentarii ad pandectas*. van der Linden (1806), 10.

[78] Gerbenzon and Algra (1972), pp. 224–226.

Slavery and all other sorts of personal servitude, of whatever nature or under whatever denomination are not to be tolerated in the Kingdom.[79]

One contemporary scholar used this article to pose himself a hypothetical (?) question: what would happen if a slave from the colonies, who has become free by coming to the territory of the Kingdom, went back to the colonies? Was he a slave or a free person over there? The answer given was in favour of freedom, and three reasons were advanced to substantiate this claim. First, the author believed that it was the intent of the Dutch legislator of 1838 to fully reinstate the freedom principle, as it was enunciated by jurists such as Van Leeuwen in the seventeenth century. The stowaway case of 1736 and the Placaet of 1776 were handily discarded by the author. The decisions regarding stowaways had not created a rigid precedent according to him, noting the court's lack of motivation for its judgments. The Placaet of 1776, meanwhile, was considered to have been abolished, if not implicitly by the French, than at least explicitly by the new civil code. If slavery would re-attach to the slave, Dutch liberty would be an empty shell. And whilst the Dutch could not, for example, force Russian courts to acknowledge the freedom that a Russian serf who had been in the Netherlands had received, the situation was judged to be different for the Dutch colonies. They belonged to the same Dutch realm. Second, the *favor libertatis* of Roman law was used as an argument. Finally, an analogy with France was made, as the author noted its 1791 promulgation of the freedom principle.[80]

6.4.3 *The Road to Abolition: The Case of the Slave Virginie*

As colonial legislation had made it nearly impossible for slaves to come to the fatherland with their masters in the nineteenth century, one is hard pressed to find evidence of any further presence of black slaves in the metropolis. For the period 1828–1845, Maduro found only one instance of a slave travelling from the Antilles to the Netherlands. Few years later, one of the very scarce instances of black slaves travelling to the metropolis did make it to the highest echelons of the Dutch government.[81]

In 1852, the Dutch Minister of the Colonies received a request from the governor-general *ad interim* of Surinam, Ph. De Kanter (1804–1852). The governor asked for advice and a decision regarding the case of the slave Virginie. Virginie had travelled with her master to the Netherlands few years before, and now claimed her freedom

[79] The translation is my own. Art. 2, second part Dutch Civil Code of 1838 ("Slavernij en alle andere persoonlijke dienstbaarheden, van welken aard of onder welke benaming ook bekend, worden in het rijk niet geduld")

[80] Den Tex and Van Hall (1840), p. 1840.

[81] The account of the case is taken from Oostindie and Maduro (1986), pp. 157–164.

in the colonies on the basis of that visit.[82] The slave's master, Baron Raders (1794–1868), a one-time governor of Surinam himself, sent a letter opposing this.[83] He staked his claim on the *placaet* of 1776 and the fact that he knew of several slaves who had gone to the motherland, but did not consider themselves to have been freed on the basis of that visit. All these arguments were contradicted by the *procureur-generaal* of Surinam. On the issue of the freedom principle, he simply referred to Art. 2 of the Dutch civil code to assert the lasting freedom of the slave, even upon return to the colonies. However, the Minister of the Colonies still doubted. He asked additional advice from a former judge of a Surinam court, consulted again with the *procureur-generaal* and even discussed the matter with the Minister of Justice. Only after all these persons confirmed the same, did he decide that Virginie was indeed free after having been on Dutch soil.[84]

Virginie's case proves two things. Legally speaking, the Dutch freedom principle was clearly confirmed. This is not so surprising. The official abolition of slavery was near, and the only reason abolition took until 1863 was because a compensation scheme for slave owners had not yet been agreed on.[85] At the same time, the examples of Raders show that Virginie was lucky, as she found out about the Dutch freedom principle one way or another. This lot was certainly not shared by the few companions who travelled, just like her, as slaves to the Netherlands, but did not know about the principle. In that sense, Dutch soil only became completely free once slavery itself was abolished in 1863.

6.5 Conclusion

By the middle of the seventeenth century, the Dutch freedom tradition could be found in the writings of a great many scholars, and it continued to be reiterated in tracts during the eighteenth century.

However, when the Dutch came into contact with slaves on their soil, such confirmations of clear soil were clearly more difficult to find. Before the second half of the eighteenth century, the evidence is patchy, and the black presence must have been minimal. The cases we traced showed that some black people had clearly heard of the freedom precedent, but there was no clear legal affirmation. Quite the contrary, as elsewhere, Dutch courts did not seem inclined to afford much compassion to stowaways arriving in the Republic.

---

[82] Ibid. The letter of De Kanter, which includes the main legal arguments of the parties, is reprinted on page 160.

[83] Rather ironically, this same Baron Raders was also part of a Dutch state commission that was brought into live in 1853 by the Dutch king William III in order to make proposals on the abolition of slavery across the Dutch colonial possessions. Priester (1987), p. 156.

[84] Ibid.

[85] Jansz (2005), pp. 508–511.

The record only becomes clearer when the freedom principle was perceived as a legal problem in the early 1770s. This was clearly a problem of the Republic's own making, as its lawyers seemed to confirm the legality of the freedom principle in two particular cases. Clearly, this went against the vested colonial interests of the province of Holland and the colonial interests behind it. Thus, Holland was pivotal in partially restricting the freedom principle through the 1776 statute. On the short term, the instrument seems to have been enforced well, with the Dutch trying to tie the loose ends that had been left by the resolutions of 1771 and 1773. After a few years however, the attitude of casual neglect towards the legal anomaly seems to have come back.

It took until 1838 before the freedom principle was clearly restored in The Netherlands, at a time when the black presence had once more become minimal to non-existent. Even then, late cases such as the 1852 example of Virginie show that there was still opposition against the possibilities of the freedom principle to disrupt ties of colonial ownership.

6.6 The Southern Netherlands: A Tradition Largely Untested

In contrast to France, England and the United Provinces, the Spanish and later Austrian Netherlands never really took part in the Atlantic slave trade. Antwerp faltered as a colonial market at the end of the sixteenth century to the benefit of Amsterdam, and it took well until the start of the Austrian period in the beginning of the eighteenth century before a Belgian port, namely Ostend, would become important again. Despite the attempts of Ostend merchants to become a factor of importance in the colonial slave trade, this never materialised.[86]

Given those preconditions, the black presence in the Southern Netherlands can only have been minimal. No scholar has assessed the numbers yet, and we only know that there were a few black people (whose personal status we do not know) to be found around Belgian ports in the eighteenth century.[87] The life of coloured people in the Southern Netherlands is mostly shrouded in darkness, though their occasional appearance in paintings confirms that some must have been present on the soil of the country.[88] If we were to have the opportunity to test whether the freedom principle remained valid here, such a case would have to be largely accidental.

---

[86]Huyghebaert (1981), p. 175; Drescher (2009), p. 146.

[87]Huyghebaert (1981).

[88]One example of this is a painting of the governess Maria Elisabeth of Austria. The painting, by the hand of the Dutch artist Leonard Schenk, shows her during her *Blijde Intrede* (Joyous Entry) in Brussels. Here, we see her being accompanied by two young, black boys who are holding her train. Given the case discussed below and Maria Elisabeth's involvement in the proclamation of the freedom principle, we could gauge that the boys were probably once given to her but were not to be considered as slaves anymore. The painting is reprinted in Schreuder (2017), p. 29.

Theoretically speaking, not much seemed to have changed in legal thought on the issue of the freedom principle. Whilst the quality of legal scholarship in the Southern Netherlands was generally unimpressive in the eighteenth century, two of the few famous scholars of that century, Georges de Ghewiet (1651–1745) and Dominique Sohet (1728–1811) argued in favour of a broad vision of the freedom principle.[89]

In his *Institutions du droit Belge*, de Ghewiet discussed the issue of personal servitude or slavery (confounding the two in a title "Des serfs de fait ou esclaves", set against *servitude réelle* or, as he called them, *serfs de coutume*). According to him, slavery or personal servitude had been abolished by an *ordonnance* of 1132 (a wrong assessment, as we already pointed out). From the moment a slave arrived in the Southern Netherlands, he became free ("Dès qu'un Esclave arive dans ces Pays, il devient eo ipso libre"). Given that de Ghewiet's work was meant to instruct French jurists on the peculiarities of the areas conquered by Louis XIV in the War of Devolution (1667–1668), he had one *caveat*, namely that the French Edict of 1716 had been registered by the Parlement of Flanders.[90]

We find much the same in Sohet's work, which was an attempt to compare the laws of the Prince-Bishopric of Liège (itself part of the Holy Roman Empire) with the customs of the eastern provinces of the Southern Netherlands. In his *Instituts de droit pour les pays, de Liège, de Luxembourg, Namur et autres*, we find that thanks to "universal agreement" amongst Christians, slavery and personal servitude had ended around 1250. Whenever slaves from other countries would come to these provinces, they became free from the moment they entered.[91]

Through sheer chance, the authorities of the Austrian Netherlands were faced with the freedom principle at one moment in the eighteenth century.[92] In 1733, one Juan Blanco, the captain of an English ship, arrived in the port of Ostend with his slave Antonio Bartholomeo de Lion (who came from Mexico). Blanco permitted his slave to attend a church service in the city. After the church service was over, an Italian soldier brought the slave to the drum major of the army regiment which was present in the city. The drum major was a black person, which gives the impression that Antonio's origins probably lay in Africa as well. Whilst chatting, Juan Blanco arrived, and he hit his slave several times with a stick to get him back aboard the ship. At that point, the slave decided to flee. Maybe the drum major had told him that slaves became free upon arrival in the Southern Netherlands? Anyhow, his master found out and had Antonio thrown in prison. The slave then petitioned the local nobleman François-Dominique Vilain de Gand (known as the *Comte de Gand*), the governor of Ostend, for his freedom. de Gand must have felt unsure how to proceed, as he sent a letter to Maria-Elisabeth of Austria, the governor of the Austrian

---

[89]On de Ghewiet and de Sohet, see Gilissen (1981), p. 361. For the importance of legal writing in the Southern Netherlands during the eighteenth century, see Van den Broeck (1990).

[90]de Ghewiet (1736)., Partie prémiére, Tit. II, XXXV. As said before, de Ghewiet's reference to an 1132 (actually 1232) *ordonnance* is incorrect. de Ghewiet cited Gudelinus, Christinaeus, Knobbaert and the customs of Antwerp in favour of the freedom principle.

[91]Sohet (1770), Livre I, Tit. LXX. Sohet referred to Voet.

[92]The only person who seems to have noted this case is Ernest Nys. Nys (1890), pp. 144–146.

Netherlands between 1725 and 1741. She then asked the *Geheime Raad*, one of her central advisory organs, for guidance.[93]

In its advice, the *Geheime Raad* started by noting that, according to popular opinion ("la commune opinion et même l'opinion vulgaire passé en loi tacite"), slaves coming to the Southern Netherlands became free upon arrival. It did not consider this to be decisive and wanted to back this up by references to the most eminent jurists of France, the United Provinces and the Austrian Netherlands. A plethora of scholars was mentioned. From France, Jean Bodin, Antoine Mornac (1554–1619), André Du Chesne (1584–1640), one Bouchet, Bernard Automne (1574–1666) and a certain Carolus were all referred to.[94] From the Dutch Republic, Groenewegen van der Made and Arnold Vinnius were quoted. Finally, Zypaeus was mentioned as well (including the references he made). To back this all up, the case that was discussed by the Great Council of Malines in 1532 was referred to as a precedent. Finally, the customs of Antwerp were mentioned. The council considered this final element to be the most decisive. They referred to the period when Antwerp had flourished, when it was an important city in international commerce. The council was convinced that Antwerp's freedom provision could only have been moulded by cases concerning slaves that must have happened in the city's glorious past, and in which the slave received his freedom from the municipal authorities.[95]

These arguments seem to have swayed the governor, as she concurred that Antonio Bartholomeo de Lion was held to be free as from the moment he had entered the city of Ostend, following the laws and customs of the Southern Netherlands ("est à réputer pour une personne de libre condition dès son entrée dans la ville d'Ostende, suivant les lois et usages des États de Sa Majesté dans les provinces des Pays-Bas de son obéissance"). This ruling is scarcely surprising. In a society which was excluded from the spoils of the Atlantic slave trade, there were no interest groups striving for a relaxation of the freedom principle. Lacking this factor, giving freedom to those few slaves asking for it in the Southern Netherlands must have been evident.[96]

As an interesting anecdote, Belgium also has a codification of the freedom principle. In 1794, French troops occupied the Southern Netherlands (a second time) after having defeated the First Coalition in the Battle of Fleurus. At first, the French

[93] *Recueil des ordonnances des Pays-Bas autrichiens. 3ième série, IV,* 503–505. The *Geheime Raad* was one of the three councils established in 1531 to assist the ruling monarch/governor of the (then still united) XVII Provinces in his tasks of government (the others being the *Raad van State* and the *Raad van Financiën*). The *Geheime Raad* was composed of jurists who mainly helped with the administration of justice and police in this region. See Coppens et al. (1994), pp. 295–324.

[94] On Mornac and Automne, see Arabeyre (2007), pp. 26–27, 580. André Du Chesne was a famous historian and geographer. There were several Bouchets in the sixteenth and seventeenth century (historians, poets, and even a councillor in the Parlement of Paris), but the name does not feature in the *Dictionnaire historique des jurists français*. The reference to one Carolus is even more obscure. This author wrote a work called *de Grassaliis Regalium Franciae libri* duo in 1538. The work does not seem to have been preserved, nor do we know anything more about its author (unfortunately so, because if the reference is correct, this would have been a very early pronouncement of the French freedom principle).

[95] *Recueil des ordonnances des Pays-Bas autrichiens. 3ième série, IV,* 503–505

[96] Ibid.

occupiers decided to let the region keep its existing laws and customs. However, the Southern Netherlands were annexed on 1 October 1795, and French legislation was to replace the existing one over time. For French legislation that was enacted after 1789 but before the annexation, a transition period of one and a half year was to be respected before it became applicable in this region. The French eventually decided to speed up this process. The French Minister of Justice Philippe-Antoine Merlin de Douai had to make an *état général* of all the French revolutionary laws which were not yet published in the conquered territories, but which had to be applied there.[97] The so-called *Code Merlin* was ready on January 26, 1797, and in it, we find the "*Loi portant que tout homme est libre en France*" of 28 September 1791. That is not to say that the French consciously thought this over, as if anything, the period in which the French decided how and when to transplant the revolutionary era legislation to its new territories, was known for its legal uncertainty, both in the promulgation and application of laws.[98] Be that as it may, the French codification of the freedom principle was thus transplanted to the Southern Netherlands, and has since formed part of its legislation.[99]

References

Arabeyre P (2007) Dictionnaire historique des juristes français (XIIe-XXe siècle). Presses Universitaires de France, Paris

Arntzenius HJ (1783) Institutiones iuris belgici civilis. Abrahamum Groenewolt and Iacobum Dikema, Groningen

Berkvens AMJA, Hallebeek J, Sirks AJB (2012) Het Franse Nederland: de inlijving 1810–1813: de juridische en bestuurlijke gevolgen van de 'Réunion' met Frankrijk. Uitgeverij Verloren, Hilversum

Beyerman JJ (1977) Vrijlating van een slavin (en een slaaf) bij notariële akte (2 December 1658). Weekbl voor privaatrecht, Notar en Regist 108:566–568

Blakely A (1993) Blacks in the Dutch world: the evolution of racial imagery in a modern society. Indiana University Press, Bloomington

Buve RTJ (1963) Surinaamse slaven en vrije negers in Amsterdam gedurende de achttiende eeuw. Bijdr tot Taal-, Land- en Volkenkd 119:8–17

Coppens EC (1997) Één grote onzekerheid. De invoering van de Franse wetgeving in de Zuidelijke Nederlanden na 1795. In: Moorman van Kappen O, Coppens EC (eds) De Bataafse omwenteling en het recht. Gerard Noodt Instituut, Nijmegen

Coppens H, Aerts E, Baelde M (1994) De centrale overheidsinstellingen van de Habsburgse Nederlanden 1482–1795. I. Algemeen rijksarchief, Brussel

de Ghewiet G (1736) Institutions du droit belgique. C.-M. Cramé, Lille

De Jong GF (1971) The Dutch reformed church and Negro slavery in colonial America. Church Hist 40:423–436

[97] Gilissen (1981), pp. 403–404.

[98] For more on the Code Merlin, see Heirbaut (2011), pp. 13–31; Coppens (1997).

[99] *Recueil de lois et règlemens pour les neuf départemens réunies par la loi du 9 Vendémiaire, an IV, Tome premier* (Paris: Impremerie de la République, 1797), 440. To be fully correct, it is unknown to me if any enslaved persons might have entered the Southern Netherlands after Napoléon reinstated colonial slavery and resuscitated the *police des noirs*.

de Smidt JT, van der Lee T (eds) (1973) Plakkaten, ordonnantiën en andere wetten, uit- gevaardigd in Suriname, 1667–1816. Emmering, Amsterdam

Den Tex CA, Van Hall J (1840) Regtsgeleerd bijblad, behoorende tot de Nederlandsche jaarboeken voor regtsgeleerdheid en wetgeving, Tweede Deel, Voor het jaar 1840. Johannes Müller, Amsterdam

Drescher S (1994) The long goodbye: Dutch capitalism and antislavery in comparative perspective. Am Hist Rev 99:44–69

Drescher S (2009) Abolition: a history of slavery and antislavery. Cambridge University Press, Cambridge

Fatah-Black K, van Rossum M (2014) Slavery in a 'slave free enclave'? Historical links between the Dutch Republic, Empire and slavery, 1580s–1860s. WerkstattGeschichte 66–67:55–74

Fruin R, Colenbrander HT (1922) Geschiedenis der staatsinstellingen in Nederland tot den val der Republiek. Nijhoff,'s-Gravenhage

Gane P (ed) (1955) The selective Voet: being the Commentary on the Pandects. Butterworth, Durban

Gerbenzon P, Algra NE (1972) Voortgangh des rechtes: de ontwikkeling van het Nederlandse recht tegen de achtergrond van de Westeuropese cultuur. Tjeenk Willink, Groningen

Gilissen J (1981) Historische inleiding tot het recht. Kluwer Rechtswetenschappen, Antwerpen

Heirbaut D (2011) De Franse overheersing in België. Pro Mem 13:13–31

Hondius D (2008) 'Swart' in Nederland: Afrikanen en Creolen in de Noordelijke Nederlanden vanaf de middeleeuwen tot de twintigste eeuw. In: Kolfin E, Schreuder E (eds) Black is beautiful: Rubens tot Dumas. De Nieuwe Kerk, Amsterdam, p 387

Hondius D (2011) Access to the Netherlands of enslaved and free black Africans: exploring legal and social historical practices in the sixteenth-nineteenth centuries. Slavery Abol 32:377–395

Huussen AH (1999) The Dutch constitution of 1798 and the problem of slavery. Tijdschr voor Rechtsgeschiedenis 67:99–114

Huyghebaert N (1981) De eerste zwarten te Sint-Andries. Biekorf 81:175–177

Israel J (1995) The Dutch Republic: its rise, greatness, and fall 1477–1806. Oxford University Press, Oxford

Jansz U (2005) Onze natuurgenoten overzee. De afschaffing van de slavernij in de Nederlandse koloniën als mensenrechtenvraagstuk. Tijdschr voor Geschied 118:497–512

Jordaan HR (2012) Slavernij en vrijheid op Curaçao: de dynamiek van een achttiende-eeuws Atlantisch handelsknooppunt. Faculty of Humanities, Leiden University, Leiden Institute for History

Kunst AJM (1967) Historische ontwikkeling van het recht. Deel I. W.E.J, Tjeenk Willink, Zwolle

Mok I (2017) Waarom kwam Quaco in Nederland pas na 1 jaar en 6 weken vrij? In: Cultuursporen. https://www.cultuursporen.nl/2016/11/slavernij-in-de-republiek-1-de-wet-van-1776/. Accessed 22 September 2018

Nys E (1890) L'esclavage noir devant les jurisconsultes et les cours de justice (première partie). Rev droit Int législation comparée 22:57–69

Oostindie G (2005) Paradise overseas: the Dutch Caribbean: colonialism and its transatlantic legacies. Macmillan Caribbean, Oxford

Oostindie G, Maduro E (1986) In het land van de overheerser II Antillianen en Surinamers in Nederland 1634/1667–1954. Foris Publications, Dordrecht

Ponte M (2019) 'Al de swarten die hier ter stede comen' Een Afro-Atlantische gemeenschap in zeventiende-eeuws Amsterdam. Tijdschr voor Soc en Econ Geschiedenis/ Low Ctries J Soc Econ Hist 15:33–62

Priester LR (1987) De Nederlandse houding ten aanzien van de slavenhandel en slavernij, 1596–1863: het gedrag van de slavenhandelaren van de Commercie Compagnie van Middelburg in de 18e eeuw. Commissie Regionale Geschiedbeoefening Zeeland, Middelburg

Schoeman K (2012) Portrait of a slave society: the cape of good hope, 1717–1795. Protea Boekhuis, Pretoria

Schorsch J (2004) Jews and blacks in the early modern world. Cambridge University Press, Cambridge

Schreuder E (2017) Cupido en Sideron: twee Moren aan het Hof van Oranje. Uitgeverij Balans, Amsterdam
Sirks AJB (2012) The supreme court of Holland and Zeeland judging cases in the early eighteenth century. In: Brand P, Getzler J (eds) Judges and judging in the history of the common law and civil law. Cambridge University Press, Cambridge, p 363
Sohet D (1770) Instituts de droit pour les pays, de Liege, de Luxembourg, Namur et autres. Guillaume-Joseph Lafontaine, Namur
van Bynkershoek C (1926) Observationes tumultuariae. Tjeenk Willink, Haarlem
van der Linden J (1793) Commentarii ad pandectas. Wild, Utrecht
van der Linden J (1806) Regtsgeleerd, practicaal en koopmans handboek. Johannes Allart, Amsterdam
Van de Voort JP (1973) De Westindische Plantages van 1720 tot 1795: Financiën en Handel. De Witte, Eindhoven
Van den Broeck J (1990) De historiografie van het recht in de Zuidelijke Nederlanden tijdens de 18de eeuw. Wetenschappelijk comité voor rechtsgeschiedenis, Koninklijke academie voor wetenschappen, letteren en schone kunsten van België, Brussel
van Kralingen H-J (2014) Some remarks on slavery and legal history. Leiden Law Blog
Van Oosten MS (1962) Systematisch compendium der Observationes Tumultuariae van Cornelis Van Bijnkershoek. Tjeenk Willink, Haarlem
Voet J (1707) Commentarius ad pandectas. Abrahamum de Hondt, Den Haag

Chapter 7
A Legal Comparison of the Freedom Principle—Similarities and Differences

7.1 Introduction

In the past chapters, we have traced the waxing and waning of the freedom principle in England, France and the Low Countries. We discussed its origins in the late Middle Ages and then looked at its development over two phases: first, when the respective countries were not (or to a very limited extent) involved in the Atlantic slave trade themselves (1500–1650), and the black presence in Western Europe was consequently very small. Second, we discussed how the principle evolved when these countries were heavily implicated in the Atlantic slave trade, and had extensive American possessions, which led to an increase in the black community in each of the countries involved. This chapter compares the different experiences. Using a comparative law approach, we will ask the following question: what are the main similarities and differences with respect to the origins and development of the freedom principle in the jurisdictions discussed?

7.2 The Legal Origins of the Freedom Principle

Let us first look at the origins of the freedom principle. Did each and every country have, in law, a principle which held that slaves became free as soon as they crossed into their territory by the middle of the seventeenth century, or not?

As a prerequisite for such a principle, slavery would normally first have to be precluded in domestic law.[1] In this regards, although neither of them formally abrogated slavery, France, England and the Low Countries are broadly similar. In the early middle ages, the same forces were at work in each of these countries (religious,

[1] I use the term "normally", given that we noted how Spanish American colonies, which acknowledged slavery, sometimes freed slaves from Dutch colonies coming to their territory. That, of course, has primarily to do with the weakening of an imperial opponent, and not with the impossibility of slavery in Spanish America.

F. Batselé, *Liberty, Slavery and the Law in Early Modern Western Europe*, Studies in the History of Law and Justice 17, https://doi.org/10.1007/978-3-030-36855-5_7

economic and military, if we are to follow Marc Bloch), as many free peasants saw a deterioration in their condition at the moment when slaves saw theirs ameliorate. Likewise, enslavement in a just war disappeared from the theatre of war between Christian nations. As a result, in the twelfth century at the latest, the only kind of unfreedom known to the great majority of the domestic population in these countries was serfdom, not slavery. In France and the Low Countries, there were many local varieties in an unfreedom which was defined by *formariage*, *mainmorte* and various dues. In England, common law developed the elaborate law of villeinage. First in the Low Countries, but later on in France and England as well, unfreedom started to decline, as the use of free labour became economically more interesting. In France, there was a partial exception to all this, as slavery, though not of "Frenchmen", lingered on for a longer period in the Southern fringes of the kingdom.

Although the great majority of the population in each of these countries could thus count themselves as being personally free by 1650, serfdom nor slavery was formally abolished in the Early Modern Period. Mainly in France do we find the mistaken idea that slavery had been abolished by royal legislation, because of the fact that Louis X's 1315 *ordonnance* was being misinterpreted by the likes of Bodin, centuries after the law itself was made.[2]

However, slavery was nowhere part of the domestic laws, and it is clear that it was not considered to be acceptable for the domestic population anymore. In France, we can see this in the sentiment expressed due to the enslavement of French persons by the Barbary States. Likewise, in England, the failure of the Vagrancy Act 1547 showed that instituting a form of domestic slavery was no option.

It is difficult to see how the galleys fit into this picture. Condemnations to the galleys could be seen as exceptions to disallowing slavery for the domestic population, but the French did not consider their *forçats* to be in exactly the same state as Turkish slaves. Likewise, whilst the English talked much about galley slavery, not much came of it in reality, and it was even less of an issue in the United Provinces.

In any case, what is clear is that none of the countries under consideration still recognised slavery as part of their domestic legal order and that the only kind of unfreedom recognised in any of them was serfdom or villeinage, which had nearly disappeared itself by the middle of the seventeenth century.

This raises the question whether slaves who came to one of these countries from the outside also became free upon their arrival. In essence, this is a question of private international law. In the fifteenth and sixteenth century, this issue would mainly arise when slaves from Spain and Portugal, where slavery was allowed by domestic laws and where black slaves were to be found across the country, came to England, France or the Low Countries. Did these countries recognise a status which was conferred by Spanish or Portuguese law? Here, things do seem to differ a bit.

In France and the Low Countries, we found a strong freedom tradition. The origins seem eerily similar, as both countries had strong cities with municipal charters. In the sixteenth century, the provisions of such charters became national principles of law, which could be applied to free slaves rather than serfs, the original target of such provisions.

[2]George de Ghewiet also believed slavery to have been abolished in the Southern Netherlands by a misinterpreted *ordonnance* of 1232.

In the case of France, municipal charters containing some form of freedom principle were especially important for those cities which had most contacts with Spanish territories. This explains the central role of the French city of Toulouse. Although these freedom provisions were not universally shared amongst all cities, they were internalised by national, domestic law in the sixteenth century. It is most likely that this elevation happened because of the Habsburg-French rivalry, combined with the antislavery sentiment caused by the experience of Barbary enslavement.

For the Low Countries, there was also an evolution from a municipal to a national freedom principle. Just like France, it had cities with municipal freedom provisions. Unlike France, the dichotomy between cities that did not recognise slavery on the one hand, and Iberians holding slaves on the other hand, only came to the fore in the sixteenth century. This was due to Antwerp's role in international commerce. It is in this context that we find governor Mary's decision not to return the Portuguese ambassador's slave. Mary's decision in favour of liberty did not seem to have been aroused by anti-Portuguese sentiment, but probably had more to do with her keeping the domestic context in mind.

At the same time, both France and the United Provinces (upon its independence in the latter quarter of the sixteenth century) were not involved in the colonial slave trade in the sixteenth century, so the idea of the freedom principle cannot have been seen as very problematic from the ruler's perspective. The Iberian powers were the opponents of the French and Dutch in the later sixteenth century, and the idea of the "Black legend" was present in both countries.[3]

This does fail to explain why the idea also spread in the Southern (Spanish) Netherlands, where the Spaniards had more of an interest in guarding property rights. It might have been that the freedom principle did not matter a great deal to the Spanish rulers of this region. The merchants holding slaves in Antwerp were primarily Portuguese, and the precedent of Malines predates the Spanish-Portuguese Union of the Crowns in 1580. Second, the presence of Spanish slaves in Antwerp must have been almost negligent by the end of the sixteenth century. On the one hand, the city's prosperity declined and the Scheldt estuary was controlled by the Dutch Republic, on the other hand, the city of Seville (and later Cadiz) enjoyed a monopoly on Spanish colonial trade.[4]

To continue, in both France and the Low Countries, the freedom principle was not to be found in central legislation.[5] We can find expressions of the idea in court cases, such as the 1571 case that was discussed by the Parlement of Guyenne, or the Great Council of Malines' advice of 1532. Subsequently, the idea was picked up by scholars in both countries, as a web of cross-references between such scholars quickly spread, even crossing state boundaries.

[3]Emmer (2007), pp. 34–39, Brion Davis (1966), pp. 111–114.

[4]Israel (1995), pp. 171–172, 242, 262–263.

[5]One has to take into account that it is primarily with our current mind-set that custom is perceived as a less important source of law. In the sixteenth century, custom was accorded a high status by many scholars Kelly (1992), pp. 184–186.

Interestingly, whilst we find "blanket" freedom principle enunciations in legal tracts of both countries, the freedom principle was sometimes qualified in one way or another. In the case of France, this was often done by positing a link between baptism and freedom. In the Low Countries, we sometimes find the requirement for a slave to petition the authorities himself in order to receive his freedom. One reason to explain this might have been that the French writers expounding on the freedom principle were making use of fifteenth century Italian works which made a link between baptism and slavery, as Nys suggested.[6] Another reason, which I would suggest, could be that scholars were taking the particularities of their region into account. Whereas French persons were sometimes enslaved by Barbary pirates, the inverse held true as well, the French likewise capturing Barbary Muslims in the Mediterranean. A religious exception to the freedom principle, to explain for the presence of Muslim slaves, makes sense then. In the Low Countries, the "Muslim factor" was less relevant due to geographical reasons. If scholars wanted to expound on the freedom principle, they must have come across the provisions of the municipal laws of Antwerp, the most important city of the Low Countries in the sixteenth century. These provisions necessitated that slaves had to petition the authorities themselves in order to receive their freedom, in case their masters did not voluntarily acknowledge their slaves' freedom. Scholars might well have elevated this municipal qualification into a national nuance on the freedom principle.

I am more reserved to say that, legally speaking, England also had the same freedom tradition as part of its legal system. Much obviously depends on one's interpretation of Cartwright's case, and the extent to which it was known to contemporaries. Personally, I am rather doubtful about its value. As noted, the case was only mentioned for the first time in *Somerset v. Stewart*, more than 200 years after it had happened (discounting the seemingly little known reference by John Cook). Thus, if it really happened in the first place, it was certainly not well-known by contemporaries. Second, it could be explained in several ways. Originally, it was even understood as a limitation on the means of punishment, rather than as a recognition of the freedom principle. Finally, it is a bit unclear what exactly is meant with "*England was too pure an Air for Slaves to breath in*". The first time we find the enunciation of "*As soon as a slave sets foot on English soil, he is free*" in a common law judgment, is only in 1705.[7]

At the same time, statutory law (as elsewhere) was silent on the issue. Doctrine does show some discussion regarding the situation of slaves coming to England, but what we find is quite limited. Lord Coke and Matthew Hale did not refer to the freedom principle in their works on the English common law. Before the second half of the seventeenth century, we thus have to revert to William Harrison's statement. However, he was not a lawyer, and many scholars considered his statement to be overblown. It is only in the second half of the seventeenth century that we find some

[6] Nys (1890), pp. 62–63.

[7] *Smith v. Brown and Cooper* (1705), 2 Salkeld 666. As I mentioned, even in that case, I believe that Holt's statement was not as broadly meant as one would presume. The case itself did not come to a final conclusion either.

enunciations of the English freedom principle, and two of those scholars might have been influenced by civilian thinking through their legal education. More importantly, even these pronouncements usually only mentioned a very qualified freedom principle. Those few English writers expounding on what happened if a slave came into their realm, such as Charles Molloy, did acknowledge that full chattel slavery could not be allowed to subsist in England. At the same time, these writers were very unsure whether and to what extent the right of service continued whilst the slave was in the metropolis. These were generally opinions which favoured neither full emancipation, nor a full continuation of the rights attached to slavery.

I do need to qualify this statement in one respect. England might not have had the same popular maxims as the continent, but that does not mean that, viewed from the point of private international law, slavery would have been permitted to exist in England. Rather, the issue remained more of an uncertainty. That did not deter Somerset's legal counsel, who were craftily able to construct the idea of a freedom tradition in England, even though, in law, the basis of the freedom principle was less secure than in France or the Low Countries. How do we explain this difference?

In my opinion, the difference is not so much caused by differences in the approach that courts would take when faced with Iberian slaves, but rather has to do with geography and coincidence. The fact that French and Dutch courts had a chance to pronounce themselves on the status of slaves coming to their jurisdiction, was because there were Iberian slaves to be found in the first place. France's border with Spain guaranteed a continued trickle of Spanish slaves crossing the border, and Antwerp's early role in the colonial trade meant there was a Lusitanian merchant presence.

The English attitude towards the Iberian powers had soured by the end of the sixteenth century, as England was amongst those countries refuting Iberian claims to Atlantic territory, and in this they were no different than France or the United Provinces.[8] But the chance of Iberian slaves coming to England must have been relatively small, and without slaves, there could be no legal judgment, and little doctrinal discussion.[9] The first time English courts had to bother themselves with black slaves in England was at the end of the seventeenth century. At that moment, English claimants were involved, and their country was already well involved in the Atlantic slave trade.

---

[8]Neff (2014), pp. 126–135.

[9]In fact, the only case I know of a foreigner claiming his runaway slave in England dates from 1259. In this case, an Italian knight (Roger de Lynton) asked for a royal order to assist in the search of his Ethiopian runaway slave Bartholomew. Permission was granted by the king. We can only guess whether such a case would have had the same outcome in the sixteenth century. It does show that in the 13th century, notwithstanding that slavery had disappeared from England, a status acquired under foreign law was respected Bush (1996), pp. 615–620. The relative neglect of English writers on questions of private international law related to a personal status conferred by the laws of another country is also discussed in the work of the pro-slavery writer Thomas Cobb (1823–1862). See Cobb (1858), pp. 146–147, 156. Cobb likewise linked this neglect to geography, as Britain was more secluded from foreigners, simply due to its island location.

This proposition is not meant to be revolutionary. English judges might well have come to the conclusion that Spanish slaves became free if they touched English soil. From a strict legal perspective however, barring English judgments, the freedom principle was better grounded in French and Dutch rulings and scholarly writing, whereas it was less so in England by the second half of the seventeenth century.[10]

7.3 The Freedom Principle and the Atlantic Slave Trade

Before the second half of the seventeenth century, in each of the countries under discussion, the number of slaves coming from other countries was negligent, if not almost non-existent in the case of England. All that changed in the period 1650–1800. In this era, the European powers made massive use of slave labour in their colonies. Slavery was considered to be legal in the colonies, as we confirmed through our survey of both international law and colonial slave laws between the sixteenth-eighteenth centuries. Especially towards the end of this period, colonial proprietors living in the English, French and Dutch colonies often returned to their respective metropolises and took one or more slaves with them. Likewise, slaves sometimes managed to make it to the motherland by themselves or ended up there in one or another way. What does a comparison of the behaviour of metropolitan courts and legislators, as well as the reality "on the ground" teach us?

7.3.1 The Reaction of the Legislators

First, there was an important similarity between all countries under discussion. As a domestic principle of law, slavery was not revived. This is easy to explain. If not much was left of personal unfreedom around the middle of the seventeenth century, even less of it remained in the next century and a half. Reinstating slavery as a domestic principle was simply unfeasible.

Second, the reaction of legislators can also serve as an example to further my claim that the "roots" of the freedom principle were stronger in France and the Low Countries than in England. The earliest governmental decisions in France, as well as

[10] Articles of Léon Vignols on the French freedom principle led me to the *Histoire abrégée des traités de paix, entre les puissances de l'Europe, depuis la paix de Westphalie* of the French diplomats Christoph-Guillaume Koch (1737–1813) and Frédéric Schoell (1766–1833). This was an authoritative collection of peace treaties between European powers. Curiously, when the treaties on the abolishment of the slave trade are discussed, Schoell also confirms this view. He notes that whereas the French had "always" had a maxim confirming that slaves became free upon touching the soil of France, he held that this was only adopted in England after *Somerset's case*. I do disagree on the breath of his claims regarding Somerset, but it does show that even this contemporary writer noted the difference between France and England (although the counter-argument would be that there might have been a flavour of French chauvinism in his pronouncement) Koch and Schöll (1817), 178.

the 1775 report of the States of Holland and the 1733 advice of the *Geheime Raad* prove that the highest authorities of the state at the least took note of the freedom principle.[11] At the same time, early (aborted) attempts in England to make legislation on black slaves present in England seemingly did not refer to the freedom principle, and the idea we get is that at least parts of Parliament considered slavery to be legal in England.[12]

Only two of the countries under discussion, namely France and the United Provinces, effectively made legislation to regulate the status of blacks in their country. The reaction of the French legislature was the most elaborate. Before 1716, various decisions recognised the freedom principle. In 1716, the freedom principle was restricted for the first time, although the "default condition" remained freedom. The approach partially changed in 1738. The freedom principle was completely abrogated, as the default condition in case the procedural requirements of the declaration of 1738 were not met, was the reshipment of the slave to the colonies *au profit du roi*. In 1777, the French legislature switched its approach, as race was used instead of status, in an attempt to rid the country of its black presence. Racial bias explained part of this change, but it was also an attempt to finally get cooperation from the Parisian courts.

Contrary to what one would expect, the Dutch States General or the particular States did not seem to uphold the freedom principle in the earliest stages of the black presence in the Dutch Republic. Although the "roots" of the freedom principle were comparable to France, I have found less of an early tug between colonists taking slaves with them, and the Dutch authorities declaring these slaves to be free, although the Dutch Cape Colony sources confirm that the notion of the freedom principle was known by some colonists. The difference is notable, but much work on the Dutch archives remains to be done to ascertain this difference. The Dutch legislator only intervened in 1776, at the height of the black presence in the United Provinces. The result, the placaet of 1776, was similar to the French edict of 1716 and the declaration of 1738. Exceptions to the freedom principle were created, although the default condition in case the requirements of the law were not respected remained freedom.

There were some other similarities between the Dutch and French legislation. For example, when it came to stowaways, both countries were harsh: the edict of 1716 and the placaet of 1776 confirmed that stowaways could not get their freedom simply by coming to the metropolis. Finally, the actors pushing for legislation were eerily similar in the French and Dutch case. Certainly in an early period, the influence of the Atlantic cities, Nantes in particular, was clear in the legislative restrictions on the French freedom principle. Likewise, Holland, the province with the biggest financial stake in the Dutch colonies, clearly pushed through restrictions on the Dutch freedom principle mostly on its own.

---

[11] Boulle and Peabody (2014), pp. 29–31; *Rapport op de Missive van Gouverneur en Raaden van Suriname, concerneerende de vryheid der Slaaven die in het Vaderland zyn geweest, 19 juli 1775,* 2*; Recueil des ordonnances des Pays-Bas autrichiens. 3ième série, IV*, 503–505.

[12] Paley (2010).

More interesting than the content of these legislative measures, which we discussed in full in the relevant chapters, is the following question: why did France and the United Provinces legislate on the issue in the first place, and why did this not happen in the Southern Netherlands and England?

Explaining why the authorities in the Southern Netherlands did not issue legislation, is the easiest part: there simply was no reason to do so. In contrast to the Dutch, English or French, the interests of the Southern Netherlands in the Atlantic slave trade were negligent. During the Spanish period, and especially so after the demise of Antwerp, Spanish ports dealt with the colonial slave trade. During the Austrian period, despite the best wishes of the city of Ostend, the Austrians did not acquire any important colonies. Slave arrivals in this region were accidental then, and there was no interest group that would have wanted to sway the governor to abrogate the freedom principle.

This explanation does not hold true for England. The Atlantic slave trade was economically important, and there was a virulent colonial lobby to be found in England as well. Seymour Drescher has tried to address the reasons for this lack of legislation.[13] According to him, the difference lay in the political context. He believed that the French monarchy could draft legislation unilaterally, without having to consult the wider public opinion. For this reason, the French monarchy was accessible to highly organized domestic elites (read: the plantation lobby), which could ask for laws drafted in their favour. As the English Parliament had to take a wider range of interests into account, Drescher held that "the masters utterly failed to win support for legislation affirming their property rights".[14]

I will not contend with Drescher's statement but rather qualify it. My contention would be that, in contrast to France or the United Provinces, there was less of an incentive for any pro-slavery lobby to appeal to Parliament and ask for legislation in the first place. I would explain this by using an analogy which Peabody also made in her *There Are no Slaves in France*. When describing the approach of the French government to the issue of black slavery, she noted that "The government moved the issue of blacks in France to the back burner only to return it when it occasionally boiled over. Nobody found a way to remove the pot from the stove".[15] She used this analogy to explain that the French government only intervened with the issue of black slaves in France at moments when the problems connected to this black presence came to the fore. To me, this analogy seems very useful to explain when and why a government intervened in the issue of blacks coming to the metropolis for every country under discussion, namely at "moments of crisis".

[13]His account was mainly written in the context of legal restraints placed upon black entry (done in France by the *Police des Noirs*, but never done in England). In more recent work, Drescher also made some other comparative remarks between the French, Dutch and English approach to slaves arriving in the metropolis Drescher (2009), pp. 94–102.

[14]Drescher (1990), p. 424. Sue Peabody further added that this lack of regard to the public opinion explained why the French courts (and in particular, the Parlement of Paris), had such a strong role in the shaping of legislation on this subject Peabody (1996), p. 7.

[15]Peabody (1996), p. 13.

In France, we find three such moments. The first one was in 1715–1716, when the early confirmations of the French freedom principle clashed with the attempts of colonists to take slaves to France. Planter interests, exemplified by Nantes' Gérard Mellier, managed to have legislation in their favour passed. In 1738, there was the highly publicised case of Jean Boucaux, which brought to light many violations of the edict of 1716, and triggered the government to impose stricter limits. Finally, right before the declaration of 1776, we noted how various scholars described clashes between slavery and the freedom principle: the tensions between the Admiralty of France and royal orders, another well-known case (Pampy and Julienne v. Mèndes France) and liberty given to the slave of a well-connected owner. All these examples explain why the issue of black slaves received governmental attention again.

Likewise, the States General only intervened when there was a "moment of crisis". In this case, the crisis was a creation of its own. The States General had given liberty to some individual slaves in the early 1770s, but the way in which its resolutions were drafted apparently convinced several other slaves that a stay in the Republic had given them their freedom. At this point, the States of Holland jumped in. Not only were their colonial interests at stake (given their role in the *Sociëteit van Suriname*), domestic Amsterdam creditors could suffer from liberty being given to mortgaged slaves as well. As a result, Holland drafted legislation to crackdown on the idea of the freedom principle, and to limit the damage the States General had done.

My contention is that there was no such crisis in England, or at least not before 1772. In the early stages, unlike France, we do not find a government granting freedom to slaves arriving in the country. Likewise, neither the courts nor society at large really curbed slave ownership in England. In particular, the Yorke-Talbot opinion can be mentioned, which must have soothed the troubles of many slave-owners. Finally, there are no indications that the English Parliament ever made the same "mistake" as the Dutch States General did, by granting confusingly-drafted acts of freedom to individual slaves. In short, there were no compelling reasons for the slave-owners to appeal to Parliament in the first place. A crisis did erupt at one point, namely during *Somerset's case*. At the closing stages of the hearings, Mansfield even advised the colonisers that, if they wanted the issue to be conclusively settled, they should appeal to Parliament. Why was no legislation made at this point? Van Cleve has shown that the slave owners did appeal to Parliament, but that their request was denied. Likewise, he thinks that the slave owners did not try very hard at this point, as they had assumed that *Somerset's case* would turn in their favour. Afterwards, when the outcome of Somerset went wrong for the colonists, Parliament did not intervene either. The way to explain why Parliament did not do so, at a time when the Dutch and French government did not have qualms to legislate on this issue, would be to note a defining factor of England. Abolitionism had already started to become important in England early on, but less so elsewhere. After Somerset's case, Parliament was probably already too internally divided on the issue to make legislation.[16] In effect, when the issue of slaves in England did "boil over", Parliament preferred to keep its hands off the pot.

[16]Drescher (1990), pp. 420–422, Van Cleve (2006), pp. 630–631.

7.3.2 The Reaction of the Courts

How did the courts deal with issues of personal status? First, neither of them contended that slavery was part of domestic law. There was one exception to this rule. In the case of *Pearne v. Lisle*, we have seen how Lord Hardwicke equated villeinage and slavery, in order to prove that colonial slavery was lawful and slaves were property in both England and the colonies.[17] This was an exception to the normal approach of English courts, and has to be seen within the context of Hardwicke's imperial vision of the relationship between colonial and English law.

If courts were faced with slavery, they had to deal with it as an issue of private international law. Here, we find some interesting differences. When faced with slave status arising from colonial law, English courts made use of English law. Likewise, when the Parisian courts had to deal with a status which was regulated by the Code Noir in the colonies, they used French law. The Edict of 1716 and the Declaration of 1738 had given the French courts clear guidelines how they had to deal with these issues, but this did not change the situation in the Parisian courts, which reverted to applying the French freedom principle. The Dutch approach was a bit different. In the 1736 case that came before the Supreme Court of Holland and Zeeland, the applicable law was not Dutch law, but Roman-Dutch colonial slave law. Unfortunately, we do not know whether this approach was only used in cases of stowaways, or whether it was extended to other cases as well (for the period after 1776, the Dutch *placaet* gave explicit guidelines on stowaways, and recourse to Dutch law would then have become the more obvious option).

Some arguments used by counsel were different, and some were similar. For example, lawyers tried to use extra-legal arguments on both sides of the continent. In *Somerset v. Stewart*, we find Wallace's assertion that a broad judgment against the slaveholders would cause mass financial losses. In the same manner, Monsieur Verdelin's lawyer believed that a decision in favour of slaves would cause uproar in the colonies. The same fear for colonial repercussions also featured in Bynkershoek's observations.

At the same time, there were some interesting distinctions in arguments used. In the two best reported English cases (*Chamberline v. Harvey* and *Somerset v. Stewart*), the crux of the argument is the question to what extent black slavery could be equated with English villeinage. The slave's lawyer would hold that it could not be equated, thus "albifying" villeinage, as one scholar called it.[18] The master's lawyers would use villeinage as an argument in favour of respecting an unfree status, slavery, conferred under colonial law.[19] In the French published cases, we do see references to serfdom,

[17] Of course, there were virtually no English villeins left, so the domestic effect of such a ruling was limited.

[18] The idea thus being that only (white) Englishmen could have ever been villeins, but that no new villeins could now be created out of the black slaves in England Rabin (2014).

[19] The best example is Hargrave's memorial for Somerset, which attempts to show the distinction between slavery and villeinage in no less than 22 pages Hargrave (1772), pp. 25–47.

but it is hardly the backbone of the argument.[20] One reason for this might be that the English law of villeinage was a well-developed part of the common law, and that English lords had been more effective in tying their villeins to the land. The characteristics of French serfdom were more dependent from region to region, and some of the lord's rights over his serfs had been abolished over time.

Unlike in England, in the French cases, the freedom principle is taken for granted. For example, in the case of *Jean Boucaux v. Verdelin*, both lawyers and the *procureur du roi* acknowledged that, in principle, the French soil rendered slaves free. The real discussion in court then, was whether there was an exception to the French freedom principle at hand.[21] The edict of 1716 and the declaration of 1738 were, of course, the easiest means to assert such an exception.[22] Another tack was possible as well, such as the one used by the lawyer of the slave Francisque. He tried to show that Indian slaves did not fall under the restrictions on the freedom principle, by focusing on his Indian heritage.

Why this difference in arguments? This is mostly an issue about the possible means to get to the same result. If a slave wanted freedom in France, the question was whether the French freedom principle applied or not. This straightforward way of asserting the freedom principle was lacking in England, and lawyers had to use a two-step approach. They had to plead that the only kind of unfreedom recognised by English law is villeinage and then that the status of blacks coming to England ought to be governed by English law, but that these black persons were no villeins. Following those two steps, the slave's lawyer could then assert that the slave was free, whilst the opposing lawyer could argue that the slave's status ought to be respected up to the limits of what the law of villeinage allowed for. We do not know enough of the arguments used by Dutch lawyers. The stowaway's lawyer referred to the precedent of the Great Council of Malines to assert the freedom principle, and in the case of Blondin and his family we also find the idea of the freedom principle for non-stowaways, which is more in line with the arguments used in France.

The substantive outcomes of court decisions varied as well. In France, we noted how there was a bifurcation. The Parisian courts constantly upheld the French freedom principle, freeing every slave who petitioned them. Whilst French courts did not motivate their judgments, we can infer that the Parisian courts did so on the basis of non-registration of the edict of 1716 and the declaration of 1738. This is clearer after 1738, given that the declaration of 1738 required the courts to declare that slaves were confiscated *au profit du roi,* in case the administrative provisions of the Declaration were not met. We lack exact data for the admiralty courts at the Atlantic seaside, but can presume that they respected the legislation, given their respective *Parlements*' registration of the laws, and the example of Catherine Morgan's case.

[20] For example, see de Pitaval (1750), 349–351.

[21] As the Admiralty of France routinely freed slaves, the *procureur du Roi* did not even bother to make elaborate statements in most of the cases. He simply sided with the slave's lawyer and asserted that "Je n'empêche pour le Roi les conclusions du suppliant être adjugées" Boulle and Peabody (2014), pp. 79–81.

[22] Verdelin's lawyer even tried to assert that the Code Noir could be used to justify the exception.

If French courts either clearly refuted or clearly recognised colonial slavery, the English courts went somewhere in between—that is, if we follow Van Cleve's reasoning, as most other scholars believe that the case law was contradictory or unsettled—. The few cases that came before Dutch courts all upheld slavery, but again, we only know of cases involving stowaways, a special category by any measure.[23] Given that we do not hear of Blondin & Cicero anymore after the States of Holland asked the Holland courts to assist their creditors in retrieving them, we can suppose that the courts did not protect them.

Finally, in contrast to their English counterparts, French courts could pronounce a judgment in favour of the slave's liberty, without this having legal consequences for the colonies.[24] The relationship between French metropolitan law and colonial law on slavery was quite clear, given that there was explicit royal legislation, the *Code Noir*. Likewise, a Dutch decision would not have had adverse legal consequences on colonial slavery, which was explicitly regulated by provisions of Roman law. English courts did not have this luxury, and the pronouncements made by them on slavery might well have reflected an individual judge's beliefs on the relationship between English colonial and metropolitan law.[25] This was a belief in "one imperial law" according to Hardwicke, but one of strict independence between colonial and English law in Holt's vision. Likewise, this approach might explain why Mansfield grounded his ruling in (the lack of) positive law, not common law.

7.3.3 *Other Differences and Similarities*

The most remarkable difference might be the sheer amount of cases we have come across.[26] In the Low Countries, we only discussed a handful of them. In England, about a dozen. In sheer contrast, we know that there were 154 cases in the Admiralty of France alone between 1730 and 1790! And to this, we can add a hitherto unknown number of cases at the other admiralty courts. How do we explain these remarkable differences?

A first explanation comes down both to sheer numbers and the state of research: in the United Provinces, the black presence was rather small, which explains the smaller number of cases. At the same time, we need to bear in mind the state of

[23] Bosschaert's report did mention that, in cases not involving stowaways, the courts could be asked to send a slave back to the colonies as well. *Rapport op de Missive van Gouverneur en Raaden van Suriname, concerneerende de vryheid der Slaaven die in het Vaderland zyn geweest, 19 juli 1775*, 4.

[24] Such decisions could of course be said to have had socio-political consequences for the colonies. If slaves knew that coming to France might render them free, one could expect that more slaves would try to reach France. This problem could have been foreclosed by the stowaway provisions in the French Edict of 1716, but the Parisian refusal to register the law in the first place barred this.

[25] Van Cleve (2006).

[26] I wish to thank Professor Sue Peabody for some of her very useful suggestions concerning these differences. Private correspondence with Professor Sue Peabody, 27/04/2017.

research. The focus in England has been on the reported cases that came before the central courts, and it might be that there still are quite some other cases which came before local courts. In the Unites Provinces, we can be reasonably sure that no more cases came before the Supreme Court of Holland and Zeeland (thanks to the notes of Van Bynkershoek and Willem Pauw), but it is highly likely that municipal court archives would be able to tell us of more cases which involved black servants/slaves taken to the Republic.

Even taking that factor into account, this does not explain the stark difference between France and England. The main reason to explain the difference between those two countries probably has to do with the Yorke-Talbot opinion. Given the clout of its writers, it is highly probable that the well-known opinion foreclosed most lawyers or clients' appetite to assert a slave's freedom in court, as they must have judged that their chances of winning would be minimal.[27] For example, it is highly relevant to note that in the two cases right before *Somerset v. Stewart* (the case of Jonathan Strong and *Hylas v. Newton*), Granville Sharp remarked that the slave's lawyers pointed to the Yorke-Talbot opinion. In *Hylas v. Newton*, the lawyers even only asked money damages because they were cowed by the opinion.[28]

In contrast, the several well-known cases in France, those with memorials being printed or to be found in collections such as the *Causes célèbres* (*Jean Boucaux v. Verdelin*), all went in favour of freedom. The case of Francisque was even decided by the Parlement of Paris, the most important court of the country. Next to that, the French admiralty's registration effort in 1762 must have highlighted questions of personal status. We find no well-known cases in the Low Countries, and *Somerset's case* was the first and only (very) well-known case in England.

Another difference which might come into play in explaining the different number of cases is monetary. In England, we noted how Mansfield (in *The King v. The inhabitants of Thomas Ditton*) said that he had never awarded back wages to slaves, and no other judge seems to have awarded this either. In Paris, on the other hand, many slaves did ask for back wages in their requests, although probably only a small number of slaves eventually received them. As most slaves did not boast large financial reserves, the incentive for a lawyer to take a slave case might have been smaller in England than in Paris, unless all lawyers involved were acting out of humanitarian motives.[29] If such in not the case, the hopes of profit, combined with the prospect of a certain favourable verdict, might have swayed some Parisian lawyers to take on these cases.[30]

Finally, one must keep in mind that, in all countries under discussion, the slaves that were taken to the metropolis were often the master's favourites, and thus in a relatively good position vis-à-vis plantation slaves. The chance of conflict between the slaves and their masters was rather low, and even if a conflict arose, the power balance was heavily skewed in favour of the master. He could always use private

---

[27]On the fact that the opinion was well known in the legal community, see Glasson (2010).

[28]Wise (2006), pp. 24, 46.

[29]As mentioned before this humanitarian motive would be a fruitful avenue for further research.

[30]For France, see Peabody (1996), pp. 88–105.

violence to try and take the slave back to the colonies against his will. This can be illustrated by some of the cases described by Granville Sharp before Somerset, where Sharp was only able to petition the authorities just before the slave was irretrievably gone.[31]

Another similarity was the legal uncertainty concerning the relationship between baptism and freedom. Not all European colonisers wrestled with this problem, as Portugal routinely baptised its slaves before sending them to the Americas.[32] The idea started to fade at the end of the seventeenth century in France, because of the Code Noir's provisions on baptism. In England the idea seems to have lived on for a longer time, and the Yorke-Talbot opinion, which was likely inspired by missionaries, tried to get rid of it. For the Low Countries, we have seen how baptism was certainly taken into consideration in the sixteenth century precedents, but did not find it discussed later on. The idea was disposed of by a decision of the Classis of Amsterdam, though it is unclear whether this was also done with the metropolitan context in mind.

The role of scholars in the promulgation of the freedom principle was less important at the time of the Atlantic slave trade. In the sixteenth century, scholars were largely responsible for spreading the idea of the freedom principle, on the basis of the few available precedents, and by creating a web of cross-references. In the eighteenth century, most scholars simply continued to reiterate the statements of their predecessors, but took note of the exceptions created by their respective national governments.[33] In England meanwhile, scholars such as Blackstone visibly struggled with the issue. This also helps to prove my assertion that in England, the debate on the recognition of slavery as an issue of private international law was more unsettled than elsewhere.

Finally, another recurring theme were the limitations imposed, if and when the freedom principle was recognised. Even if a slave was recognised as free when he came on metropolitan soil, the free air did not necessarily follow him upon return to the colonies. In France, we noted how an early case in 1707 recognized the French freedom principle, but did not extend it to a slave who had voluntarily returned to the colonies and had not claimed his liberty whilst in France. Even in Furcy's case, this argument was discussed. Likewise, the Dutch placaet of 1776 limited the results of freedom granted in the metropolis. Returnees were treated as manumitted persons, rather than as *vrye luyden*. Up to Virginie's case of 1852, the issue was uncertain in the Republic. Again, the same held true in England. In two of the cases after *Somerset's case*, namely *Williams v. Brown* and *The Slave Grace*, we find the idea that a slave did not take his freedom privilege back with him to the colonies.

---

[31] On private violence of masters, see for example Cairns (2013), pp. 168–169.

[32] For a discussion on the origins of the principle, next to the work of Ernest Nys, see Brion Davis (1966), pp. 98–106.

[33] For example, De Ghewiet in France or Van der Linden in the United Provinces took note of the exceptions created by their governments.

7.3.4 Law in Books Versus Law in Society

Whilst the focus of this work has been on the law, as it was moulded by "Judges, Legislators and Professors", to use the words of the eminent legal historian R. C. Van Caenegem, I do believe that my approach needs to be relativized. Clearly, one should also take note of the broader perspective. Such an approach also allows me to point to the danger of *Hineininterpretierung*. Lawyers nowadays are used to treating legislation as the highest source of law, and often closely evaluate the exact words of a statute, in order to know its application. Legal historians are very wary of using the same framework when looking at the Early Modern Period. Centralised legislation was often part of a dialogue between the centre and the local echelons of society. Legislative acts were not always well-published, and did not really lend themselves to a word-per-word exegesis, much as lawyers do nowadays. Finally, the law was often a coincidence, very much dependent on the historic conditions at the moment of promulgation, and not necessarily preceded by discussions on long-term policy.[34] Because of such factors, we need to go "behind the law" and look at everyday conditions as well.

In all of the cases discussed, only the Parisian courts consistently upheld the freedom principle, whilst English courts went for a "middle of the road" solution. The courts of the United Provinces were clearly ambivalent concerning the application of the freedom principle as well. Such a narrow focus tends however to obscure one point. Let us revisit the number of black people who came to Europe. For England, there were somewhere between 10,000 and 20,000 black people. In France, at its height, a presence of 4000–5000 blacks. For the United Provinces, a total of 700 blacks at the very least. A sizeable part of these persons came as slaves. Combine this number with some of the sixteenth century pronouncements of the freedom principle, which held that "*Slaves become free as soon as they set foot on our land*". Clearly, this was not the lot of the great majority of the personally unfree part of this black presence. All indicators show that many legal professionals and, more general, society at large condoned the presence of slaves.

The Low Countries? In the sixteenth century, we found instances of sales of slaves and manumissions in Antwerp. In the United Provinces, we noted much the same. Several notaries at least did not consider slavery to be illegal in the metropolis, for how else could they make notarial deeds dealing with the presence of such slaves? Finally, Oostindie's numbers showed that 627 out of the 656 Suriname slaves who came to the metropolis, also returned to the colonies.

England? The same holds true. The issue has been best discussed for Scotland by J. W. Cairns, but proof of manumissions can be found in England as well.[35] Most remarkably, we noted that there is evidence which strongly suggests that small slave markets once existed in several English cities. Likewise, various advertisements for runaway slaves (although the term slave was not necessarily directly used) were to be

[34] On all of these remarks regarding the role of central legislation in the Ancien Régime, see Martyn (2014).

[35] Drescher (1989).

found in newspapers. Again, the number of slave cases was negligent in comparison with the true size of the enslaved population.

Even in France, the many pronouncements in favour of liberty have to be taken into perspective. First of all for Paris. It has to borne in mind that at the same moment when the Admiralty of France was freeing slaves, its clerks were registering declarations of the arrival of slaves, much as they were doing elsewhere in France. Second, numbers give us the same sense of perspective. It is certainly true that Parisian courts freed at least 154 slaves and registered 93 acts of enfranchisements. However, there were at least 606 slaves who arrived in Nantes between 1740 and 1777, 653 in La Rochelle between 1719 and 1777, and 1024 in Bordeaux between 1720 and 1770.[36] And that number does not even take those slaves which were not registered into account.

Even after the Age of Revolution, we noted that slaves sometimes came to the metropolis. Certainly, in countries such as England, where abolitionism had become a popular movement in the final quarter of the eighteenth century, this was more difficult. But even there, masters could use the trick of an indentured servitude for a while, in order to be able to take some blacks with them to the colonies. More clearly, we noted how small numbers of black slaves could still be found in both the United Provinces and France in the early nineteenth century. Only right before these countries abolished slavery in their empires, was the personal status of slaves who came to the metropolis conclusively settled.

All in all, the gap between a doctrinal pronouncement of the freedom principle and the reality on the ground was incredibly large. For the great majority of slaves, the European soil was as unfree as that of the colonies.

References

Boulle PH, Peabody S (2014) Le droit des noirs en France au temps de l'esclavage: textes choisis et commentés. L'Harmattan, Paris

Brion Davis D (1966) The problem of slavery in western culture. Cornell University Press, Ithaca

Bush JA (1996) The first slave (and why he matters). Cardozo Law Rev 18:599–629

Cairns JW (2013) Slavery without a code noir: Scotland 1700–1778. In: Larkin FM, Dawson NM (eds) Lawyers, the law and history [Irish legal history society]. Four Courts Press, pp 148–178

Cobb TRR (1858) An Inquiry into the law of Negro slavery in the united states of America. T. & J. W. Johnson & Co.—W. T, Williams, Philadelphia

de Pitaval FG (1750) Causes célèbres et intéressantes, avec les jugemens qui les ont décidées, Tome quatorzième. Jean Neaulme, The Hague

Drescher S (2009) Abolition: a history of slavery and antislavery. Cambridge University Press, Cambridge

Drescher S (1990) The ending of the slave trade and the evolution of european scientific racism. Soc Sci Hist 14:415–450

Drescher S (1989) Manumission in a society without slave law: eighteenth century England. Slavery Abol 10:85–101

Emmer PC (2007) De Nederlandse slavenhandel, 1500–1850. Arbeiderspers, Amsterdam

[36]Koufinkana (2008), pp. 47–48.

Glasson T (2010) Baptism doth not bestow freedom: missionary anglicanism, slavery, and the Yorke-Talbot opinion, 1701–1730. William Mary Q 67:279–318

Hargrave F (1772) An argument in the case of James Sommersett. In: Negro A, Otridge W, London

Israel J (1995) The dutch republic: its rise, greatness, and fall 1477–1806. Oxford University Press, Oxford

Kelly JM (1992) A short history of western legal theory. Clarendon Press, Oxford

Koch C, Schöll MSF (1817) Histoire abrégée des traités de paix entre les puissances de l'Europe, depuis la paix de Westphalie. Tome 11. Gide, Paris

Koufinkana M (2008) Les esclaves noirs en France sous l'Ancien régime: XVIe–XVIIIe siècles. L'Harmattan, Paris

Martyn G (2014) De wet in het ancien régime: autoritatieve formele rechtsbron of pragmatische programmaverklaring? In: Martyn G (ed) Recht en wet tijdens het ancien régime: le droit et la loi pendant l'Ancien Régime. Algemeen rijksarchief, Brussel, pp 149–165

Neff SC (2014) Justice among nations: a history of international law. Harvard University Press, Cambridge

Nys E (1890) L'esclavage noir devant les jurisconsultes et les cours de justice (première partie). Rev droit Int législation comparée 22:57–69

Paley R (2010) Parliament and slavery, 1660–c.1710. Slavery Abol 31:257–281

Peabody S (1996) There are no slaves in France: the political culture of race and slavery in the ancien régime. Oxford University Press, New York

Rabin D (2014) Empire on trial: slavery, villeinage and law in imperial Britain. In: Dorsett S, McLaren J (eds) Legal histories of the british empire—laws, engagements and legacies. Routledge, Abingdon, pp 203–217

Van Cleve G (2006) Somerset's case and its antecedents in imperial perspective. Law Hist Rev 24:601–645

Wise SM (2006) Though the heavens may fall: the landmark trial that led to the end of human slavery. Pimlico, London

Chapter 8
General Conclusion—The Soil of Europe: Free or Unfree?

The goal of this book was to enquire how the so-called freedom principle developed in the legal order of France, England and the Low Countries during the Early Modern Period. This principle held that slaves became free upon crossing certain territorial borders. Let me briefly recall the flow of the argument, and the conclusions reached.

In the first chapter, we have set out the prerequisites for our study.

We started by setting out the definition of slavery, in order to delineate the subject of our study. For that purpose, we used the internationally recognised definition of slavery, as set out in the 1926 Slavery Convention: "(1) Slavery is the status or condition of a person over whom any or all of the powers attaching to the right of ownership are exercised". Whilst noting the ambiguity of some of the characteristics ascribed to being in the state of slavery, the definition was found useful in order to delineate slavery from serfdom, that institution which was also pervasive in Medieval Europe.

We then looked at the legal justification of slavery by lawyers and philosophers, from Greek times to the dawn of the Atlantic slave trade and beyond. The key term here was "continuity". Only in the second half of the eighteenth century, with Vattel's *Le Droit des Gens,* did we start to see some moral qualms regarding the institution of slavery. And before? The institution was broadly seen as legitimate, but the pendulum swung between two conceptions. Scholars as diverse as Sepúlveda, Thomas Aquinas, and to a certain extent even at times Hugo Grotius, showed that Aristotle's idea of "natural slavery" never fully perished away before the decline of slavery in the nineteenth century. Yet, certainly in the seventeenth and eighteenth century, the dominant attitude seems to have been more in line with the Roman inclination. Slavery was not part of natural law, according to which men were born free. But be it as a result of the sinful nature of men, or a more secular attitude towards the *ius gentium,* slavery was generally recognized as part of international law. In that regard at least, differences between Roman thinkers, Grotians, and even Vattel in the eighteenth century, were more cosmetic than fundamental.

One of the greatest legal edifices of the Christian Middle Ages, the development of just war doctrines, did however show one of the changes in comparison with earlier times. In contrast to Greek and Roman life, slavery did start to progressively

F. Batselé, *Liberty, Slavery and the Law in Early Modern Western Europe*, Studies in the History of Law and Justice 17, https://doi.org/10.1007/978-3-030-36855-5_8

disappear in Western Europe. As a result, writers started taking note of this at the end of the Middle Ages, pointing towards the European custom of not enslaving each other's troops any longer, and instead developing intricate systems of ransom and hostage-taking. Whilst the Catholic Church played a role in this development, it was primarily a complex set of economic and political reasons that helped towards this development.

That did not mean that unfreedom suddenly disappeared in Western Europe. Instead, we took cognizance of the debate concerning the transition from slavery to serfdom in Western Europe. If the institution was still well alive going into the Carolingian Era, it had practically perished in all but the fringes of Southern France by the twelfth century. The reasons behind this transition remain somewhat shrouded in mystery. Be it because of economic reasons (Marc Bloch's predominant factor), because of a transformation in society after the Roman era (more Marxist), or a "feudal transformation" around the year 1000, slavery disappeared and serfdom came in its place. The chaotic circumstances of the Dark Ages defy all-encompassing definitions, and the exact meaning of what a serf was could change significantly from one place to another. Some of the general characteristics (and with the risk of anachronisms) can be noted here. England, France and the Low Countries all knew the distinction between personal unfree status, and land to which servile dues were connected. Likewise, whilst economically speaking, the serf or villeins condition could really lie anywhere on the specter of economic prosperity, a serf owed some form of service or dues to his master. The decline of slavery was no pre-ordained path though, as the example of Spain and Portugal, where Christian and Muslim continued enslaving one another during the course of the Middle Ages, has shown.

Despite the disappearance of slavery in France, England and the Low Countries, we noted how scholars as diverse as Zouche, Grotius and Vattel still took slavery into account in their writings. One can fairly presume that what they had in mind, was the then growing commerce in men erupting on the boards of the Atlantic. First the Portuguese and the Spanish, but soon afterwards the English, French and Dutch all started using black slave labor to fuel their Atlantic economies. Even though slavery had disappeared from their metropolitan soil, there were remarkably little moral or legal qualms in any of these countries to resuscitate slavery in the Atlantic, some early writing criticizing the Spanish slave trade notwithstanding. Either through metropolitan acquiescence (England), royal intervention (France) or a reversal to Roman law (Dutch Republic), Atlantic colonies soon developed elaborate ways to regulate the lives of black slaves on their soil. The expansion of these systems raised one obvious question: would colonial slavery be recognized when a slave touched the soil of Europe?

This book has tried to answer that question in the second and third part, before engaging in a broad, comparative approach in the final part.

The second part focused on unearthing the origins of what have been seen as "freedom principle traditions", focusing whether and how the principle was legally grounded.

For England, we focused first on the decline of villeinage after the Black Death. As the institution of villeinage became progressively worn out due to manumissions, popular attitudes in favor of personal freedom, cities, and the rise of wage labor, villeinage eventually became an empty shell. Formally, the institution has never been abrogated, but it simply became devoid of any persons to regulate. A short lived attempt to resuscitate domestic slavery with the Vagrancy Act of 1547 utterly failed. Likewise, whilst a horrible condition nonetheless, the impressment of sailors for Britain's growing naval power could not be equated with slavery. However, it is one thing not to allow slavery for domestic purposes, but another thing altogether to have a principle holding that slaves on English soil, immediately become free. It was concluded that the legal foundations for such a principle were, if not weak, non-existent in English law. Lawyers before 1650 did not seem to take cognizance of it, and most simply rehashed the existing law of villeinage in their work, with or without noting that the institution had mostly fallen into disuse. Only the curious Cartwright's case begged to differ, with its pronunciation that England was too pure an Air for Slaves to breathe in. I criticized the value of the case for two reasons: first of all because of its veracity, which is uncertain, though I personally veered towards believing that it did take place. But more importantly, it did not seem to have been picked up by English lawyers for a long time and was thus of limited influence, as even the well prepared team of Somerset had to admit that they only knew of the case through Rushwordt's account.

Things stood rather differently in France. Whilst the claim was sometimes made from the sixteenth century onwards, slavery was certainly not legally abrogated by the French King in 1315. Though still often repeated in literature, the famous ordonnance of 3 July 1315 had a far more limited scope, and dealt with serfs, not slaves. That serfdom was indeed on the decline in France. Whilst it was still recognized in law up until the end of the eighteenth century, most of the serfs has progressively become free by the end of the Middle Ages. Meanwhile, cities became nuclei of economic activity in the later Middle Ages. Many of them had city charters, which incorporated a well-known provisions of early medieval law: a lord who did not exercise his *droit de poursuite* within a year and a day after the fleeing of his serf, could not exercise this right anymore afterwards. Obviously, such a principle was earlier implemented in practice in cities than elsewhere. Whilst the principle was meant to apply to the lord-serf relation, it was transformed in the South of France. Driven by the trickle of slaves coming in from Spain, first Toulouse and later also some other cities tried to implement their freedom provisions on slaves as well. Though the path was bumpy, a souring in relations between France and Aragon in the sixteenth century ensured that Toulouse could eventually continue to force its privilege. Likewise, in that century, the freedom principle was elevated from a municipal to a national principle in France. Examples abound. Toulouse continued to free slaves, as shown by Jean Bodin, but the Parlement of Bordeaux (in 1571) did so as well. These and a variety of other instances started referring to France as a land of freedom, where slaves became free as soon as they entered. It was not long before legal scholars started noting this, and Bodin, Grotius and Loisel are but a few of those holding that slaves became free as soon as they entered France. Lofty idealism aside, one should not forget that this might have been inspired by more mundane reasons. Slavery was primarily known to Frenchmen because of Barbary pirates enslaving Frenchmen, and the consequences of the freedom principle were very limited as long as only Spain and Portugal were involved in the slaving business.

Finally, the Low Countries were subject to many of the same forces. Serfdom was also in decline here in the later Middle Ages, and even disappeared in some regions a bit earlier than elsewhere, undoubtedly driven by the relative affluence of cities in this region. Likewise, slavery was never abolished by the French king, or any count or duke in any of the regions of the Low Countries. As in France and England, freedom provisions were present in some city charters, most importantly in that of the affluent city of Antwerp. It was here that the freedom principle was tested, and also mostly confirmed, in a case that has been forgotten in the literature. As Antwerp became home to not only a number of Sephardic Jews leaving Iberia after the expulsion decrees, but also became one of the gateways to the New World in the sixteenth century, there was a black, unfree presence on the city streets. When one such slave, belonging to the Portuguese ambassador escaped, it was the supreme court of the XVII Provinces, the Great Council of Malines that had to decide on the status of slavery in the Low Countries. In the end, its decision was rather limited: the request of the Portuguese ambassador for help in retrieving his slave had to be ignored, as slavery was unknown in the XVII Provinces. However, this lit the fuse for the development of a freedom tradition in scholarly writing. Soon after the Great Council made its decision, a great many scholars started seeing this decision as proof that slaves coming to the XVII Provinces became free as soon as they set foot on the soil. And yet, practice did show a more nuanced understanding of slavery. Both in daily life in Antwerp, as well as in Middelburg in 1596, lofty legal pronouncements were filtered through the lens of economic necessities, and some isolated instances of slavery seem to have continued mostly unabated.

In the third chapter, which dealt with the period 1650-1800, we tested where the rubber hit the road. Even in the case of France and the Low Countries, dealings with slavery had mostly been accidental and occasional in nature. However, with the rise of England, the Dutch Republic and France as slave traders themselves, the freedom principle was put to the test.

Even allowing for the inherent uncertainty in numbers, England was clearly the country where the black presence was the highest, with a clear concentration in London. Parliament's answer to the legal problem of unfree blacks on English soil was one of complete silence. The English common law courts were mostly left to settle the status of slavery in England. They clearly wrestled with this task all the way from the earliest cases at the end of the seventeenth century, up until the final abolition of slavery across the English Empire in 1833. Whilst there is a good argument to make in favour of a confused state of the law up until Somerset, Van Cleve's conflict of laws framework is very attractive. Common law courts seemed to be creating some form of "near slavery", in which some consequences of slavery were allowed in England, but some were not. Meanwhile, different judges had different ideas about the colonial repercussions of decisions under English common law, and might have taken this into account when making their decisions. What is sure is that the freedom principle stood at its nadir in England with the advent of the Yorke-Talbot Opinion, which, as a matter of private international law, can be seen as a statement in favour of recognising slavery on English soil. But even if Somerset clarified that Yorke-Talbot was clearly not written in stone, neither did Mansfield free all the English slaves. For that, abolitionist efforts in changing people's mind, and agency by black slaves fleeing their masters were more seminal. This abolitionist attitude went bottom-up through the English court system, as first local courts and only few decades before eventual abolition, the superior English common law courts, became convinced that England itself was indeed a land where the soil had to be free.

In the case of France, we find a strange, early dichotomy. Despite the seemingly strong freedom tradition, I showed how the issue of Turkish galley slaves remained remarkably non-controversial in France. The weak sophistry by the Count of Maurepas aside, who argued that there was an exception to French freedom for those slaves that were bought from countries where the slave trade was established (an argument equally valid for African slaves), the lack of contemporary discussion between French freedom and galley slavery remains surprising. This is all the more so, given that the early presence of black slaves does show this tug towards reasserting the freedom principle, as slaves were freed in the few lucky cases where their case was heard. This early, more liberal attitude did not stay in place long. The French king made his first inroads into the freedom principle in 1716, before mostly voiding the principle of any value in 1738. Whilst these laws were influenced by those regions in France having the most benefits from the slave trade, a more "racial" attitude soon came in its place. With the declaration of 1777, the King tried to eradicate France of any black presence, but this and subsequent attempts ended in failure. This failure was, by the way, broader than just 1777. Before then, it could be said that Paris boycotted the King's legislation, by consequently declaring slaves free who petitioned for it. But look at Nantes or Bordeaux, and one gets the reverse image: complacent, even positive about the royal legislation before 1777, but unhappy with the negative effects of the declaration of 1777 on what was seen as slaveholder property. Although the issue was formally put to rest with the re-recognition of the French freedom principle during the Revolutionary era, subsequent French governments almost continuously switched in their attitude towards the freedom principle. As in England, it was only just before the second abolition in 1848 that the freedom principle was fully guaranteed.

Finally, there are the Low Countries. The Southern Netherlands' attitude remained mostly similar by confirming the freedom principle. However, given the very minimal involvement of this region in the colonial ventures, and the consequent minimal to non-existent black population, the question remained mostly theoretical. We know more about the United Provinces. Somewhat surprisingly, the early battle between the freedom principle and slaveholders' interests was also rather subdued here. The cases of slaves claiming their freedom remained minimal before the second half of the eighteenth century, although indications of a recognised freedom tradition did come up at times. What is certain though, is that the Dutch had no qualms with sending stowaways back to the colonies, in a clear show of defending colonial property. This monograph has also engaged in an extensive discussion of the Dutch placaet of 1776, which had hitherto remained largely untouched in archival records. We have shown how, although formally enacted by the States General, the process was fully pushed by the province of Holland. Fearful of the precedential value of some particular cases in which slaves had received their freedom, Holland forcefully pushed the case for itself, its bankers, and its Surinam planters. The result was clear limitations to the freedom principle, and subsequent cases show a concerted effort to enforce the placaet. The placaet quickly seems to have been forgotten, and the legal issues concerning black slaves in the Republic subsided, and probably became less of an issue as the English temporarily took over Surinam during the Napoleonic Era. Whilst the Dutch civil code of 1838 solved the question in favour of a clear and unambiguous confirmation of the freedom principle, we know little of the previous 30 years, and should point out that by 1838, slavery had fallen into moral disrepute already in Europe.

Finally, in the previous chapter, we considerably expanded upon previous work in the field by engaging in a wide-ranging legal comparison of the freedom principle from a pan-Western European perspective. Although much of the literature has tended to equate the strength of freedom traditions in different countries, my comparison has shown that this needs to be nuanced. Clearly, the legal foundations of the freedom principle were already well-grounded in sixteenth century France and the Low Countries, but less so in England. Whilst the unclear case of Cartwright is the closest we have of a confirmation of the freedom principle in England, we found a stronger string of cases and scholars asserting the freedom principle in the Low Countries and France. One should however not assume that the English common law was more "tolerant" of foreign slaves. In fact, much of the reason why the tradition could develop elsewhere was because Spanish and Portuguese connections ensured a small stream of foreign slaves touching Dutch and French soil, something which was less the case in England. The application of the freedom principle during the heyday of the Atlantic slave trade also showed interesting differences and similarities. I have proposed that legislators only intervened in the issue during "moments of crisis", namely when planter interests managed to capture the ear of those powerful enough to make legislation. This happened in France in 1716 and 1738 (the 1777 declaration also following upon a "crisis", but not much to the benefit of the planters), and in the Dutch Republic in 1776. In the case of England, my contention is that such a crisis did not appear before 1772, many planters probably being satisfied with the "near slavery" status quo, as well as the Yorke-Talbot Opinion. Likewise, court outcomes varied substantially. Only in Paris did slaves consistently receive their freedom, whilst the courts of Nantes, Bordeaux, London and the Dutch Republic cannot be seen as upholders of slave's rights.

However, what struck me the most during the researching and writing process of this monograph, was the contrast between the law in a strict sense, and the broader situation on the ground. The great majority of slaves did or could not petition for its freedom in a metropolitan court, and a large number were taken back to the colonies, continuing their lives as slaves. That situation as it existed for the thousands of black slaves who were once on European metropolitan soil, necessitates me to make an admittedly bleak conclusion. Most certainly, it was not the case that slaves coming to France, England or the Low Countries in the Early Modern Period immediately received freedom upon touching the soil of these countries, as some sixteenth century scholars held. Slaves had to assert this right in court, and the outcome was uncertain everywhere but in Paris for a while. Governments did not protect the slaves either, as both the French and the Dutch government limited their freedom, and English Parliament turned a blind eye towards slavery. True, the air of Europe did become progressively "clearer" starting from the end of the eighteenth century, first in England and later on in France and the United Provinces. But if slaves hoped to receive recognition by the law that a stay in the metropolis had given them permanent, unencumbered and universal liberty, they would only get this guarantee at a very late stage. It was only right before the abolition of slavery, when the institution itself was in decay, that slaves coming to the metropolis could be assured of their freedom. Only then was the soil truly free.

9783030368548